ssed condition, wearing the minimum of clothing and breathing directly from an oxygen
:.' See p. 232)

WHENSOEVER

50 years of the RAF Mountain Rescue Service 1943 – 1993

Flight Lieutenant George Graham shown in the Llandwrog jeep, probably in 1943.

WHENSOEVER

50 years of the RAF Mountain Rescue Service 1943 – 1993

Frank Card

Paintings and cartoons by Pat Donovan
Maps drawn by Tony Jones

THE ERNEST PRESS

Published by The Ernest Press 1993

ISBN 0 948153 23 7

British Library Cataloguing-in-Publication Data
A catalogue record for this book is available
from the British Library

Typeset by EMS Phototypesetting, Berwick upon Tweed
Printed by St Edmundsbury Press

CONTENTS

To the memory of the late George Desmond Graham 1913-1980

DISCLAIMER

Much of the material in this book is based on RAF records, local and national, and on human memory; neither is infallible. The writer apologises for any errors of fact caused thereby.

FOREWORD

Air Vice-Marshal R J Honey CB CBE FIPM RAF
Air Secretary and Air Officer Commanding Personnel Management Centre

One cold, snowy winter evening many years ago, I was sharing accommodation in North Wales with the RAF Valley Mountain Rescue Team. This was a good arrangement for me and my climbing partner because the Mountain Rescue Team always lived well and maintained a constant supply of hot tea and hot food 24 hours a day. At midnight, on that cold, snowy night the team were called out to search for a party overdue on the Glyders. I then witnessed the sudden transformation of a group of noisy, larking individuals into a highly professional body of men. Suddenly the banter vanished as each man quickly collected his equipment, completed his pre-assigned tasks and was away into the falling snow. We were also dragooned into the team. At the rendezvous, the team leader quickly took control of the civilian elements involved and within minutes we were organised and on the mountain searching. A few hours later we found the missing party safe and well, if a little cold and hungry.

Such was my first working contact with the RAF Mountain Rescue Service, an organisation which sets the benchmark for similar organisations throughout the world.

This book describes in graphic detail the history of the RAF Mountain Rescue Teams from their genesis in ad hoc arrangements to the present highly professional rescues. It is a story of courage and dedication which should inspire us all. I commend it to you.

INTRODUCTION

Late in 1950, a group of National Service men was waiting outside one of the wooden administration buildings at RAF Compton Bassett, then the training school for wireless operators. The course was over; people had passed or not; postings came next.

"Card!"

"Yes, flight sergeant."

"You a Scot, Card?"

"No, flight sergeant."

"'Ard luck! Montrose."

Still very conscious of the wireless operator's sparks on the right sleeve and the LAC's propellers on both, I found my way overnight to RAF Montrose on the steam-hauled 'Aberdonian', to learn that I, who had never climbed anything higher than the South Downs, was now the wireless operator of the Mountain Rescue Team. Within weeks I was away from the radio equipment and up on the hill.

Wherever climbers meet, from Pete's Eats in Llanberis to the Kingshouse in Glen Coe, by way of the Old Dungeon Ghyll in the shadow of Langdale Pikes, eventually the talk is likely to veer round to the RAF Mountain Rescue Service; many, from absolute tyros to the most expert mountaineers and rock-climbers, have reason to be grateful that the service exists. This is the story of that service, from the wartime beginnings of standard blue battledress and half-trained non-climbers to the present time when both kit and training are superb, and the men and women who use it are widely respected, not just as rescuers but as mountaineers in their own right.

Inevitably, it has been possible to include only a tiny proportion of the incidents that have happened over the years; even some which would be regarded as outstanding feats have had to be omitted, and to those who find that their favourite is not here, I can only say sorry, but some painful decisions had to be made. I do believe, however, that I have included all those which could be regarded as 'watershed' incidents: those that changed people's way of thinking.

In here is Mountain Rescue. Out there is the Royal Air Force.
– A Deputy Team Leader, to the writer, in 1990.

ALL FOR THE WANT OF A NAIL

If it's climbing you go there's a tale you should know
That will make you both quiver and quail
Of a hole in your toe where a clinker should go
And it's all for the want of a nail.

You're a thousand feet high and you're nearing the sky
And you can't get a grip on the shale.
Only ten feet away there's a perfect belay
And it's all for the want of a nail.

There's scarcely a grip for a small fingertip
And a thousand foot drop if you fail.
There's a pumping machine where your heart should have been
And it's all for the want of a nail.

The Good Lord looked down and he laughed like a clown:
There'll soon be a rucksack for sale
For if boots don't deceive us this guy's going to leave us
And it's all for the want of a nail.

They scraped what was left from a hard granite cleft
And gathered it up in a pail,
And the toast that they drank to the body that stank
Was 'it's all for the want of a nail'.

They buried him high where the cliffs meet the sky;
Put round him a white wooden rail.
And if you succeed to get there you'll read:
"It was all for the want of a nail."

Now it is gone, my sad little song,
This is the end of my tale.
Don't ever go with a hole in your toe –
Use Vibrams, they never will fail.

From the RAF Leuchars Mountain Rescue Team songbook (and probably a few more besides).

ACKNOWLEDGEMENTS

My thanks go first to the present and previous Inspectors of Land Rescue, Squadron Leader Brian Canfer and Squadron Leader Bill Gault, the latter now at RCC Pitreavie, both of whom made us welcome during our researches; to Mike Holton, Group Captain Tony Smyth retired and Johnnie Lees, whose knowledge of the crucial period of 1951 is profound; to Dr Tony Jones for great assistance with the North Wales research, with civilian mountain rescue generally, and for his splendid maps; to Hugh Budgen, with technical help on aircraft ancient and modern; to Pat Donovan, a former RAF mountain rescuer, for his drawings; and to Derek Bottomer, Erdmute Brewer, Squadron Leader David Dattner retired, Sandy Gordon Cumming, John Hinde, David Lofts, Pete McGowan, Colin Pibworth, Squadron Leader John Sims retired, Dan Stewart and Tom White for the time they gave me in conversation.

Many past and present members contributed much, including: T I Anderson; Harry Appleby; Noel Bailey; Jack Baines (who is also my publisher and can spot the misspelling of a Welsh village name a mile away); John "Campi" Barrows; Geoff Barry; Flight Sergeant Bill Batson; David J Beardsall; Alan Bell; John M Brailsford; Teuch Brewer; George Bruce; Bob Buchanan; Alan Coley; Sergeant Dan Carroll; Air Commodore David Crichton retired; Ian Cunningham; Peter Dear; Ray Dingley; Sergeant Paul Duckworth; Jack Emmerson; Flight Sergeant Tony Emsley; Squadron Leader K Fitton retired; Keith Ford; John T Foster; Glyn Gianelli; Trevor Goldsbrough; K C Gordon; Joss Gosling; Squadron Leader M J Harden retired; Harry Hawthorn; Corporal Peter Higgins; Geoff Hodges; David Horton; Harry S Hunter; Peter Kay; Derek Keegan; Robin Kelly; Harry Kirk; Jimmy Kirkham; Flight Sergeant Peter Kirkpatrick; Keith Laidler; Gordon Leigh; Erik Lock; Trevor Mann; Ian Martin; J Mooring; Ken McCoy; Tony Newbould; John Norrie; Has Oldham; Ken Ovenden; Geordie Paterson; William Patrick; Ron Peart; Group Captain D J B Pierce; Willis Rae; Mick Randall; Brian Riley; Ted Robinson; Vic Salvadori; Dr T O Scudamore; Warrant Officer Ray Sefton; Lieutenant Commander Robert Sharp RN retired; Walter Shepherd; Chris Shorrocks; Bill Simpson; Harold Sinden; Flight Sergeant Jim Smith; Corporal 'Smudge' Smith; Corporal Graham Stamp; Ralph Stephenson; Charles Stringfellow; Ian Sykes; Flight Sergeant Tom Taylor; Arthur Thwaites; Bill Trench; Wing Commander G J Turnbull, Consultant Psychiatrist, Princess Alexandra Hospital, RAF Wroughton; Derek Walker, General Secretary, British Mountaineering Council; Ivor Warn; Peter Williams; T A Williams; Sergeant Peter Winn; Flight Sergeant David Whalley; Gerald White. Many others wrote or telephoned, and I am grateful to them all.

Invaluable information and help also came from Alf Card; The Rt Hon Lord Cledwyn; Ron Collier; David Cuthbertson; Dr David Davidson; Eddie Doylerush; Jack Drummond; the Duke of Kent; Ken Dwyer; Commander A B Erskine RN retired; Brigadier G Finch retired; General Medical Council (Miss K Barlow); Joyce Gilbert; George Hare of Caernarfon Air World; Gerald Hartley; Alastair Hetherington, former editor of The Guardian; The Rev. F L Jenkins; Air Vice Marshal A V R Johnstone retired; Christine Lewis; Bob Lloyd Williams; Hamish MacInnes; John Nixon, HM Prison Service, Haverigg Camp (formerly RAF Millom); John Quartly; Air Commodore H A Probert retired and Basil Aldridge of the RAF Historical Society; RAF Personnel Management Centre, Innsworth (Mrs S C Raftree); John Ellis Roberts; Robin Trangmar; Jon Whalley; Peter Worledge; Dr Mark Nichols, Archivist, Cambridge University Library; Adrian Allen, Assistant Archivist, University of Liverpool; Adrian Gibbs, Records Department, Royal College of Surgeons.

Finally, grateful thanks to my co-researcher and proof-reader my wife, Jo; and to all members of the existing teams, who have always made us very welcome though we must sometimes have got in the way. If nothing else, I have regained my palate for RAF tea.

The early Montrose team in 1944. L to r, standing: Cpl H Sinden, Flt Lt S Duff, Sqn Ldr B A E Harley (senior medical officer), Flt Lt Thompson, LAC S Elder (driver); on roof: Sgt G Watson (wireless operator); on bonnet: Cpl A Innes. *Photo: Crown Copyright*

An exercise completed, the Harpur Hill team returns to the base camp. As well as the radio van and the ambulance, the fleet consists of the Bedford (l) and the jeep (r.)
Photo: Daily Express (from Sqn Ldr K Fitton ret'd)

CHAPTER I – DISCOVERING VIRTUE

The wartime years, 1939–45

> Prosperity doth best discover vice, but adversity doth best discover virtue.
> Francis Bacon 1561–1626: *Of Adversity*

1 – The Pioneers: Scotland

Montrose, a nice, quiet, grey-stone town on the Scottish east coast, was wrapped in mist early on that Saturday morning in 1938. The mist swirled across the airfield as the corporal went from billet to billet. LAC Jack Drummond, flight mechanic, was woken out of a deep sleep by a shout, then an urgent hand shaking his shoulder. Someone was standing by his bed.

"Come on airman!" said the corporal, "we've got to look for a crashed aircraft. Get dressed."

Others were being roused as well. He looked at his watch, and groaned. It was five o'clock. He and many others had been out the previous evening, and were hung-over. Outside the billet there was a 3-ton truck, and they piled in, still bleary. They were told that they were on their way to Cairn o' Mount to look for a Hawker Audax of their unit, 8 Flying Training School, which had crashed round there somewhere. The lorry, in the cold mist of the Montrose dawn, turned out of the gates of RAF Montrose and towards the hills.

There was then no RAF Mountain Rescue Service. There was scarcely a civilian mountain rescue service. Drummond and his mates went up into the hills with no climbing gear and, for the most part, no climbing experience. But Drummond's incident, which he remembers vividly after fifty-five years, was exactly the sort for which the Mountain Rescue Service was formed, five years later, in the intense aerial activity of the Second World War.

Cairn o' Mount, when the RAF Montrose Mountain Rescue Team was formed seven years after this incident, was to become one of its regular training grounds; the writer remembers it well.

A young Royal Auxiliary Air Force Spitfire pilot in 602 (City of Glasgow) Squadron, Flight Lieutenant Sandy Johnstone, was also roped in to a scratch team. In 1939, before World War II broke out, he was an instructor at Prestwick. An Avro Anson, no. L9153, from 269 Squadron at Abbotsinch crashed on Meikle Millyea (2448 feet), in the Rhinns of Kells west of the New Galloway-Ayr road. The pilot was an instructor colleague of Johnstone's, Flying Officer Iain Douglas Shields, and he had as crew two leading aircraftmen, Gordon Eric Betts and Henry Gilbert Stewart Briggs, and, unusually, a civilian wireless operator, Norman Edgar Duff.[1]

For a whole day the aircraft remained missing, and Johnstone and his fellow flyers conducted continuous aerial searches, without success. At eight the next morning, a shepherd, William McCubbin, left his cottage as usual. From his door he could see Meikle Millyea, and this morning his attention was taken by a wisp of smoke rising from the side of it. Curious, he called his dogs and started walking.

He reached the spot after an hour, to find a horrifying scene. The Anson had totally burnt out. Three of the crew had been thrown out and were dead.

The nearest cottage was some distance away, but on the way there McCubbin met the postman, Robert Dalziel, doing his rounds in his car. Dalziel turned the car round and went to the police station in St John's Town of Dalry, as it is known locally. Sergeant Hutchinson was just about to go out with a search party, so instead he telephoned Prestwick to give the Air Force the news, then started organising a recovery party.

When the news came through at Prestwick, Sandy Johnstone and his colleagues were weary after a day's continuous flying. One of the officers at Prestwick was Squadron Leader D F McIntyre. It was McIntyre who in 1933 had been one of two pilots first to fly over Everest, in open-cockpit Westland biplanes; this was in the face of considerable opposition from the establishment of the climbing world, particularly the Everest Committee.[2]

McIntyre set about getting a stretcher-party of 40 together, which included Johnstone. They met McCubbin by arrangement, and he guided them to the wreck. 'He guided them to the wreck'. Those few words make it sound easy. In fact, for a party of non-climbers (except for the leader), without proper clothing or equipment, it was a dreadful night. Temperatures were below zero, and Sandy Johnstone remembers vividly his breath freezing and ice forming on his clothes. These consisted of his Sidcot flying suit[3] over flannel trousers and a sports jacket, with ordinary brogues without studs. He remembers also having to wade waist-deep through icy streams. Each of the party was issued with a pork pie and a hurricane lamp; Johnstone lost the former and broke the latter when he fell down a steep slope in the pitch darkness.

Reaching the scene at nightfall, they decided that it was not practical to do a stretcher-carry over that terrain in the dark. What added to the almost bizarre aspects of this episode was that nearby was another crashed aircraft, a civilian Tiger Moth. The pilot, Hugh Barrow, had spotted the Anson and gone down to have a closer look; then he had been caught in an air pocket and completely lost control. The aeroplane ended up nose-down in a bog, and Barrow and his passenger, John Mackenzie were able to crawl out unscathed. They found Mrs McCubbin in the cottage; she gave them tea and sympathy and set them on their way.

Overnight, a few of the stretcher-party were found room in the tiny McCubbin cottage, and others slept, frozen, in a nearby barn. They were the lucky ones, for

Later marks of 'Faithful Annie', the Avro Anson, replaced the greenhouse effect with airliner windows. The last production Anson, a Mark T21, here leaves the Avro works at Woodford, piloted by the chairman Sir Roy Dobson, to be delivered to 22 Group Communications Flight on 27th May 1952. It was sold for scrap on the 27th June 1960. *Photo: courtesy of British Aerospace*

the barn was only small, and some had to sleep in the open with only topcoats over them. At the McCubbin cottage in the morning, things started to look a little better. Somehow, Mrs McCubbin found enough tea and eggs for 40 men.

They then brought the bodies down carrying the stretchers three miles over the rough terrain before they even reached a track of any sort. A group of shepherds showed them a better route back, skirting the western side of the Rhinns of Kells, then to the narrow road which runs along the shore of Loch Doon and eventually to the main road. One man by this stage was in a piteous state; he had fallen in a bog during the night, his wet clothes had frozen on him, he was suffering from cramp pains and he collapsed when he reached the road.

2 – The Pioneers: England

Late in 1940 an airman was posted to RAF Millom, on the fringes of the Lake District. Arthur Thwaites was quite happy to get this posting. He had been climbing since he was about seven: now, twenty years later, he glanced up at Black Combe which glowered down on the town as he went through the gates. He knew the area well and was looking forward to some good 48-hour passes.

He found an aerodrome still under construction. It was not until the following year that it was fully open as No. 2 Bombing & Gunnery School, using Bothas initially, but, when they were found to be causing many problems, Ansons. It was dangerously close to the Lake District hills.

On November 2nd 1941 a scratch team was put together to search for an Oxford which had crashed. Nobody survived from the aircraft, but this was the trigger which prompted the setting-up of a regular team. Within the RAF at that time, it was no-one's specific task – except that of the officer commanding the nearest RAF station – to do anything about rescuing possible survivors from hill crashes. RAF Millom finally got together a team of eight or ten men, and an officer was detailed to find volunteers. The team was allocated two drivers with Bedford 3-ton lorries. Volunteers stayed away in droves. There were not many hill men on the station, and the hills shrouded in mist and rain were a fearsome sight.

When it became clear that would-be rescue operations were less than successful, two experienced climbers with local knowledge, a sergeant from Barrow-in-Furness and Corporal Arthur Thwaites, an electrician, eventually put their names forward. As the team became established it was given the priorities firstly, of seeking and extracting survivors, and secondly of removing the IFF. This was an electronic device which identified the aircraft to the anti-aircraft units down below. It was fitted with a small explosive charge which shot it clear of the aircraft on crashing; an early 'black box'.

When the service as a whole was finally recognised in 1943, Millom was one of the two English teams, and soon became the home of two very competent climbers, Scottie Dwyer and John Lloyd. No doubt they and their fellow-members would have appreciated the irony that, years later, RAF Millom was to become HM Prison, Haverigg Camp.

Then there were RAF Harpur Hill and Flight Lieutenant David Crichton. Crichton, who had graduated from Edinburgh in 1939, was awarded the MBE in January 1946 for services to RAF Mountain Rescue over the previous three years. Doc Crichton, a Scot, already had a 'mention in despatches' for work during a bomb dump explosion at Burton-on-Trent, and he had received the King's commendation for bravery in the 1945 honours.

A newspaper item of the time said that Doc Crichton's team covered...

> ...a large area of the Peaks of Derbyshire and the Pennines...and...has rescued many crashed airmen. His section carried out the recent rescue of injured aviators from Kinderscout [sic], one of the highest and most treacherous points in the Peaks.

At Harpur Hill was 28 Maintenance Unit, of which Crichton was the Medical Officer. Crichton developed the practice in 1942 of taking two medical orderlies with him in an ambulance when a crash was reported. Then, as aerial activity increased, volunteers were brought in and he had a permanent NCO, Sergeant Thornton.

From those beginnings grew a regular group of volunteer rescuers with little in

George Graham giving instruction in rock-climbing

Flt Lt David Crichton, medical officer, in charge Harpur Hill MRT

the way of climbing equipment or experience. Crichton, in an interview some years ago, recalled going to an old retired sailor in Buxton to learn how to splice ropes. He had not started as a mountaineer or even a fell-walker, but had had to learn from the beginning; as indeed had his team members. At one stage the Ministry received a grateful letter from the US Army Air Force, thanking them for the services of RAF Mountain Rescue to an American pilot in the Peak. This was the first that the Ministry had heard that the service existed.

By the time that the Air Ministry recognised the need for – indeed the actual existence of – Mountain Rescue, Harpur Hill had attended about 40 crashes, and had acquired a jeep, some proper clothing, a rocket gun and radios. The jeep, it has been suggested, came from the grateful Americans. Like the more well-known Llandwrog, Harpur Hill, identifying the necessity for a sledge stretcher, designed and built one. The team had also acquired an example of the Humber ambulance which was standard issue to the officially-recognised teams.

David Crichton, now retired, said that there was never any intention on his part of pioneering anything such as mountain rescue: the commitment grew as the need grew. He started getting calls from police and farmers about aircraft crashes in their areas, and he as the medical officer turned out with medical orderlies to do what could be done.

He continued:

As conditions in the hills became a bit difficult at times for myself and a couple of nursing orderlies with an ordinary small ambulance, I gradually acquired the help of odd airmen who might be available when a crash call came in – and this grew into a band of volunteers and tradesmen and technicians from all sorts of trades and crafts, who were prepared to go out at any time, even at the end of a hard day's work, and be on duty again in the morning after a hard night out on a rescue job.[4]

Crichton has good memories of the people he organised into scratch teams then:

My MRS volunteers were such a wonderful lot of chaps that they deserve to be remembered – but then, so did so many others during the war.[5]

Successive station commanders, despite the lack of official recognition, were sympathetic to the needs of Crichton's teams, and an alarm system was operated that summoned tradesmen from their sections whenever there was a call-out.

3 – The Pioneers: Wales

In 1941 AC1 Noel Bailey was fresh from his Flight Mechanic's course at RAF Kirkham, and was posted to RAF Llandwrog in North Wales. His job in 'B' Flight was to look after Lysanders which were used as target tugs.

An Orderly Room clerk's voice came over the Tannoy one day:

An aircraft from this station is overdue and believed lost in the mountains. Volunteers are required to form a rescue party to go and bring down any survivors. Please report to the Medical Officer in thirty minutes. I repeat:....

Bailey saw the flight sergeant in charge of the workshop, and in half an hour he was with a group of other young airmen outside Station Headquarters. They were briefed by a young medical officer, Flying Officer Graham, then climbed into the lorries.

Bailey has a lasting memory of Graham on this and subsequent episodes as a friendly man – given the great social gulf that existed between officers and other ranks in 1941 – with a lock of fair hair that insisted on falling across his forehead, especially in the wet in the mountains.

Neither Bailey nor most of the other men on that very early scratch team had any experience of climbing or even hill walking, and their equipment and clothing did not extend beyond standard blue battledress, greatcoats and rubber boots. Graham carried the standard doctor's little black bag and a small compass which Bailey remembers looked rather like a Boy Scout's compass. They could see, when they reached the site, that the aircraft and its contents had completely disintegrated into hundreds of small pieces. Graham gathered the group round him. Their job, he said, was simply to collect every tiny piece of human remains which they could find. They were not to concern themselves which piece came from which body: that was his job. He would identify the remains and put them together for burial.

Flt Lt Graham (top rt.) instructs in stretcher lowcring

McTigue BEM points the way in this rather self-conscious pose

l to r: Cpl Gregory McTigue, Flt Lt Graham, LAC Jackson, LAC Cummings. The rescue party pauses for consultation over a map. Note the regulation wartime headlamp mask. At night in the tricky North Welsh lanes – hazardous at the best of times – the jeep was effectively being driven on one masked headlamp and two tiny sidelamps, and use of the central unmasked lamp would not have been approved.

They started searching and collecting. Bailey remembers picking up a suede flying boot; it felt heavy. Reluctantly, he looked, and as he had feared, found the owner's foot still in there. Descending over loose shale and rock and wet grass was hazardous in slippery rubber boots when carrying heavy general service stretchers with their loads.

Over the months, Graham's initiative continued. His inexperienced team members quickly learnt to keep in sight of the people on either side when searching in poor visibility.

The Douglas Boston was an American twin-engined bomber which saw service in the Royal Air Force; it was one of the first with a tricycle undercarriage (one nose wheel, two under the wings) in the RAF. Such a configuration is standard now, but was a novelty in 1942.

Sergeant Mervyn Sims, a Canadian, was the pilot of Boston Z2186 from 418 Squadron. He was taking it on a training flight from RAF Bradwell Bay, Essex, on October 17th 1942, and took off at 11.15am. Flying in cloud over North Wales at something above 3000 feet, he hit Carnedd Dafydd.

When he came to, he was in acute pain. He could see virtually nothing except swirling mist, a few yards of rock and grass, the broken remains of his Boston, and the bodies of his crew of two, Flight Lieutenant Lowenworth and Sergeant Walker. As far as he could tell, they were dead; anyway, they certainly did not respond to his calls. He could not move; any attempt to do so brought unbelievable pain in his back, his head, and his limbs. He was bleeding profusely from various cuts. Nothing happened for a very long time. His shock was made worse by the fact that the crash was totally unexpected. He had been given a course to take him well clear of Snowdonia. He tried shouting; the mist mocked him, seeming to shout back, and shouting only compounded the pain in his head. Despite the pain and the cold, he was not too depressed. The mist was intermittent, and from time to time he could hear aircraft passing nearby, some of which would be out looking for him. He slept, after a fashion and his lacerations had stopped bleeding.

Sims woke again to find that it was dusk; he was very cold and hungry: thirst he could alleviate to some extent by collecting the condensed mist. Clenching his teeth against the pain, he managed to edge nearer a part of the wreck and cover himself with a sheet of aluminium alloy. The early hours of the morning were the worst: the intensity of the damp cold made him sick and the night seemed endless. Light eventually began to show, but the mist was as thick as ever. He was now thinking more rationally, and tried to work out how he came to be there, but the night's cold had permeated every part of his body. Suddenly, depression hit him. He was not going to survive; a new thought.

As the day wore on, so slowly, he waited for the sound of aircraft engines to start again; it did not. The mist was much thicker now, too heavy, he knew, for an

The Llandwrog team is scrambled in 1943.

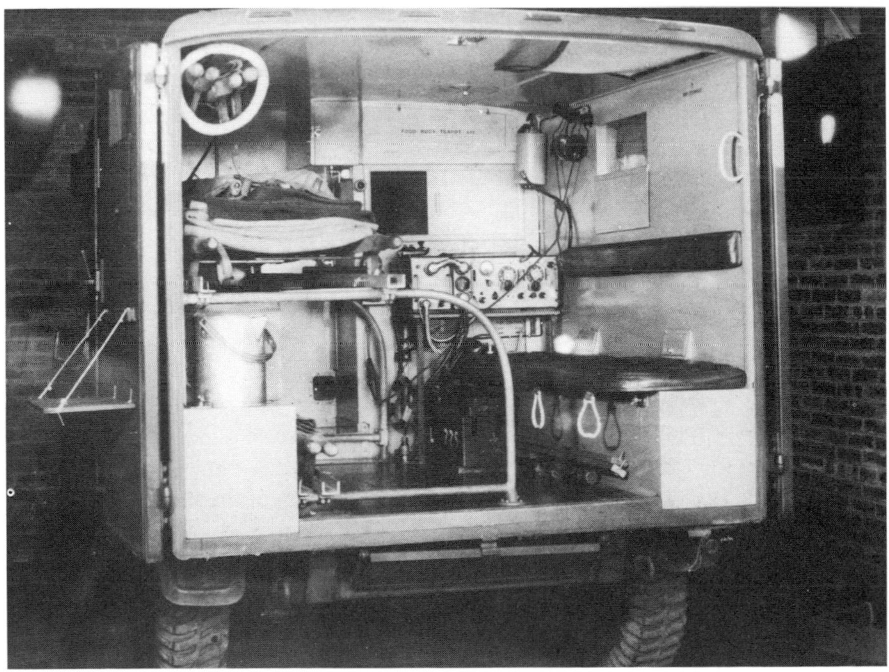

The interior of the Humber ambulance in use towards the end of the war; it doubled as a radio van in some teams, as can be seen here. There is provision for only two stretchers with casualties to be carried, and presumably when the casualties were taken to hospital, radio communication was lost.

aircraft search. He drifted in and out of consciousness throughout the day, trying not to look at the broken bodies of the two other members of the crew, one visible in the wreck, one hanging out. Night fell again. He had gone through the barriers of pain and cold, and he slept, fitfully.

The next morning a young airman and his local girlfriend were walking on Carnedd Dafydd. They saw the dark shape of the wreck, with torn metal gleaming in the sunlight, the first sunlight for two days. They approached, and saw the three bodies. Closer still, they saw that one was alive. The young man started running back down the hill.

Doctor Mostyn Williams had his practice in Bethesda. As a doctor, he had a special wartime petrol allowance. Driving towards the Nant Francon Pass in the direction of Capel Curig, he approached the lake, Llyn Ogwen, and was surprised to see a young man running at full tilt off the hillside, then stand in the road, waving him down. Williams wound down the window. The young airman breathlessly explained about the wreck, and about the pilot, still alive.

"Right, hop in!" Williams said. A little way down the road, by Llyn Ogwen, he turned off to a small track which leads to Ogwen Cottage, a local mecca for mountaineers and mountain rescuers. There he raised the alarm. Then the two men set off up the hill towards the peak of Carnedd Dafydd. The doctor's companion was vague about the exact location of the wreck, but eventually they saw the girl waving.

Mervyn Sims was suffering from exposure, a broken back, a broken leg, a fractured skull and concussion, and a broken thumb, as well as assorted lacerations. Some of his injuries had started to turn gangrenous by the time the two men reached him. Dr Williams was still attending to Sims when a party from RAF Llandwrog, led by a medical officer, reached the scene, and Sims was placed on a stretcher and taken down the hill where an ambulance awaited him, ready to take him to a warm ward and white sheets, hot drinks and care.

Williams had met this particular medical officer before. Twenty-nine-year-old Flight Lieutenant George Graham, worried about the lack of a properly set-up search-and-rescue scheme, was continuing to train his informal team in his own way, drawing upon pre-war mountaineering experience in Switzerland. Graham was a man who impressed as soon as you met him. He had a big, powerful voice; he was 'a man who knew what he wanted'.[6] For his semi-private enterprise, he had been using a large, clumsy Albion ambulance, quite unsuitable for mountain roads, and a pick-up truck. He and his team had been attending crashes and going on exercises with no waterproof clothing, no torches, no climbing footwear.

Over a period, he had, with scant regard for RAF protocol, been writing to the Air Ministry pointing out the deficiencies in his equipment. In the first instance, the Air Ministry wrote back pointing out that this was not the proper thing for a rather junior medical officer to do. He should put his request in writing to his own Commanding Officer, who would, if he thought it worthwhile, send it on to

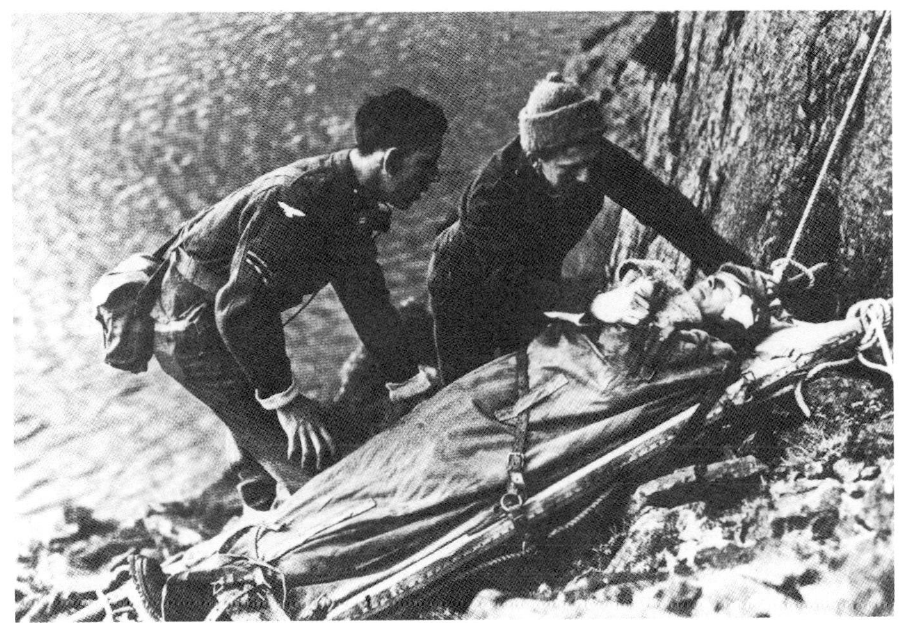

Graham and McTigue attend to a "casualty" during a Llandwrog exercise.

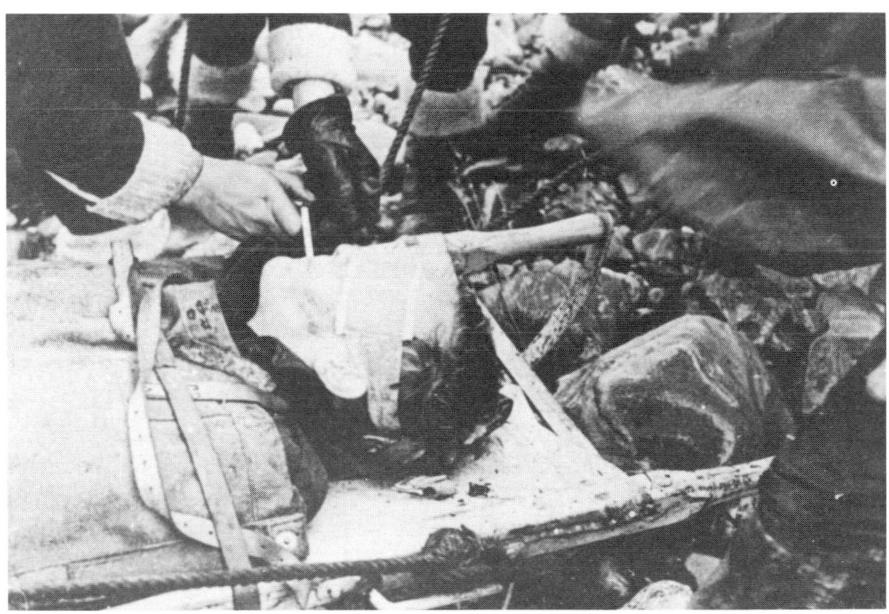

A casualty – almost certainly aircrew – is made comfortable...

Group Headquarters, who would in turn, if they thought it had merit, pass it on to Flying Training Command, who would only then, perhaps, forward it to the Air Ministry. 'Don't do that again!'

Graham immediately wrote back explaining why it had been necessary to write in the first place. This exchange of correspondence continued for some time. Eventually, in desperation, Whitehall asked Wing Commander Ruffell Smith of Flying Training Command to call on Graham and find out what he was up to and what his real requirements were. Ruffell Smith, unusually both a doctor and a pilot, flew down to Llandwrog from Command Headquarters at Reading, had a long talk with Graham, and in equal measure to Graham's and the Air Ministry's surprise, agreed that his requirements were real and justified. As a result, Command supplied a more suitable ambulance, jeeps, 1″ maps, compasses, Verey pistols, waterproofs and boots.

Allied troops landed in North Africa; Casablanca fell. On the same day, by coincidence, 'Casablanca' was released, with Humphrey Bogart, Ingrid Bergman and Claude Raines. This was in November 1942, a month after the Mervyn Sims crash. At about the same time, a Hawker Henley target tug no. L3334 from 1605 Flight at RAF Towyn was reported to have crashed at Cwm Silyn, not far from the village of Llanllyfni. Graham organised another party from RAF Llandwrog; they searched, but without success. Then the same evening Graham was told that an Anson was down on Moel Eilio, just south of Llanberis, two valleys away. This was no. N4981 from 9(0)AFU (Observers Advanced Flying Unit), based at RAF Penrhos. The unit was about to have a distressing time. This particular Anson was only the first of a series of twelve from the unit – the equivalent of one squadron – to crash over a period of nineteen months. Thirty-one aircrew gone, and all on non-operational duties.

The records of crashes in the 40s in Snowdonia, show an inordinate number of Ansons. That does not necessarily mean that Ansons were more prone to fall out of the sky than other types; in fact it was a very tough and reliable aircraft. But nearby RAF Llandwrog was the home of No. 9 Air Gunnery School; RAF Penrhos, as we have seen, of 9(0)AFU; other stations had Anson squadrons for different training purposes; and the Anson was a training aircraft.

Local people found N4981 on the south side of Moel Eilio, with all the crew dead but one. On a navigational exercise, it had flown into a narrow valley whilst in cloud, and been unable to climb out. With Graham from Llandwrog tied up on the Henley search, the survivor could not be properly treated, and died. The Henley was found the next day, wedged high up in a gully. The pilot's body was inaccessible to normal mortals; a quarryman recovered it on the following day. The local quarrymen of the time, when suspended on ropes, could perform prodigious feats on rock faces.

Just outside the village of Llandwrog is Caernarfon Airport, approached by a long straight road with typical seaside bungalows on the right and the beach on

Jackson, McTigue, Graham, Scudamore, Hanley and Martin, Llandwrog 1943.

the left. As airports go, it's not much. Some derelict buildings which have the unmistakable stamp of wartime RAF architecture; a Vampire at the gate, looking very much the worse for wear and weather; a small control tower which also has a vintage RAF look about it, though spruced up; and a single runway still in use out of the three used during World War II. There is a small, friendly museum, run by George Hare, with a compact but comprehensive RAF Mountain Rescue display. This includes George Graham's first log on loan from RAF Valley.

Here, when all three runways were in use, George Graham had become a familiar sight leading his Sick Quarters staff out on another search, followed by the search-and-carry element from other trades. Tall and thin, he usually sat in the front passenger seat of the jeep, wearing a woollen hat from which a lock of blond hair escaped over his forehead.

It had become obvious in all mountainous areas that some sort of search and rescue initiative was necessary, and other stations made their own arrangements. In some cases, it was felt that army personnel or members of the RAF Regiment – because of their training – would form the best teams. But endurance was not the only criterion. SAR (Search and Rescue) experience has, over the years, shown that special skills are required, and special equipment. Knowledge is needed of the risks endemic in broken airframes, in leaking fuel, in scattered armaments; knowledge is needed too of first-aid. This range of skills was best found among the ranks of the Royal Air Force.

By the end of 1942 Graham's scratch teams had on many occasions gone into the hills to rescue the injured, or, more often, to bring down the dead. Twelve flyers had been rescued and 35 bodies recovered from 11 crashes. But the first of several Foel Grach incidents showed that more was needed. This was in January 1943, when Graham had just been awarded an MBE for his work.

A mountain rescue organisation already existed, in fact, though not for airmen. The Rucksack Club had formed a committee in 1933 to look at current arrangements and to suggest improvements; and fortuitously had found that the Fell and Rock Club was doing the same thing. The two clubs joined forces and formed an organisation with units and equipment strategically placed. When rescuing climbers and walkers, there are three enemies: time, weather, mountain. When rescuing aviators, there is a fourth: the aircraft itself, which can cause physical injury on impact, can explode, or can catch fire. Quite often it does all three.

Pilot Officer Ken Archer and George Graham often passed a word in the mess. Archer, like many of the other officers and the NCOs, was pleased to hear of Graham's MBE and to congratulate him. They were interested in his unique enterprise, but probably Archer, like many other flyers, believed that accidents happened to other people. Nevertheless, it was a comfort to see this energetic, well-trained team, fired with Graham's slightly eccentric enthusiasm. Archer was not thinking of Graham, though, when he took out Anson EG110 from Llandwrog on the evening of January 14th 1943 with a pupil navigator aboard. The navigator later reported that he was having radio trouble and could not get a fix. Both men looking anxiously out of the cockpit window saw that the weather was closing in; Archer suspected that they were icing up and he could not climb above the weather; and Snowdonia was, they knew, uncomfortably close. But which way?

The Anson hit a gully at about 2400 feet on the north-east slopes of Foel Grach, just above the Dulyn Reservoir east of Bethesda. This was at about 8.45 pm. It was pitch dark, and the weather was not good. Ken Archer and the pupil navigator, Sergeant Patterson, both New Zealanders, talked, then slept. They had got no response from the other aircrew.

Dawn eventually broke. It was a long time before Archer could get himself together. Patterson clearly was in no condition to move. The other two crew members, Sergeant Brocklehurst the wireless operator and Sergeant Barnett, seemed to be dead. It was not until 2 pm that Archer, concussed and with lacerations to his face and scalp, managed to stagger down to Rowlyn Farm near Tal-y-Bont some miles away. The farmer, horrified at his appearance, made a telephone call to RAF Llandwrog, and Graham went to Tal-y-Bont with two nursing orderlies, arriving at about 4.30 pm. Archer, by then irrational, could not describe where the wreck was, except that he had climbed a ridge (probably Craig y Dulyn) and seen two lakes. The three men searched the mountainside far into the night, but at about 2 am there was a heavy snowstorm and Graham felt he had to call a halt. By dawn the weather had improved and they started again with another thirty men from RAF Llandwrog and some civilians.

Now Graham had vehicles to help him get closer to the base of the mountain. One large lorry, however, could not take the bends in the narrow, twisty lane from Tal-y-Bont. Graham, therefore, had to take the party on foot for the remaining eight miles, leaving behind their food. He split the groups up, sending one party to search the area which he had covered the previous night, and leading another party over a different mountain, Foel Fras. As they started searching, they heard an aircraft. This was a Beaufighter from 456 Squadron at RAF Valley which had been sent to help, but there was no radio communication between the Beaufighter and Graham's team. The first party soon found the aircraft. Two of the crew were dead, with exposure and injuries, but Patterson had survived.

For him, though, the torment was not yet over. Graham was with the other party, and communications were so poor that he could not immediately be contacted. It was a further hour and a half before he could join that party and give Patterson some medical attention. Then Patterson had to be taken down the mountainside, on what was known as a Stretcher, General Service. There were three hours of very hard walking before the team reached the ambulance. To make matters yet worse, the RAF ambulance was unable to climb the steep track and the help of a civilian vehicle was needed. Twice, therefore, the need had been clearly seen for specialised vehicles.

Both Archer and Patterson got through this experience, but Patterson was so badly injured that he had to be invalided back to New Zealand. Archer was flying again in June, and survived the war to return to farming in New Zealand.

When he had time to sit back and think about this particular incident, Graham took a piece of paper and made some brief notes:

Inadequate communications between parties
Too long to raise a search party
Unsuitable vehicles
Unsuitable stretchers
Difficulty of searching at night or in poor weather.

From those thoughts grew his plans for a properly set-up team. He set his proposals out and put them forward.[7] Then he climbed into his Bentley open tourer and went home to his wife Evelyn, in their rooms in Ted Thomas's farm at Bethesda-Bach, a mile or two up the road towards Caernarfon, with the satisfaction of a job well done.

Graham had proposed that he should get together a regular team to be properly equipped, properly trained and on a regular stand-by basis. His proposal was accepted, and a first trial was held near Tal-y-Bont, not far from where Ken Archer's Anson hit Foel Grach. The trial was held on February 26th 1943, only six weeks after Ken Archer's crash. Later that year the press were invited in, and the Liverpool Daily Post was enthusiastic about Graham and his team.

RAF Mountain Rescue was on its way.

4 – A Grossly Inaccurate Pinpoint

On June 2nd 1943 Graham's MBE for his mountain rescue work was gazetted. A month and a bit later the team was launched with Air Ministry approval, but until this point the team organised on an ad hoc basis by Graham, using what equipment he could get hold of, had successfully rescued 33 aircrew from 22 crashes.

On the day that the Llandwrog team was properly and officially established, George Graham sat down in his office in Sick Quarters and opened a lined foolscap notebook. He wrote in it a stark first entry:

1943
July 6th Mountain Rescue Service formed.

He was still lumbered with the cumbersome general service stretcher, and the Air Ministry had given a choice of footwear which amounted to army boots or wellingtons (far-fetched though that seems now). But in other respects he had been able to effect some very tangible improvements in equipment. Ropes, maps, compasses and windproof clothing were issued. The search parties had portable radios, and RT (voice) and WT (Morse) equipment were installed in the Humber ambulance. To a large extent this was due to the sympathetic help of Wing Commander Ruffell Smith, who had been sent to Llandwrog initially to shut Graham up. Ruffell Smith visited Llandwrog on the very first inspection only a month after the opening.

The official opening was celebrated with an exercise, in which the team was called out at 4.45 am to attend a dummy crash on the central peak of The Rivals. The Humber ambulance was driven to the Lleyn Peninsula, then followed the track from Llithfaen village to the dip between the two northerly peaks. When it could go no further, a base camp was set up and Graham sent search parties out from there. Visibility above the height reached by the Humber, about 1500 feet, was, said Graham in his log, 'nil owing to cloud and darkness'. One major request of his was vindicated. Radio contact was maintained between the search parties and the Humber by RT, and between the Humber and RAF Llandwrog by WT.

The search parties returned as dawn was breaking. Camp was broken and the group drove out to Porth Dinllaen, a point on Caernarfon Bay about fourteen miles across the sea from RAF Llandwrog. Again, WT contact was established with Llandwrog. Then at 7.45 am the wireless operator received a message

Llandwrog's Humber ambulance with the tent extension which gave the doctors and orderlies working room. (Tal y Fan in background) *Photo: the late Gordon Leigh, courtesy Edward Doylerush*

from Llandwrog which gave Graham an immediate opportunity to put his team into action. A Lancaster had crashed, said 9 Group, at 4.00 am, near Llangernyw, which is on the road from Llanwrst to Abergele. They packed up and left immediately in heavy rain, arriving at 10 am. The Lancaster had exploded on impact and the wreckage was scattered over a wide area. The remains of three of the crew had been found by a local army unit; there might have been others who had bailed out.

Graham tried to establish how many had actually been on the aircraft, but suffering his first operational disappointment, found that his operator was unable to get in WT contact at that point with Llandwrog. The wireless operator believed that the aerial socket was shorting somewhere because of the rain. Graham found a telephone, and ringing Llandwrog asked for an aircraft to be sent out. He soon made RT contact with the aircraft when it approached and it was brought to the crash scene by Verey lights. No parachutes could be spotted by the crew or the team and later another three bodies were found. At 6 pm, the team returned to RAF Llandwrog. Graham had every reason to be pleased with the way his enterprise had gone on its first day.

Six days later, they returned to the spot. The prime reason was to establish the cause of the WT failure. They had no better success than before, but it was not raining. The operator eventually found that the aerial was shorting at the base of the mast. Whilst they were there, they had a further search and found more human remains which were buried at the spot.

Despite the improved organisation, the team was not always successful. When Blackburn Botha L6202 from Hooton Park crashed on 29th August, the subsequent operation was something of a disaster. On the 29th, at 5 pm, Flying Control told Graham that an aircraft from Hooton Park had located the Botha between two lakes three miles north of Capel Curig and seven miles east of Bethesda; this would place it near Llyn Eigiau. The team left at 5.30 pm, reaching Tal-y-Bont at 6.45 pm. The first problem happened before they had got very far: the jeep skidded into a kerb, buckling a wheel. The wireless operator had to set up his aerial, tune in the equipment, and send a message back to RAF Llandwrog for the jeep spare wheel to be brought out by the ambulance.

Behind Tal-y-Bont there is a narrow road which winds its way south-west and up towards Llyn Eigiau. As it gets near to the lake, it becomes nothing more than a mountain track: as they wanted to get to the western end of Llyn Eigiau, this is what they followed. Looking through the windscreen of the jeep, Graham was surprised to see a deep ravine across the track. The convoy stopped, and Graham checked the map. The ravine was not marked. Problem number two.

Graham and the drivers got out with their torches and had a look. It was quite deep, and they estimated that it would take the best part of a day to level the slopes out sufficiently to get the vehicles across. Reluctantly, therefore, Graham decided to set up the Mountain Headquarters at that point. A little further on, closer to the lake, is Hafod-y-rhiw, a couple of cottages. People there told Graham that a shepherd and his boy had already set out to find the crash. Graham, with Pilot Officer Bowen, Corporal McTigue and AC Hughes, spent two hours searching what seemed at the time to be the most likely area – the slopes of Pen Llithrig y Wrach. But this was problem number three: the wreck was not there. By the time they had finished at midnight, the weather had deteriorated and there was much driving rain. On the way back they found that the engineer officer with the crash party had found accommodation at Hafod-y-rhiw, and they made arrangements to start again at five with a combined group.

Graham, when they returned to the Mountain Headquarters at 1 am, found that the light ambulance which was due to bring the spare wheel had not arrived. He and LAC Martin took the jeep and drove down into Tal-y-Bont, where they met the ambulance. The driver informed them then of problem number four: on the way from Llandwrog to Tal-y-Bont, the ambulance had shed a wheel. He added that the back axle had been grossly overfilled with oil which was streaming out at each side and, he thought, was probably responsible for the loosening of the nuts. The jeep wheel was changed, and the two vehicles turned up the mountain lane, which brought them to problem number five: the ambulance could not manage the slopes. It was pushed into a cul-de-sac and left; they then took the jeep back up to the mountain ravine, and found a different track which enabled them to by-pass it.

A further search was started at 5 am, in gale and rain. After another four and a half hours, the team returned to Mountain Headquarters, but not without problems six, seven and eight: 2 airmen lost, 1 injured. All subsequently recovered.[8]

The wireless operator called up Llandwrog, asking them to get more information from Hooton Park. Graham was on his way in the jeep to the station to collect some more food and, he hoped, to pick up that information. Information there was none. Back at Tal-y-Bont, at mid-day whilst Graham was still away, a message was passed on by the police. The crash, it seemed, had been spotted some two miles south of MHQ. Bowen therefore led a small party up there and was soon followed by Graham on his return from Llandwrog. The weather was bright and clear when Bowen's group and Graham met on the hill, and had to conclude that the message must have been based on surmise. Problem number nine.

The afternoon dragged on to 6 pm at which time Graham was in touch with Flying Officer Perry in charge of an RAF detachment from 34MU which happened to be at Bethesda. Whilst he was there, the police waved down the Humber to pass on yet another message: that the crash had been found, somewhere near Capel Curig, by none other than the 34MU detachment. The message was passed on to Graham, who was immediately able to obtain a denial. Problem number ten. The denial was passed back to the Humber to prevent the wastage of any more time.

An arrangement was made with 34MU – which was why Graham was there in the first place – that they would provide a party to search the western slopes of the Carneddau, whilst the MR team would move onto the eastern slopes. Graham therefore called all parties into headquarters. One party he sent across Glearffordd, to the hut at Melynllyn (still there but now roofless), so that they could use it as a base from which to search the cwm at western end of Llyn Eigiau. In the meantime the vehicles used the track to go round the mountain to the hut. Graham and Bowen made their way to the top of Foel Grach at about 10 pm; but again, there was no trace of any aircraft, and they descended in cloud and darkness. All parties were issued with rum when they gathered again at MHQ at 1 am.

The log at this point is showing signs of tiredness. Graham's handwriting is getting larger and starting to wander across the page. It was clearly being updated whenever an opportunity presented itself, and the writing becomes more and more weary.

Nothing happened again until mid-day; it was now August 31st. Most of the team, for the whole morning, were catching up on their sleep, helped by the rum ration. Then at 12 noon they were told that the Hooton Park aircraft had been found. Graham was taken up on an air reconnaissance, and confirmed that the aeroplane was on the south slope of Llwytmor, 500 feet from the top, about five miles north-north-west of the original reported location. The convoy was taken along the steep track which runs up the Anafon valley. They parked, and the team, once again, started climbing. On the way they passed the bleached wreckage of a Junkers 88 which had crashed there in 1940 after being attacked by a Spitfire. It had made a good forced landing and the crew, including a Gestapo officer, all survived. The aeroplane was being used for reconnaissance, surveying and photographing the damage to Liverpool after a bomber raid the previous week.

The Botha was finally reached at 6 pm: all of the crew had died instantly. Graham called up the main crash party and commented in his log:

> Some time passed before the whole party was collected at the crash owing to the poor physique and age of the airmen used (mainly ACH/GD).[9]

The bodies were tied to the heavy general duty stretchers. However, the descent was very steep, and when, by midnight, Graham judged that progress had not been sufficient and the team was exhausted, he decided to leave the stretchers and bodies on the hillside overnight. They were to be ferried off the hill by the jeep, but at that point it was discovered that Cumming, the jeep driver who had been sent back to fetch more torches, was missing. Problem number eleven.

Graham then, when everyone was at the limit of their endurance, had to organise a search for Cumming. He was eventually found, exhausted after having lost his bearings. It was not until 4 am that the team returned to Llandwrog; and by 9 am, some of them were back on the hill acting as guides for a fresh stretcher party to recover the bodies.

Graham's final comment in his log is that this was the longest continual operation in which the team had been employed, and he adds:

> The long delay in finding the crash was due entirely to having been given a grossly inaccurate pinpoint.[10]

Thirty-two years later, a climber found the pilot's ring with his initials engraved on it, near to what was left of the wreckage.

5 – Graham's Graveyard

Many of the crashes took place in or near the Welsh mountain cwms. The reasons for this are not so simple as was first thought.

During the Ice Age, only the peaks of the mountains showed above the ice. These peaks were, through repeated and intense frosting and thawing, prised apart to form pinnacles. Under the ice, the fragments of rock from these pinnacles acted like emery paper on the rock floor, cutting a deep ice-filled bowl. When, after many thousands of years, the ice retreated, what was left was a great amphitheatre, very often with a small lake: in Wales, a cwm; in Scotland, a corrie; in France, a cirque. Snowdon is surrounded by cwms. Llyn Dulyn (Black Lake), which Ken Archer had reported seeing the previous January, became notorious for aircraft crashes. Myths grew up about the Black Art, as some saw it, of flying over mountains, particularly over cwms and corries often with their icy lakes.

Much more is now known on this subject than was known in the 1940s. Then the belief largely was that as cwm lakes such as Llyn Dulyn are extremely cold, being totally untouched by the sun, a downdraught is created over the slopes. This, went the theory, creates a suction effect which can cause aircraft, which are apparently flying safely above, to be dragged into the side of the hill. Such a downdraught is a katabatic wind, and the same effect can be seen on opening a freezer door and watching the cold air fall out and sink slowly to the floor. However, a katabatic wind in Britain rarely reaches more than a few knots, not fast enough to cause that catastrophic effect. That is far more likely to be caused by rotor streaming or standing waves.

Rotor streaming happens when there is a very strong wind extending through the height of the mountain. In certain atmospheric conditions at about the height of the summit air is then accelerated, from the top of the hill and above, to many times the speed of the wind. This leads to very rapid accelerations and downdraughts – turbulence – in layers level with the hill top and often two or three times that height, which can cause sudden loss of control in an aircraft.

Standing waves occur, again when atmospheric conditions are right, on the lee side of a hill, and are in a fixed position with the air moving over them. The airflow follows the contours of the standing waves, with little apparent relationship to the contour of the ground beneath. Vertical currents so caused can be quite strong, and can extend as high as 80,000 feet.[11] In places there are two corries back-to-back. Over the millennia the hillsides have been worn away, leaving a sharp edge between the two valleys. In such a situation, the airflow is even more disrupted.

When flying in cloud over mountains the problems are unseen and therefore compounded, and that is probably what brought Ken Archer and his crew to grief. On the other hand, clouds often form in the crests of lee waves or under standing waves, and can themselves be a warning of the danger. For helicopters these problems can be even more hazardous, particularly at the start of a search with full tanks and therefore lower power margins. The pilot must often make several approaches to assess the situation before going into the cwm. He may even find that he cannot hover in the cwm, and therefore a rescue from there has to be done by a mountain rescue team on foot with a long haul to get there and a steep descent. Since climbers find fascinating challenges in cwms and corries, they are a double hazard.

The team had been involved in eight crashes by the end of October, one of them including the Botha search of 2½ days. In the light of experience, identifying black and yellow bands had, by this time, been painted onto the ambulance roof to help both searching aircraft and search parties on the hill. A new medical officer had been posted to the parent station, RAF Penrhos, during the year: Flying Officer Tom Scudamore. The adjutant during this period at Llandwrog was Flight Lieutenant Cledwyn Hughes (now Lord Cledwyn of Penrhos), who remembers Graham well and kept contact with Scudamore for a long time.

Squadron Leader Collins called Scudamore in soon after he had arrived.

"Look," he said, "We have a satellite station called Llandwrog. I'll be sending you over there from time to time to do sick parade, because the MO, a chap called Graham, is a bit of a nuisance. He's very keen on mountaineering, and he's either on an aircraft crash or he's taking the medical orderlies on exercises. So you'll have to go over there and do sick parade whilst he's on exercises."

Scudamore went, then, to Llandwrog to meet Graham. Graham explained the Mountain Rescue organisation which he had developed, and showed Scudamore the vehicles – the two jeeps and the Humber four-wheel-drive ambulance which he had had since early that year.

"You must come out with us on exercises and crashes." said Graham. "We'll get a civilian medical practitioner to stand by for emergencies. You come out with us – we needn't tell Squadron-Leader Collins."

Scudamore reflects now:

That is how I became involved. I went out on exercises and crashes. Not being a mountaineer or a rock-climber I reckon I'm a very lucky RAF medical officer, being in the right place at the right time.[12]

George Graham had enjoyed his leave in November, 1943. He had been to Evelyn Ann's home at Crosby to see her through her second birth but sadly now had to leave the family behind in the UK whilst he went abroad. Still, he was well-pleased with the way his Mountain Rescue team was shaping up and happy that it was being left in the hands of Tom Scudamore, now effectively his deputy. Just before Graham was due back from leave, Scudamore was taking sick parade at Llandwrog. Sergeant Harvey, the senior NCO in the Sick Quarters there, told him that there was a crash, and Scudamore could hear the team vehicles getting ready outside.

Graham arrived back at RAF Llandwrog early on December 2nd to find that the team was out and had been since the previous day, seeking an Anson from RAF Jurby on the Isle of Man which had crashed two evenings earlier. Two of the crew, with facial injuries, had walked down to Bethesda. They were taken into a shop and given first-aid and tea. Their Anson had been flying across Wales on a west-to-east bearing. They had only one bearing, so it could have been almost anywhere, but the Observer Corps thought that they had heard an aircraft coming to grief in the area of Carnedd Dafydd and Carnedd Llewelyn.

Sick Quarters sent out a light ambulance to pick up the two crew members, and in the meantime the team was setting up a base camp. They searched for many hours on Carnedd Llewelyn and Foel Grach, but called a halt at 11 pm, returning to Llandwrog for a meal, a change of clothes and a rest. At 7.30 am they were out again, starting on Carnedd Dafydd in a snowstorn. During the morning, Graham was taken up in an aircraft to act as observer over Carnedd Dafydd, but the weather made this impractical. Then, later that morning, the constable on duty at Bethesda Police Station was surprised to find in front of him at the desk a young aviator with torn flying suit and alarming cuts to face and hands: the third member of the crew. After two nights in the cold, he had been able to summon up enough strength to start walking.

Graham questioned the crewman. From this, with his by now intimate knowledge of the local geography, he was able to get a more precise picture of where the wreck might be, and he established also that there was a fourth survivor. Time, therefore, was of the essence.

"You haven't", he said to Scudamore, "searched the Graveyard!"

Interested to learn where Graham's Graveyard was, Scudamore went in the jeep with Graham driving. (That, he remembers, was a mistake. Graham's driving was alarmingly fast, with a propensity to cut corners.) They went along the Conwy Valley, turning off onto a mountain track which was impassable except to jeeps and four-wheel-drive Humber ambulances and the like, and stopped at the shepherd's hut between Llyn Dulyn and Melynllyn.

There was a very extensive search with the team being helped by reinforcements from Llandwrog. After 20 minutes searching on Foel Grach in the mist, Graham's and Scudamore's parties met, and the two medical officers had a discussion. They were still talking when the mist suddenly lifted as it can in North Wales, and there only about 400 yards away was the Anson. There was no sign of life. The two officers walked over to the wreck, and found someone in the gun turret wrapped in parachutes. They looked closely; he was not dead, but fast asleep. Woken and offered rum, he declined, saying cheerfully, "Sorry, I never touch the stuff". He was suffering, after two days, from dehydration and starvation, and he had a fractured foot but otherwise he was in fair shape. Llandwrog was told of the find, and the Humber was sent to the crash site with stretcher bearers, blankets, hot water bottles and sweet tea. He was loaded in darkness into the Humber, which took him to Llandwrog's Sick Quarters where he joined his colleagues. All four survived: Sergeant J Knight, pilot; Sergeant Gilbert, navigator; LACs Reid and Thompson, pupil navigators.

There was an odd sequel to this story. Some time after the episode, Scudamore received a letter from a survivor, thanking him and the team for their help. This man was now in the Army Pioneer Corps. In his letter, he said that the medical board, when he came out of hospital and showed a reluctance to fly again, had decided that he suffered from a 'lack of moral fibre', and should be transferred.

The name of Graham is a common surname in Carlisle, where George came into the world in 1913. He was born at Grosvenor College, where his father was headmaster.

After matriculating in November 1933, he took third class honours in Part I of the Natural Sciences Tripos in 1936 at Clare College, Cambridge. This, with success in the First MB examinations, qualified him for the BA, which he took in June 1936, followed by his Second MB in 1939. George Desmond Graham, his medical training over and his primary qualifications of MRCS and LRCP filed safely away, was living then in Liverpool.[13] By 1940, however, he had moved to London and was working and living at the London Fever Hospital, Islington, from where he took the further degrees of MB and BChir. It was also from here in November that he married, in her home town of Blundellsands, Crosby, a girl he had met when training: the 24-year-old teacher Evelyn Ann Russell.[14]

On the 18th February 1941, when he was 27, he was commissioned into the Royal Air Force Volunteer Reserve as a flying officer in the medical branch. Exactly a year later he was given the war substantive rank of flight lieutenant, and that same year he was posted to RAF Llandwrog as a medical officer.[15] By then, he and Evelyn Ann had a son, John, and the three of them lived in a farmhouse not far from the airfield, Graham becoming a familiar sight in his Bentley tourer.

Graham's wartime career after he got the Mountain Rescue Service started shows that his Welsh initiative was no flash in the pan. The next incident happened just two months after Mountain Rescue in the UK was given official approval. But before his posting abroad, he had ensured that Tom Scudamore was well-settled and running the team.

6 – Burma Drop

Equipped with an odd mixture of Lockheed Hudsons, Consolidated Liberators, Westland Lysanders and Douglas Dakotas, 357 Squadron worked out of Dum Dum, Calcutta and elsewhere, specialising in dropping agents and supplies to the resistance in the Japanese-occupied territories of Burma. This was Operation Buffin.

Four Hudsons from 357 Squadron were going out over the Sino-Burmese border on March 14th 1944, and one of the dispatchers was Flight Sergeant Tom E 'Chalky' White. Another was his friend, Flight Sergeant Joe Wilkinson. Both were parachute instructors drafted into 357 Squadron to act as dispatchers. All were dropping supplies to the guerillas who were being trained to support the local war lord against the Chinese communists. White had come up from Chaklaha by Liberator and Hudson over the first three days of March. Then almost immediately he was involved in a flurry of activity, going out six times over the next ten days.

The crews, as usual, received information on weight of containers and order of dispatch, had a meal, collected flying equipment and drove to the airield. After

Douglas Dakota IV at RAF Cosford in RAF wartime livery. This was Field Marshal Montgomery's personal aircraft in various fields of war. *Photo: H J Budgen*

loading and checking they waited for departure time and chatted and smoked. Then, one after another, the four Hudsons taxied out to dispersal, and then on to the main runway. Throttles were opened, the aircraft gathered speed down the runway, bounced, and then were airborne. They climbed and turned in the gathering tropical dusk, the navigators already getting bearings and setting routes. The ground crews were left with the diminishing sound of the Hudsons' eight Pratt & Whitney Twin Wasps as they pulled the aircraft up and over the jungle. Red points of light glowed in the darkness as the men lit up and talked quietly and thoughtfully on their way back for a beer and then bed.

Early the next morning, through the tropical dawn, the ground crews awaited the return of their aircraft. Three Hudsons returned, one was missing. The crew of Hudson AM949 – squadron callsign A-Able – included three Canadians: the pilot and captain Flying Officer R B Palmer, the navigator Flying Officer W Prosser, and the wireless operator/air gunner Flight Lieutenant L Patterson. The rest of the crew were RAF: the co-pilot Flight Lieutenant J C S Ponsford, the second wireless operator Warrant Officer B A Ogilvie, and Joe Wilkinson.

Time dragged on; rumours abounded. Then an agent called in on the radio to say that the missing Hudson AM949 had crashed in the target area at 3 am. Two of the crew were seriously injured, and the others were dead. The agent asked for a doctor to be sent. The only medical officer at Dum Dum with parachuting experience was on stand down and could not be contacted. There was, however, another medical officer, who had been posted out from the UK, only days before. In fact, rumour had it that he was the chap who had started the Mountain Rescue Service in North Wales – RAF Llandwrog, was it? – which had built up something of a reputation with the crews.

Graham, on his return from another airield, immediately volunteered to parachute to the crash scene, though he had never parachuted in his life and even his flying experience was very limited. White, concerned about Graham's total lack of parachuting experience and keen also to see if he could do anything for his friend Joe, quickly offered to go with Graham, and to give him what parachuting instruction he could in the very limited time available. For both men, permission had to be obtained from Air Headquarters in Delhi. Take-off was scheduled for 11.30 pm; the two men met for the first time at 9 pm. Two men, one a mountain rescuer who had never parachuted, the other a parachutist with no mountain experience, though young and fit.

In the two and a half hours available, White gave Graham such parachuting instruction as he could, and the two drew special kit: boots, bush hats and revolvers, cyanide pills, and silver rupees as 'escape money'.

After the all-round farewells, they were driven out to the airield and the various containers were loaded into the Hudson F-Freddie. More parachute instruction, on such basics as how to leave the aeroplane, followed. Then came the take-off, under the pilot Flight Lieutenant J A King, with firstly an hour's flight through cloud to Chittagong. There they landed and had a meal, with the Hudson being checked and refuelled. A further departure took place in time for the expected arrival time of 5 am. The two men, once aloft, had time to check their equipment again and try to get a little sleep.

Chalky White, writing only three and a half years after the event, said:

With the first streaks of dawn over the hills, we prepared ourselves and the containers for the descent. As we completed the final check and opened the rear hatch, the target, complete with ground signals appeared dead ahead, and the pilot began a dummy run to check wind-drift. The rope holding the first container in position was cut, and the MO steadied it ready for dispatch. As the aircraft came in on its dropping run, the ground appeared to rush past as we gazed down through the hatch, and a quick glance behind showed the two wireless operators gazing intently at us as we awaited the signal to jump. The red light flashed on, and I shouted Action Stations into the ear of the MO. The green replaced the red, and as I shouted GO the MO pushed out the first container and followed it himself, with myself and the second container close behind. Our parachutes burst open just below the aircraft as we breathed in the cold mountain air somewhere behind Japanese lines in Burma.

White, with his great parachuting experience, manoeuvred himself close enough to Graham to be able to shout instructions to him: telling him when to yank the cords and spill air.

We drifted slightly off the target area and made rather a fast, but safe, landing on a slope

Flt Sgt Tom "Chalky" White, who made a parachute drop with Graham into the Burmese jungle in 1944 to rescue a British airman. This photograph was sent to his wife from India in 1948. *Photo: T E White*

George Graham at the Aircrew Mountain Centre in Kashmir in 1944. He has lost much weight compared with pictures taken in Llandwrog only a few months earlier; his 4-week jungle walk with White intervened. *Photo: Tony Smyth*

leading to the DZ[16]. The MO narrowly missed a tree, hitting his head slightly as he went into a 'rugby roll' on a mound of earth, but he was quite blasé about his first descent.[17]

The target area was a 6,000-foot ridge. Soon after their landing they were met by some local people who did not speak English nor any dialect which Chalky White knew. They were in fact the guerilla group under the command of Colonel Yang Yan Sang. At the request of the British intelligence officer, Major Leach, they were there to take the two men, on mules, to the crash, some four miles away – an hour's journey. White and Graham waved to King in the Hudson. The wings dipped in farewell and it turned back towards Calcutta.

At the crash scene White found Captain Cole, whom he had dispatched only a few days earlier. The only crew member still alive now, Cole explained, was the Canadian navigator, Prosser, and he had a fractured skull, a fractured right ankle and various burns and bruises. The other who had survived the crash, Ponsford, had since died. So White's friend Joe Wilkinson, with the rest, was dead.

Whilst White learnt about the crash and the burying of the casualties, Graham was tending the comatose Prosser and found that the Americans had given efficient first-aid treatment to a terrible injury. He cleaned up the head wound and filled it with crushed M & B tablets, covered by Elasto-plast. He made a plaster cast using bamboo splints for the leg from the toes to the knee. During this Prosser was delirious and had to be held down. Then Graham and White settled down to sleep, with Leach watching over Prosser. The only illumination during the night vigils, which were taken in turn, was a wick burning in a saucer of pig fat.

Later that day they were joined by an American officer, Lieutenant Parsons, and some radio messages were sent back to Calcutta. The following day, they visited the wreck to see if they could find out the cause of the crash. It was rapidly being dismantled by some local people, so Graham noted the readings on some of the instruments and salvaged as many as possible.

Next morning Prosser was weaker. An American doctor, Captain Hockman, arrived by mule the following morning after a five-day trek from his HQ in China. Graham and Hockman fixed up a nasal feeding device, using rubber tubing taken from the wreck. Prosser seemed to show some improvement that evening.

Whilst White carried coded messages for the agents, and on one occasion was invited to dinner at the headquarters of Colonel Yang (how incongruously civilised that sounds now, in the context of the time), Graham and Hockman continued to treat Prosser, but his condition had worsened. There seemed little chance of his survival and his condition continued to worsen until a crude but effective enema seemed to lead to a slight improvement.

The following morning, they learnt from a messenger that the Japanese and the Burmese pro-Japanese troops were trying to enter the area, and were trying also to persuade the headmen to provide labour for road-building. Graham and White therefore decided that they would have to evacuate Prosser should the enemy approach any closer. A litter was built and supplies got together, with mules made available by the guerilla chief. After two days, it looked as if the Japanese were beginning to move forward, and the party moved out with twelve litter bearers. It was a very slow journey in the heavy rain and both men and mules were constantly slipping. The first village was reached at about six that evening.

The next day, they again started at nine, resting once, and stopping at 6 pm at a compound. After that, they made an earlier start, and covered thirty miles the following day before stopping and resting overnight in a village schoolroom. Their deep and much-needed sleep was cut short at 6.30 am. The schoolroom was needed by the children; it gave a bizarre touch of everyday life to an extraordinary situation.

On day four they reached the headquarters of the guerilla officer who was supposed to supply the medical needs of the Chinese Army in the area, and who was also supposed to be a friend of Hockman. For some reason, he seemed to be unwilling to help beyond the absolute minimum. The party paid off the guerillas who had brought them so far, but the colonel, who was expected to replace the twelve coolies and the mules with twelve more coolies and more mules, insisted that eight coolies would be enough.

Day five, therefore, was very slow, including as it did the journey's highest mountain. The target was the American unit to which Hockman belonged. Finally they did reach it; Prosser was treated and a day's rest was taken. The Americans wanted to build an airstrip so that Prosser could be taken out, but the Chinese army would not allow this – understandably, since it would give their position away. This meant a further five days' trek, which, after the five days already experienced, seemed like the end of the world. Fresh mules and more men were provided by the Americans, as well as information on the terrain which lay ahead. Graham's Colt .45 had to be used to encourage the unhelpful coolies, but the party eventually arrived at the day's objective. After a welcome sleep they woke up in the morning to find that the coolies had all left, fortunately leaving the mules and the baggage.

The local Sheriff was ordered to replace the missing men, and finally produced four, with the promise of four more to come. White went on ahead with the mules, leaving Graham and Prosser to follow. The extra coolies did not turn up as promised, and Graham therefore took off with only four, feeding them with rum from time to time to keep them going. At one stage, he left the track and found a village, where he was able to obtain more men.

Graham and White were due to be staying that night with Lieutenant Watson, an American attached to the Chinese army. After a very difficult journey, White met Watson, unloaded the mules and, taking a haversack of emergency rations started to retrace his steps in the hope of finding Graham. Unsuccessful and depressed, he returned to Watson's quarters to sleep. He was woken up at about 1.30 am with Graham's welcome shout: "Chalky, Chalky!"

Graham approached the Chinese army for a fatigue party during the day, which, after the ritual display of reluctance, was forthcoming. This enabled Graham and White with Prosser to reach the next American outpost, commanded by Lieutenant Colonel Lines, who invited them to stay, but Graham decided that in Prosser's interest they should press on and get the patient to India. The party started off again at 8 am, aiming for a deserted village about twenty miles away. They reached it, and had a hot meal. By this time Prosser was much stronger.

One could be excused for thinking that this journey could not produce anything harder than it had already; one would have been wrong. The next route was to Shunning, the headquarters of the US 'Y' force. Hard as it was, it had its consolation:

> This was the toughest trek of them all, as not only was it very mountainous, but one minute we would be stripped to the waist in sweltering heat, and the next, freezing in a hailstorm on the top of a mountain. We had a wonderful reception from the Americans when we reached the thickly-populated valley, and the MO decided to give Prosser a day's rest before travelling by weapons-carrier to the US-Chinese hospital at Yunshien.[18]

Then followed three days' drive to Yunnanni Airport, and after a day's wait they were able to board a C-46 Commando bound for India. Bad weather and a faulty undercarriage forced the aircraft back to Kunming Airport, where they stayed. They were able to restore some semblance of normality to life by seeing *Madame Curie* at the base cinema. Next day, a month after Graham and White had started out, they were able to reboard the Commando. They flew over the 'Hump', the Himalayan ridge which runs for hundreds of miles along the Burma-India border, to an airfield in Assam, thence by Dakota to Calcutta. Prosser was on oxygen, and Graham was trying all the way to keep his patient cool with the ventilators. At Calcutta they were met by an ambulance which took them to the British General Hospital.

Graham and White by then had the sort of close bond that is established only when people go through great hardship together. White, nearly fifty years later, has a clear memory of the man with whom he went through this odd corner of war history:

'Doc' Graham and I were only together for this particular operation, yet I found him a most charming and efficient medical officer. When you consider this was his first parachute jump, with no preliminary instructions apart from a few minutes with me before 'take-off' it speaks volumes for his courage and dedication.[19]

Graham went out and came back with a gift for White, a cigarette case engraved inside '17th March 1944 – from G.D.G.', which he had bought with the remnants of the solid silver escape rupees with which they went into the jungle. With its Indian floral design on the outside, and White's initials TEW, it sits in the palm of the hand now, strangely evoking those extraordinary events of nearly fifty years ago. Graham was awarded the Distinguished Service Order; White the Conspicuous Gallantry Medal. Their pilot, King, received a bar to his Distinguished Flying Cross for this and other operations. Within a day or two of his return, Graham had submitted a lucid and well-constructed report to the Station Commander.

Although Graham's and White's jungle foray was off-the-cuff, an Air/Jungle Rescue Service did in fact exist in Burma. Whilst it was formed specifically to recover aircrew speedily from either enemy-occupied territory or from remote parts of Burma away from roads and tracks, it had gone a long way in teaching aircrews how to combat the dangers of the jungle in the event of a crash. Exercises were conducted in which aircrews were provided with jungle aid, were dropped in the jungle and left to find their way to some rendezvous from where they were later picked up. As more aircraft became available a combined Air/Sea/Jungle Rescue Service was established similar in many respects to the Air Sea Rescue Organisation of Coastal Command[20]

During 1944, it was noticed that aircrew were more susceptible to the problems of tropical climate than other people under fire. What were the reasons: more nervous strain? higher alcohol consumption? Whatever the reasons, it was becoming a serious matter, and – putting humanitarian considerations aside – aircrew were expensive to replace. The problem landed on the desk of Air Vice Marshal Goddard at Air Headquarters India.

By chance, Goddard had recently spent a leave in Kashmir where he went on a trekking trip up the Sind River. He and his companions had walked about ten miles each day and camped each night in magnificent scenery. He returned refreshed in mind and body, and immediately thought of that leave when confronted with the problem of the jaded aircrew. This, he thought, is what my airmen need after three summers in Bengal. He drafted the sort of organisation that would make the scheme work and left it with his staff officer while he returned to London, thence to Washington. He never saw the scheme in practice.

In his absence a circular went out under his name, asking for volunteers to run the Aircrew Mountain Centre (AMC). One of those to see it was Wing Commander Tony Smyth, an experienced mountaineer. He had just spent a month in Tibet, and had returned to Calcutta from there. Smyth had three months in which to occupy himself before repatriation; what could be better? he thought. Borrowing a Hurricane, he flew to Group Headquarters. Somewhat to his surprise – no other officer had applied – he got the job.

A location was found. Goddard, before his departure, had given the scheme a high priority, and Smyth found wheels oiled and doors opened to an extent he had seldom known before. He was allocated a Harvard in which he had an eventful flight to Rawalpindi, from where the rest of the journey was by car. On his way, anticipating the start of the scheme, he was setting up staging posts for the AMC students and stores. For the last part of his rugged journey, Smyth was given a ½-ton four-wheel-drive Humber van; the same as the vehicle then used as an ambulance at Llandwrog and Harpur Hill.

At the future site of AMC, he arranged for houseboats and cookboats to be brought upriver, and selected climbing and skiing instructors, not all of whom were RAF, and administrative staff. His leading mountaineer was Wilfred Noyce, later to be on Sir John Hunt's Everest expedition of 1953. The basis of the scheme was that students would be away from their units for 28 days, which allowed for a journey of about seven days in each direction and fourteen days at AMC. They would be given mountaineering, trekking and skiing experience, depending on the time of year.

Shortly after the Burma drop, first Graham and then White were posted to AMC. Graham arrived with the vague reputation of having started the Mountain Rescue Service, but it was not until this book was being researched that Smyth learnt how true this was.

On one of those ski-treks, Sergeant Bill Surrey, an instructor, broke a leg.

Graham, with his usual resourcefulness, made a sledge with which to take Surrey back; perhaps his Llandwrog experience of sledge stretchers was useful. On another, he tried to milk a herd of yaks. His party was hot, dry and thirsty, and he and the group lifted the long curtains of hair on the side of each beast, only to find that all were male. Another doctor in the party made a comment about FFI Inspections[21]

During a quiet spell at the centre, caused by a period of unusually severe snowfalls in the winter of 1944-45, the opportunity was taken by the authorities to post some people away, and Doc Graham was the first of these. He remains something of an enigma. He did not tell his new CO, Tony Smyth, of his mountain rescue initiative in Wales, although if the men chatted as men usually do in remote postings he would soon have learnt of Smyth's mountaineering experience. Neither did he tell Smyth about the Burmese incident, nor the DSO which that earned him.

At first glance, Smyth's impression of Graham as 'an extreme introvert' seems odd. Here we have a man who, from our North Wales evidence, was ebullient and outgoing, not lacking in self-confidence and capable of standing up to the highest authority if he knew he was right. Did his character change? Certainly not immediately after the Prosser incident, if White's recollection and Graham's excellent report are any guide.

There is something of a gap in our knowledge after the posting away from Tony Smyth's unit. He was made acting squadron-leader on December 12th 1944, but did not return to the UK until March 1946 when he went straight into hospital at Dumfries. What happened between the time he left Smyth and the time he arrived in the UK? Even allowing for the end-of-war logistical chaos, that seems a long time. Had he been on the run in the jungle? A prisoner of the Japanese? On another dangerous Graham enterprise? It would be nice to know, but both the records and the authorities are silent on the matter.

By October 1946 the address had changed to Northampton, and then, after what seems to have been a long period of treatment, he finally relinquished his commission on September 23rd 1947.

Prosser went back to Canada, spending many weeks in hospital, and he and White corresponded a little. Prosser died in July 1990 of cancer, survived by his wife and two children. George Graham, who had saved Prosser's life and those of many others, had died ten years earlier than Prosser, on October 10th 1980, of a stomach cancer, in the Cheadle Royal Hospital. He died in obscurity, in a psychiatric hospital, having had no further contact with the Mountain Rescue Service which he had played such a large part in shaping. Both Cheadle Royal Hospital and the War Pensions Directorate of the Department of Social Security, for reasons of confidentiality, felt unable to give any further details, though he had been dead twelve years when these words were written. Sadly, no contact could be established by the writer with either Evelyn Ann or the sons.

Standing l to r: Campi Barrows, Flt Lt S Cummings, Unknown, Sgt Hans Pick.
Photo: the late Gordon Leigh

Flt Lt John Lloyd during his short period with Llandwrog before his posting to Millom.
Photo: the late Gordon Leigh

7: The Ball Starts Rolling

In January of 1944, six months after Graham had been given the green light, the Air Ministry formally announced the new service.[22] Military crashes had accounted for 571 aircrew deaths on the mountains of Britain in 1943 alone, despite the efforts of the Graham and Crichton teams. The network, therefore, was expanded greatly over the next twelve months.

Like Graham before him, Scudamore also received the occasional visit from Wing Commander Ruffell Smith, who would fly down from Reading. He would come into Scudamore's surgery, sit on the examination couch swinging his legs, and chat. "What do you need this time, Tom?" Scudamore would give him a list – Verey pistols perhaps, compasses – and Ruffell Smith would nod, say that was reasonable, and make his notes. But before he left, Ruffell Smith would say: "Right, now who wants to go on leave?"

Perhaps Scudamore felt that Corporal Jackson, a Londoner, could do with a break. Ernie Jackson would go off to Station Headquarters to get a 48-hour pass, and then join Ruffell Smith in his aircraft to Reading, considerably shortening his journey. Before long the items Scudamore had asked for would arrive.

A little after Graham left for India, another officer, to the total surprise of Scudamore, suddenly appeared on the doorstep of Sick Quarters. Flight Lieutenant John Lloyd was a mountaineer and rock-climber, and had gone to the

Air Ministry to ask if there was any way in which he could use his talents for the Air Force. Right, said the Ministry, you'd better go down to Llandwrog – Graham's just been posted away. Scudamore confesses that at first he was 'shattered', but fortunately the two men got on well together. Lloyd tried – unsuccessfully, says Scudamore – to teach the other man rock-climbing.

Sergeant Grant's instructions, on a February day in 1944, were to take his Anson LT433 from RAF Cark, near Barrow-in-Furness, down to a northern part of Anglesey to provide trainees with a navigational exercise. The route was given, and he was to fly at 1500 feet. Sitting next to him was Warrant Officer Redman, the regular wireless operator; behind him, at the wireless operator's table, were Pilot Officer Byrne, the pupil wireless operator, and Sergeeant Birch, the navigator. They drifted well east of the prescribed route and found themselves over North Wales.

Grant found climbing difficult – it was a cold day and perhaps this Anson, too, was icing up – and before he could get clear of the hills he suddenly became aware of a rocky crag directly ahead. Desperately he tried to drop the aircraft down onto a grassy slope that he could just see. It slithered and banged, spun round; the world, it seemed, was turning over. After an age, the Anson stopped, but not before it had hit part of the crag head-on. They were on the slopes of Pen Llithrig-y-Wrach at about 2500 feet. The roof of the Anson's cockpit hit the ground, and came down onto Grant's head, pushing it sharply onto his chest.

When silence descended, Redman thought that he was lying on damp grass, and he could not understand how this could be. He was in acute pain and seemed to be bleeding everywhere. Byrne and Birch were on the floor of the aircraft, among tangled metal, papers, maps, pencils, the remains of the smashed table and bits of the transmitter and receiver. They both started shivering.

After an unknown length of time – it was about 10.30 am – Byrne and Birch heard Welsh voices outside. In shock, they were unable to call out or to move. The local people saw the terrible injuries that Redman and suffered and put overcoats over him. Someone ran to the nearest cottage to make and bring tea. This was taken in to Byrne and Birch with more overcoats; people felt it best not to move them. The temperature outside was freezing. Someone looked into the inverted and smashed cockpit and saw Grant. The weight of the aircraft had pushed his head forward onto his chest. His tongue was protruding between his teeth and his face and ears were a livid colour. Somebody had phoned either the police or the RAF.

The Flying Control Officer put a call through to Scudamore at 11.35 am, and the advance party was on its way within minutes. They called at Conwy Police Station and picked up PC Jones who was to guide them through the mountain tracks. He took them to a farm where they established base camp. The farmer, another Jones, told them about the three survivors and the dead pilot and about the local people who were doing what they could. Scudamore unloaded stretchers and first-aid equipment, and sent the Humber back to find the jeep which had been misdirected. Scudamore's stretcher party reached the crash site at about 1.45 pm.

It was immediately clear to Scudamore that there was nothing he could do for Grant, and he turned to Redman, lying on the grass. He had gone through the windscreen and his scalp was very badly lacerated. There were other injuries, and his condition was serious. Scudamore gave him some Omnopon (papaveretum, a pain-killer), then he was put on a stretcher to be taken to the Humber, and on to hospital as soon as the civilians returned. Scudamore called up the Humber on his walkie-talkie and spoke to the wireless operator, the blond Corporal Sid Baker, an old hand who had been in the Air Force since 1936. He was to come to the crash site with two more stretchers and the civilians. However, Baker told him that the civilians seemed to have lost enthusiasm and disappeared. He had, therefore, called up Llandwrog on his own initiative and asked for a crash party.

Scudamore then got inside the aircraft to see to Byrne and Birch, still in shock. They were both injured, and Scudamore gave them both Omnopon and wrapped them in all the blankets available. That was at 2 pm. It was not until 5 pm that the Humber party returned and Byrne could be taken out and removed to the Humber. When the Byrne stretcher party was on its way, Grant's body was extracted, with some difficulty, from the smashed cockpit and laid on the grass, covered with a blanket, to be collected later. Birch was fed on Horlicks tablets whilst he waited his turn for removal. It was 6.30 pm before the party returned to take him to the ambulance, and it was 7 pm, in diminishing light, before he was on the stretcher and being taken down the laborious route to the base camp by Jones, Baker, LAC Martin and LAC Jackson. The Londoner Ernie Jackson had been an ambulance driver in the Blitz, before going into the army as a medical orderly and then becoming an air ambulance orderly in the Middle East. All that was before being posted to Wales.

Like Byrne, Birch finally reached the farmhouse base, where Mr and Mrs Jones had been looking after the party. More tea was produced, with bully beef sandwiches. Since it was about 8 pm and they had had no breakfast, this was more than welcome. Both Byrne and Birch were in remarkably good spirits, commented Scudamore in the log. The crash party – including J C 'Campi' Barrows on his first MR operation; the first of many – eventually arrived at 9.15 pm.

The delay in its arrival exposed yet more weaknesses in the transport arrangements. RAF Llandwrog had sent the fourteen men out in a coach, which suggests that whoever made the transport allocation did not know much about Welsh mountain roads. The coach had been unable to negotiate the track and the party had had to walk six miles. The drawbacks were obvious. Firstly, it delayed the arrival of the crash party, and secondly, they arrived exhausted before starting work. Fortunately, on this particular occasion there was a kind and helpful couple on hand, Mr and Mrs Jones, who again were pleased to aid their recovery with adequate cups of tea.

Baker and Jackson then led the crash party up to the crash site, collecting the body of the dead pilot. Byrne and Birch were taken in the Humber to hospital where they were expected. By the time Scudamore arrived at the hospital Redman had already been operated on, and was still in shock.

Two days later, Scudamore was on his way to the Air Ministry in London, to lecture on 'The Mountain Rescue of Aircraft Crashes'. He had been asked by Air Marshal Sir Harold Whittingham, who was then the Director General of Medical Services. This was at rather short notice, and Scudamore just grabbed some of George Graham's old notes and went. He found himself talking to senior medical personnel, including the Matron-in-Chief of the Royal Air Force. The audience, he adds wryly, also included, '...many junior officers like group captains and wing commanders. It was rather a terrifying experience.'

Scudamore told them about his experience with the Grant crash only a couple of days before. Sir Harold, in thanking him for coming, said that it was obvious that the Mountain Rescue Service should continue and expand. It seemed to Scudamore during this visit that whilst the medical branch knew very well of his existence and where he was, the admin people did not – probably explaining why they had sent John Lloyd down a little earlier.

From early in 1944, many miles away from Llandwrog, people at RAF Millom and in the Lake District gradually became accustomed to a new character. He would leave the station on a bicycle and point it towards the hills. Two things made him instantly noticeable: a bald and shining pate, and coils of rope draped over his shoulders. If anyone had occasion to speak to him, he had what his long-time friend, Willis Rae, called a 'crunching Scottish accent'. This new member of the Millom team was a bomb armourer, George (Scottie) Dwyer, later a noted mountaineer and British Mountaineering Council guide. He had been climbing in North Wales and elsewhere from quite an early age, and was posted to RAF Millom in February 1944. Within the month he was on the team. He was only the first of many RAF mountain rescue people to make his mark in the wider world of mountaineering. Dwyer's pre-war and wartime climbs in Scotland, Wales and England had made him already well-known in the tight-knit climbing fraternity.

The very first entry in his diary reads, in pencil and in a boyish hand:

Jan 1. 1934
Being the beginning of numerous excursions among the Hills and Mountains.
Jan 1. Spent the New Year in the proper manner at Shiel Bothy in Glen Isla in the company of T Harley and J Chalmers.
Climbed Beinn a' Ghlo with Chalmers, Cunny, & Davidson saw 'Spectre of the Brocken'.

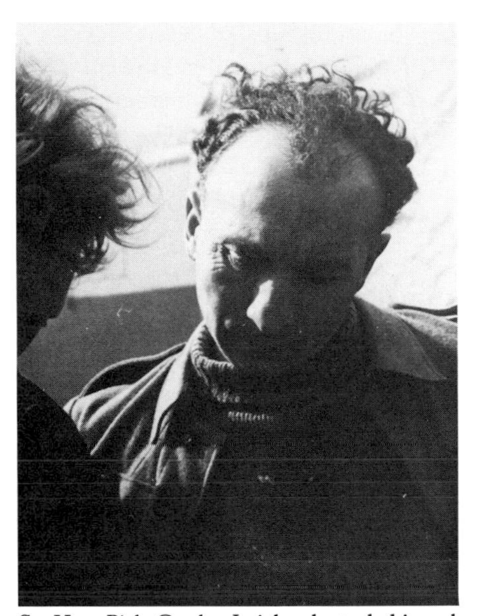

Sgt Hans Pick. Gordon Leigh, who took this and other photographs, and gave the writer much information, sadly died before the book was completed. *Photo: the late Gordon Leigh*

Scottie Dwyer (l) and Willis Rae, 11/3/45. *Photo: Willis Rae*

Dwyer saw the Spectre – that eerie phenomenon when the climber's shadow appears against the mist – again in August 1939, during his first Alpine climbs, in Switzerland:

Aug 6th. With Bell climbed Gisighorn a lot of fresh snow had fallen on the mountains, saw Brocken Spectre repeatedly today.

He and Campi Barrows, a flight mechanic, were friends, and early in 1944 when stationed at Binbrook had seen a feature in a daily newspaper on the Llandwrog team, with Mick McTigue operating the walkie-talkie. They both put in for a posting to a station with a Mountain Rescue team: Dwyer asked for North Wales, Barrows asked for the Lakes. When they finally came through, the postings were the reverse. It can often seem to someone in this situation that there is a clerk in the records office who takes a perverse delight in playing this sort of trick.

Dwyer's first time out with the team was on March 12th 1944, when there was a report of a crash at Coniston. On the first day, in rain and mist, they were unsuccessful, but the following day they found the wreck and removed the dead crew.

On April 25th an Anson from RAF Millom's 20(0)AFU on a night navigational exercise ended up on Llandwrog's patch, on Drum, near Tal-y-Bont in the Conwy Valley, close to where last August's Botha had crashed. The team had been on standby since the previous evening, and some of them, as usual in those circumstances, slept in the sick bay. (Some, especially Scudamore, had wondered in the intervening period how Graham was getting on in the Far East. Nobody had any idea of the privations he had been through.) At 9.30 pm the MO took a telephone call from the police. In one area of the Conwy Valley people were quite used to hearing explosions since the moorland was used by the army for night exercises with live ammunition. However, during this particular night there had been a bang which was louder than the usual, and people reported it. It was treated with a little caution, since the exercises in the past had caused one or two false alarms. By dawn a crash had been confirmed and the team left. There was rain in the hills, with low cloud.

Gordon Leigh remembers backing up a long, narrow mountain track. This was a technique learnt through hard experience, so that if there were any survivors the ambulance could make a quick getaway and not have to turn round in the narrow road. The mountain rescue fleet then included a 20-cwt truck as well as the ambulance. It was fitted out purely as a stretcher-carrier. With the convoy on that day, recalls Leigh, were two medical officers and Sergeant Hans Pick.

Hans Pick was a refugee from Austria, who had been in an Alpine Division of the Austrian army. He was now in the British Army, seconded to the Air Force as Mountain Rescue instructor. His task was to tour the burgeoning network of teams and inject some mountaineering expertise where little more than enthusiasm, toughness and bravery had existed.

McTigue and Leigh were the first on the crash scene after an arduous climb. The Anson had ploughed into the hillside just below the summit. As the climbing party extracted the bodies from the wreck, Leigh radioed their identities to Baker in the radio van, who then relayed them to RAF Llandwrog, from where they were passed on to RAF Millom.

Barrows remembers Leigh with affection: 'He taught me a lot on the Welsh hills and was our best hill man. Pity he only stayed a few months.'[23] For on May 15th 1944, Gordon Leigh was posted away from Llandwrog to the South Coast as part of the D-Day preparations. He was attached to the Fleet Air Arm, where he remained for the rest of the war. Scudamore, by then a flight-lieutenant, was on a course on tropical medicine at RAF Halton, and another medical officer, Flight Lieutenant R O Swaine, had been drafted in to Llandwrog from RAF Barrow.

Sergeant W C Harvey took a call from the Senior Flying Control Officer in the early hours of May 16th: a Wellington, HF519, belonging to 26 OTU from RAF Wrexham had flown into a hill about a mile north-east of Llanwrst while trying to get a visual fix. Harvey told the stand-in MO, who to Harvey's surprise, even shock, said he would not be going out. An hour later, the team left without the medical officer, Sergeant Harvey (the NCO in charge of Sick Quarters) having put Mick McTigue, a source of great strength, in charge. They called, as usual, at the local police station for a precise location, but found that all the police were at the crash. The fire station staff were able to direct them and they arrived at the crash site at 3.20 am.

It was not difficult to find. About 100 yards from a farm, the aircraft was still burning. It had flown straight into the side of a small hill. It was very dark and the police and then the MR team had trouble locating any of the crew. Eventually five bodies were found and McTigue ordered a search of the surrounding fields; they had expected to find six. They were concerned also that some of the local people might have been caught in the crash. Dawn broke, and they found the sixth crewman in the wreckage. All except one were Canadians.

It was three days later that Scudamore returned from his course. He was annoyed to learn that there had been a call-out, that there had been no medical officer present, and that no report had been written. He told McTigue and Harvey to write a full report in the log: in fact McTigue wrote it and Harvey endorsed it. At the same time, recalls Scudamore, the locum had become excited and was threatening to charge the team's drivers with dangerous driving.

The Medical Officer senior to Scudamore, a couple of days later, was equally concerned. He made it plain that it was expected of a medical officer running a Mountain Rescue team always to attend a flying accident if possible, though he conceded that the officer concerned had had a vaccination not long before, and this might have influenced his decision. The CO, Group Captain G W Bentley, made an even more terse comment: 'Thank you. I have received the Chief Instructor's report and have taken the action I consider necessary.'[24]

Squadron Leader Harley, a Volunteer Reserve MO, had been to Llandwrog to see how the team there was organised, and on his return he quickly set about getting something similar for Montrose. It was becoming obvious that something had to be done to speed up the rescue of crashed aircrew in the Grampians, and he was instrumental in getting things moving there. Probably that is the reason he found himself a few months later at RAF Millom. Sergeant Hans Pick was sent to start things off at Montrose and to give the fledgling team a grounding in rock-climbing. D-Day – June 6th 1944 – arrived during his time there. Harold Sinden, a medical orderly, was on the hill resting with Pick and some trainees when news came over the radio of the Normandy landings. Pick let out a great whoop of joy and the team quickly learnt that he had in the past few years acquired some very colourful English expressions.

From this day on, people in the UK quickly became used to seeing the black and white identifying stripes on the wings of the invasion force aircraft.

8 – Crescendo

Preparations for D-Day – Operation Overlord – were reaching a peak. Only five days before the Normandy landings, on June 1st 1944, Scudamore said: 'MO and SSQ staff had retired to bed and were trying to sleep through a heavy thunderstorm. Rain was torrential and lightning flashes were dazzling and continuous. Aircraft were returning to base from a detail one by one.'[25] The phone rang at 1.10 am: would Flight Lieutenant Scudamore please report at Flying Control immediately. He roused McTigue and Cumming, and the three men drove over to Flying Control. There they learnt that an aircraft had overshot the runway and finished up in the sea – not the first to do so.

Harvey and Jackson were told to join the three at the beach. There Scudamore found a small group of airmen who told him that they had seen Verey lights from the crashed plane about a mile out to sea. These had since ceased and even the lightning revealed nothing. Also there were the senior officers in charge of night flying, who, deciding that there was nothing further to be done, turned to go back inside. Scudamore and McTigue looked at their departing backs in disbelief.

A nearby Air Sea Rescue unit had been informed, Scudamore learnt, but no sighting had been made of its pinnace as yet. In the best Mountain Rescue tradition, he liberated a dinghy from the nearest aircraft, an Anson, on the aerodrome, and Harvey arranged for the various team vehicles to point their headlights out to sea – the blackout regulations had become fairly relaxed by this time. The dinghy was launched, Flight Lieutenant Scudamore commanding, with Cumming and two others; all, according to the skipper, very willing volunteers. It was a strange, almost bizarre, occasion. Headlamps shining out from the beach; occasional flashes from the sea, some way out; lightning and thunder from time to time with heavy rain; and, strangest of all, the sea luminous with glowing plankton.

Verey lights were seen again. As they approached the lights, they could see that they came from another dinghy. A cheerful voice came across the water through the torrential rain: "We're all here, all five of us!" The two dinghies were hitched together, and Scudamore checked the ditched crew for injuries; there were no problems. Cigarettes were handed out and the two dinghies started for the shore.

Closer inshore, Scudamore suddenly saw two figures in the water, swimming towards him. As they reached the dinghies, he recognised Flying Officer H King, the Air Sea Rescue Officer, and the recently-promoted Corporal Ernie Jackson of the Mountain Rescue Team. Exhausted, they joined the dinghy crew, hauled aboard by willing hands. There seems to have been something of a carnival atmosphere on that warm June night; perhaps everybody there, career airmen and conscripts alike, smelt the beginning of the end in the air. Within the year the war was over.

All, rescuers and rescued, were taken to sick quarters and peeled off their clothes in the warmth of the operating theatre. An issue of rum was followed by tea. Writing up the log, however, Scudamore decided that there was a lesson to be drawn from the incident. This was the third occasion on which the Air Sea

Rescue launch had been unable to get near to a ditched aircraft which was just offshore. As it happened, there was an inspection by the Air Officer Commanding on that day, and Scudamore suggested to him that an amphibious jeep, permanently stationed there, might be the best solution. The suggestion was noted, but nothing came of it.

During that same day, Scudamore received a telephone call which left him rather shocked: an engineering officer told him that he ought to be severely reprimanded.

"Why, what's the matter?" asked Scudamore.

"Last night you had the audacity to remove a dinghy from one of my aircraft. Do you realise that that aircraft could have taken off and those people could have ditched and drowned?"

"Do you realise what that dinghy was being used for?"

The engineering officer was not impressed.

"Don't you ever do that again."

"If you give me a boat," replied Scudamore "I won't have to do it again."

There is no hint of censure in the log although the entry was seen and commented on generally by Squadron Leader Collins, and Scudamore heard nothing more of the incident. Probably the other officers concerned realised that it would have been embarrassing to report that they were on the scene and made no effort to find out if the ditched crew were safe or not.

On June 6th 1944 the RAF dropped 5,200 tons of bombs on coastal defence gun emplacements in Normandy. They were followed in the dawn light by the USAF daytime bombers, attacking other shore defences. From midnight, three airborne divisions were landing: the British 6th Airborne Division north-east of Caen, and two American divisions north of Carentan. Then came the shore attacks. One of the American beaches was Omaha Beach, near Bayeux, where they suffered very severe losses.

Once the first assaults were over there was a secondary priority: to get the severely injured back to Britain. The standard transport for this sort of work, for both the RAF and the United States Army Air Force (USAAF), was the Douglas Dakota, the C47. One of these, in American livery, left France full of American casualties on June 8th bound for Prestwick. All had what would have been called in another war, another army, a Blighty one. At Prestwick the casualties were to be transferred to a long-haul aircraft for the final journey back home to the USA. Flying up the Scottish west coast, Prestwick getting nearer all the time, both the crew and the wounded soldiers felt their spirits rising.

On the approach to Prestwick the visibility was very poor. The Dakota was very low – too low – preparing to cross the peninsula of The Rhinns, passing within sight of Stranraer then Ayr and on to Prestwick. All the way down the coast of the peninsula, on either side of Portpatrick, are high cliffs. The Dakota flew straight into them; all on board were killed instantly. Five miles away, at RAF West Freugh, a call was received: can you get some airmen together to collect the bodies?

A group of volunteers was gathered, and they were taken to the top of the cliffs. It was immediately clear that the wreck could not be reached from there, or at least not without special equipment which West Freugh did not have. A lorry was sent back to West Freugh, and there loaded with inflatable dinghies. These were taken down to the beach and launched, then paddled round to the foot of the cliff where the impact had occurred. One after another, the bodies were put on to the dinghies, two at a time, and taken out to the local lifeboat which had arrived on the scene. Some time after this, an American staff officer called at RAF West Freugh to thank the RAF on behalf of the USAAF, and to express appreciation of the way in which the whole operation had been carried out.

There was, by this stage, already a Mountain Rescue Team at RAF Wigtown covering South-West Scotland, but this incident made it clear that there was need for one at West Freugh. With the CO's encouragement, a permanent team of volunteers was established, and remained there on an unofficial basis until the one at Dumfries was closed in 1946.

The very comprehensive Mountain and Cave Rescue Handbook was not quite accurate when it said:

> It will be realised that from 1935 when the first mountain rescue posts were established up to the mid 1950 era, in most cases the friends and associates of the injured climber, walker or pot-holer carried out the rescue using equipment from the nearest mountain rescue post. Apart from the Keswick Mountain Rescue Team founded in 1947 and the Coniston Mountain Rescue Team founded in 1952 *there were no mountain rescue teams available.*[26] (My italics.)

By the end of World War II the RAF had teams established in all of the main climbing areas, always willing to help a civilian climber in trouble. The first non-flying rescue or attempted rescue that can be traced was on June 16th 1944, just a fortnight after the seaborne rescue. At this time, far away in London, the first V1 flying bombs – doodlebugs – were dropping. Even further away, the Allied forces were struggling to break out of the Normandy beachhead. But on Cadair Idris, south of Dolgellau, there was another problem.

The police phoned Llandwrog at about 1.30 in the morning. A girl was stranded on a ledge on Cadair Idris. John Lloyd went out with Mick McTigue, leaving the Humber to deal with any emergencies. They called on the farmer who had first reported to the police and he led them to the cliff; however, he seemed uncertain which way she had climbed from that point. He and the police had already tried to reach the girl but were unable to do so. Dawn was breaking as, in driving rain and variable mist, Lloyd and McTigue climbed a gully for a preliminary search; then they returned to the foot of the cliff. By this time, someone who had seen the girl on the previous evening had arrived, and he led them up to a ledge high up beside another gully, at about 2500 feet. To get onto this ledge, Lloyd had to descend to it from above, and he was able to establish beyond doubt that it was the ledge in question; but the girl was not there.

Puzzled and more than a little concerned, they returned in the bitter cold to the farmhouse where they found her sitting comfortably in the warm. She told them that after three hours or so, she had managed to pull herself together and climb away from the ledge up the difficult rocks above. Lloyd and McTigue returned to Llandwrog at four pm, having been out for fourteen and a half hours.

Lloyd afterwards felt that some sort of explanation for his decision to go out on a non-flying rescue might be called for, and commented in the log:

The decision [to respond] was made for the following reasons:

1 There is little doubt that the MRS has the most efficient equipment and is the best organisation for dealing with mountain casualties of all sorts up to a radius of 40 miles from this station.

2 The police in this neighbourhood are of the utmost value to us in locating aircraft crashes, and it is felt that our present relations with the police would deteriorate if we refused to help them with civilian accidents which are primarily their responsibility.[27]

Without knowing it, he had set the pattern for the next 46 years and more.

Further developments happened in the south of the Principality towards the end of this month of June. A medical officer, Squadron Leader Winterbottom, returned from India and set up a team at RAF Madley. This, though based in Herefordshire, covered what is now St Athan's patch.

At about the time that John Lloyd and Mick McTigue were sitting in the farmhouse at the foot of Cadair Idris, sipping the tea supplied by the farmer's wife, the Tannoy at RAF Millom crackled and spoke: "Mountain Rescue – report to Flying Control! Mountain Rescue – report to Flying Control!"

Cockermouth police had telephoned to say that someone had reported a low-flying aircraft, which then crashed somewhere on Red Pike. The team left Millom just after 2.30 pm, calling in at two police stations. At the second, Keswick, they learnt that the wreck had been located on Red Pike and that bodies were being brought down to the Fish Hotel, Buttermere. At the hotel, they found that this work was being done by forty soldiers from the Carrier Training Centre under Lieutenant Anderdon. Anderdon assured Squadron Leader G A Van-Someren, the Senior Medical Officer who was leading the team, that his soldiers would continue the work. Four bodies, he said, had been found so far. Van-Someren telephoned Millom to say that in view of the army's assistance, no support party would be needed, but that the engineering officer should come in a vehicle suitable for carrying bodies. Base camp was established at the outlet of Buttermere, about 2,000 feet below the wreckage. The aircraft was a Wellington, HZ715, from 22OTU, RAF Wellesbourne Mountford.

After tea and sandwiches, Van-Someren, Anderdon and the five-strong Mountain Rescue Party started on the climb with a sledge stretcher and a standard stretcher. They met two parties of soldiers on the way, each party carrying down a body on an improvised stretcher. Van-Someren stopped the second party, gave them the standard stretcher, and told them to send up another party and stretcher from the base camp. As they got near the 2,000-foot cloud base, they could see the wreck; against the sky could just be distinguished the lattice construction of a Wellington. Close up, they found two bodies which had been thrown clear, but they could see, on closer inspection, that there were four more in the fuselage. They had reached the wreck at 6.45 pm, and it was a full hour before they had completed tying three bodies onto the one sledge stretcher they had with them. There was neither sight nor sound of the soldiers who were due to return.

They started the descent, Lieutenant Anderdon going ahead with the promise that he would send up more men and stretchers. They had been descending with their prodigious load for near an hour and a half when they saw a solitary figure approaching up the hill – the engineering officer, Flying Officer Ward. Van-Someren left the stretcher party in the care of Corporal Elems, a nursing orderly, and took Ward up to the wreck. The unfortunate Elems had been continuing the descent with his party for nearly three quarters of an hour, when the stretcher collapsed under the load. At this point they were still 1,000 feet above base camp, so they had descended less than half of the way in two hours. Elems left the bodies and the broken stretcher there and went down with the party to the base camp. Divested of the load, they made the rest of the descent in less than half an hour, at 10.15 pm.

Van-Someren, in his later report, suggested amendments to the stretcher, including a third runner down the centre and lateral bracing.

It would be understandable if Elems had been rather rattled by having a stretcher with three bodies on it collapse in mid-lower. His mood would certainly not have been improved by what he found at the base camp. The only people there were the wireless operator and driver, who told him that Lieutenant Anderdon had decided to call it a day, taking his men with him.

Pondering his next move, Elems found that he had been joined by someone else. This man introduced himself as Church – H F Church, a mountaineer. He listened to what Elems had to say, and offered to get some climbing friends together from a climbers' hostel at Newlands, west of Keswick. Gratefully, Elems accepted, and the driver took Elems and Church there in the jeep. On the way there was some tyre trouble, and almost unbelievably the jeep did not have a spare wheel. Elems and Church were therefore dropped at Newlands whilst the

11,461 Vickers-Armstrong Wellingtons were built. MF628 subsequently went to the RAF Museum, Hendon. *Photo: H J Budgen*

driver went on to Keswick where he could obtain a spare.

At about this time, Van-Someren and Ward had reached the wreck. With some RAF and Home Guard men who were there, they started to bring the remaining three bodies down using a canvas stretcher provided by the police. They descended the first 500 feet, but Van-Someren was getting very anxious about the non-appearance of the stretchers. He made the full descent in an hour, getting to base camp at about eleven at night. There he was filled in on events by the wireless operator. He felt very badly let down by Lieutenant Anderdon, and said so in his report later.

Van-Someren telephoned RAF Millom to say that they would not be able to complete the job that night. He was told to stay there overnight and arrangements were made for a support party to come out the next morning. In the meantime a nursing orderly and a driver were still up on the hill with the wreck and three bodies. Van-Someren started on the 2,000-foot climb yet again and met them at the point where the three bodies and the broken sledge stretcher had been left; they had started coming down with the heaviest of the bodies. They had realised that something had gone badly wrong and decided wisely that they might as well find their way back to base camp.

This group travelled light down to base camp, reaching it at about midnight. Soon they could hear vehicles, and were surprised to find that the jeep was being closely followed by a lorry bearing the name of a Cockermouth coal merchant, and by another vehicle. All were full: the passengers were mountaineers, Home

Guard, soldiers, the product of Church's efforts. As the strange convoy pulled up, Van-Someren went over to speak to them all. He thanked them for turning out so late at night; but, he said, it was too dark for a safe climb and descent with stretchers over a route which consisted largely of rocky track. Therefore, he suggested, the best thing to do was to disperse; he thanked them again, and they went. Most of the party slept in the Fish Hotel's hayloft, with some in the Humber ambulance. The hotel had also made washing facilities freely available and had shown much forbearance when faced with muddy hobnailed boots.

The following morning, Dwyer was called out as one of the Support Party which included Flying Officer Ward and thirteen pupil aircrew sergeants. They arrived at the base camp to find a note left by Van-Someren. He had gone up to the half-way point with two stretchers, and wanted some of the Support Party to go to that point, the rest to the wreck. The whole job was finished by 3.30 pm and the two parties returned to Millom. Using pupil aircrew as stretcher-fodder was commonplace at Millom at that time. One can hardly imagine anything more likely to put a potential navigator or bomb-aimer off his training course or planned career than being sent up onto a misty, wet, dark, dangerous hill, and told to rake around in the burnt-out skeleton of an Anson or a Botha to find the charred or shredded remains of the young men who had been flying it not long before.

'The Air-crew Pupil N.C.O.'s did not make a good working party,' Van-Someren wrote in his report:

It is felt that strength, diligence, speed, discipline and enthusiasm are necessities for this work, and that these qualities will only be found in either trained volunteers or in persons such as those of the Mountain Rescue Party who are often out on this work and who take a pride in it. Moreover, it is an open question whether it be wise to bring inexperienced aircrew personnel into contact with the grisly gruesome objects with which the Support Party must deal.[28]

He suggested therefore that the SMO be authorised to have thirty men on the team drawn from the permanent staff, chosen so that 20 were likely at any one time to be available and therefore no section would be crippled by loss of staff. He added that a by-product of this would be that all members would be able to hold their own clothing and equipment.

Clearly this had been an operation which had shown up some serious weaknesses; at the same time it had demonstrated some impressive devotion to duty from the party of men who were inexperienced in climbing terms. As Johnnie Lees was to do twelve years later, Van-Someren put the case for sending the convoy out even before the exact location of the crash was known. He, like Lees, suggested that they should make for a given police station to pick up later information. He argued also for more use of walkie-talkies to avoid unnecessary long journeys between parties, and for the taking of rations and water no matter how brief the call-out seemed likely to be. Finally Van-Someren's report commented angrily on the lack of spare wheel for either jeep or Humber; it was only by chance that the jeep driver had been able to borrow one from the Driving and Maintenance School at Keswick.

As so often happens with these incidents, there is an odd post-script. During research for this book in July 1992, John Nixon, who is a prison officer at what was RAF Millom, found the remains of an RAF bomb at the Red Pike crash site. But the Wellington had been on a navigational exercise. Why would it be carrying a bomb?

9 – The Beginning of the End

In 1944, at Llandwrog, Scudamore was waiting for an opportunity to try out the new and experimental Duff stretcher (designed by Dr D G Duff of Fort William, an old climbing companion of Dwyer's), and this was granted to him on July 12th. Responding to a call, the team, after a several hours' search in drizzling rain, found Anson MG804 from 8(0)AFU at RAF Mona, on Foel Fras at 3000 feet, in cloud and with very bad visibility. On a night navigational exercise, the aircraft had crashed at 2.45 am; the wreck was not found until 8.30 am.

Scudamore found the air bomber, Sergeant Dalton, lying outside the aircraft, shouting and semi-conscious, clearly badly concussed. He was given morphia and kept warm. Whilst Scudamore and an orderly were looking after Dalton, they were startled to see three other members of the crew come out of the aircraft. The pilot, Flight Sergeant Biffin, had a fractured jaw and a foot injury; the navigator, Pilot Officer Sidthorp and the wireless operator, Sergeant Lorrimer, had less severe injuries. Inside was Flight Sergeant Standring, the staff wireless operator, who had died from shock and head injuries, shortly before the rescue party arrived. The Duff stretcher was used for Dalton. Although Scudamore had asked RAF Mona for a carrying party at 10 am, the party did not arrive until 6.30 pm. Dalton had to be given a second dose of morphia *en route*, and they reached the mountain headquarters at 8.30 pm, nearly eighteen hours after the crash. From there, Dalton and Biffin were taken to hospital.

The Duff, in this first version, was only moderately successful, showing a tendency to distort. Dr Duff demonstrated two modified versions only a few weeks later, and while the distortion problem had been overcome, the modifications made the stretcher too heavy.

There was more concern about the eight and a half hours which the carrying party had taken to arrive, and Scudamore was questioned on this. He replied that the Austrian mountain soldier Sergeant Hans Pick was now training a number of volunteers so that a full party, including stretcher-bearers, would be available from Llandwrog.

Gradually, the service was assuming the shape which we see today.

As the war progressed, a change in the pattern of crashes began to be seen in north Wales. Overwhelmingly until mid-1944, the aircraft concerned had been Ansons but now, others were appearing. Already in February there had been a Mosquito, the fast and popular twin-engined fighter-bomber with the unique moulded-plywood construction.

The Avro Lancaster, Handley Page Halifax and Short Stirling were the RAF's heavy bombers for the second half of the war, with the American-made Liberator. Normally, a Halifax would carry a crew of seven or eight, and it was not the aircrews' favourite, with neither the height nor the bomb capacity of the Lancaster, and it was gradually withdrawn from operations over Germany after 1943[29]. The Llandwrog team had to deal with two Halifaxes in a few days. The first, LL283 from Dishforth, Yorkshire, fell out of the sky in flames north-west of Porthmadoc, in the early hours of the morning of August 31st 1944. Scudamore and the team learnt that the wreckage was scattered over three fields on a small hill. As they approached through the darkness they could see a fire – actually one of the tyres – still burning. They were on a narrow track which the police had pointed out to them, but this petered out about a mile from the wreckage. Walking the rest of the way to the main part of the aircraft, they searched through the wreckage and found the mutilated body of Sergeant Pack, the flight engineer. Unlike the rest of the crew, he had for some reason been unable to bale out and had gone down with the plummeting, torching Halifax. Perhaps he had been caught in the fire right from the start. They were about to carry the body across the fields when somebody from a local cottage appeared on the scene. He showed them another track which enabled the team to bring the ambulance right up to the wreck. This track passed through a farm, and Scudamore took the opportunity of calling there and asking for the use of their telephone; then speaking to Flying Control at Llandwrog, since radio communication had been proving difficult that night. Not only could they not contact Llandwrog, but also could not speak to the reconnaissance Anson up above.

Flying Control had some news for him. Two of the crew who had baled out were being looked after at Porthmadoc Casualty Reception Station, an army establishment. Scudamore took Flight Sergeant Murphy and a policeman with him in the jeep, and found Sergeant Swan, another flight engineer, and Sergeant Morris, an air gunner, in bed there. Morris had had an injury to the side of his head, and was very confused and dazed, but Swan appeared to be unhurt and was able to tell them that he had seen another air gunner, Flight Sergeant Lowe, also leave the aircraft. By this time it was 8.30 am.

Scudamore and Murphy were still at the casualty station when an NCO came into the ward and told Scudamore that he was wanted on the telephone. The caller told him that an airman had knocked on the door of a farm called Tyddin-Mawr in Cwm Ystradllyn and was being looked after by the family. Scudamore, Murphy and the policeman found their way there, and met Warrant Officer Hogan, the wireless operator. Hogan kept insisting that he felt fine except for a

A P-47 Thunderbolt, similar to that which came down on Arran Fawddwy in September 1944. This belongs to Stephen Grey's fighter collection. *Photo: H J Budgen*

painful left foot, but there was something not quite rational in the way he was speaking, and Scudamore was certain that he was, in fact, in shock. Hogan, too, was taken to the casualty station and on their arrival they found that in the meantime, Lowe had been taken there with injuries to his left leg and right buttock.

10 am now. Another telephone call. Another farmer's wife had been disturbed and was doing what she could. Flying Officer Buck, the bomb aimer, and Sergeant Abson, the navigator, had called at a farm called Braich Dinas, having walked down the Cwm Pennant Valley. An army ambulance took Scudamore to Braich Dinas where he found the two airmen who seemed to be very cheerful with only minor injuries. They too were taken to Porthmadoc. There, at 12.30 pm, Scudamore took another message, this time from the police inspector at Porthmadoc. The eighth crew member had been seen somewhere on the mountains – he would be the last. He, it was thought, was dead.

No sooner had Scudamore put down the telephone than it rang again; this was Flying Control at RAF Llandwrog. The crew of the reconnaissance Anson had seen a body with a parachute attached and the map reference given would put it very near the Braich Dinas farm. Scudamore and the main team went back to start a search, beginning with the northern end of the Cwm Pennant Valley, leaving the support party at the casualty station. Searching through heavy hail, they established that, despite what the Anson crew had said, there was no body in the vicinity of Braich Dinas. Whilst they were doing this, the orderly officer in charge of the support party received an exact location for the body, and took the men out to retrieve it from Cwm Ystradllyn. Scudamore and the team, returning from Braich Dinas, then went up the valley, meeting the support party coming down with the body on a stretcher. This was of Flight Lieutenant McGuire, the pilot. He had landed badly, hitting his head very hard and dislocating his spine. Scudamore judged that death had been mercifully instantaneous.

The Porthmadoc Casualty Reception Station had served as an excellent headquarters and sick quarters, and the staff had worked well with the RAF Llandwrog team.

Then, only three days later on September 3rd, a Halifax no. JD417 from Lindholme, also in Yorkshire, crashed on The Rivals at about 1150 feet while on a navigation exercise. All six aboard were dead and were taken to the Llandwrog mortuary. In mid-September, a Republic P47 Thunderbolt, an American fighter, went missing. It was not until a week later that a shepherd reported seeing a crashed aircraft with a body on a very inaccessible cliff face on Aran Fawddy. The team investigated, searching the area in heavy rain. As darkness approached, they called the search off as it was known that the pilot was dead, and returned the next day. In close succession, they dealt with a Mosquito on Foel Fras (September 25th), a Wellington reported but not found (October 12th), a Mosquito with a Belgian pilot on Mynydd Mawr (November 1st), and an American C47 above Llyn Dulyn on Foel Grach. There were no survivors from any of the wrecks.

The record of the service with its own motor vehicles has not been particularly good; but then the conditions under which they have to be driven are so often far worse than normal, as are the roads used. A return journey was made to the C47 crash to collect the bodies on November 23rd, and the Humber ambulance carrying the bodies of 2nd Lieutenant W G Gough, Lieutenant R A Rolfe, Flight Sergeant K H McLaren and Corporal H Lavitski had an accident on the way back.

En route from Le Bourget to Burtonwood, the C47, like many an earlier crash, had been reported on an east-west bearing that would take it across Graham's Graveyard. Sure enough, when the team arrived within sight of Craig Dulyn above the twin lakes, there high up in the crag Campy Barrows could see a shining silver bird-like object which had flown straight into the cliff-face and was now resting on a ledge. It took the team more than a month to drag the wing sections down the valley. The rest of the aircraft stayed there a long time before finally breaking up and falling into the dark, cold waters. Until that happened, it was visible on a sunny day as far away as Llandudno.

In the mountainous areas of the United Kingdom there are many wrecks, a large proportion dating from the war. These became objects of interest, and the seeing and plotting and recording of wrecks, especially wartime ones, soon developed into a sizeable movement with its own literature – books and magazines. Some have even given the movement a spurious scientific name, 'wreckology'. Perhaps, if we are generous, we can assume that the word is used ironically. But perhaps not. This particular aircraft quickly became an object of interest in this respect, and most of it is now in the Fort Perch Air Museum at New Brighton.

It was October 22nd before Millom MRT was called on again to look for a wrecked aeroplane; on this occasion a Halifax. At 10 pm the team went out to Cockley Beck Farm at the head of the Duddon Valley. They started searching at about midnight but it was a dark and misty night. Drawing a blank, they returned to the farm at about 5 am, had a meal and waited for daybreak. When the four search parties started again at first light, Scottie Dwyer's group met the farmer, who showed them where the wreck was and how to get to it. The other three parties were sent back to collect the vehicles and take them to a point in Little Langdale, near to Ambleside and closer to the crash site.

The fuselage was found almost on the summit of Carrs, and on the rocky ground and scree below were the wings, engines and the rest of the wreckage. All eight bodies were taken out of the fuselage but there was insufficient time to get them all down that day, largely because of the extremely rough ground and the inexperience of the team.

Dwyer stayed overnight with one from his enormous network of friendly bed-and-breakfast landladies; in ten years of climbing he had, like many other young climbers, gradually accumulated these invaluable contacts dotted all over Mid and North Wales, the Peaks, the Lakes and the Scottish Highlands. Where there was not a bed-and-breakfast landlady, there was a pub with inexpensive accommodation and, even in wartime it seemed, an inexhaustible supply of pints, usually drawn by someone with a keen interest in climbing and climbers, like Sid Cross of the Old Dungeon Ghyll. Scottie left the team that evening, and: '...went over to Langdale and stayed at Mrs Myers that night.'[30]

On the following morning, he walked over to Little Langdale to rejoin the team. The whole operation seems to have been fairly leisurely and because of the late start on this day, they were able to bring only three bodies down. Three aircrew members of the team joined Dwyer that night at the Myers' establishment. The job was finished the next day, with the remaining five bodies recovered.

Only a week after the Halifax crashed on Carrs, Hans Pick arrived at Millom to continue his peripatetic training task, and stayed for ten days. A further week after he had finished his job and gone, on November 17th, Millom were out again, at 10 pm. This was rather more successful than the Carrs call-out.

An Anson, no. MG464 from 5(0)AS RAF Jurby, with a crew of four had hit the side of Grisedale Pike, near Keswick, in cloud. Two of the crew were injured, one seriously; the other had broken legs. The remaining two, badly shaken but otherwise unhurt, eventually were able to find their way down into the valley. It took the team all night – nearly twelve hours – to locate the crash. The more seriously injured crew-member had died during the night; perhaps he could have been saved if the wreck had been found earlier. The injured one was carried down by stretcher and taken to Mark Hewitts Hospital at Keswick.

By this time, Squadron Leader Harley, who had been Station Commander at Montrose, was at Millom, and on the day of this operation had just returned from the Air Ministry, where had been held what was probably the very first Mountain Rescue Conference. No records exist, except that Scudamore noted in the Llandwrog diary that medical equipment was discussed.

Then, next month, without any warning, there is a different sort of entry in Dwyer's climbing diary:

Dec. [1944]
2nd. Nell and I got married at Keighley.
3rd. With Nell, went from Bradford to Bangor on our honeymoon, weather was bad.

Many of Dwyer's climbing companions had been women, including on some of the most severe climbs. This seems to disprove a general impression that the world of hard rock-climbing before the war was exclusively a male domain. Dwyer returned to camp on December 10th; the following day yet another Anson crashed on Kinder Scout, this time from a Polish squadron. All survived, two with injuries.

By February 1945, an officer in Whitehall who had been made responsible for these matters, Flight Lieutenant Gill, was able to tell the Air Ministry that the teams now in existence were Kinloss, Topcliffe, Wick, Cark (transferred from Millom), Llandwrog, Montrose, Wigtown and Madley. The network had spread rapidly.

But where was Harpur Hill which had been operating for nearly three years? Not in this list, certainly. But during all the activity at Llandwrog, Millom and elsewhere, Harpur Hill MRT was also developing under Crichton's guidance. In his case, however, there was the disadvantage that the team did not officially exist, and it was only when they were involved in searches for the American aircraft, prompting a letter of thanks from the American authorities to the Air Ministry, that the Ministry 'gave us official existence and more lavish equipment'.

Why, then, was Harpur Hill not recognised in Whitehall until April 1945? There was no other team in the Peak District at the time.

10 – The End of the Beginning

Just before the turn of the year, Millom had welcomed a new officer – the genial and popular John Lloyd, from Llandwrog, leaving Scudamore again in sole charge there. Flight Lieutenant John Lloyd, the tall, bespectacled doctor with a ready grin, and Corporal George Dwyer, the intense, self-sufficient bomb armourer with the shining bald head, knew of each other's reputation and soon established a rapport that went beyond the common task in MR.

Initially Dwyer was the only member of the Millom team with any serious mountaineering experience. It is clear from his climbing diary that the small matter of wartime national service was hardly allowed to interfere with his great passion for climbing. Neither was the matter of marriage. No doubt because of his diary-keeping experience, he was also the keeper of the MRT log at Millom and then Cark. It is obvious from his diary that Dwyer had no interest in aircraft. Nowhere does he name the aircraft whose crashes he attended; for that information you have to go to the MRT log.

He returned from his honeymoon leave on January 4th, and within a few days was plunged into a busy time. On the 8th an Anson from RAF Wigtown crashed early in the morning on Bootle Fell, only five miles or so from RAF Millom. An aircraft was sent out and was able to locate the crash. The team was guided to the site by signal cartridges, fired from the search aircraft at regular intervals. Three crew members were rescued and were taken down by stretcher to the ambulance; the other was, in Dwyer's words, 'beyond help'. The pilot's leg was trapped in the wreckage and part of the aircraft had to be sawn away to get the man out.

The following day the team was sent out again to find an aircraft, another Anson, this time from RAF Walney, which had been missing since the previous week. An independent aircraft had reported its position. Again the team piled into the MRT convoy vehicles and were taken to Whicham Valley. The information had been that the crashed plane was in the area between Black and White Combe, only a short distance from Bootle Fell, yesterday's scene. However, they were unable to find it. Flying Officer Wragg, who was leading the search, found a telephone and asked RAF Cark to send out the aircraft which had first seen the crash site. This it did, and markers were dropped which led the team to the crash, on the north side of the corrie of Black Combe. By this time it was too late to recover the bodies, which could be seen in the wreck. Next day Dwyer and another NCO from the team, Corporal Beattie, acted as guides to a second party which brought the bodies down.

Over the following weekend, the team moved to its new base, RAF Cark. Willis Rae, who was to become a lifelong friend of Dwyer, had recently joined the team. Nobody in the team quite knew why it was moving – RAF Millom was remaining open – but the general opinion was that there would be more opportunity for climbing, and after all that was what really mattered. At one point Rae had an attack of what he recalls now as a fit of organisational zeal, and drew up a roster so that all members – not just the keen climbers – would get their chance to do some real rock-climbing. Dwyer caught sight of the roster, and went to see Rae, fuming.

"What the hell are you playing at?"

Rae explained.

"Look," said Dwyer, "those bods do their stuff when it matters. Apart from that, they couldn't care less about the hills – not like you and me and Doc Lloyd. This bloody roster will mean that you and I get less rock-climbing together, for Christ's sake!"

The roster was quickly scrapped. Lloyd, recalls Rae, laughed 'like a drain' when he was told.

Life in the MRT at Cark remained busy. Within days of the move they had serviced a squeaker (radio beacon) on Skiddaw, extracted bodies from a Fleet Air Arm aircraft after an all-night search and tested a new stretcher. Later that same year, in July, they were to experiment with the use of police dogs in searching for bodies. However, very soon the intensity of air activity, and therefore of MRT activity, died down.

Squeaker trips, though, remained gratifyingly frequent. The squeakers were powered by batteries and these had to be replaced every week or ten days. The heavy lead batteries had to be lugged up the hill in a rucksack which took a four-man crew. Two of them would be keen climbers: at Cark that meant Dwyer and Rae, as often as not. Once the squeaker chore was over, the day's real climbing would begin.

A squeaker trip was often combined with an exercise. On one occasion in 1945, the outing had a third purpose: to show a Very Important Person from the Air Ministry how Mountain Rescue went about its task. Lloyd gave the team an informal briefing: here was somebody who, come what may, had to be impressed. Fortunately for the team, but less so for the VIP, the weather conditions were at their grisliest. The party went over Hardknott and Wrynose Pass, the notorious road between Eskdale and Ambleside which, says Rae, was at that time in a truly appalling condition. Driving up there in good weather conditions was exciting enough, and the team's guest was white-knuckled and ashen-faced by the time they reached the top. Clinging to the side of an open-sided jeep on a twisty and precipitous mountain road in heavy mist and rain is not the most comfortable of experiences.

After some impressive-looking equipment testing, two groups were sent out in opposite directions over the fells of the Carrs, Swirl Howe and Wetherlam, which were of course invisible from the starting-point. Hearing from the parties on their return that high up they had seen the wreck of a crashed bomber in which Millom MRT had been involved some time earlier can only have made a deeper impression on the man from the ministry.

It was believed that only RAF aircraft could pick up the signal from squeakers. Be that as it may, Rae and Doc Lloyd, with some team members, had to go out to pick up the pieces from an American Grumman Avenger which had hit the screes above Wastwater in dense mist. About two weeks later, Lloyd's telephone rang. It was the police near Wastwater. Apparently, they said, a young lad had been on the hill and seen human remains there – a torso, it was believed. Again, Lloyd and Rae went out, with a medical orderly. Lloyd had an idea, and they first

A Grumman Avenger TBM-3E in US Navy colours, when owned by the Old Flying Machine Company. The Avenger was one of the first American aircraft to boast a power-operated turret. Carrier-borne, it was a very successful torpedo bomber. *Photo: H J Budgen*

made their way to the base of a cliff below the strike point of the Avenger. There was some debris there; then they found a foot. Rae looked down at this sad little remnant of what had been a young vigorous human being only a fortnight earlier, far away from his home in the States. Then slowly he and Lloyd looked across Waswater and the fells. They were looking superb on that day. Back on the road, the crash marks of the aircraft on the north-west face of The Screes were clearly visible. Even now, if you know where to look, black burn marks can be seen. The foot was the nearest they came to finding the torso about which police kept reminding them for some weeks.

They received another visitor in 1945: Flying Officer Gordon F Parkinson. Parkie was a Royal Canadian Air Force officer who in 1938 had made the first ascent of *Diagonal Route* on Dinas Mot (on the south side of the Llanberis Pass) with A Birtwistle, and was also on the first exploration of *Bow-shaped Slab* on Clogwyn Du'r Arddu (on the north side of the Pass) with J Menlove Edwards. He visited the team, interested to see what was going on, climbed *Sinister Slabs* on Bowfell with Rae and returned to climb with the team at every opportunity when he was not flying.

He and Dwyer were superb climbers with, perhaps, a touch of the prima donna about them. On 18th April Dwyer records that he, Parkinson and Corporal Valentine 'mucked about on A Buttress [of Dow Crag] for a while'. Less than a month later, by which time Parkinson had received his promotion to flight lieutenant, he and Dwyer completed their new A Buttress route, Parkinson leading, and named it *Southern Circuit.* Dwyer made it clear that he had wanted to lead and after that they did not often climb together.

1944 had not ended too well for the MRT at Llandwrog, but the new year began on a happier note. Mick McTigue – Corporal Gregory McTigue, a nursing orderly – had been with George Graham in his very early days of getting scratch teams together, and although he never thought of himself as a climber had been a tremendous support to three successive medical officers in running the team. Some time during 1944, his name was put forward by Scudamore for a British Empire Medal, and this was announced in the December and carefully recorded by Scudamore in the log. He was the first of many NCOs to receive the award for Mountain Rescue work.

Scudamore, when he learnt that the team was in the running for a BEM, had asked for two, the other being for Ernie Jackson. They were rationed, however, and the one available went to McTigue as the senior of the two corporals. Campy Barrows believes that McTigue probably attended more air crashes than anyone else in the service. Later a flight sergeant, he died in a road accident in 1979.

It was February 1st 1945. The U-boat war in the North Atlantic was in its final phase. The German army had just been defeated in the Ardennes in its last great offensive. Winston Churchill was resting in Malta on his way to the Yalta Conference.

Piloted by 1st Lieutenant N B Sowell with a crew consisting of 2nd Lieutenant K W Carty, 2nd Lieutenant W H Cardwell, Corporal J D Arnold and Corporal R H Aquirre, a B26G Marauder had taken off from Morrison Field, West Palm Beach, Florida, to add to the Americans' fleet of bombers in Europe. It was finding its way from Florida to RAF Burtonwood by way of Trinidad, Brazil, Dakar, Marrakesh and Cornwall. It left St Mawgan, Cornwall at 12.28 pm for the final leg to Burtonwood, Lancashire where it would be allocated to a unit. The Martin Marauder was a medium bomber, high-speed for its time, used also by the RAF. Popular with the crews, it had a low combat-loss rate.

In the meantime, down below, life carried on.

The Crosville bus stopped at Nant Peris. The conductor on his platform, finger on the bell-push, gave a last glance out for late passengers on their way to Llanberis or Caernarfon, but something caught his attention above. Hanging on the grab-rail, he leaned out and looked up. Somewhere up there was an aircraft, lower than usual. The driver glanced back, wondering about the delay, but the conductor gestured to him and he switched off his engine and dropped down from his cab to join the other man.

It was plainer now, without the bus's engine running. An aeroplane was circling, far too low for comfort with Snowdon to the south and the Glyders to the east. Over the four years since the war had started, aircraft with young men from all over the world had hit crags every week, it seemed. They, like everybody

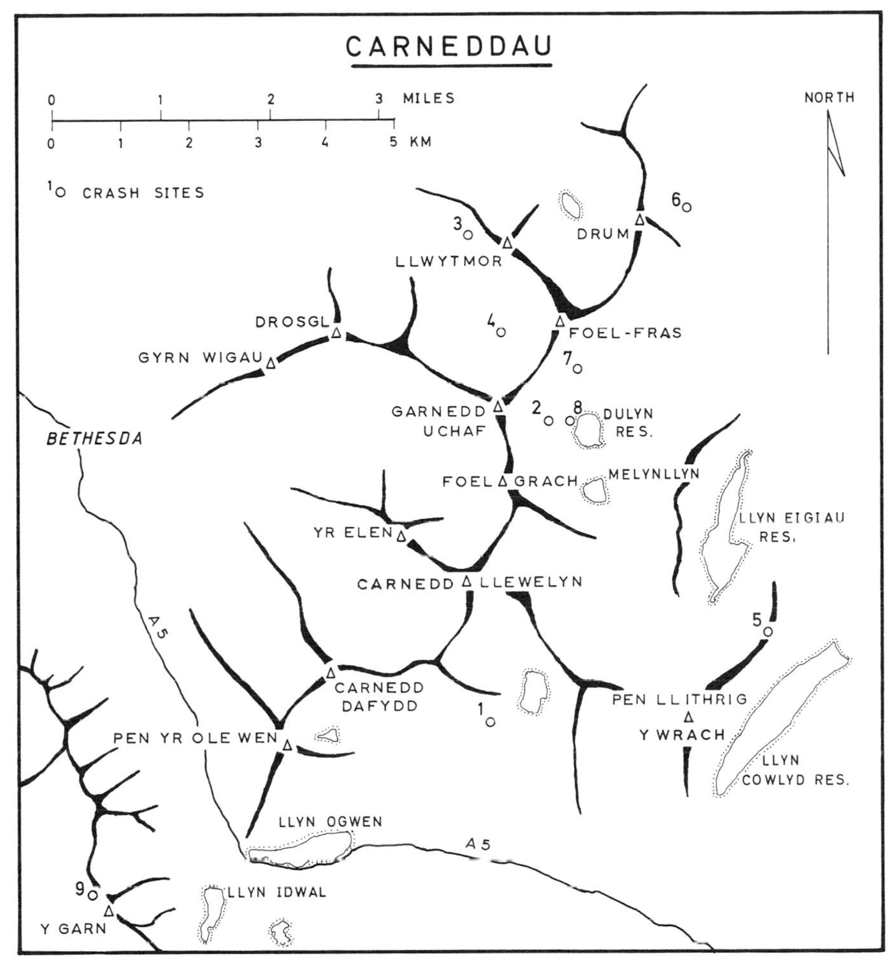

MAP 1 GRAHAM'S GRAVEYARD, 1942-45 (THE CARNEDDAU)

This area became notorious among air crew during World War II, and the numbers mark the various crashes described in these pages all handled by the RAF Llandwrog/Llanbedr Mountain Rescue Team.

1. Sgt Mervyn Sims's Douglas Boston Z2186 17/10/42
2. PO Ken Archer's Avro Anson I EG110 14/1/43
3. Blackburn Botha L6202 29/8/43
4. Sgt J Knight's Anson I EF909 30/11/43
5. Sgt Grant's Anson I LT433 20/2/44
6. Sgt R W T Smith's Anson IV AX583 24/4/44
7. Flt Sgt Biffin's Anson I MG804 12/7/44
8. 2nd Lt W G Gough's Douglas C-47B Skytrain 43-48473 23/11/44
9. 1st Lt N B Sowell's Martin B-26G Marauder 44-68072 2/2/45

else in North Wales, had got used to the jeeps and 3-tonners and ambulances with their brass bells from RAF Llandwrog going off in convoy through the lanes and mountain tracks, off to find a wrecked plane, sometimes with someone still alive there. Now, with the war apparently moving into the final phase...

The conductor thought that the aeroplane was getting lower in the cloud as it went off to the north towards Bethesda. Then there was an almighty explosion. He called in at the nearest police station.

A Marauder was missing.

On the last leg north from Mawgan, heavier wind than expected had blown the aircraft west of the proper route. The pilot, believing he was well clear of the Welsh mountains, descended. Llandwrog Mountain Rescue Team was not alerted until 2.45 the next afternoon; bits of evidence were being pieced together. Tom Scudamore set up his Mountain Headquarters at Nant Peris. The wireless operator stayed with the Humber there, and Scudamore sent three parties of two, with darkness approaching, to Elidir Fawr, Foel Goch and Y Garn respectively, near Ogwen. The Foel Goch party found pieces of wreckage and human remains at 6.45, as darkness fell, near Y Garn, at the rim of a precipice. Scudamore himself nearly stepped over the edge in the dark. The weather had deteriorated – high wind, hail, rain – and Scudamore recalled all three parties. All returned to Llandwrog for a few hours just after midnight.

Next morning the weather had changed. In pleasant warm sunshine, they returned to the crash site and could see in daylight that the Marauder had hit the grassy slope at the top of Y Garn at 3000 feet, and had then fallen over the 1000-foot cliff where it burned out. They found four bodies at the base of the cliff and a torso at the top. The team lowered sledge stretchers – one Duff and one the Pick version of the General Service – down the cliff-face to recover the four charred and mutilated bodies, and took them down to a hut near Ogwen Cottage, arriving there as darkness fell. This part of the team was now about fifteen miles from the base camp with the team vehicles, which came to pick them up. By this time the weather had again deteriorated into high wind and torrential rain.

It had been a gruelling day for the team. They found their way to the Ogwen Youth Hostel and stood around shivering whilst food and tea were prepared. Suddenly, there was the warden of the hostel offering them accommodation. It was a busy weekend for the hostel, with cyclists, walkers and climbers filling the common room. Nevertheless, the warden put aside a room for the men and looked after them well. Large pieces of the Marauder wreckage were to be seen in Cwm Cywion many years later.

A Liberator, laden with depth charges and ammunition, crashed in the hills behind Montrose. The Montrose team was called out, some of them by means of a message thrown onto the screen at the local cinema. Within half an hour they were on their way, and as they approached they could see that the crash was still burning. They parked the vehicles as near as they could and started climbing to be met by the rear gunner, who told them that there were three other survivors; the pilot, the navigator and the wireless operator. A further hour's climbing brought them to the wreck, where they found the three men.

The medical officer was Flight Lieutenant Stewart Duff, who was in charge of the team. With unexploded depth-charges and ammunition still in the burning wreck, he attended to the injuries, and the casualties were taken by stretcher down to the base camp and to the ambulance. Duff remarked afterwards that but for the prompt action of his team, two of the crew might well have died of exposure.

11 – The Storm Subsides

VE Day – the end of the European war – was 8th May 1945. In general an irreverent atmosphere pervaded the armed forces. Mountain Rescue, always a little apart from and not totally respectful towards the RAF generally, probably led the way in this. On VE day itself at RAF Cark everybody had expected a day off, but it did not happen. At about this time there was a camp concert, one of the 'turns' being the CO playing his musical saw. When the expected day off failed to happen, someone (believed to be Parkinson) was heard to comment that the CO was too busy tuning his bloody saw. VE day on camp then, was something of a disaster, hence the trip to Langdale, which turned out to be another disaster.

Dwyer took the Mountain Rescue Team to Langdale; the weather was not conducive to climbing and a jeep broke down so they all stayed indoors in Sid Cross's familiar Old Dungeon Ghyll Hotel and had a few pints on the house. A group of soldiers in there was also celebrating at the landlord's expense. The Cark team persuaded the soldiery that a little rock-climbing would round off the day nicely and so in the afternoon they were prised away from their free Bulman's bitter and led on to Middlefell Buttress. Emboldened by Bulman's, they tackled the Buttress with more enthusiasm than skill. One of the soldiers fell off the Buttress sideways; this was more or less at ground level, but still he broke a leg and was taken to Kendal Infirmary.

Scottie Dwyer set up after the war as a British Mountaineering Council guide – the first. A modest little entry in the BMC's journal, *Mountaineering*, of September 1947 records Dwyer and four others being awarded this qualification. He died in 1976 aged about 65 after a notable mountaineering career.

Finally, before we leave Willis Rae, is there a bond between mountaineers and met. office people? Rae married a met. officer WAAF; not the only mountain rescuer to do so, as we shall see.

The North American Mustang was a single-seater fighter, designed more on the European long and slim pattern rather than the then traditional American short and fat: a product perhaps, since it was a war-time design, of cross-fertilisation between the various allied air forces. For its time, it was very fast.

On the 17th May 1945 a P51 Mustang from the USAAF's 333rd Fighter Squadron power-dived out of formation onto the Dolgellau-Bala road, probably due to oxygen starvation. The nearby station, RAF Llanbedr, had no medical officer and asked the Scudamore team to deal with it. By then Sergeant Harvey had been posted and there was a new team leader in place. When they arrived, a local doctor who was on standby for Llanbedr was already there with a party of men. The crash had straddled the road, and pieces of wreckage, including the Packard engine, were found by Valley MRT thirty years later in a fir plantation.

Coincidentally, it was to Llanbedr that the Llandwrog team was to be moved when 9(0)AFU (Observers Advanced Flying Unit) Satellite was disbanded and RAF Llandwrog closed a few weeks later. During this period, so much had happened in the outside world. Hitler shot himself through the mouth in his bunker, with Eva Braun lying poisoned beside him, at the end of April. Germany surrendered in May. At its peak, RAF Llandwrog had housed a thousand people with the roar of the Cheetahs bouncing off the control tower and the Ansons bouncing along the runway – with their apprehensive trainee pilots and navigators and wireless operators – before climbing over the sandy beach and the sea, and curving back for their navigational exercises over the Carneddau and the Glyders. Soon it would all be finished; a ghost airfield.

It is at about this time that Crichton's Harpur Hill team is recorded, in the in-house history, as being formed; but as we have seen, it had been operating since 1942 and for some reason had failed to get recognition in January 1944 when the Air Ministry promulgation was issued. It must have been in May 1945, therefore, that it got belated recognition after its very existence was drawn to the Air Ministry's attention by the Americans. Perhaps the fact of Crichton's King's Commendation for the work he did on the bomb explosion at Fauld brought the matter to someone's attention.

Harpur Hill became very swift in responding to calls. David Crichton claims that he could assemble everyone and get them on their way within five minutes of a call-out. He adds that the Buxton police were very helpful:

> ... holding up traffic and allowing us to use bells on our vehicles, in the knowledge that we would not abuse the privilege. There was one occasion when in conditions of very low cloud we heard an aircraft flying dangerously low overhead straight towards a neighbouring hill called, I believe, Axe Edge, and we were assembled and ready to leave before the crash call even came in.[31]

Less than three weeks after the Mustang incident, Scudamore was on his way to Llanbedr to get things ready. He had not been there more than twenty-four hours before he was told, by the Americans at RAF Valley, about an American Army Air Force B17 Flying Fortress from 511 Bomber Squadron which had crashed on Cadair Idris.

In one of the last call-outs before the move to RAF Llanbedr, the Llandwrog MRT attended the crash of a P-51 Mustang which power-dived out of formation, probably because of oxygen starvation, on Arran Fawddwy in May 1945. *Photo: H J Budgen*

This B-24 Liberator, belonging to the Cosford Aerospace Museum, is in Indian Air Force 6 Squadron markings. *Photo: H J Budgen*

"Look," the caller said, "we've lost a B17 and wonder if you can help us. We understand you have a Mountain Rescue unit there."

The caller went on to say that there were twenty on board, going home on leave. They had taken off from Valley, the captain keeping in touch. After about five minutes he had said:

"We are now circling through cloud. We are setting our course for the States."

That was the last that was heard.

The team, still based at Llandwrog, called in at Llanbedr to collect the MO, then went to the crash site, where they found the B17 high up on Craig Cwm Llwyd, about 100 feet from the summit of Cadair Idris. All twenty aboard were dead, badly charred and mutilated, many of them scattered over the mountain-side. Whilst searching, Scudamore found a piece of charred paper blowing in the wind – the plane's manifest, giving details of the crew and passengers. The American forces at RAF Valley were contacted; they expressed their thanks and said they would send someone out to identify the bodies.

"You'll have a bit of a job," said Scudamore, "because they're not burnt, they're charred. To put it bluntly, if you touched a skull with your finger it would go straight through. The bone has been reduced to ashes."

"No trouble at all, " replied the American officer at the other end. "We'll come and identify them."

A dentist arrived and was able to make his identifications from the teeth, fillings and dentures. Afterwards, he and his colleagues, writing down the names, were saying:

"John N M I Lewis...

"Mark N M I Evans...

"Tom N M I Marshall[32]..."

After a while, Scudamore could not restrain his curiosity: "What's all this N M I business?"

"Don't you know? That means No Middle Initial."

Then the team moved to Llanbedr. Sergeant Harvey had gone by this time, replaced by Flight Sergeant Murphy. There was a Met. Officer at Llandwrog, Section Officer Mary Jones: during Scudamore's time at Llandbedr, he and Mary Jones married.

It seems that the move, as often used to happen, stirred up the RAF's personnel records, because Barrows found himself, as flight mechanic, at the receiving end of a posting to the Middle East. Tom Scudamore, who recalls Barrows with gratitude, produced a special letter praising Barrows's hard and useful work with MR. This secured Barrows a pleasant six months' posting to an officers' rest and leave centre and ski school in the Austrian Alps. Barrows's personal records show that during his time at Llandwrog and Llanbedr, he attended twenty-four aircraft crashes and three climbing accidents, as well as hundreds of squeaker runs to service radio beacons.

As the year goes on, already we can see an acute reduction of air activity following the end of the European war, and then of the Far Eastern war. An incident in August 1945 showed how much more time was available to make full investigations; it also showed, incidentally, how even experts can be misled.

The Llanbedr Flying Control Officer telephoned Scudamore at 7.00 pm on August 2nd to say that a pilot flying over Carnedd Dafydd had reported seeing a crashed Liberator below. The map reference given, Scudamore commented, was roughly where Mervyn Sims's Boston crashed in 1942, where he spent those two terrible nights, before the young man and his girl-friend and Doctor Williams found him. The team was told to wait until RAF Valley had been able to check the sighting. Nothing was heard. After an hour, an exasperated Scudamore telephoned Valley: no such reconnaissance was being made. The team went out without further delay – after all, if the pilot's sighting was correct, someone's life might be at stake – and set up Mountain HQ at Llyn Ogwen at 11 pm. Three separate parties searched thoroughly under a beautiful star-studded sky; only Sims's old Boston was found. On the team's return after searching all night, Corporal Ernie Jackson was taken on a reconnaissance flight over Carnedd Dafydd; again, he could find only the Boston.

The pilot who first had raised the alarm came over to Llanbedr in an Airspeed Oxford and took Scudamore out. He pointed out a wreck on Craig y Dulyn above Llyn Dulyn, which Scudamore immediately recognised as the Dakota which he and the team had attended in November 1944. He made a recommendation from this experience, with just a touch of impatience in the report language:

> Old mountain crashes, inaccessible and unsalvageable, should be so marked that pilots can recognise them from the air as such. This will minimise unnecessary journeys by rescue parties.[33]

One hopes that at the very least the pilot concerned stood the team a round of drinks after their night's unnecessary work. A member of the Harpur Hill team of a slightly later time, 'Lofty' Bircham, has commented that there also, false alarms based on old wrecks were a problem.

Then on the 12th September 1945, Admiral Lord Louis Mountbatten, the Supreme Commander in South-east Asia, held a surrender ceremony at Singapore.

The storm was over. What was to happen in the calm?

Chapter 1 – Footnotes

[1] Letter to writer 29/5/92
[2] Walter Unsworth: Everest; Clydesdale & McIntyre: The Pilot's Book of Everest
[3] Sidcot: after the inventor, Sidney Cotton (eccentric RAF officer who frequently used to fly in trench coat and trilby)
[4] Letter to R C Collier 28/7/78
[5] Letter to writer 11/2/92
[6] Tom Scudamore: Recorded message to writer 17/4/92
[7] Appendix 3
[8] Llandwrog MRT log 30/8/43 0930
[9] Llandwrog log 31/8/43
[10] Llandwrog log 1/9/43
[11] Squadron Leader B J Canfer, Inspector of Land Rescue; and Steve Jordan, RAF Valley
[12] Recorded message to writer 17/4/92
[13] General Medical Council
[14] Public Record Office, London
[15] Personnel Management Centre, Innsworth
[16] Dropping zone
[17] Article by T E White, 1947
[18] Article by T E White, 1947
[19] Letter to writer 10/12/91
[20] 221 Group records, Burma, July 1945; Public Record Office, Kew
[21] FFI = Freedom From Infection (a check for venereal disease)
[22] See Appendix 4
[23] Letter to writer 16/4/92
[24] Llandwrog log
[25] Llandwrog log 1/6/44
[26] Mountain and Cave Rescue Handbook 1990 (Mountain Rescue Committee)
[27] Llandwrog log 19/6/44
[28] Undated report after the call-out
[29] Martin Middlebrook: The Berlin Raids (Viking 1988)
[30] Dwyer's climbing diary 22/10/44
[31] Letter to Ron Collier 26/7/78
[32] Fictitious names
[33] Llanbedr log 5/8/45

CHAPTER II: THE MORE THINGS CHANGE

Post-war Problems 1946-51

Plus ça change, plus c'est la même chose. Alphonse Karr 1808-1890 (Les Guêpes, 1849) (The more things change, the more they are the same.)

1 – The Calm after the Storm

By the end of 1945, the wartime pattern of flying had gone; peace-time civilian flying was not yet under way and the post-war boom in walking, rock-climbing and mountaineering had yet to start. The original *raison d'être*, then, of the service had all but gone. Its future teetered in the balance. What was to prevent it being consigned to oblivion, at best, a mere footnote in some historian's tome on the air war of 1939-45?

Crichton at Harpur Hill helped to keep up the interest of the team by such activities as public demonstrations of the work. There was one in Buxton in October. Then on November 23rd 1945 a distinguished aviator, Wing Commander R D Speares DSO DFC and bar, Croix de Guerre with Palm, was alone in his Anson XI NL185 from Bomber Command HQ Flight on his way to RAF Feltwell. In bad visibility, he crashed between Jacob's Ladder and Edale, south of Kinder Scout, and was killed outright. Crichton's team was called out on the following day, and brought Speares's body down on a sledge stretcher.

Just over a month later, on December 28th, a Peak District farming family was surprised by a knock at the door during the afternoon. They were startled to find on the doorstep a man in flying gear, obviously injured and in distress. He was unable to speak coherently, but managed to convey that there were more survivors in the wreck, although he could not indicate where this was. The farmer telephoned the police at Chapel Milton, who in turn telephoned RAF Harpur Hill. Crichton took the call at 5.20 pm and within twenty minutes he was on his way with the team. He had only the vaguest idea of where the aircraft might be, and split the team up into search parties. They covered about 20 square miles, searching Edale Head, Jacob's Ladder and Green Clough. When, after eight hours or more, the parties were showing signs of tiredness, he called them in for a rest: it was then 3 am.

They started again at dawn, searching Brown Knoll, about half a mile south of Jacob's Ladder, in extreme cold and dense fog; at 11 am they found an Airspeed Oxford at about 1700 feet, with the aircrew in a poor state from serious injuries and exposure.

Crichton had set up base camp on the south-western side of Brown Knoll, but that side was too steep for the arduous stretcher work necessary. He therefore sent the vehicles to the north-western aspect, where they found they could get the jeeps within a mile of the wreck. The injured men were put on the jeeps, then transferred to the Humber ambulance which took them to the RAF Hospital at Wilmslow, arriving there at 3.30 pm. When he was able to check two weeks later, all had made good progress. It had been a classic rescue: aircrew were rescued who might well otherwise have died of exposure. But Crichton's report concludes with a comment which can only have come from a hurt and angry man:

I am still very much concerned, and profoundly disappointed. Firstly because we still have not been acknowledged in Air Ministry Orders as a Mountain Rescue unit and, secondly, because we still have no wireless call-signs but have to use practice call-signs which are of local value only.[1]

Nevertheless, the team cannot have been entirely unrecognised: Crichton was about to receive his MBE for services to Mountain Rescue and the team's ambulance was the standard Humber Mountain Rescue ambulance, which seems to suggest that in some quarters at least it was treated as a real, grown-up Mountain Rescue Team.

The letter from 42 Group, dated January 3rd 1946, read:

My dear Crichton
Hearty congratulations on your well deserved honour. I know the arduous work you have done in connection with the Mountain Rescue Service and I have no doubt that you have been honoured for this in particular. Knowing the surrounding country and the average weather at Harpur Hill, I can well imagine the difficulties you and your team must have had to overcome from time to time in order to carry out the tasks confronting you.

Formed on an ad hoc basis in 1944, West Freugh MRT never received the amount of attention accorded to other teams. Nevertheless, in September 1946 it became an official team responsible for Central and South-West Scotland and the Lake District. The team leader was Warrant Officer Bill Pitcairn, an aircrew man who shortly afterwards became the service's chief instructor, taking over from Hans Pick, who had also in his time been responsible for West Freugh.

A patient, Commissioned Wardmaster C R Alwright, was being put into a Dominie air ambulance X7394, named Merlin V, from 782 Squadron (Navy) on the morning of August 30th 1946, to be taken from Abbotsinch to Stretton Naval Air Station near Warrington. The biplane, a development of the Dragon Rapide and even by then looking rather dated, turned south to find its route. Before very long, radio contact was lost.

At RAF West Freugh late that evening, LAC Keith Ford was in bed when he heard the Tannoy call for the Mountain Rescue Team. Getting dressed quickly, he made his way to the section, then through the darkness the team convoy headed eastwards towards Dalbeattie. Corporal Jack Sinclair had got married some weeks earlier, but this was the first time that he had had an opportunity to spend a night with his wife. He had said that if a call-out occurred, he was to be

Members of the West Freugh MRT in 1946. Centre is WO Bill Pitcairn who became Air Ministry instructor in 1947. First left is Keith Ford. *Photo: K S Ford*

collected. Pitcairn and the team took him at his word, and the convoy pulled up outside his parents' house in Gatehouse of Fleet and knocked at the door in the early hours of the morning. He rushed out of the house, clambered into the jeep and was driven off, waving to his startled and rather worried bride.

Beyond Dalbeattie is Criffel Hill (1868 feet), which seemed then to be the most likely position. Two ladies nearby had heard an aircraft, and, they thought, a crash coming from the direction of the hill. They got in touch with the police, and Criffel Hill was searched, without result. Then Sergeant John Howe, the wireless operator, received a message that it was now believed that the Dominie had crashed in the Lake District. The convoy was quickly reloaded and turned south. In the meantime, some members of the Barrow team who only a short time previously had gone to Jurby to set up the Isle of Man coverage, were flown back to RAF Barrow to pick up equipment, and then got into their vehicles to be taken to the familiar Lake District manor in support of West Freugh. The Navy had sent out search aircraft and an Anson eventually spotted the wreckage on Scafell Pike, at 3210 feet the highest in England. The Barrow team reached the crash site first and were bringing down the bodies as West Freugh arrived there.

It was only days after this that West Freugh became 'official', and Bill Pitcairn stepped up the training. He had a formidable reputation for navigating, and Keith Ford can remember him taking a party in thick fog, entirely by compass, to within 100 yards of the pick-up point.

2 – The 1947 Exercise

1946 began quietly in North Wales and many who had been involved with the service for two busy years or so must have been wondering whether the whole edifice would be dismantled, now that the war was just a horrible memory. Scudamore's team went to a crashed Wellington in January; all the crew were dead. A Spitfire force-landed on the beach near Tal-y-Bont in April with no harm to the pilot. During this period they had been experiencing prolonged radio trouble, and sometimes the Humber had been unable to make contact with RAF Llanbedr. However, soon thereafter they began to be equipped with the 1154 transmitter and the 1155 receiver, the standard equipment for the RAF bomber fleet. Llanbedr tested theirs in May and were well pleased.

Flight Lieutenant Tom Scudamore was posted to Middlesbrough on August 30th 1946 to be made up to Squadron Leader before demobilisation, and to be replaced at Llanbedr by Flying Officer J A B Mounsey. Mounsey had, with his team leader Warrant Officer Campion, been in place only two weeks or so when they were told, at 11 pm on September 17th, that a prisoner of war from the POW camp at Dolgellau had fallen on Cadair Idris. They had to search by torchlight, with the help of the climber's friend who had also fallen but had been able to raise the alarm. Although they found footmarks which might have belonged to the fallen man, they reached the summit without finding him. They rested there until 6 am, then started descending by the Fox's Path. Half way down they found the body.

The first team covering South Wales had been formed at RAF Madley, in June 1944. In 1947 it was moved to RAF St Athan, where it has been ever since. That year, a young engine-fitter called John Hinde, a keen climber, applied to join the St Athan team but was refused because he was on a course. Despite having made that application, he now admits rather looking down on the Saints at the time:

> I wondered about the mountains in South Wales but I didn't really regard them as mountains you know, because by that time I knew the English Lake District and I knew Snowdonia well, and I didn't think the Mountain Rescue Team at St Athan would be doing the sort of stuff that I wanted to.[2]

John Hinde was later, after a tempestuous early career, to become one of the service's leading NCOs. During his early days in the Air Force, he had the reputation of being something of a tearaway with a disciplinary problem. It is difficult to reconcile that young tearaway with the tall, almost gaunt, quiet-spoken man in the Outward Bound Centre at Loch Eil where he leads parties of children and businessmen and shows them what mountaincraft is about. Hinde started walking on Kinder Scout when he was about eleven, at the beginning of the war, inspired by Frank Smythe's *The Spirit of the Hills.*

> I didn't know anybody in the whole town who was a mountaineer or even a hill walker – there just weren't any. So, I got an old German army rucksack and loaded this up with a

blanket, biscuits or something like that, unsuitable foods, and I'd go off for the weekend. Very little money. I was a very early member of the Youth Hostels Association. I felt a stranger, because there was nobody with that interest. I felt a sort of freak.[2]

In 1947 Sergeant Hans Pick was replaced as trainer-in-chief by Warrant Officer Bill Pitcairn from West Freugh, and it was with Pitcairn's guidance that the first big exercise was mounted. This was held north of Llandovery, South Wales, on May 31st 1947. The objectives were:

To test the organisation and training of mountain rescue units in large scale and small scale searching, and at the same time to investigate the practical use of a helicopter in mountain search and rescue.

It included the teams from RAF St Athan, Llanbedr and, in the year following Crichton's departure, Harpur Hill, as well as a Sikorsky R6 from RAF Thorney Island. This was the first time a helicopter had been used in a Mountain Rescue exercise. Not included was the West Freugh team: Pitcairn was so confident of its efficiency that he felt he could safely leave it out. The assumption was that an aircraft had crashed in the mountains at about 1700 feet twelve miles north of Llandovery, the position being indicated by ground signalling strips on a grassy slope. All three teams set up forward bases on the evening before and Pitcairn briefed them. He gave them route cards and they were equipped with Type 39 walkie-talkies, maps, compasses, first-aid kits and, in theory at least, rations.

The various routes were designed to bring all the search parties to positions along the sides of a triangle near the simulated crash at about the same time. Also then, the Sikorsky was to fly from RAF St Athan to the forward base of the St Athan team, where it was due to land in a prepared field at about 9.30 am. The 'crash site' was chosen because it seemed to be just accessible by jeep using a mountain track, so if there was any problem with the experimental helicopter, the whole exercise would not have to be aborted. Then the parties were to be directed to the site by radio, either from one of the forward bases or from a link radio. They were to be split up into 'casualties', searchers and stretcher parties. The 'casualties' would plant themselves in various places; the searchers were to carry out a small-scale square search using radio and compasses; and the stretcher parties were to stand by with sledge stretchers brought in by a medical officer and a nursing orderly. The final phase was to be a first-aid and casualty evacuation practice under a medical officer. Then all search parties were to walk to St Athan forward base to be joined by the vehicles from the other teams.

The Air Ministry observers, Squadron Leader Cook and Flight Lieutenant Beck, had arrived at St Athan on the morning before the exercise. Later in the morning a Lancaster from Thorney Island brought a helicopter maintenance party, a supply of jerricans for refuelling the helicopters and two observers from the Survival and Rescue Training Unit, Squadron Leader Barwood and Flight Lieutenant Wilson. Then came two Sikorsky R6 helicopters, not one as in the original plan. The convoy left St Athan for the forward base at about 2 pm. The first serious setback occurred when one of the vehicles, borrowed from the RAF St Athan pool, broke down, and the team did not arrive at the base camp until 7 pm. Then St Athan's wireless operator was having difficulty in getting in touch with the parties from Llanbedr and Harpur Hill. Believing that the surrounding hills were to blame, he arranged for the van to be moved to higher ground the next day.

Pitcairn went to brief the other two teams, but did not return until 6.30 am, having spent most of the night digging the jeep out of a bog. Thus he got no rest, since at 7 am preparations – checking kit, checking walkie-talkie communications with the radio van – had started. By 8 am the search parties were ready to go and the radio van moved to the new site. It was a clear and almost windless morning, and very soon became hot.

One of the helicopters landed in the chosen field at 9.15 am, and refuelled. The pilot, Wing Commander Burns, uneasy about the conditions, made a short test flight to establish the best way of climbing out of the valley. On his return he landed twice in a very confined space for the benefit of press photographers. Burns finally left at 10.45 am with the weary Pitcairn who was carrying an Army portable radio. After two legs of a creeping search they found the crash site and Pitcairn was put down. Burns in successive journeys went to collect Flying Officer Chandler (the officer in charge of St Athan MRT), an army observer Major Nelson and a press photographer. Now Pitcairn was guiding the search parties to the crash site by radio. All of the St Athan and Llanbedr parties arrived within ten minutes of the estimated time, but by 1 pm only one of the Harpur Hill parties was there, and it was obvious that the others were lost.

A party in jeeps with stretchers and with fuel and oil for the helicopter started out from the St Athan base at midday. After an hour's driving on an appalling track which would have been impassable for any vehicle other than a jeep, the search parties at the crash site were spotted. It was not easy to judge where best to leave the twisty track and go cross-country without running into trouble, but a helicopter was able to hover over the nearest part of the road to the crash site.

By this time it was extremely hot. One of the missing Harpur Hill parties had been found exhausted and a jeep was sent back to help them. At the crash site, preparations were starting for the square search. It was clear, however, that many of the men were really in no condition or mood to continue, being extremely tired. The Harpur Hill contingent were particularly affected, though they were not alone. They made it clear to Pitcairn and the officers that they were not inclined to do any more cross-country walking, with or without sledge stretchers. Neither, they added, were they going to walk the ten miles back to base.

Taking the three groups, an average of seven or eight miles had been walked; not a great deal on the face of it. But it had included an aggregate climb of 3,000 feet with corresponding descents on an oppressively hot day. To make matters worse, many of the Harpur Hill people had not bothered to use Pitcairn's route cards or compasses, so they had walked much further than they needed. But the fault did not lie with the men alone. They had not been given any food since 5 pm the previous evening: the team had left Harpur Hill without bread and so no sandwiches were provided; neither had they had breakfast on the day of the exercise. Even taking the generous view and assuming that lack of food was an oversight, St Athan was not too far away, and evening and breakfast rations could surely have been obtained there. In the report there is no suggestion that this was even tried. Furthermore, the parties were wearing ordinary blue RAF uniform with walking shoes – both unsuited to the terrain and climate.

In the end Pitcairn reluctantly concluded that the whole exercise ought to be aborted. He discussed matters with the medical officers and decided to abandon the casualty search; this was at 4.30 pm, by which time Harpur Hill had been without food for nearly 24 hours. Search parties already out on the square search were recalled. Only three jeeps were available to evacuate everybody and that took some time. There was a further vehicle breakdown and the St Athan party did not arrive back until 8 pm.

Several experienced people were involved in the planning, organisation and monitoring of this exercise. So why were these men, mostly complete tyros in mountain conditions, allowed even to start out on this exercise by, amongst others, the Air Ministry's Mountain Rescue Instructor and two observers from the Survival and Rescue Training Unit?

The official report reached several conclusions, one being that difficulties were caused by the deprivations of demobilisation and posting, making it very difficult to keep a trained team together. A very fair point. It goes on, however, to suggest that the airmen concerned were not willing to make physical effort or to train in the essentials of mountaincraft, and resented being asked to walk a few miles and being told how to do it properly. Considering the fact that the authorities do not seem to have ensured that the teams concerned were dressed and equipped properly, or even fed for over 24 hours, that seems to the present writer to be a prime example of buck-passing. The report concludes:

> It is essential that membership of Mountain Rescue Units should be confined to men who are keen enough to keep fit and make an effort to learn, and that on no account should the Unit be allowed to become a 'scrounge'.

It makes no recommendations as to the quality of leadership and preparation and training.

The exercise was not just a climbing search-and-rescue exercise. It was also intended to be something of a trial in the use of helicopters in such operations; a complete novelty at the time. The report is suitably enthusiastic on the use of helicopters in principle, though it comments that the R6 would lift only two people and was therefore not the right helicopter for the job.

What did impress the writer of the report was the ease with which the helicopter could be handled in confined valleys and rough country, and could be used to search in high ground which would defeat fixed-wing aircraft. He commented also on the speed with which first-aid could be delivered, the possibility of casualty evacuation, the helicopter's guidance and support of ground parties and its ability to deliver medical supplies more easily and safely than by dropping from conventional aircraft. One other comment might produce a wry smile from experienced climbers. The report says that the ability to direct ground parties to a crash quickly 'would be of much greater value in more rugged conditions than are met in the United Kingdom'. Anybody who thinks rugged conditions cannot be met in the UK has never climbed in the Snowdon range or the Western Highlands of Scotland, especially in mid-winter.

Finally, one can only regret that John Hinde had not been able to join the Saints team when he went to St Athan that year on a course. Although young, he already had several years' hard climbing experience and might have done something to avert an embarrassing fiasco.

Perhaps acting on the lessons from that disastrous exercise, less than a year later (on January 12th 1948), the Air Ministry wrote to all teams – then St Athan, Llanbedr, Harpur Hill, Topcliffe, Wigtown, Kinloss:

Participation in Mountain Rescue operations calls for an exacting standard of operational and physical fitness which can be achieved only by constant and regular practice in Mountain Search and Rescue under all conditions of weather, both by day and night. The following scale of exercises is, therefore, recommended:–
(a) At least one day exercise per week.
(b) One combined day and night exercise per month.
(c) Various methods of search to be practised as frequently as possible.

Later that same year, the Harpur Hill team went to the crash of a USAF Superfortress near Snake Pass, where thirteen died. It was an arduous recovery and Major General Leon W Johnson, who then commanded the 3rd Air Division, wrote a letter of commendation to the Air Ministry, which was passed on to RAF Harpur Hill and to the then team leader, Flight Sergeant G H Thompson. The following year George Thompson received the BEM.

3 – The Superfortress on Strachur

In 1948, John Hinde had finished his apprenticeship at RAF St Athan.

They said where do you want to be posted? Most people wanted to go to the London area, so I said: Scotland! Because I'd never actually climbed in Scotland....
Right, you're off to Kinloss! So they gave me a pass to get to Kinloss.... We used to change at Aviemore at that time. We used to get a train to Grantown on Spey, down to Forres, then a train to Kinloss and I saw my first sight of the Scottish mountains from the great pinewoods of Strathspey. And I saw these Cairngorms and as soon as I was there I thought this is where I'm going to live. And this is over forty years ago...and I'm still here.[2]

Hinde, however, was away sick – unusually for him – at the time of the Superfortress call-out in January 1949. AC William Patrick, flight mechanic, heard on the Tannoy on the Monday morning that the team was needed. A Boeing B29-BN Superfortress – a huge aircraft for its time – from the American 301st Bomber Group had clipped the tops of the hills above Strachur, on the banks of Loch Fyne. It had been on its way back to the United States, probably from RAF Brize Norton, and had been circling for some time.

The aircraft had been flying up the west coast of Scotland on its way to Keflavik, the staging post. Since the accident had only just happened, the team were given only an approximate location. A flight was arranged to Glasgow, then the Navy were to take them across the Firth of Clyde to a spot as near the crash as possible. An aircraft was loaded with a minimum of gear, the rest to follow by lorry, and the well rehearsed routine of preparing the convoy for the road started. People were pulled away from their jobs, with their NCOs muttering under their breath but having learnt to accept the inevitable. Kit was thrown into the lorry. The ambulance and radio vans were checked.

Just before take-off another telephone call was received – a second call from the Air Ministry: the whole thing was off. The Americans had telephoned, thanked the RAF for its intended help and trouble, but they would look after the whole matter themselves. Vehicles and the aircraft were unloaded, men went back to sections, stores were replaced in the MR section. Just as the incident was beginning to fade in the memory, three days later another call was received: would the team go to the crash site after all?

"What's been happening in the meantime?"

"Nothing," they were told.

"Nothing?"

"Nothing. Nobody's been there, nobody's visited the crash."

Puzzled, the team started preparations again. Enquiries established an exact location; a shepherd had heard the crash and seen the wreck but, superstitiously perhaps, had refused to go anywhere near it.

Whereas on the Monday time had been all-important, now it was less so, and it was decided to travel by road overnight so that all the equipment could be used from the outset. Again the convoy vehicles were loaded and the long journey begun. Strachur was reached in the early hours of the Friday morning; accommodation had been arranged, and they were shown to a village hall. As they parked they were surprised to find a large number of Royal Navy 3-tonners and about 200 naval personnel. Patrick recalls now that they seemed to be milling around and not quite knowing what to do. The officers were wearing gunnery field-kit – long black shiny gaiters and webbing belt to carry a revolver. There was more than a whiff of rum in the air.

Flight Sergeant Donald Siddons, the 29-year-old team leader, explained that the Kinloss team were going up onto the hill and over various shoulders to reach the crash. The naval ratings were then immediately informed by their officers that they were to go as well. The sailors peered up through the thick mist, and the general reaction was: "We're not going up there!" The mood was becoming ugly, and Patrick remembers the naval officers drawing revolvers to herd the ratings over the first shoulder. The Kinloss team made the mistake of laughing at this. There were twenty RAF men, 200 naval ratings.

Having got their men up as far as the first shoulder, the naval officers seemed to disappear, and then the ratings threatened the Kinloss men: "We'll get you on the way back." Patrick admits now that the team was frightened. To make matters worse for Patrick, this was his first call-out. Not only did he have the possible vengeance of 200 tanked-up naval ratings somewhere ahead of him, but he had to face the sight of mass death for the first time. He did not know how he would react to either and was glad to have alongside him Corporal McKay, a former ghillie, who was a very strong member of the team. Patrick stuck to him throughout this climb. As they came over the brow of the last hill, the horrible carnage of the crash became only too clear to them. The aircraft had been carrying twenty high-ranking officers, and fully laden with fuel for the journey to the USA, it had exploded and scattered the wreckage over a wide area.

The American Air Force had supplied some very good body-bags, and the team first went round gathering arms, legs, torsos. The uniforms had very senior rank insignia and in many cases solid gold pilots' wings. The team had been told that the pilot of the aircraft was a 20-stone man; it was not difficult to identify him. Having finished their work with the bodies, the team then started to collect belongings: photographs, wallets, money. The latter notes were often of high denomination, such as $500 and $1000. There were many brand new top quality Whitney blankets, some of them in their original wrappings, and Patrick can remember too a silver salver.

The team became aware that there was a stranger with them. Siddons and McKay asked who he was, and he replied that he was a padre, a major, in the USAAF.

"Why," asked the Kinloss NCOs, "haven't you or any of your people been up here before?"

"None of your goddam business," came the rather unpadre-like answer.

Handing the papers and other belongings over to this officer, the team then busied themselves with collecting other material, but were surprised to find after a few minutes that he had gone some way away and lit a small fire on which he was burning the papers. Already edgy from the brush with the Navy, the team members were now angry.

"What the hell do you think you're doing?" they asked.

Again he indicated that it was none of their business. "I'm an American major, and I'll report you" he went on when they pressed him. A chorus of voices told him what to do with his report. "We're a volunteer unit – don't speak to us like

Fl Sgt Don Siddons, Kinloss team leader, in Sept 1951. *Photo: Joss Gosling*

that!" An 'incident' was fast approaching but the bellicose major soon left the scene. The team busied itself with more clearance work, concerned that some apparently important evidence had been destroyed. But why?

The first batch of bodies was taken down on stretchers as darkness approached, and when they reached the hall the team found that the naval contingent had gone. It was decided to go back up the hill immediately, even in darkness, to recover the rest of the bodies in the hope of avoiding a bloody confrontation with the Navy. The job was done without too much difficulty and Siddons and his team returned to the hall tired but satisfied and had just handed over the bodies when they could see the sailors returning. The RAF piled into the convoy vehicles and left; discretion was the better part of valour and anyway they were not sorry to leave the now appalling smell. They had been told that there were twenty bodies and they had actually collected that number of torsos. A big military funeral for the twenty dead, with all the pomp accorded to senior officers, followed in the United States.

However, a few weeks later, someone visited the crash site and, looking around, found another body. So there had been twenty-one aboard, not twenty. Had someone arranged a free (and illegal) ride back to the States? Whatever the truth, clearly the USAAF did not want the embarrassment of admitting that another had been aboard. Who knew what sort of enquiries and witch hunts that might spark off? The torso was quietly buried on the hill above Strachur.

Another odd thing about this particular operation was that there was neither sight nor sound of the press. It is difficult to believe that no reporters would have been told by their stringers about the crash of such a huge aircraft with so many important people aboard. Were reporters kept away? if so, why? And how?

And one last question: Why were the passengers on this Superfortress all carrying loaded Lugers?

4 – The Morphia Question

Rising out of the Balmoral Deer Forest is Lochnagar. Because of its shape when seen from the north, it was originally called Beinn Chiochan (Hill of the Breasts), but the Victorians changed that.

John Hinde's climbing companions at Kinloss included Flight Lieutenant James Carden, Flying Officer James and Johnny Maskell. On Saturday February 12th 1949 this group went out on exercise, taking the convoy up Glen Muick to the Spittal of Glenmuick. Then they set off for the Meikle Pap Bealach from where they crossed the Lochnagar corrie and kicked steps up the easy *Black Spout* Gully. Next day Hinde with James, Bunny Downhill and Geordie Haggard again took the jeep from Ballater to the Spittal of Glenmuick, but followed a slightly different route to Lochnagar's summit, taking the steeper left-hand branch of the Black Spout and finishing by the *Crumbling Cranny* exit. Here they could see that an earlier party had tunnelled through a cornice.

Hinde now says:

> We should never have been there at all, but in excuse we had no benefit of an avalanche warning service and we did have the written categorical guidance of an eminent climber, 'Avalanches do not occur on British mountains'.[3]

He was about to become involved in one of his first Scottish rescues, but for the moment could do little but marvel at the beauty of the pure blue above the pure white of the plateau. He was soon shaken out of his reflective and peaceful mood. At the col they met two battered and bloodied climbers, supporting each other, trying to make their way to Glen Muick to get help for their two injured friends who were still in the corrie. They had all been caught by an avalanche in *Raeburn's Gully*.

The four men had been climbing *Raeburn's Gully* on two ropes well below the cornice when it collapsed and sent all four down about six hundred feet. The worst injured had been the second man on the first rope. He had been belayed onto icicles at the crux and dragged out of the cave by the rope as the leader fell past. Downhill and Haggard took two men to Glenmuick, whilst Hinde and James descended to the avalanche debris below *Raeburn's Gully*. One man had a broken leg and Hinde gave him morphia from a tubonic ampoule, before splinting his leg with the RAF-issue British Bulldog ice-axe, the piece of MR equipment that all experienced climbers hated as much as the notorious Boots Grooved Heel. Hoping that the British Bulldog was at least strong enough to act

In 1949 Kinloss went to the crash of a Fleet Air Arm Firefly, which killed both members of the crew. *Photo: H J Budgen*

as a splint (he had broken the ash shaft of one not long before when cutting steps) Hinde looked around him and spotted the injured man's much superior ice-axe in the snow.

The last man had only burnt hands and Hinde returned with him over the bealach and down to the Spittal of Glenmuick. By that time the rest of the team had been alerted and were waiting with vehicles. They went up to carry the injured man down on the stretcher.

The Hinde party later went up again to meet the stretcher party and helped in carrying the stretcher down on the lower part of the descent. By this time, they had met John Robertson, fighter pilot turned stalker, who came back up with them. It was the early hours of the morning before they got back to Ballater but by then many people had turned out, forty or so, forming a long diagonal line of blinding white light across the snow, all with their Tilley lamps. An eerie and impressive sight, Hinde remembers.

At 11.45 am on a Monday in May 1949, the team was put on standby. Flight Lieutenant Reid and Flight Sergeant Don Siddons were told that a Fleet Air Arm aircraft, a Firefly no. Z2108 from 766 Squadron, was overdue. It had left Lossiemouth on a training flight with Lieutenant A A Dowell and Lieutenant R M Osborne, and had not returned. Initially the search was by police, gamekeepers and estate workers; then the Kinloss team set up headquarters by the shores of Loch Muick, for a search of Lochnagar and White Mounth. They took with them John Robertson who believed he had heard the aircraft droning overhead, then a crash. The help of an experienced ghillie or gamekeeper is invaluable; if he is also familiar with aircraft that is a bonus.

The searchers had to cope with blizzard conditions, then higher up with thick mist. Because of the weather, the police and gamekeepers called off their search but the RAF team continued to comb Lochnagar. They were groping their way about the hillside when the mist suddenly lifted. One member of the team glanced to one side and saw a tailplane just visible over some boulders. A little further away was the cockpit and inside the mutilated bodies of the two officers. Ponies from the estate were used to bring the bodies down.

A year later, there was need of morphia again. Staying in the Glencoe Hostel, Gerald Hartley, Peter Bryce Thompson, Harold Drasdo and Ken Kennedy decided that the next day they would tackle Buachaille Etive Mor by the North Buttress. All four were experienced climbers. It was March 5th 1950.

Buachaille Etive Mor consists of a 2½ mile ridge linking four summits, the north-eastern of which, Stob Dearg (3403 feet) overlooks Rannoch Moor. They reached the summit by 10 am, had something to eat and admired the view. Their descent was by Curved Ridge, and half an hour later they reached D Gully. The 22-year-old engineer Gerald Hartley decided that he would glissade down. After about fifteen feet his ice-axe snagged something and was whipped out of his hands. Left with no means of braking, he slid helplessly, gathering speed for about another 250 feet, until his friends saw him disappear over a precipice. He dropped about fifty feet onto a narrow ledge, but a further drop threatened should he make a wrong move. Thompson, Drasdo and Kennedy went down to him as quickly as they could and found him lying there on the ledge with head injuries and an apparently broken arm. Clearly it would have been unwise to move him.

Leaving Thompson and Drasdo to look after Hartley, Kennedy went down to the foot of the mountain and along the track to the Kingshouse, the climbers' inn. However, in 1950 the Kingshouse did not possess such a modern luxury as a telephone, so the innkeeper drove him to the Clachaig Inn, another climbers' inn which also served as the base to a sub-unit of RAF Kinloss MRT. Whilst the innkeeper there was telephoning the police, Kennedy was given a sleeping bag, blankets, first-aid kit, food, drink and a hot-water bottle, and driven back to the foot of the Buachaille. Burdened with his load, he climbed back up to *D Gully* and his three companions, a feat which earned him the admiration of the RAF team. With this weight to carry, his was something of a heroic climb, and by the time he reached his companions some five hours had passed since Hartley's fall.

Thompson and Drasdo wrapped Hartley in blankets and slid him into the sleeping bag, tended his injuries as best they could, and fed him. They were worried about the narrowness of the ledge, and roped him securely to a knob of rock.

Buachaille Etive Mor. 'D' Gully is directly below the summit. *Photo: P. Hodgkiss*

At the Clachaig Inn, a search party had been formed by a policeman who was a keen climber; he recruited four climbers staying there. They climbed in darkness and were relieved when the moon made an appearance at 11 pm. It was 2 am, though, before they got within reach of the summit and still they had not found the group. Probably the instructions given quickly by Kennedy had been misinterpreted or had not been clear enough, but they were certainly not helped by the thick mist. Reluctantly, the five turned and started to descend. In the meantime, RAF Kinloss had been told and at 1.45 am, the convoy was on the road for the 160-mile run (the Ballachulish Bridge had not then been built).

Reaching the foot of the Buachaille, Don Siddons and his team set up camp and cooked breakfast. It was still dark at 6 am as the RAF men started climbing, joined by the original search party of five and by Kennedy acting as a guide. As they got nearer, they were able to see the Hartley party flashing torches and reached them at 10.30 am. Hartley was strapped to a sledge stretcher, then hauled, painfully slowly, up the face. It was 2.30 pm before they reached the summit; twenty-four hours after Hartley's fall.

He was made comfortable and given morphia. After a short rest, the descent began down the south side, watched by an interested crowd from Glen Etive through binoculars and telescopes. They reached the Glen Etive road at 5.00 pm and Gerald Hartley was taken to Fort William Hospital with concussion and shock; thirty hours had passed since his fall. He still remembers Don Siddons and the Kinloss team with gratitude.[4]

In the year after the Gerald Hartley incident, in August 1951, the Director General of Medical Services instructed that morphia was to be removed from first-aid outfits. The instruction added, optimistically:

> Under normal circumstances a medical officer should be readily available, who will have at hand supplies of all drugs which may be required in an emergency. It is not therefore intended to press for the supply of drugs for Mountain Rescue Teams.[5]

In 1951 civilian rescuers felt it necessary on several occasions to break the law in this respect, since in many cases it was not possible to get a doctor in time to such out of the way spots as *Raeburn's Gully* and to Buachaille Etive Mor. Eventually the Home Office agreed under pressure from the British Mountaineering Council and the Mountain Rescue Committee of British Climbing Clubs that the rule could be waived. In January 1952 the Committee could once again issue ampoules of morphia, which were kept in locked wooden boxes in civilian mountain rescue posts, but this concession did not extend to the RAF teams.

The point was made that the circumstances for RAF rescuers are the same, with the additional complications of often having to deal with aircraft crashes, which can cause more complicated and distressing injuries than rock falls. For a while, the RAF teams had to rely on the civilian teams to administer morphia and this was clearly unsatisfactory. In many cases, it was not possible for the RAF medical officer to be on the scene.

Before very long, the rule was relaxed for the RAF teams as well.

5 – Black Easter

The Americans had left RAF Valley, and the North Wales MRT moved there from RAF Llanbedr on September 26th 1949. During the early weeks the team experimented with heating, taking an old 40-gallon oil-drum, piercing it with holes in the side and bottom, and filling it with coke. Corporal 'Wacker' Bailey, the cook, turned out some good meals on it; especially, recalls Squadron Leader M J Harden[6], rice pudding. The heating experiment was so successful that they recommended it to the other teams, and suggested an issue of coke for the winter months.

Activities tended to be in a minor key. The matter of driving standards came up again when one night the jeep took a bend in Bangor a little too wide and ended up in the window of a grocery shop. According to one account, quite a few tins of sardines helped to vary the MR diet for some time.

Then the service reached a crisis-point at Easter time in 1951, both in North Wales and in the Scottish Highlands; the reasons were very different. That Valley showed up so well in North Wales, during what has come to be known as Black Easter, can probably be credited to the training skills of a medical officer in charge of Valley at the time, Flying Officer Mike Mason.

Mike Mason demonstrating a 'Tyrolean', Pont Ogwen, 1950. *Photo: Colin Pibworth*

The previous year had seen only five incidents, of which four had been climbing or walking mishaps; all four, as it happened, on Lliwedd, though on different occasions. But things took off in 1951, and in one short public holiday Valley was to see as much action as it had seen in the whole of 1950.

January started with a bang, right on cue on the 1st, when an avalanche on Y Garn, started by two parties tunnelling through the cornice, killed one climber and injured four more. Less than a fortnight later, six walkers went missing on Snowdon, but were found safe, sound and warm in the Summit Hotel. In February, four climbers met with an accident which killed two of them. Later that month, a climber went missing somewhere in the Snowdon area, but could not be found. The same happened to a walker on Cadair Idris in the first week of March.

For many the movable feast of Easter is the first opportunity to get out onto the hill for a prolonged period. When the holiday falls early in the year it can catch the dying throes of winter. For the year-round climber, of course, that is not a problem, more of a challenge. But for the climber whose boots are hung up in the shed throughout the winter, the natural hazards of the mountain are multiplied.

That was the situation at Easter 1951 when Good Friday fell on March 23rd. Precipitation through the winter had been high, with heavy snowfall on high ground. In North Wales and the Lake District, the snow was unusually deep: in addition, the post-war explosion of activity in the mountains was really under way. However, many of the people who escaped out of the cities into Snowdonia that long weekend were ill-prepared. As ever, those who were not well-versed in climbing or hill-walking often underestimated the wrath of the hills in the apparently cosy British Isles. Equally, they were liable to dismiss or forget the warnings of experienced people.

It was fortunate, therefore, that Mason had recently taken over at Valley. He had climbing experience before joining the RAF and had found the state of readiness at Valley to be appalling. He immediately instigated an effective training programme and made himself unpopular in the Air Ministry by pestering for equipment: he did not see why his team should be expected to buy their own or go without. He and John Berkeley at West Freugh had tried on more than one occasion to get RAF Mountaineering Association involved in the MR training, but had received the cold shoulder every time. The Air Ministry feared that if 'real' mountaineers were allowed into the service, it would be taken over as a cheap means of indulging a hobby at the taxpayer's expense – of treating it as a 'jolly', to use a favourite RAF expression.

To put into perspective the achievement of Mason and Valley during that disastrous Easter, let us look first at the whole picture. The British Mountaineering Council, in its journal 'Mountaineering' later that year, commented:

> The continued snowfall meant unusual cornices and dangerous ice slopes, which ordinary fell-walkers were quite unable to cope with; even with ice-axes, some of the slopes, quite safe under normal conditions, had become very dangerous.[7]

The chapter of events really started on Thursday, March 22nd, the day before Good Friday. A party of seven experienced climbers was descending the South Gully on Tryfan. They were unroped. Most of the party were on the edge of the gully as there was hard snow in it and they were using rock handholds on the steep side-wall. One woman, however, chose to descend in the centre of the gully. She slipped and fell 500 feet, and was dead when her companions reached her.

That evening, a bad storm raged.

On the Saturday, at 1 pm, two people fell at the foot of Clogwyn D'ur Arddu on the north-west slope of Snowdon. Several members of the Climbers' Club including Chris Briggs, who was to be distinguished for many years in Welsh mountain rescue, picked up first-aid equipment and went to see what they could do. One of the victims was dead, the other severely injured. On the descent, the party was told of another accident, also on Snowdon, this time in Trinity Gully. Three experienced climbers had passed the first 600 feet without difficulty, cutting steps in the snow as they went. However, near the point where the gully finished and the angle levelled out, the snow turned to ice and the wind began blowing too fiercely to face, so that they decided to descend. However they found that they had cut the ascending steps too wide apart to provide a safe descent in that gale; they would need to cut intermediate steps as they went down. It was therefore just as difficult to go back as to go on up and many blows of the axe were needed to cut a step. By this time the gale was so strong that they had to guess how long a lull would be before swinging the axe. Eventually the leader guessed wrong; he was blown off, causing all three climbers to fall the whole height of the cliff. One was dead; the leader was unconscious for a while, but the two survivors were able to walk to the Pen-y-Gwyrd Hotel, where Chris Briggs was landlord, and there was a Mountain Rescue Post.

The Chris Briggs party, in the meantime, went up again to take some photographs, and on their descent found that someone else had slipped at the point where the first two had fallen earlier that afternoon. He too died. Later that evening a man was climbing Snowdon by the Watkin Path, which runs up the south side of Snowdon from Nant Gwynant. He fell 50 feet, having slipped on frozen snow, and was fortunate to be found by a party of Rover Scouts from Dublin. They made a stretcher from ropes and started to carry him down to Llanberis where they were staying. However, they found the path at Clogwyn Station on the Snowdon Railway impassable due to ice and climbed back to the Summit Hotel.

Whilst all this was going on, another party led by an Everest mountaineer, Jack Longland, had ascended from Glaslyn. They had made two attempts to descend and then decided to spend the night at the hotel, where they met the Irish Scouts and the injured man. The party then numbered twenty-one.

At seven the next morning, Easter Sunday, sixteen of them left for Llanberis, leaving four with the casualty. At Clogwyn, where the ice had proved so difficult the day before, they cut big steps all the way across. When they finally reached Llanberis, they found Chris Briggs with the police and what *Mountaineering* described as: ...the splendidly trained and equipped RAF Mountain Rescue Unit.... What, then, had the Valley MRT been doing up to this point?

Mike Holton, a RAFMA member and a civil servant, brought into the Air Ministry later to strengthen the hand of the mountaineers, said:

> Their [Valley's] contribution to the life saving on Snowdon at Easter 1951 was phenomenal – if overlooked. Even the ... account of accidents that holiday taken from 'Mountaineering' Vol. 1 No. 10 does not pay adequate tribute. Yet, by November that year, their strength had declined and they had only two experienced men: Flying Officer Bill Brooks, the team leader [ie team officer i/c] and Medical Officer, and SAC Colin Pibworth. Incidentally, I remember very clearly from Michael Mason ... that the work over Easter on Snowdon had been done by using the team members' own clothing and climbing equipment because the service issue at that time was inadequate. The stretchers used above the snow line were borrowed from the mountain rescue posts, and casualties were transferred to the heavy modified service stretchers as soon as this was practical so as to release the civilian stretchers. As a result of this experience it was Mason who began to press in particular for better equipment....[8]

It is a little strange that the BMC Journal made so little mention of the Valley contribution. Pibworth remembers the conditions:

There was a fair amount of snow on the ground – not in condition for hard things, but more than enough to cause problems for an ever increasing number of hill-walkers (who did not have the correct gear or common sense).[9]

The Valley team was on exercise that weekend, under the team leader Sergeant Charlie Staff. Base camp on the Thursday was near a bridge just off the A5 outside Bethesda. In the early hours of the next day they were searching for two of their own members who were overdue at base. A party led by Colin Pibworth was dropped off at the east end of Llyn Ogwen at 2 am, and 'stumbled off into the night'. They did not go onto the tops but checked Cwm Lloer and Cwm Llugwy, then went back to base by road. Pibworth remembers it as a black, windy and very wet night. Back at the base camp, they stuck their heads through the tent flaps, to find everybody, including the missing two, fast asleep. The latter had walked in just after Pibworth and his party had started up the hill, and the recall, because of the usual radio inefficiency of the time, had not been picked up.

Over that weekend Valley recovered three bodies and four casualties, the results of three accidents, then were stood by for a fourth accident which was resolved by a civilian team. They were probably responsible for preventing other tragedies by giving advice, and helped another party without ice-axes on the Snowdon Horseshoe trying to cross an icy stretch. On the Sunday and Monday they remained on standby at Ogwen where they would be fairly certain of seeing any recall pyrotechnics: '... little or no reliance being given to the box of radio parts that we were obliged to carry!' Comments Pibworth now: 'Nowadays it seems ridiculous that there could be three deaths on Snowdon in a twenty-four hour period.'[9] The team was stood down and returned to RAF Valley during the afternoon of the Tuesday, 27th March.

Chris Briggs, as we have seen, commented on the superb equipment of the RAF team. It seems, though, from Holton's remarks and Mason's actions that this superb equipment was the private property of such enthusiasts as Mason and Pibworth. Pibworth in turn is happy to pay a suitable compliment to Briggs.

Briggs at PyG would have been involved of course – and he is to be congratulated for turning out any time and anywhere not with a 'trained' team of Alpinists but ad hoc volunteers from his hotel and bar![9]

Not only did Mason press the RAF for better equipment, he had already persuaded the team members to buy better equipment of their own – not easy on a ranker's pay in 1951. Mason's powers of persuasion and inspiration must have been considerable. In the case of Colin Pibworth, they were unnecessary; he was already very experienced and well equipped. Mike Holton, on his arrival in the Air Ministry:

... found Mason's name to be unpopular as he had been banging away and bombarding, trying to shift the usual bureaucratic complacency before and immediately after the Beinn Eighe incident. This made the progress we made on equipment over the next six months easier to achieve: selection of custom-designed boots, stretchers and nylon rope, and adoption of the MRC's drill for the use of morphia.[8]

It was during Mike Mason's brief time at Valley, Colin Pibworth recalls, that they were called out on another dramatic civilian rescue. Pibworth, then a young airman, was later to become a team leader both in the UK and abroad. Now long retired, he lives in a tiny bungalow high up in the hills behind Caernarfon, surrounded by sophisticated CB equipment, the roof bristling with aerials, alone but for a cat called Tenzing. (Why Tenzing? 'Because he's a bit of a cloimber!')

We had a call out at Valley during the winter. There had been an avalanche on the Glyders. Two separate roped parties had gone up under the face of Y Garn and they'd cut a hole through the cornice of overhanging snow at the top, and of course the day had been immaculate – sunshine, blue sky – and they were in the shadow away from the sun. One party got through and went on to the top and eventually the other one got through.... But the first party said they were going down again to have another go. They went down, cut another hole, ... and the whole lot came down with both parties. They came down in it and one member must have gone down to Ogwen and raised the alarm and we got called out of course. We arrived at 8 pm and not having any avalanche equipment at all, – no spades, no shovels, – we were digging with ice axes. I ended up on one bloke's face, following the rope down through the snow. There was no question of rescuing them. If you get caught in snow and you've been swept down you can move about, swim, kick ... but as soon as it stops it all compacts and that's it. If you happen to be face downwards with arms behind your back you can't do anything, and it's not so clever. But we did manage to get one person from this. He hadn't been killed but had been slightly damaged, and stayed at the site.'[10]

Before, during and after this period, paralleling Black Easter in Snowdonia, the Kinloss MRT in Scotland was going through the trauma of Beinn Eighe. These two events, happening so close together in time, sent shock waves through the Mountain Rescue management in Whitehall.

6 – Beinn Eighe

Right from the start, the signs were that 1951 could be a busy year for Kinloss, which had been covering Northern Scotland since 1944. On the first Saturday in February the team, led by Flight Lieutenant P Dawes and Flight Sergeant Don Siddons, left RAF Kinloss for the usual exercise, to be based at Ballater. They were getting the overnight accommodation ready when they were told that a climber was missing in the Glen Dessarry deer forest. Not having anough rations with them for an extended search, and with the roads judged to be too treacherous for a return to Kinloss that evening, the team stayed at Ballater overnight, leaving for Kinloss at 7 am. It was a disastrous journey, both the lorry and the ambulance getting stuck in snowdrifts and having to be dug out, and it was 2 pm before Kinloss was reached. After loading rations and equipment they made their way to Fort William, arriving at 6.30 pm. Staying there overnight, they then moved up to Loch Arkaig to begin searching. A whole day had been lost.

The missing man was not a climber but an estate factor, the Honourable John Cross, and it was whilst he was inspecting estate fences that he went missing. When the alarm was raised, a young local shepherd filled an oil lamp and put it outside his cottage every night in the hope that it would guide Cross home.

Then followed three days of sweep searches in the wild countryside of the area; then on the fourth day a party led by 22-year-old Joss Gosling from Bristol found a rock fall which he estimated to be of about five tons. They dug for two hours, and Cross's brother, Viscount Cross, arrived with some bloodhounds, but there was no scent. Digging continued the next day. Two more fruitless days were spent searching; then there was a five day break at Kinloss for the RAF, after which the team returned to the search area. The search was finally abandoned three days after that. Apart from the RAF, searchers had included estate shepherds and stalkers, police and Cross's friends. It was a long time before his body was finally found and a funeral could be held.

It seems odd now that a mountain rescue team should go out on exercise with insufficient rations and equipment even to start a search. Now, of course, these things can be brought up quickly by helicopter and team leaders have credit cards for emergency purchases.

Three weeks later, on March 11th Gosling was woken up at 11.30 pm. A climber was missing at Braemar. Don Siddons told him that they would be leaving at 9 am, so Gosling, still struggling against his disturbed sleep, packed his kit, then returned thankfully to bed. But less than an hour later he was woken up again to the news that the team was now going to leave at 6, not 9 am. The convoy drove to Alltdorie Shooting Lodge. There had been heavy snow over the weekend, then sixteen degrees of frost on the Sunday night. These conditions were to make matters very difficult for the searchers, especially in the actual recovery of the body. Gosling had a foot injury, so was left behind at the lodge as cook whilst the team left for Coire na Ciche on Beinn a' Bhuird (3924 feet). There they met members of the Cairngorm Club bringing down the body of Dr Donald McConnach, a young registrar at Aberdeen Royal Infirmary. He had been with a party returning from a climb when the snow gave way beneath his boots and he fell 500 feet, the first 200 feet over snow and the rest over a precipice. His companions had alerted a civilian mountain rescue team at Aberdeen and the Kinloss MRT was brought in soon afterwards.

It was now, in contrast to the previous harsh conditions, a bright sunny day, and the Kinloss team took over the stretcher-carrying task stripped to the waist. It had been a tragic time for the McConnach family: his brother had died in Nairobi only two months earlier in January.

The team slept on the floor of the lounge of the Loirston Hotel that night, and

Lancaster (NX611) VII: as used by French squadrons. *Photo: H J Budgen*

returned to Kinloss the next day, the 13th. They were held up in Ballater by trouble with the Humber and the Bedford and finally reached Kinloss at 5 pm. The team had just about finished unloading and were thinking about getting a meal when they heard the distant roar of a Lancaster's four Merlins on the main runway, and they glanced casually at it as it gathered speed, bounced a couple of times, then was in the air, turning to find its course.

Lancaster TX264 of 120 Squadron had been converted, like many others after the war, to fulfil a reconnaissance role. Coded BS-D, and with the call sign D Dog, it left RAF Kinloss just after 6 pm of Tuesday March 13th. Piloted by 24-year-old Flight Lieutenant Harry Reid DFC, it was to go to the Rockall and Faroes area for a navigational exercise, by way of Cape Wrath, the Kyle of Tongue and the Moray Firth. He had with him a crew of eight: a second pilot, a navigator, a flight engineer and four signallers.

There is probably no more remote spot on the mainland coast than Cape Wrath. Murdo Nicholson, the assistant lighthouse keeper, was one of that special breed which can stand this sort of isolation. At midnight that night, reading in bed, he cocked his head: a heavy aircraft was going over – 'a familiar noise, sounded like a Lanc'. He thought no more of it until he had occasion to be reminded a couple of days later.

At 1.27 am Reid radioed back to Kinloss giving his position, which was 60 miles north of Cape Wrath. That was the last anyone heard from 'D Dog'. Gosling, looking forward to breakfast, heard a Tannoy broadcast at 6.50 am, only the day after they returned from Beinn a' Bhuird. At the MT section Dawes, looking gloomy, told them that the missing aircraft was one from their own station; many of them knew Harry Reid and some of the other crew members. 'D Dog' had been due back at midnight. They packed their kit in the vehicles, then went off to their sections to work, telling their immediate superiors that they were on standby. Still weary from the McConnach climb, they were not sorry that they were not going out straight away.

During this day two aircraft searched the likely sea area, and air and sea searches continued for the next two days. Early in the morning of March 14th, a young boy living at Torridon, looking out of his bedroom window, had seen a distant red flash in the sky. He had assumed that it was something to do with the boats on the nearby lochs, and gone back to sleep. Then on Saturday March 17th, he saw in the *Daily Mail* news of the missing aircraft:

MISSING PLANE SOUGHT
North Coast at the alert

Torridon is 'round the corner' on the west coast, the boy's curiosity was roused and he spoke to the local postmaster. That man took it seriously enough to pass the message on to RAF Kinloss, which had in the meantime been receiving similar reports. It was now possible to concentrate the search on a specific area – Beinn Eighe (3313 feet), near to Kinlochewe. An Airspeed Oxford was sent out and soon the wreck was seen.

To understand both the difficulties the team faced and the mistakes that it made, it is necessary to understand the topography of Beinn Eighe. Beinn Eighe is the collective name for a series of peaks forming an east-west ridge and bearing many steep north-facing corries.

The Kinloss MRT went out at 8.30 am on the 17th, so no time had been wasted between the boy's reporting of the flash and their call-out. They set up camp behind the Kinlochewe Hotel and Gosling's party walked along the deer path between Beinn Eighe and Liathach (3456 feet), the neighbouring mountain, scanning the southern slopes with binoculars. In the meantime, a second party found some wreckage in Coire Mhic Fhearchair, the most westerly of the north-facing corries. Next morning they tackled it from the north, walking along the track in Glen Grudie, across the shoulder of Ruadh-stac Mor. They found themselves in a corrie – "the wildest corrie I have ever seen," said Gosling – with at the back a massive wall, 1000 feet at its highest. Three colossal and overlapping buttresses occupied the greater part towards the right, the western end, and on this day disappeared up into the mist. They were in Coire Mhic Fhearchair. At the foot of the Western Buttress, on a steep snow-covered slope were the port wing and undercarriage, and scattered around were two engines and various cowlings.[11] Four of the party tried to climb the right-hand gully between the Central and Western Buttresses, but ice and mist forced them back.

On the following day, they found that the wind had brought down the

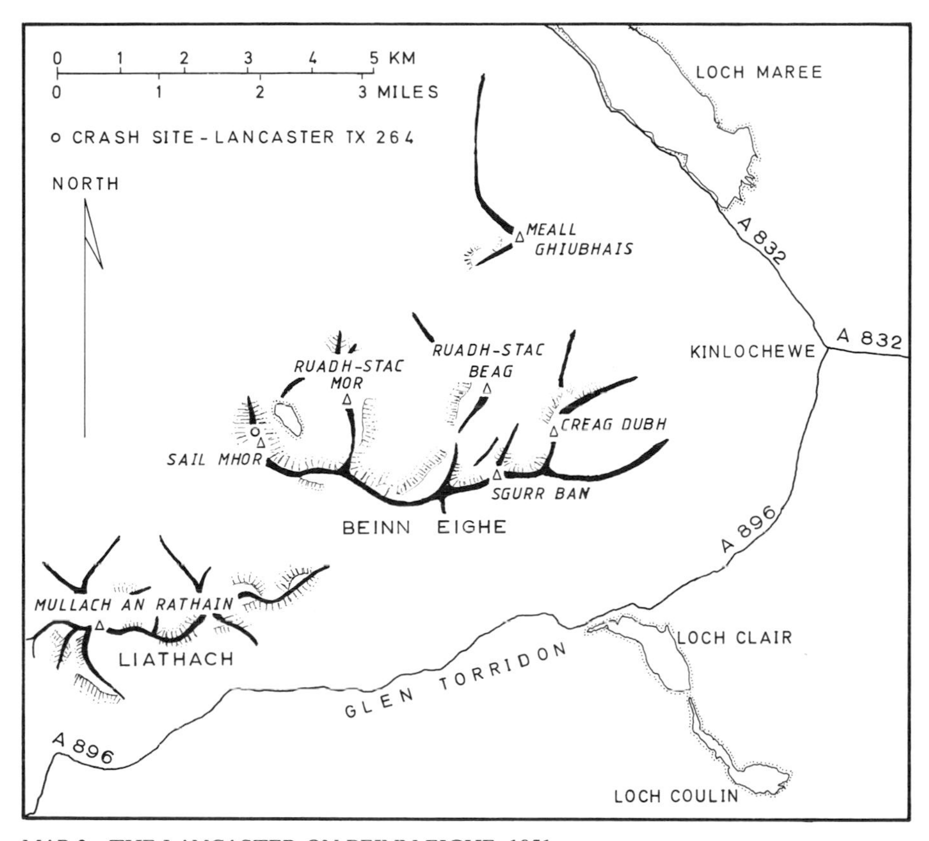

MAP 2 THE LANCASTER ON BEINN EIGHE, 1951

The crash point of Flt Lt Harry Reid's Avro Lancaster GR3 TX264 on Sail Mhor, Beinn Eighe, Ross and Cromarty, 13/3/51

starboard wing and parts of the mainplane, but there was no sign of the fuselage. A party again tried to climb and got higher than the previous day. They could see the burnt out fuselage from that point, but could not get to it. After this, the team abandoned attempts for the time being, and returned to Kinloss on March 20th. In the light of subsequent events, that was a pity, especially as in the meantime the team leadership had declined offers of help from St Andrews University and Moray Mountaineering Clubs. Several accounts written since say that they returned to Kinloss because of a fall suffered by Siddons. There is no record of that in Gosling's diary and he has no recollection of it.

On the 24th, Dr Brewster, the president of the Moray club, telephoned the Officer Commanding at Kinloss and informed him that some members of the club intended to attempt to reach the wreck on their own initiative. Later that day, Dawes called on Dr Brewster to tell him exactly where it was. At about this time, two experienced climbers were in the vicinity: Captain Mike Banks, a Royal Marine Commando and a mountaineering instructor, and Lieutenant Angus Erskine of the Royal Navy. Both were members of the RN Mountaineering Club. From one or two sources, largely the barman at the Kinlochewe Hotel, they heard about a crashed aircraft, and about Kinloss MRT's fruitless attempts to reach it. Banks and Erskine decided they would do so, but even they, much more experienced than the Kinloss team, found the task far from easy. Reaching part of the wreck, they found a body spreadeagled near the cairn of Sail Mhor, a peaceful sight which Banks found very moving.

Afterwards Banks was extremely critical of the Kinloss team. Certainly they were lacking in mountaincraft. They were lacking also in good equipment. The present writer, as a member of the RAF Edzell team during the time of this incident, climbed in army battledress, which the RAF seemed to think suitable clothing for a Scottish Highland winter (and summer, if it comes to that). This, with smocks and boots and seaboot stockings and white polo neck aircrew sweater, was standard issue. Only the enthusiastic mountaineers (and Edzell had none) had good gear, and that was because they bought it. Ice-axes were unheard of at Edzell. Kinloss had six or so but a report after this incident said that nobody knew how to use them. Dawes wore only black walking shoes, not climbing boots of any sort. It is not true, as at least one newspaper has said since, that all of the team worked in walking shoes. The Kinloss MR section also possessed snow shoes and sledge stretchers. It is only fair to add that Don Siddons himself, although a walker, was not a mountaineer; though in a newspaper interview in 1949 (after the Firefly search) he claimed to have started in aircrew rescue work during the war in the Austrian Alps.

Another comment that Banks made concerned the team's use of walkie-talkies; rather oddly he added: '...although what on earth use these would be on a mountain escaped me'[12]. One can only assume that at the time he had never been involved in a search and rescue operation, for how else would he suggest that search parties keep in touch with each other?

The Kinloss team returned to the area on March 30th, after ten days, probably in response to the rising tide of criticism and innuendo, leaving Kinloss in fine weather. They found a route up Sail Mhor and then on to the ridge. Siddons with one of his drivers, Gavin Main, continued up the ridge, then called for three more with a rope. Gosling went with Mike Davidson and Junior Christie, and found that Siddons and Main had one of the bodies. This was lowered by rope down to the main party, which took it 1200 feet down a snow slope. At last something tangible had been achieved. Over the three days a further three bodies, including that of Harry Reid, were retrieved and taken down to a track, from where they were carried down to road level with the help of a pony. By April

The Kinloss team in Coire Mhic Fhearchair, Beinn Eighe, on the first day of the Lancaster call-out: Sunday 18th March 1951. *Photo: Joss Gosling*

Coire Mhic Fhearchair, 21st April 1951. *Photo: Joss Gosling*

3rd the weather had deteriorated and they did not attempt to reach the top that day.

On the 4th Gosling and Andy Fairweather left Bridge of Grudie for Coire Mhic Fhearchair and another party set off from the south. Both were defeated by very strong winds and poor visibility. Again, it had not been a good day for the team and next day they returned to Kinloss for the funerals of three of the crew members of D Dog. It was fifteen days before they returned to Beinn Eighe again.

Then Gosling was in a party of five which again started from Bridge of Grudie and tried to reach Coire Mhic Fhearchair from the north. As Mike Holton commented years later: '...anyone familiar with the mountain and conditions would have known that that was not the way to try to approach Beinn Eighe.'[13] Why was the team persisting in this, even after a month? Were they still ignoring expert advice and offers of help? Why were they approaching Beinn Eighe still from the wrong side? Holton again:

> The tragedy is that the Kinloss team attempted to reach the crash by the most difficult ascent, which only experts would have tackled, and it would have been more practical to have followed Banks's route to make a recce, though it seems they were not equipped for this in winter conditions.[14]

By this time the comments had gone beyond muttering and had reached a clamour.

Gosling's party found the snow still deep, although the thaw had started. They pressed on, searching for the tailplane and rear turret, but without success. Then on Sunday, April 22nd, they started from the more acceptable southern side, from the Torridon road and this time they reached the wreck, finding human remains, instruments and engines. But again strong wind increased and they stopped digging – another ignominious return to Kinloss. They were not to see Beinn Eighe again for over two months, although there was still a body there somewhere.

The next visit was early in July, when another engine and parts of the rear turret were found. There was still a large snowdrift unsearched and Gosling suspected that something hidden there would be revealed when the thaw was complete. Nearly two months after, on August 27th, they were back. Again Gosling, in a party of six, approached from the Torridon road side and found the last body. It had been there for five months. Having recovered it, they then sent the remaining large pieces of fuselage and wing hurtling down the gully, which later was to be known as Fuselage Gully, into the scree below, where it could do no harm, and where much of it remains to this day.

Five of the crew of TX264 are buried in Kinloss cemetery, set in the peaceful grounds of the ruined abbey there. They are Sergeant W D Beck, Sergeant J W Bell, Sergeant R Clucas, Flight Sergeant J Naismith and Flight Lieutenant P Tennison, and they are in the section reserved for the many aircrew who have

The Lancaster's propellor & memorial at Kinloss. *Photo: Frank Card*

Where five of the Lancaster's crew are buried, in the shadow of the ancient abbey at Kinloss. *Photo: Frank Card*

died flying from RAF Kinloss over the years. Thus ended the episode which, above all others, was to shake the service to its core. The contrast between this and Valley's performance in Wales during the same period was not lost on various influential people. But whilst arguments raged in Whitehall, the work of the teams had to go on. Notwithstanding the criticisms of the team, in the New Year SAC Malcolm Brown received the British Empire Medal at a special award ceremony at RAF Kinloss for his work on the operation, an award often unfairly omitted from any list of MR honours.

On August 28th 1985, a group of officer cadets, led by Sergeant Jim Morning, were airlifted onto the summit of Beinn Eighe by a Sea King from 202 Squadron. One of D Dog's propellers was recovered and put into a lifting net and taken by the helicopter to the road, whence it was taken to RAF Kinloss. The twisted three-bladed propeller now stands outside the wooden Mountain Rescue Section building as a memorial to D Dog's crew.

7 – After Beinn Eighe

Much has been made of the fact that Dawes and Siddons declined offers of expert help during the Beinn Eighe episode. In this, one can only speculate on their motives. But whatever the criticisms may be, we must remember three things. Firstly, this was an operation outside the competence of the team: they were not trained to the standard necessary, neither did they have the equipment for it. The fact that Valley in North Wales at the same time showed up so well by comparison was to the credit of a mountaineer officer, helped by an experienced SAC who happened to be there, and who ensured that his team was properly equipped. Secondly, Dawes and Siddons were not alone in refusing the help of competent mountaineers. The RAF itself had declined the help that the RAF Mountaineering Association had for some time been offering, probably out of fear that dedicated mountaineers would exploit the service as a cheap means of indulging their strange pastime. Thirdly, the weather at that time was extremely severe even by local standards, and even experienced climbers such as Banks and Erskine found themselves in some difficulty.

Senior officers often held the opinion that what was needed for mountain rescue work was not skilled mountaineers but stretcher fodder. Another factor was that there was no officer in Air Ministry with exclusive responsibility for MR – no equivalent of the present day Inspector of Land Rescue. The most senior person with that sort of responsibility was in fact Bill Pitcairn's successor, Flight Sergeant J D Archibald, an experienced climber and a good instructor, but without the clout that is imparted by rings on the sleeve. Tragically, he was killed in a civilian air crash shortly after obtaining his commission in 1952.

Since the end of the war, with the decline in military flying, the Air Ministry had been resisting initiatives to improve Mountain Rescue expertise. Particularly it had developed a policy of not encouraging the use of volunteers with good mountain experience. Mike Holton, as a National Service radar mechanic and a RAFMA member, was one such: he had no response to his enquiries. After demobilisation in 1950, Holton stayed in the RAFMA and was soon on the committee. He remembers much discussion of the problem at the time. The Vice-President was Wing Commander Bentley Beauman, a well-known climber, then in the Air Ministry. Beauman went to see the Vice Chief of the Air Staff to suggest that the RAFMA's offer of help be accepted: he too heard no more. The official line was that rescue should not be made too specialist a subject. Most of the team NCOs were hill-walkers, not mountaineers.

The local gossip in the Torridon area was still buzzing when Lieutenant Angus Erskine, Mike Banks's companion, was so moved by the obvious lack of expertise that, taking his naval career in his hands, he wrote RAFMA's president a letter which was eventually picked up by Wing Commander Tony Smyth, the Chairman; the same Tony Smyth who had been George Graham's CO at the Aircrew Mountain Centre in India in 1944. This letter gave Smyth the ammunition he had long needed. Like others in RAFMA, Smyth had for some time been uneasy about Mountain Rescue organisation: at a RAFMA committee meeting in Glen Coe in August of the previous year (1950), he and Flight Lieutenant Gordon Parish had discussed the problems with Sergeant J R Lees, a leading rock-climber.

"Could you do any better?" had asked Smyth of Lees.

"I'm sure I could," Lees had answered.

Then they had discussed the problems of non-mountaineers in mountain rescue teams and the shape the service ought to assume.

Prompted by the Erskine letter and helped by the Glen Coe discussion, Smyth drafted a letter to the President of RAFMA, Air Chief Marshal Sir Ralph Cochrane, complaining about the 'uselessness' of the Mountain Rescue Service as it was then constituted. He suggested that:

1 MR should have an Inspector at squadron leader level, who should be housed in the Directorate of Navigation, and should be provided with a Land Rover and given office facilities.
2 Each MR team should have a permanent staff of a Sergeant (Physical Education) and an airman (Stores), with one Land Rover.
3 An instruction book should be written.
4 A yearly course on mountain techniques should be run with the help of RAFMA.
5 The intervention of God would be needed to help any Station Commander who did not co-operate.

To Smyth's horror, Cochrane passed the letter straight to the Air Council and this did set the cat amongst the pigeons. Fortunately for Smyth and the service, it was adopted almost without alteration.[15] Within the year the suggestions were accepted practically as they stood.

The change of attitude towards RAFMA's expertise and offer of help happened very quickly. On May 9th 1951, before the last Beinn Eighe body had been recovered, came a letter from Wing Commander Watts, the senior officer in the general search and rescue organisation, to Tony Smyth:

As a result of our experiences during the last winter it has been decided to hold a conference in the Air Ministry to examine means of improving our organisation, and the best way of training these teams.
We have been wondering whether the RAF Mountaineering Association might be able to assist us in this matter....[16]

Smyth replied, with a pleasure which he did not attempt to disguise, and just a touch of understandable 'told you so':

I was delighted to receive your letter of May 9th as we have been suggesting to your predecessors in AD rescue that a knowledge of rock-climbing was necessary for Mountain Rescue teams. This winter has emphasised our contention.... We shall, of course, do everything we can to help.

Later, he added: '....I think we can provide an officer and a number of airmen to act as instructors in rock climbing....' He suggested Capel Curig as the venue.[17]

In a later letter he was able to confirm that the idea had the official approval of RAFMA. He commented:

I hear that the recovery of bodies from the Lancaster which crashed on Ben Eighe in the Torridonians was seriously held up through lack of mountaineers. This is another case where mountaineering knowledge was necessary.[18]

One very influential figure was T Graham Brown, Professor Emeritus of Physiology at the University of Cardiff, described in Lees's climbing diary as 'a grand old chap'. The Professor was a noted alpinist who was most famous with Frank Smythe for first ascents on the Brenva face of Mont Blanc and had also taken part in first ascents in the Himalayas and Alaska. Says Mike Holton: 'TGB was to the latter [Mont Blanc] as Whymper was to the Matterhorn.'[19]

He was concerned at the shortcomings of the RAF service and was in touch with many RAFMA (RAF Mountaineering Association) members, including Dan Stewart and Mike Holton. His involvement with RAFMA began about two years before Beinn Eighe and he was a vice-president at that time. Getting wind of the Beinn Eighe fiasco, on May 31st he telephoned Sir Ralph Cochrane, who was not only President of RAFMA but also Vice Chief of the Air Staff. This led to dinner and a long talk at the Athenaeum. Cochrane subsequently wrote answering some of Graham Brown's queries on number and distribution of teams. The professor's key suggestion was that the RAF should encourage young doctors into the Mountain Rescue Service and post them into teams, and should screen new RAF recruits and RAFMA members, and when possible post them also into teams.

Before the next month was out, on June 29th 1951, the first Mountain Rescue

L to r: Colin Pibworth, T Graham Brown and Gordon Parish in Glencoe, Feb 1950. All members of the RAF Mountaineering Association; Pibworth was already in the RAF Valley MRT; Graham Brown had much influence on the shape of the service after Beinn Eighe. *Photo: Colin Pibworth*

Conference had taken place in Air Ministry. Amongst those present were Smyth and Mike Mason (both from the Flying College at Manby and representing RAFMA), Dawes and Siddons from Kinloss, Air Commodore Merer and Wing Commander Watts. One objective was to seek opinions of the teams and to hear at first-hand the problems they faced. The system then was that resonsibility for administering the teams lay with the Command under which the individual stations fell. Should this responsibility be delegated to one selected Command? Some saw difficulties in this but there was general agreement on a need for an inspecting officer, preferably experienced in mountaineering, to visit teams and oversee efficiency and to standardise training and equipment. It was agreed that liaison between the MRTs and the civil authorities was 'adequate'. There was a move to formalise what was already the de facto situation: officers i/c to be medical officers.

Tony Smyth offered to find RAFMA members who were willing to serve in Mountain Rescue, but mentioned that many NCOs were probably deterred from volunteering because of a fear that their promotion prospects could be harmed. Both of these points were accepted. The need for a manual was agreed. Tony Smyth strongly advocated the need of training courses and the final agreement was for a summer and a winter course at Valley or Kinloss, for ten or twelve NCOs. The RAF Medical Branch was to be approached about the carrying of morphia or paraldehyde. Expert advice was to be sought on the relative merits of the Duff and Thomas stretchers.

Picking up some of those points, Smyth wrote to Watts, proposing the first course at Valley:

I intend first to ask Flight Lieutenant Gordon Parish and, failing him, Flying Officer Mason to lead the course – both are doctors.
With reference to S/Ldr Sinclair's letter ... on the subject of the Rescue Manual, I have only one name to suggest and he is not at the moment a serving officer. He is in fact Michael Holton Esq. . . . He is a Civil Servant of officer status at the present moment employed with the Ministry of Food. He has all the mountaineering qualifications coupled with an ability to write, a University degree and a fair knowledge of the RAF having served in it for many years. He is on our Committee and has already asked whether there would be any chance of getting a transfer to the Air Ministry on this question.[20]

The manual Smyth referred to here came out in 1953: Mike Holton's AMP 299. In November, by when Holton had been seconded to the Air Ministry from the Ministry of Food, he met Professor T Graham Brown for lunch. The professor had written on October 24th 1951 from the Physiology Institute of the University College in Cardiff to arrange this, adding: 'I have been beating up recruits for MR, and I think that you will get some really first class men next October, but not this year.'[21] He then went on to talks with the two senior officers responsible for rescue services, finding them 'decent, but sticky and timid'.[22]

There was due to be another dinner between Graham Brown and Cochrane in December: it fell through because of confusion over dates, but in view of subsequent events it seems possible that it was a diplomatic cancellation. Cochrane had arranged to send the Beinn Eighe papers and photographs to Graham Brown but he wrote in February 1952 to say that they had been sent back to the unit, adding that in talking with Air Commodore Merer, who controlled Search and Rescue, he found that many of the steps which they had been discussing had in fact already been taken. Merer, he went on, had in particular been considering the possibility of appointing a trained mountaineer as inspector of the teams. The letter reads like a brush-off, thinks Holton: 'Don't worry about this, old chap, we've got it under control'.

The second conference was on January 14th 1952. Ex-LAC Mike Holton was present, doubtless relishing, after two years' National Service in the ranks, the delicious irony of working in this high-powered company in the rarified atmosphere of a committee room in the Air Ministry. Another newcomer was Squadron Leader David Dattner, who had recently taken over at Kinloss from Dawes and was acquiring a reputation for his unorthodox methods of what we would now call paramedic training. Later he was to be Inspector of Mountain Rescue.

Discussion concentrated this time on mundane matters like boots and vehicles. Life was beginning to settle down after Beinn Eighe. Brown's BEM for Beinn

Eighe had by then been awarded but did not receive a mention. But the problems were not over; bureaucracy was dragging its feet. On April 3rd Tony Smyth, wearing his RAFMA hat, wrote to Sir Ralph Cochrane again.

We are getting deeply depressed about Mountain Rescue. The main cause for this is the failure of P. Staff and Records to effect any postings to stations which have Mountain Rescue Teams. Let me deal first with the airmen; we circularised our members and obtained thirty volunteers who wish to be posted to team stations. These were forwarded to Records who stated that six were eligible. Of these only one has actually been posted. The officer situation is no better. At the moment officers running teams are mostly doctors and of the nine officers i/c teams, seven will be released at the end of 1952. We know of no one coming forward to take their places. I do know however that there is no shortage of new doctors coming up for National Service who would be willing to volunteer for the RAF if offered a certainty of mountaineering – as it is the Army will get them. Graham Brown will bear this out.

The situation regarding NCOs in teams is also parlous. At the moment the establishment is filled by some sergeant who is surplus or no good at anything else. In the nine teams there are only three who can claim to be good at their jobs, and it is a job which is becoming more and more technical and specialised every day. There is an urgent need for establishing the trade of Mountain Rescue Specialist for this alone will attract men of the calibre we want.[23]

Eventually, this reached Group Captain W P Welsh, whose reactions were indignant. Firstly he said that for airmen, the department had received 20 names, not 30, and only six were eligible; he asked for further details. Then:

There has never been any difficulty in the past regarding the replacement of officers i/c teams who need not, themselves, be mountaineers. Regarding National Service doctors, they may be of great value to us but I think it would be quite wrong to offer them a 'certainty of mountaineering' as a bait to join the RAF.

Smyth's statement about NCOs calls for some substantiation. The NCO is the one and only member of each team who is established. Normal methods of removing them are therefore available if they are inefficient.

I think the suggestion of instituting a trade of Mountain Rescue Specialist is quite fantastic. We should make the best use of mountaineers we have in the RAF and build up and maintain a good liaison with civil rescue organisations. Air Commodore Merer has already done a lot to this end.

After commending the help received from RAFMA, he goes on:

I am at a loss to understand why Smyth chose to unload all these somewhat distorted facts onto VCAS[24]. Firstly, he is in no authoritative position to do so. Secondly he is in regular correspondence with AD Rescue[25] to whom he is always at liberty to make suggestions or requests. He has never mentioned to us the subjects which he has now referred to VCAS. I consider Smyth's letter inaccurate, uncalled for and impolite in that it has gone over your head to VCAS.

The reply came that wisdom should not be clouded by irritation over the mode of getting something useful done. Welsh was told to liaise with Smyth, establish the precise nature of the criticisms and work out plans for obtaining the right people for the jobs

Smyth wrote to Holton on May 1st:

Today I had a telephone call from Wing Commander Watts which was somewhat acrimonious. It turns out that the new Director wishes to see me on May 21st, and before that time I must get some more particulars of my complaints to the VCAS. At least this letter seems to have churned up the mud.

He noted the discrepancy between the numbers, and asked Holton for the names, adding:

I have already told Watts that I am not interested in Records eligibility for posting and see no reason why all the names we gave them should not be posted to Mountain Rescue Units unless the airmen concerned were about to leave the service.[26]

Holton's handwritten notes show how the discrepancy in numbers occurred. RAFMA had submitted 29 names of interested members, of whom nine were already on a station with a team and wished to stay there. No more had been heard about those people and there had been no guarantee that they would be left where they were. Of the other 20, only 18 had more than nine months to serve and of those only six were eligible for posting. Because only one member had been posted as a result of RAFMA's intervention, the Association had ceased supplying names. Quite by chance, Sergeant Lees had been posted to Valley although he was not one of the six. As an example of the difficulties, Holton offered Valley. Of the team, only three, Bill Brooks, Lees and Pibworth, were experienced mountaineers and they were working hard to pass on their knowledge and skills.[27]

Commander Angus Erskine, who as a young lieutenant was the author of the letter which was the catalyst for the reorganisation of the service, met Holton many years later by chance. Although the results of his letter had been so far-reaching, he had never been told what they were and Holton enlightened him. Years after that chance meeting he makes two comments:

Actually there was an element of humour about the incident: two members of the RN Mountaineering Club reaching the summit of Ben Eighe in winter conditions after the RAF Rescue squad had failed to do so!!
Anyway, I am the first to acknowledge that today the RAF Mountain Rescue teams are second to none in the Highlands.[28]

For that he is entitled to take a fair slice of the credit.

Over the years we have seen that various officers, not directly involved, can be very sceptical of the need for real mountaineering skills in mountain rescue. As part of his campaign to bring RAF Mountain Rescue up to scratch through the medium of RAFMA, Professor T Graham Brown wrote a memorandum[22] which remains in his papers. It is undated, but probably was drafted after a meeting with Mike Holton in December 1951. As far as can be ascertained, it was never typed up and submitted: perhaps it was intended to be merely an aide-mémoire, but it does illustrate Graham Brown's philosophy.

It starts by distinguishing between hill-walkers, climbers and mountaineers. Hill-walkers can get about safely on mountains but do not claim to know how to climb rocks safely. Climbers can climb difficult rocks safely. Mountaineers he divided into two groups: those who can climb safely on rock and snow under severe winter conditions in Scotland (English and Welsh hills he discounts); and those who can climb safely at high altitudes on rock, snow and permanent ice, and who can travel safely on broken glaciers (Alpine climbers). What, then, is the usefulness of climbers and mountaineers to a mountain rescue organisation?

Practical: in difficult cases of mountain rescue which call for rock climbing or for the facing of severe winter conditions especially in stormy weather.
General: as a means of encouraging *and feeding* the spirit of adventure, and thereby of building character and of bringing out latent qualities of leadership.

He conceded that most mountain rescues can be done efficiently by hill-walkers; nevertheless, a nucleus of experienced climbers and mountaineers is needed for occasions such as Beinn Eighe. In very severe conditions, climbers and mountaineers will not turn back, whereas walkers might feel justified in doing so. In a comment unconsciously echoed by Johnnie Lees in conversation with the writer forty-one years later, he then said:

The persistence of the former will in part be due to their greater knowledge, but perhaps in greater part it will be due to the very strong tradition of *maximum* effort in rescue which is part of the sport of mountain climbing.

8 – Early Training

Two rock-climbing courses were held at Blaen-y-Nant, Idwal in October 1951, under Lees's tutelage. Lees, with his distinctive red beret, was soon to be a familiar sight with RAF teams over the next ten years or so. These two initial courses were based under canvas about 30 miles from Valley, with extremely cold weather and occasional snow. Gosling from the Kinloss team – the horror of Beinn Eighe fresh in his mind – was there:

Friday 19 October. I climbed with Johnny Lees today and we started by doing 'The slab and arête route' (Diff) on Bochlwyd Buttress. We then climbed around to Heather Terrace of Tryfan and climbed 'The Second Pinnacle Rib' (Diff) with a very interesting slab behind the pinnacle. From the main peak we crossed to the North Peak and part way down the North Ridge until we came to the Notch Rocks and we descended the 'Notch Arête', a route with a very interesting chimney to climb down, we then dropped to the road and returned to base.[29]

A senior officer in the Air Ministry reported: 'The course attracted great publicity and the activities were widely reported in the National and Provincial press. In addition, some of their activities appeared on the TV newsreel.[30]

He had already had cause to regret that publicity. Some keen mountaineering eye had spotted the pictures which appeared in the *Daily Graphic* of December 6th and made unfavourable comments. A minute from Mike Holton provided defensive ammunition:

It is unfortunate that a better picture was not selected by the sub-editor of the paper since many other photographs were taken. Also press photographers know little about climbing style and had this particular photograph been taken ... two seconds later a much better result would have been obtained.

Of the three airmen in the photograph, Sergeant Lees, the RAF Mountaineering Association instructor, is the only experienced climber. He is, as a matter of fact, one of the best mountaineers in the Service today. His stance and rope management in the photograph are excellent. From his position he must be prepared to take a fall of his second man who, if he fell, would swing beneath Lees.

The second man, Sergeant Anderson, is doing a tricky move for a novice. He is balance climbing – using the toe nails of his boots and his finger tips. This is the correct technique for this particular move. Sergeant Anderson appears to be making a novice's mistake: he is crouching rather than standing up straight on his toes, but actually Anderson was moving into this position when the photographer caught him on the way.

The third man, LAC Christie, is the least experienced and his style needs to be improved a great deal. Once again, the photographer has caught Christie, who is leaning on the rock in a position of unstable equilibrium. He should have been standing straight, legs braced, with his left hand on the 'active' rope which, I understand, it was two seconds later when checked by the instructor.

The rope itself is correct in all positions.

There has been some slight comment in the mountaineering world about this photograph but fortunately Lees is known so well, particularly in NORTH WALES, that critics have been able to interpret the picture correctly.

The headings to the photograph are erroneous since it is not a rescue squad, the way up is not perilous, and the 'new methods' referred to are merely ordinary climbing methods.[31]

In fairness to the sub-editor responsible, one should bear in mind the need for a heading to be brief and eye-catching; in that context, it is reasonable, from the layman's point of view, to describe a rescue team as a rescue squad. Most people would regard climbing by boot toe-nails and finger-tips up a rock as perilous, even if roped, and would point to the not inconsiderable number of experienced mountaineers who fall as evidence. The reference to new methods certainly is not correct but perhaps the sub-editor was thinking in shorthand terms of methods new to the trainees, rather than to mountaineering. Still, it has to be admitted that there is something in the chemistry between journalists and mountaineers that ensures that the two can seldom mix. Lees comments on an episode the following year in his no-holds-barred way when he and his team had to take 'some of this species' on to the hill for a PR exercise. His objection chiefly is to a journalistic tendency to write mountaineers up as 'supermen' and 'heroes', and to talk of 'ice advisers' and 'living on ledges at 800 feet above sea level'.

The second course was in February 1952, over ten days, based on the Rothiemurchus Mountaineering Hut. Present amongst others were John Berkeley (later for many years a GP at Fort William, where he was, incidentally, Hinde's doctor), Mason, Holton, Lees, Gosling and Junior Christie. The first of the extended courses for prospective team leaders was in November 1952 with Lees (by now the Valley team leader) as Chief Instructor. Candidates, in line with the philosophy of the time, were eight physical training instructors, but the course was not a success. The eight members were down to seven at the start and the candidates were, by chance, the first to arrive at the scene of a Washington crash, with the bodies still smouldering and waiting to be removed. Then a few days later they had to recover the badly damaged bodies of two army climbers who had fallen in Dinas Cromlech. Hours were long and weekend work was expected. These factors combined to put off some of the non-mountaineers, probably for life. Only three finished the course. The rest, presumably, returned to quiet and stress-free lives as PTIs. It seemed silly to Lees to decree that all team leaders should be PTIs, even though he was one himself – what was needed was a good mountaineer with some admin experience. Also it was often the case that PTI recruits knew little about aircraft, whereas NCOs who had worked on aircraft were better in achieving good relations with RAF command in getting workers off for training.[32]

Then the centre for training moved away the following year to Kinloss and to that end Lees was posted to Kinloss, doing a swap with the incumbent NCO at Kinloss. The reason for the change was: '...that the terrain in the Kinloss area of responsibility is more suitable for general training than Snowdonia.[33]

Bill Trench, although not in the Air Force, soon became involved in Lees's training activities. There was one long day:

> ...when we climbed *Bow-Shaped Slab* on Cloggy starting at 6 am, driving back to Valley for a standby because of a Royal Flight and returning to climb in the Llanberis Pass in the fading light. The climbs were fierce enough. But the journey to Valley was terrifying. The old roads fringed with hedges meandering across Anglesey were not meant for high speed. This was an integral part of mountain rescue and *what an experience.*[34]

Derek Walker of the British Mountaineering Council considers that Lees was the most important man in (RAF) Mountain Rescue throughout the 50s;

> Johnny Lees taught me to climb, in fact to us young National Service men aged ... 18 to 20 he was a very powerful and influential personality.
> Johnny himself was about 28 or 29 at the time but he seemed an incredibly experienced climber to us young men. He was a guide, one of the relatively few guides in the country at that stage and he was married to Gwen Moffat, the only female guide in the country. Johnny had climbed quite a lot in the Alps and he had even been to the Himalayas with an

RAF expedition. He appeared to us to be quite brilliant at the time, because he could climb VSs while we were struggling to do diffs![35]

9 – The Fall on Glyder Fach

Mike Holton was with Valley MRT on Saturday, November 10th 1951. Mike Mason had by this time been posted away; the officer in charge was Flying Officer Bill Brooks. Holton and the team went out on exercise for ten hours on Crib Croch. When they got back to the base camp at Capel Curig there was a message for them. A climber had fallen from the *Direct Route* on Glyder Fach. This had been reported to the Mountain Rescue Post at Idwal Youth Hostel, which passed the message on to Valley. An advance party left Capel Curig at 5 pm and went to the youth hostel where the warden gave them details – alarming in that the climber seemed to have broken his neck and that the party which had collected the stretcher was too inexperienced and unqualified to move the injured man. Bill Brooks's first priority was to prevent those on the spot from causing any further injury. He, Pibworth and Holton immediately left for the site, leaving behind Corporal Chandler to give the rest of the team the information.

These three reached the foot of the climb at 6 pm, and found many people about, their torches bobbing and flashing through the dark. By then, the rescue was under the control of more experienced people and the RAF party was also relieved to find that the climber's injuries were not so severe as they had been told. He had broken his leg above the knee and was in shock. As the essentials had been done, morphia had been given and as the people with him on the rock face seemed to know what they were doing, Brooks did not go up to the casualty until he had been placed on the stretcher and part lowered.

At 7.30 pm the main party had still not arrived. Concerned, Holton and Pibworth descended in the dark towards Idwal, signalling with whistles and lamps as they went. On the way down, they became aware of someone approaching through the dark. This was Edward Williams, a member of a local mountaineering club, who had seen the MRT searching the foot of Glyder Fawr, next door to Glyder Fach. The main party had made the most elementary mistake of all: somehow, they had confused the names of Glyder Fach and Glyder Fawr.

What's best to be done? thought Holton. True, there now seemed to be enough experienced people to bring the stretcher down but on the other hand this was a very arduous job in such rugged country. It would be much better if the main RAF party could be located quickly and their strength of numbers added to the carrying party, perhaps to take over the latter half of the descent. Carrying on down, he and Pibworth found them near Llyn Idwal going towards Glyder Fach, having discovered that they were at the wrong cliff. They were very tired and Holton told them to rest there and relieve the stretcher party when it reached that point. All reached Idwal Hostel by 1030 pm and handed the casualty over to

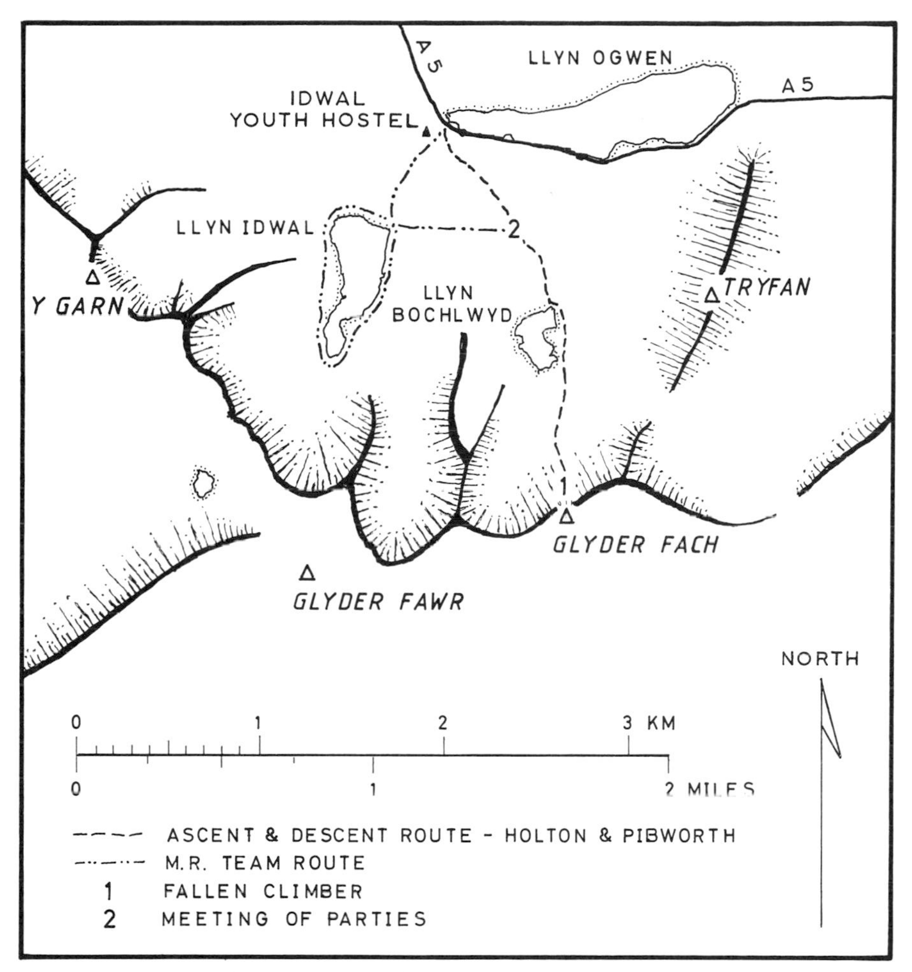

MAP 3 THE FALL ON GLYDER FACH, 1951

When a climber fell on Glyder Fach, Mike Holton and Colin Pibworth (both familiar with Wales and the language) went straight there. The main party, starting later, misheard the Welsh phonetics and went towards Glyder Fawr, circled Llyn Idwal, and were met by Holton and Pibworth who were on their way down.

police and ambulance crew.

Holton had found it quite clear where the accident was and could not really understand how the main party came to search the wrong area. The warden of the youth hostel had given the information to Holton in a clear, unhurried manner, describing the route, the climb and the mountain, with an accurate assessment of where the stretcher party would have reached. There were, conceded Holton, phonetic similarities between Glyder Fach and Glyder Fawr, but any mountaineer should have known the difference. Oddly however, the police also had got hold of the idea that the climber was on Glyder Fawr. Perhaps the warden's information had not been given quite so clearly as Holton supposed. Possibly also those phonetic similarities were, to English ears unused to the North Wales geography and language, overwhelming, especially if those ears belonged to someone other than a mountaineer. The advance party did not carry radios but even if they had it would probably not have helped, since the main party searching near Llyn Idwal had had no radio contact with base. With the benefit of hindsight, this seems strange now. Did they not try to make contact, or were they thwarted by the surrounding peaks? We do not know.

Despite the apparent weakness in communications which this incident exposed, the Vice-Chief of the Air Staff felt able to say in a memorandum only eight months later:

> I would like you to look again at the need for so many vehicles, and particularly for a W/T set. Surely, it would be sufficient to carry an R/T set with the party and have another stationed at the base of the mountain at the nearest suitable telephone. I cannot see there is any need for keeping in direct touch with the rescue centre.
> The main thing is not communications, but a light mobile team capable of getting to the scene of the accident with the equipment necessary to rescue the injured.[36]

Holton's report, written two days after the Glyder Fach incident, concluded that the weakness lay in the NCOs, and in the fact that apart from the team leader and Pibworth there were no mountaineers in the team. Had Holton not been there by chance and had there been no other climber about, it would have been impossible for Brooks, the MO, to climb up to the casualty immediately. There had been a great number of changes in the team and this meant that it had no chance of becoming a fully trained unit. Stability was needed for the service to be effective. The report said finally:

> There is no doubt about the fact that the Valley Team is not capable of carrying out rescues of this kind until there is a hard core of mountaineers in the Team itself.

There is an interesting postscript, handwritten, to the report:

> A late recollection:
> When we got down to Idwal Youth Hostel the press were there. How did they know? Later the warden told me that this invariably happened when telephone calls were made about incidents and the local operators would tip off a 'stringer'.

When Holton asked the warden how this could be, she told him politely not to be so naïve, and that it was a routine matter for the operators to let their stringers know whenever an emergency call was made. There is not much, she implied, that can be kept secret in a Welsh valley, least of all a disaster or an accident.

Valley, under Mason, had built up a good reputation for training and efficiency. Indeed, as recently as Black Easter, only eight months earlier, they had come through a hazardous long weekend with a greatly enhanced reputation. It is on the face of it a puzzle, therefore, how this particular operation could be so badly performed by the main party. Mason had left and the formidable Johnnie Lees had not yet arrived as team leader. Could it be that a crucial NCO happened not to be on duty on that day? Normally, in any context, training should be such that the machine keeps working smoothly even when the motivating force is absent. But the late forties and early fifties were a difficult time for the MRTs, as Holton hinted, with demobilisation and National Service making long-term development nigh impossible. During those intervening eight months, postings had greatly weakened the team.

Idwal Youth Hostel, which played such a part in the 1951 search and rescue, is a Mecca for mountaineers. It is where Tony Smyth started his climbing. Mr A S (Fred) Pigott, in a paper to the Alpine Club at the same meeting where Flight Lieutenant Lloyd delivered his in February 1945, described a specially designed stretcher kept at Idwal, probably the one used for the Glyder Fach rescue.

Mountain rescuers, even more than other sorts of mountaineer, often get asked why they do it. Pibworth remembers one such occasion:

> I used to go out to lectures to all sorts of people.... I went to one at Brecon, and at the end when I threw it open to questions and answers a woman at the back said "Why do you do it? Why don't you leave them? They're there of their own volition."
> I thought "What the heck have I been talking about?" It takes you aback that not everybody thinks along the same lines as we do ourselves.[37]

The present writer had exactly the same experience in June 1992, during a discussion. Why should a public service go to the help of people who do not have to be there in the first place? Is this not a misuse of the taxpayer's money? It is with difficulty that one explains that apart from the purely humanitarian aspect, the teams are there anyway for a very tangible reason: to search for and rescue aircrew. To make them effective at this, they undertake a considerable amount of unpaid training, much of which is in their own time. If, in the meantime, civilian climbers fall or go missing, then this is an opportunity for additional training which can only enhance the performance of the teams. Not only is the service inexpensive to the taxpayer (because it is mostly voluntary and unpaid), but its PR value to the RAF is incalculable. Additionally the civilian mountain rescue organisations assist the RAF teams when asked; it is only right that the RAF should return the compliment.

Chapter 2 – Footnotes

[1] Report 17/1/46
[2] Discussion with writer 18/11/90
[3] Letter to writer 30/11/91
[4] Telephone call to writer 15/3/91
[5] Squadron Leader T G Danby, 18 Group, to RAF Kinloss, 22/8/51
[6] Letter to writer 28/1/92
[7] 'Mountaineering', September 1951
[8] Letter to David Lofts in 1973
[9] Letter to writer 8/5/92
[10] Conversation with writer 13/2/92
[11] Gosling's personal records
[12] Mike Banks: *Commando Climber* (Dent)
[13] Memoire dated 9/1/74
[14] Letter to writer 20/5/92
[15] Letters to writer 3/11/91 and 16/11/91
[16] Wing Commander P H Watts DSO DFC to Wing Commander A J M Smyth, 9/5/51
[17] Smyth to Watts 10/5/51
[18] Smyth to Watts 27/5/51
[19] Letter to the writer 8/4/92
[20] Smyth to Watts 21/8/51
[21] Graham Brown to Holton 24/10/51
[22] T Graham Brown papers, Edinburgh
[23] Wing Commander Smyth to Air Chief Marshal the Honourable Sir Ralph Cochrane 3/4/52
[24] Vice-Chief of the Air Staff
[25] Assistant Director of Rescue
[26] Smyth to Holton 1/5/52
[27] Holton's undated handwritten file notes, probably after Smyth's letter of 1/5/52
[28] Letter to writer 28/12/91
[29] Gosling, climbing diary 19/10/51
[30] Acting Director Navigation & Control to Vice-Chief of the Air Staff 28/12/51
[31] M Holton to Acting Director Navigation & Control 15/12/51
[32] Letter to writer 23/1/92
[33] Deputy Director of Operations (Maritime) to Air Officer Commanding in Chief, Coastal Command 3/3/52
[34] Letter to writer received 18/1/92
[35] Letter to writer 5/2/92
[36] Vice-Chief of the Air Staff to Director of Navigation & Control, 17/6/52
[37] Conversation with writer 13/2/92

CHAPTER III – THE STONES OF SNOWDON

Wales 1952-92

Leave to Robert Browning
Beggars, fleas, and vines;
Leave to squeamish Ruskin
Popish Appenines,
Dirty stones of Venice
And his gas-lamps seven;
We've the stones of Snowdon
And the lamps of heaven.

Charles Kingsley 1819-1875: Letter to Thomas Hughes

1 – The Dublin Dakota

Aer Lingus Dakota EI-AFL, 'Saint Kevin', left Northolt for Dublin on Thursday evening January 10th 1952. On board were three crew and 20 passengers. The Douglas Dakota – known in its military versions as the DC3 or C47 – is an American airliner of pre-war design of which working examples still exist. It has the reputation of being able to take a great deal of punishment and was used during the Second World War in various roles, particularly as a transport and as a paratroop carrier.

A likely sequence of events would have been that the pilot descended to about 4,500 feet under the impression that he was passing over the Welsh coast at Nevin Beacon. But in fact he was over Snowdon and Saint Kevin got caught in some turbulence associated with the peaks. The co-pilot reached for the microphone and told the passengers to fasten their safety-belts. They were getting lower, the turbulence more violent; then through the starboard window the two pilots saw with brief horror and disbelief the end of the starboard wing break off and flip back in the slipstream. No further control was possible.

There was to be a station dance in the Naafi at RAF Valley that evening, and by 7 pm, airmen were straightening their ties and putting a last touch to the polish on their shoes, looking forward to seeing the girls arrive. At 7.15 pm a farmer, William Williams of Hafod Rhisgl, on the road from Beddgelert to Pen-y-Gwyrd, heard a crash and looking up saw a glow. Climbing up towards the glow, on the hill he knew so well, he found a crater in the bogs on Bwlch y Rhediad, and the remains of an aeroplane, still burning, with some mutilated bodies. At 8.20 pm, Air Traffic Control Valley told the Mountain Rescue Team that an Aer Lingus Dakota had crashed, probably near Porthmadog; confirmation followed almost immediately, with instructions to report to Porthmadog Police Station.

Ivor Warn, in his billet near Station Sick Quarters and the Mountain Rescue Headquarters, was part of the advance party. Reluctantly abandoning thoughts of the dance and the local girls, he got ready and climbed into the Bedford QL with eleven others. The ambulance left at 8.45 pm, followed by the Bedford. Flight Lieutenant Bill Brooks and the advance party were intercepted half an hour later by the police in Caernarfon, to be told that the crash was, in fact, on Moel Siabod and they were to go to Pen-y-Gwyrd. There is a mountain rescue post there and it is a customary meeting-point for rescues.

There they found William Williams with the police and firemen, about to move off. The vehicles – RAF, police and fire service – drove in convoy down the Nant Gwynant valley and parked where Williams indicated. There was a walk of about ½ mile and 750 feet up the hill: then through the wind and the hail, they found the crash site. It seemed to Brooks that the aeroplane had been flying almost due east, had just missed the ridge of Gallt y Wenallt and hit the bog at a fairly steep angle. Round the wreck of Saint Kevin the ground was wet and boggy and the crater had filled up within three hours of the crash.

Another Valley member later wondered whether there might have been an orchestra on the Dakota passenger list. Ken McCoy remembers being told of the weird scene which presented itself: apart from the bodies, sheet music was blowing about and shattered instruments lay amongst the wreckage. In fact, the passenger list does show one professional musician at least. The safety belts had all been secured but had sheared in the crash; one passenger's wrist-watch had stopped when the strap broke. Brooks, in his report, said that it was obvious from the almost total destruction of the aircraft that there could be no survivors. There were in fact 23 deaths.

> Small pieces were still burning when fanned by the wind. As there was a considerable amount of luggage and paper about which might get trampled into the bog it was suggested to the police sergeant that the area should be cleared of people.

This was agreed and as Warn's group arrived, fire and ambulance crews had already been up and marked the way with hurricane lamps. The civilian services were leaving as the main MRT arrived; one of the firemen said to Warn as they passed in the dark that it was a job not for stretchers but for sacks, and they were bringing empty stretchers down with them. To Warn's surprise, they were also bringing down the hurricane lamps, which did not make the RAF team's job any easier.[1]

With four stretchers taken from the team vehicles, work started on recovering human remains and documents. Working with only four men to a stretcher, the descent was extremely rough and Brooks decided not to risk another descent in the darkness and in those conditions. He called a halt until 6.30 next morning. At

The Dakota started as an airliner and is still used as such nearly 60 years later. This DC-3 belonging to Air Atlantique was seen in 1989. *Photo: H J Budgen*

dawn they started again, helped now by an officer, two NCOs and fifteen men from a nearby army camp. Five more stretcher-loads were taken down to the base camp by 9 am, then the stretchers were put on the Bedfords which carried them to a church hall serving as a temporary mortuary.

This was Warn's first aircraft crash and like most novices he did wonder what his reaction would be to so many violent deaths. In fact, he experienced very little emotion except at the sight of children's books and toys lying in the mud and blowing in the wind, and at the worst sight of all, the pilot's body, just a torso with outstretched arms. Nine bodies had so far been collected and were taken to the mortuary at a hospital in Caernarfon. By then, an ambulance party had removed items from the crash and taken them to firmer ground. The grisly work continued. Four more loaded stretchers and an Everest carrier were taken down to the base camp by 5 pm, and on to the hospital mortuary. Finally the team returned to Valley and was stood down at 10.30 pm (Friday).

Nothing happened over the weekend but soon the fire service was asking for help and the team was turned out again at 8 am on Monday morning to return to the base camp. A pump had been installed in the crater and was operating at 120 gallons a minute but this was not enough to make much reduction in the water-level. Searching continued; more mutilated bodies were recovered and as usual taken down to the base camp by stretcher parties, then on to the mortuary. Stand-down at Valley that evening was at 7.30 pm; the routine was now well-established. Again next morning at 7 am, they set out and met the firemen at the

MAP 4 THE UK TEAMS 1943-93

After the traumas of 1951, the service began to settle into a pattern. For the dates when the various teams were in operation, and for catchment areas of the current teams, see Appendices.

site. Personal belongings were recovered after a further search. Hard though the fire brigade pump was working, it was still not reducing the level enough to allow the team to search the hazardous bottom of the crater.

They removed loose wreckage from the surrounding ground, and put it in the crater. When they returned to Valley and stood down at 7.15 pm, the operation had taken three whole days and a substantial part of the Thursday night. It was not clear, because of the destruction and the boggy nature of the surroundings, how many of the twenty-three dead had been recovered; certainly not all. Brooks's report said 'approximately 10'. For a couple of years after, the spot was avoided by climbers. Colin Pibworth recalls:

> Unfortunate it was – it went all to pieces at the end. They fenced off an acre of it and a couple of padres came across from Ireland and consecrated it. They put up a little wooden plaque to the pilot and crew and passengers. That got pinched. Then the ground was very very boggy, it was dreadful. That was the whole reason why they said don't for heaven's sake go there because you are bound to find something nasty. They couldn't clear it up. It was wet and stayed wet. Through frost action the corner posts got distorted and broke up and went rusty, nobody cared for it, there was no upkeep, and eventually I think about eight years ago a warden organised a reasonably extensive draining scheme for the area. Got an army helicopter to bring in one of these miniature JCBs on crawlers, and dug a big drainage channel and the whole area is drained and is stabilising, so it's a lot safer ... but it wasn't a nice place to go to.[2]

Only a day or two after this call-out, Johnnie Lees arrived as Valley's new team leader. After the new training courses, another tangible sign to the troops of the post-Beinn Eighe, post-Black Easter Mountain Rescue Service.

Eighteen months or so later, in the summer of 1953, the Valley team was on Snowdon, coming down the Watkin Path. Suddenly Ken McCoy, a fairly new team member, gave a shout and pointed. In a stream not far from where they were walking was what looked like an aircraft undercarriage. McCoy clambered down the slope for a closer look and was able to confirm that it was indeed a large wheel and hydraulic gear, half in the water, beginning to look very weathered.[3] He took serial numbers and other details, and passed them to the airframe people at RAF Valley. A day or so later they told him that this was believed to be part of the landing gear from the Aer Lingus Dakota, though this was never confirmed. It is significant, however, that the spot where the wheel was found was not a known crash site. The reasonable assumption, therefore, is that Saint Kevin had clipped the flank of Snowdon or the adjacent Yr Aran, tearing off part of the undercarriage which ended up in the stream. Then it had carried on, losing height, coming to rest in the bogs on Bwlch y Rhediad.

Aer Lingus, in recognition of the tremendous efforts of Valley MRT, awarded the team £50, and the money was used to buy a Thomas stretcher, which was used for many years and had a brass plate attached to commemorate the gift. A sight of Aer Lingus's records of the Saint Kevin's last minutes might have been illuminating, but the airline did not respond to the request.

2 – The Anson at Cloggy

1951 and 1952 were turning out to be an eventful couple of years for Valley.

David Gwyndaf Thomas was 19, a local boy, a member of the Valley team, a promising climber and engaged to be married. On July 14th 1952 he was leading on One Pitch Gully on Cadair Idris, when he remarked to Johnny Barratt, a team driver, that the traverse was getting a bit thin. Then: "It's dodgy... It's bloody dodgy... Johnny, I think I'm coming off!" – He fell. Normally, the rope would have held him but this time it ran out over a sharp edge and was cut. He fell two hundred and fifty feet.

Ken McCoy had been climbing elsewhere with another group. They were on their way back to the base camp when they saw the red flare. They ran the last half-mile, to be told: "Gwyn's dead up there."

They ran to the foot of the route hoping but not really expecting to find that he was just injured. White with shock, the three who had been climbing with Thomas were sitting on one side of the gully, and on the other side was a crumpled shape covered with an anorak. Thomas's body was put onto a stretcher and carried down to the ambulance by Fox's Path. On the drive back to RAF Valley, they stopped at Bethesda to break the news to his fiancée. Before they had a chance to say anything, she asked casually: "Where's Gwyn?"

They all went to his funeral the next week. Ken McCoy has an abiding memory of Thomas's two young sisters, about eleven years old, in tears in the chapel. Gwyn Thomas was the first RAF Mountain Rescuer to die on team duties.[4]

There had long been rivalry between two villages in North Wales, Llanberis and Bedgellert. In the latter part of the 19th Century it came to a head. Tourism and mountaineering were, at that time, becoming major factors in the prosperity of some areas and the people of Bedgellert were claiming that their village was the principal centre in Snowdonia. Llanberis had to respond and its response was the Snowdon Railway.

The Snowdon Tramroad & Hotels Company was formed in November 1894 in order to build a rack-and-pinion railway to the summit of Snowdon and, despite persistent protests by Canon Rawnley, an Anglican cleric, it opened to the public on April 6th, 1896, running up the north-western side of the mountain from Llanberis to the summit. The start, in a blaze of publicity, was not auspicious, for on that first day there was an accident when a train hurtled down the track and the railway was closed for a year for the rack system to be modified.

About a month after Gwyn Thomas's death, George Sellars, one of the drivers peered out of the cab of one of the Swiss locomotives which had been imported 55 years before, trying to see through the heavy rain as he started the descent

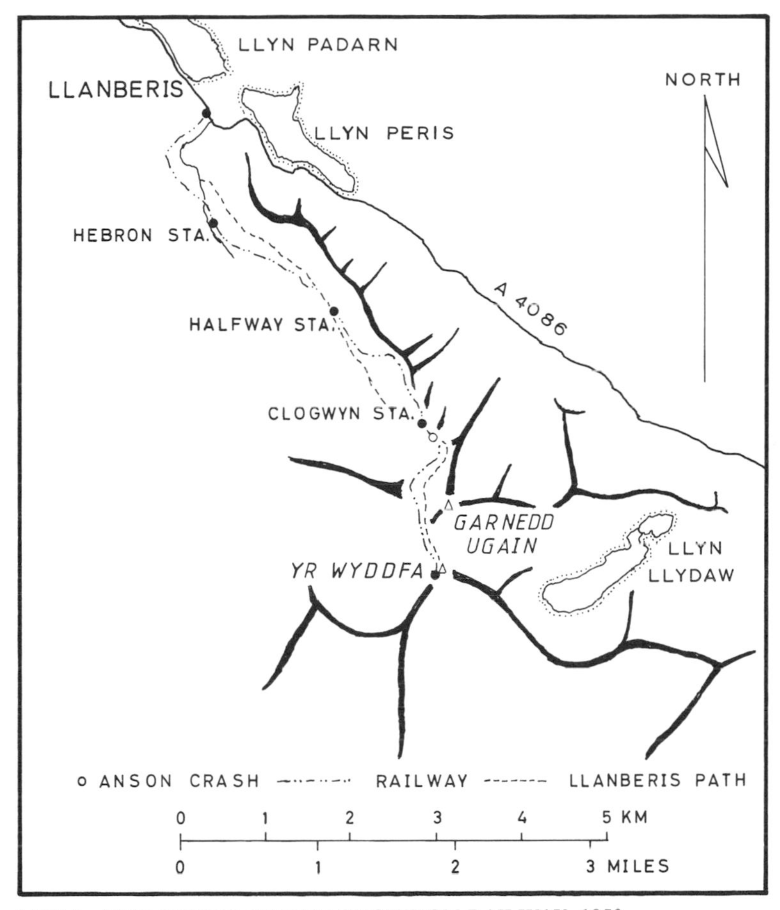

MAP 5 THE ANSON ON THE SNOWDON RAILWAY, 1952

This accident, tragic as it was, could so easily have become a major public disaster; it happened at the peak of the North Wales holiday season.

from Summit Station. Visibility was down to a few yards and he would be glad when he had arrived at Llanberis station. In the meantime, he could hear the gale hitting the mountain and the sides of the carriages. It was August 11th 1952 in the peak of the holiday season in North Wales, but not the sort of day to attract visitors to the summit of Snowdon. A few did make their way up there, had a drink or two in the hotel at the top, then caught the next train down. A few of his passengers were mountaineers who, having had an early start, had decided to descend to Llanberis earlier than planned. He glanced back; about sixty on

Anson C19, TX214: Cosford Aerospace Museum *Photo: H J Budgen*

board, he had been told.

As he approached Clogwyn Station, rounding the leftward bend at a point the railwaymen called Red Rock, he suddenly became aware of a fiery glow showing through the heavy mist. Nearer, he could see a pile of burning wreckage on the track. He braked violently and stopped; passengers grumbled. Sellars climbed down from the cab and with his fireman, Robert Owen, walked slowly towards what they could see now was a crashed aeroplane. An Anson; many were seen in North Wales. It was, he said later, embedded in the ground like a stubbed cigarette.

As they got near, they became aware of a body near the wing tip. The flames were spreading up the wing and the two men moved the body a safe distance away. They had barely finished doing this when there was an explosion. Sellars and Owen retreated rapidly and Sellars drove the train back up the hill for some distance. Two of the bodies had been blown clear, one badly burnt. John Robert Roberts, the guard, walked down to Clogwyn Station, where he telephoned the main station at Llanberis. This brought out the MRT from RAF Valley, as well as the fire brigade from Caernarfon and two ambulances, and Dr Vyrnwy Jones from Llanberis. The railway arranged for a special train to take the rescue teams to the scene and it was waiting, steamed up, when they arrived, a full water tank attached to the train as ballast against the gale.

In charge of the RAF advance party was Flight Lieutenant Brooks, the then medical officer. Just as this group was leaving on the tender, the main part of the

Sergeant J R Lees on the ferryboat across Loch Maree, August 1953. *Photo: D J Bennet*

team arrived. Ken McCoy came across a press photographer with a large mahogany brass-bound camera, wandering around, not knowing what to do, and offered to take him up. The photographer was pleased to accept and kept saying that the *Post* was always first on the scene. Approaching Clogwyn Station, they had to emerge from behind a wall. The wind picked them up bodily, rolling them about 150 feet down the hill, the pressman's gas cape went up over his head and his large and cumbersome camera with plates scattered over the area. McCoy, trying hard to keep his radio equipment together, helped to collect the photographic equipment.

As the two shaken men finally reached the wreckage, the bodies were being taken down. McCoy could see in the general detritus the RT log, a compass, the map and the pilot's helmet. He could see too that the Anson's skin had been reduced to solidified pools of aluminium. Whilst the team was manhandling the wreckage away from the track, a length of wing was caught by the gale and blown over the cliff. The Anson C19, a late version, No. VM407, had been on a flight from its home station, RAF Aldergrove, where it was part of the fleet of 23MU. Chatting to his team-mates afterwards, McCoy found that there was some discussion about one of the bodies, which had been dressed in civilian clothes, though with RAF socks. It turned out to be someone going on leave, who had hitched a lift from Aldergrove in Northern Ireland to Llandow, Glamorgan.

The train service was suspended for the rest of the day, and about 120 people were trapped in the Summit Hotel overnight.

The young men engaged in all this activity had no means of knowing that, in the meantime, a battle was taking place in the Air Ministry offices of Whitehall. Only a year after Beinn Eighe and five years after the South Wales team moved to St Athan, it was being suggested that the MRT there should be disbanded and that Valley should cover the whole of Wales. This was proposed in a minute to the Vice-Chief of the Air Staff on June 13th 1952, who agreed and also proposed some economies in radio equipment which can best be described as unrealistic. However, St Athan was reprieved by the arrival on the scene of Group Captain R E G Brittain, who was appointed to be the first Inspector of Mountain Rescue; one of the first positive results of the soul-searching that followed Beinn Eighe. Brittain was a keen mountaineer with some experience in Asia and saw immediately that to disband St Athan would throw too great a burden on Valley. He did agree to other disbandments – Jurby and Aldergrove – and to a reduction in strength of St Athan and others from 36 to 25.

Sergeant Johnnie Lees was already at Valley as Team Leader, the intention being to provide a focal point for the long-term training programme being put together by Tony Smyth, Mike Holton and Lees. Within the year, however, that focal point moved to Scotland, and Lees was posted to Kinloss in a straight swap with the then Kinloss leader, 'Chiefy' Ward. He proved to be an easy-going and popular team leader and was singled out for praise in May 1954 by Brittain's successor, Squadron Leader David Dattner. In 1955 Ward was posted away from Valley and Lees brought back in. Lees set extremely high standards for the people working under him, for himself and for those above. During the change-over period the two men clashed and Sandy Gordon-Cumming, the recently-appointed IMR (replacing Dattner), commented after an inspection:

> At present Sergeant Lees is not popular with all team members and has made several changes in the training programme. However he is an able and competent N.C.O. who has made a great success of running two other mountain rescue teams and I am quite confident that Valley will settle down under his leadership.[5]

Ken McCoy recalls Ward as a relaxed and popular NCO who was a hill-walker rather than a mountaineer. Lees, by comparison, was a hard mountaineer with the concomitant desire to achieve high mountaineering standards. He had already built a considerable reputation for himself as a mountaineer and had in fact only that year been on the RAFMA Himalayan expedition with Mike Holton, Tony Smyth, John Sims and others.

Further leadership problems emerged on the same inspection visit. The officer in charge, said Gordon-Cumming:

> ... has insufficient time to spare from his flying instructional and IRE duties adequately to run the team. I do not in any way blame him for this and he has done the best that he can.

He therefore arranged the posting in November of Flying Officer Hughes, whom he described as an experienced mountaineer and who had already had a spell in the MRT at Valley, in the November.

Then there was the recurrent theme of the standard of serviceability of the vehicles. The team could muster only one 3 ton tender which should not really have been on the road at all; one of the Land Rovers consumed a pint of oil every 30 miles; private vehicles were being used (of necessity) as troop carriers; the wireless van itself was serviceable but the equipment in it was not; and the passenger-carrying Land Rover had been on permanent loan to Sick Quarters for some time. A sorry state of affairs.

There was friction also between the team and the station command. Valley, said Gordon-Cumming:

> ... are the only team in the Mountain Rescue Service who carry out normal station duties in addition to the heavy training commitment and voluntary stand-by that their work imposes. Since it is Air Ministry policy that a nucleus of the team should be available seven days a week, a mountain rescue volunteer has to do mountain rescue stand-by duty for at least one week a month in addition to sacrificing a very large part of his remaining spare time to normal training. To expect a man to do station duties in addition to this seems to me to take an unfair advantage of the volunteer.
> ... it causes some discontent among the team that the station band, who practise two nights a week, are, in fact, excused these duties. Their spare time work is infinitely less arduous and time consuming and the argument that it is difficult to obtain volunteers for the band hardly seems fair or valid.

It was during this period, in October 1954, that the Valley team made one of the first of many animal rescues. A telephone call from the police told them that a Scottish terrier had got stuck on a ledge on the Swallow Falls. The falls were in flood at the time, and any approach was bound to be hazardous. SAC Brereton and AC1 Forkin made three attempts, on the third reaching the dog and taking it up one hundred feet to the cliff top. For that they received the RSPCA's Certificate of Merit.

Late in 1955 a young National Service man was posted to Valley. He had had a little hill-walking and climbing experience, and joined the MRT in June 1956. He stayed in it until his demobilisation in August 1957. His name is Derek Walker, now General Secretary of the British Mountaineering Council. He says: '...It was that experience in RAF Mountain Rescue which really changed my life and completely enthused me about climbing.'[6]

3 – Tensions at Valley

August 1956 was the start of a period of conflict; but the month began with an element of farce mingled with a large slice of tragedy.

On the 11th, Sergeant Lees and the Valley team were hosts to the Royal Navy in a navigational exercise in the Arenigs. After the first meal at the base camp, Lees realised that he had forgotten to get extra blankets for the sailors, and all they had was the dozen normally carried on one of the trucks. He sent someone to ring Valley so that the extra blankets could be sent out, but the orderly concerned was in the TV room in the NAAFI and did not hear the Tannoy call. On bedding down for the night, therefore, the naval personnel had to be wrapped up in what extra blankets there were plus the spare tent.

The man who had gone to make the telephone call was finally crawling into his sleeping bag at 1 am, when Sergeant Hughes of the Llanberis police turned up: a cyclist was missing on Snowdon. A small party of civilians including police had already done a preliminary search through dusk and darkness. Now they were gathering some more civilian volunteers and a further search was to begin at 8.30 am next morning. Would the RAF and Navy help? Of course the answer was Yes.

The men were roused at 5.30 am and after breakfast went to Betwys-y-Coed police station. There had been no further news from the Llanberis police and the team continued to the rendezvous agreed the previous evening. Here they were joined by Chris Briggs, who gave Lees a detailed account of the route covered the previous night by the searchers. Only one or two of the promised civilian volunteers had turned up by 8.30 am, when the combined RAF/RN party of fifteen had assembled with their walkie-talkies, pyrotechnics and first-aid equipment. Eight separate parties then went up various routes.

Very soon the body of the missing man was spotted, having obviously fallen several hundred feet from loose crags above. He was wearing thin leather-soled cycling shoes, and Lees, looking at him, judged that he had probably died instantly from his extensive injuries. A rope stretcher was made to get him down to the Thomas stretcher which was on its way up. The RAF provided transport for the civilian volunteers who had been arriving, having hitch-hiked their way there, and took them to Capel Curig Youth Hostel.

Finally, Lees apologised profusely to the Navy for forgetting the blankets.

When there is a unit on any station which comes partly or wholly under the control of any authority other than the station command, it can lead to problems and to a conflict of interests. There was such a direct clash in August 1956, only twelve days later, when a Vampire crashed on a farm at Capel Celyn, near the Ffestiniog-Bala road. RAF Valley's Senior Medical Officer went to the site straight away by helicopter, arriving there within three quarters of an hour. In the meantime, Lees's team had been called up on the Tannoy on the instructions of 18 Group. The controller at 18 Group spoke to Lees, telling him to take his team out 'as soon as possible', and Lees, as usual, provided the controller with the expected route of the convoy. Almost immediately, Lees was told by Flying Control that the team was not to leave the station. As the team was supposed to be controlled directly by RCC, this made things difficult for Lees, and on putting the telephone down he was fuming. Then a radio message was received from the SMO at Capel Celyn that he and the helicopter crew had found the remains of the Vampire's pilot. For the time being, therefore, there was no point in pushing the matter. The team was stood down at 6 pm.

Lees, however, took the long-term view, as ever. Suppose that pilot had baled out and had been somewhere in the hills, perhaps injured, with night approaching, perhaps wandering, dazed and in shock? Starting from Valley at 5.45 pm, it would have been dark by the time the convoy reached the search area. Hours would have been wasted when the team could have been travelling in the direction of the crash, as intended by 18 Group Controller. He put forward three suggestions in the log book, knowing they would be read:

1 The Mountain Rescue Section should be given all available information even if only the *possible* track (as in this instance) is known; some inferences can be drawn to make a reasonable proper search of the area. The Vampire had actually crashed within an inch of a line drawn across a large-scale map from Hawarden to Llanbedr. Following this line, the first high and remote ground was in the Arenigs, so if no other information came in he would try looking there first.
2 It takes twenty minutes for the team to assemble, so the Tannoy message should be put out as soon as the Mountain Rescue Section is informed.
3 Then the team should be sent in the direction of the incident. Even if nothing was known or even could be inferred about the route as in no. 1, they could stand by at a convenient place, such as Bangor Police Station. This would save thirty minutes.

He gave the example of a crash which had happened the previous year, on July 28th 1955. It had taken twenty-two men and the Senior Medical Officer several hours' digging to establish that the pilot had indeed been in the aircraft at the time of impact. He added that since the team's route is always known, police along the way can always stop the convoy or pass additional information to it should the occasion arise.

Flying Officer Mannings, the team's officer, supported Lees completely, saying that the suggestions he had made, if accepted, would make the team more efficient. Mannings also wanted one delicate point clarified: 'If the team is called out by RCC do we or do we not come under the full control?'[7] The OC Flying Wing's answer was that Lees's proposed procedure was what was normally done anyway. But, he added, on this occasion the whole matter was under the control of 18 Group. He had taken the matter up with 18 Group and merely wanted a closer liaison between the Mountain Rescue Team on the one hand and 18 Group on the other. Unfortunately, he added, he was at Llandwrog on this occasion and unable to provide this.

Feelings remained bruised, if hidden.

There was another Vampire crash on October 12th, when a Mark V was reported missing in the late evening. The MRT left Valley at 7.45 pm and had just set up base camp at Rhyd-Ddu, at the foot of Mynydd Mawr, or Elephant Mountain, after local people had reported a crash and a flash of light high up on the mountain. Within fifteen minutes they were climbing in the darkness and the cold with torches and Tilley lamps, then through the cloud base at five hundred feet. Just before 10 pm they reached the crash scene to find the wreckage well scattered across the top of Mynydd Mawr with the remains of the pilot. The weather was very poor and cold. There were police and other local civilians assisting, and after discussion it was decided, as nothing could be done for the pilot, to return to base camp and go up again in the morning.

The team had an early breakfast and reached the crash site again at 8.30 am. Derek Walker remembers the occasion vividly: it was his first experience of an aircraft crash or death and he was very glad to be near to Johnnie Lees. Although only about 29 at the time, Lees seemed tremendously experienced to the other team members; as indeed he was. The Vampire's engine was immediately behind the pilot and Walker can remember that there was not, in truth, much to pick up. They just went round with sacks and did their best to forget what it was they were collecting. The pilot was about 19, a fact which etched itself on Walker's mind.

By 10.15 pm the job was completed and descending to the valley they telephoned RAF Valley. All that remained now was for the team to hand over the crash site to the crash crew and take the pilot's body to the police at Caernarfon.

Then just over a week later, on October 21st, another incident was to bring those bruised feelings to the surface again. Some army cadets got lost somewhere above Aber Falls. An Auster, VF554, from the army's 663 Squadron, went on the search for them. It crashed on Bera Mawr at 4 pm and the pilot was said to be injured. An army major, whose name remained unknown, telephoned Valley at 5.45 pm asking for assistance. The team was out on an exercise; Air Traffic Control apparently did not know where the team could be found and finally contacted Mannings at 7 pm at his home. Mannings found a couple of team members who were not on the exercise and tried with the help of ATC and the police to locate the team. The team's convoy, still on its way back, got as far as Mona – only 20 minutes from Valley – before being stopped by the police.

The Mannings trio arrived at the cottage which was serving as the Rescue Base to find people drinking tea. Then they climbed up to the crash site to find the injured pilot, suffering from shock, with police and firemen. Army officers involved were arguing that the best thing to do was to leave the pilot there overnight to be picked up by helicopter in daylight. Mannings seems to have persuaded them of the folly of this. He must be got down; but how? To descend by the same route as they had climbed, carrying a stretcher, would be much too dangerous as there was a lot of loose scree and the winds were fierce. Therefore the three of them, assisted by others, carried the pilot to the rear of Llwytmor, taking many rests on the way, and then round to the rescue base which they reached at 1 am. Their ascent had taken them 40 minutes, but descent with a laden stretcher and a casualty in shock, four and a quarter hours.

As the casualty was being taken to the Caernarvon & Anglesey (C & A) hospital at Bangor at just after 1.30 am, the main team arrived, having had a number of breakdowns; at almost the same time the crash party also arrived. The team guided the crash party up to the site as the route was, in Mannings's words, 'a little dicey'.

Mannings had some blistering things to say about various people: on Air

A de Havilland Vampire flew into Mynydd Mawr at night in Oct, 1956; the crew were killed. This example was built by the English Electric Co. at Preston. *Photo: H J Budgen*

Traffic Control, who seemed 'to have their finger in for not knowing the team was out and where to contact them'; on the police, who were unable to stop the team until it got as far as Mona; on the army officers, for proposing to leave the casualty out all night, as 'without him being carried out it's doubtful if he would be alive today'; and the newspapers and the BBC for unspecified transgressions. He tried to draw something positive out of a fiasco. He suggested that the army's 663 Squadron should be contacted and asked to inform the MRT whenever they were due to go on exercise in the area. They should also, he suggested, be informed of the correct procedure for an MR operation, and of the limitations of a helicopter (in which they seemed to have limitless faith).

A few days later the OC Flying Wing, Wing Commander Curry, came back strongly. He commented firstly that a whole series of unfortunate circumstances had led up to the incidents. However, he continued, he considered that the team itself was to some extent to blame in not giving Air Traffic Control an adequate briefing. 'This' he went on, 'will not happen again, in fact HQ 18 Group are to be kept fully informed of all exercise movements.' His next comment was on the deplorable state of motor servicing in the team. He was not the first, nor would he be the last, to comment on this matter over the years. Then he picked up Mannings's comment about the police. 'I've looked into the allegations concerning the police and they did not get a direct request from anyone to intercept the team. I consider that the police were in no way to blame.' He went on, 'Provided the NCO and officer i/c the team meet the requirements [regarding the briefing of ATC] and moreover check thoroughly on the serviceability of the MT there should be no further unfortunate incidents of this nature.' On a conciliatory note he concluded: 'FO Mannings and his small posse are to be congratulated on a very good show.'

This exchange between Mannings and Curry in the log came to the attention of the Station Commander: all regretted the muddle, as muddle there undoubtedly was. However, he did not think it would happen again. Mountain Rescue MT, he went on, seems to raise an ugly unserviceable head at too regular intervals. Nevertheless, now that they had a technical officer in charge of the MRT he had great hopes. He too congratulated Mannings on a splendid job.

At this point Lees, who had been in charge of the main part of the team out on exercise, could contain himself no longer. He inserted in the log additional comments which were barely on the respectful side of insolence, remarks that could be made only by an NCO who knew he was right and was prepared to say so. Addressed to Wing Commander Curry, they started in the professional NCO's classic way:

Sir:
With all due respect may I comment on your remarks on p.37 paragraph 2. As I said on line 10 of p.33 the airman in AT control was adequately briefed in the normal manner. My detailed briefing of this airman was by chance overheard in toto by a member of the MRT who was in the MR section at the time. The fault lay not with the MRT but with an airman in ATC who did not realise the importance of the MRT booking out on a normal 36-hour exercise and his whole attitude suggested that he had heard it all before and could not worry less. When SATCO[8] spoke to me afterwards on this subject I was distressed to find that he preferred to believe his airman's story and to denigrate mine. Nevertheless I am pleased to note that since this unfortunate incident the airmen in AT movements take much more interest in our booking out and in. Ref. para 4 p.37 it is felt that controllers generally do not appreciate the MRT set-up sufficiently. FO Mannings has pointed out to the controller on this occasion that obviously one sure place to stop the returning MRT would be the Menai Bridge but this alas does not seem to have been acted upon. Perhaps Mountain Rescue SSOs[9] might be revised to cover snags for controllers, also advice to controllers in the event of MRT action at Valley. For example a call-out to a civilian climbing accident on Clogwyn at Snowdon. The Mountain Rescue/MT situation is not expected to improve materially unless MRT serviceability is given some priority on the station particularly the workshops.

J R Lees NCO i/c 4/12/56

Again, Lees was supported by Mannings, who said that the position was now more readily appreciated and ...'that a good deal of the bugs have been ironed out due to the experience gained during this incident and that of 17/11'. (Whilst the argument was going back and forth like a tennis game, other call-outs had been complicating matters.) However, continued Mannings, he was rather distressed to find that when he had visited the ATC the previous Sunday the NCO on duty had very little idea of where or how he could get hold of the team, and had not read the Orders giving the new organisation. Mannings was chasing the vehicles' servicing problem and was hopeful of improved results. Curry replied to Mannings confirming a direct conversation: 'I have spoken. I think you will agree that this matter has now been settled reasonably happily. Similar trouble will not occur again.'

But Curry and Mannings were wrong. The matter may have been dead, but it would not lie down.

Squadron Leader Butt of Air Traffic Control sent a typed note to Curry, which was inserted into the MRT log. He referred specifically to Lees's comments of December 4th. Butt said first that the telephone information regarding the exercise was received in ATC without a date. There was, he continued, no information that the MRT would not be returning on October 20th. There was ample time for the team to get **to and from** Dinas Mawddwy (the centre point of the exercise) between midday and eleven of the evening on the 20th. The fact that Mountain Rescue exercises frequently occupied two days was no justification, he felt, for assuming that this was always the case. He maintained that the controllers did appreciate the MR set-up sufficiently but it was merely one important facet of a much wider responsibility. Then he went on to defend the controller on duty on the evening in question. The controller had made (it was believed) fourteen telephone calls of which three or four were to the Menai Bridge/Llanfairfechan/Bangor area. These had failed to stop the team.

Now he turned to the comments made by Mannings. He did not expect the duty runway controller to be able to state off-hand the whereabouts of the MRT; his employment was in the control caravan and his knowledge of ATC matters was confined to emergency and other urgent matters. He concluded that the whole matter had been discussed with Mannings and agreement reached. At this point the saga ends, a truce having been called. But during all this time, with relationships on a knife-edge, other things had been happening.

Mannings, during his exchanges with Curry and Butt, had mentioned the incident of November 17th. On that day, the team was on exercise, part of which was to investigate a report that there was a wrecked Wellington somewhere up in the hills with the remains of five or six men in it. They were able to establish that the Wellington was in another area, that there had been three or four bodies only and that it had been dealt with already. The crash had happened in 1941 or 1942.

During this operation, a police sergeant from Llangollen called at the base camp to tell Lees and Ian Martin (who later became a noted team leader) of a call-out: there had been a climbing accident on *Longlands Climb* (a very severe rock-climb on Clogwyn D'ur Arddu). Mannings and Lees could not quite understand this, as the arrangement had grown up over the years that Valley would be brought in for a civilian climbing accident only if there were not enough competent civilian climbers and rescuers available. This was a Saturday evening when one would expect the bar and dining room of Chris Briggs's Pen-y-Gwyrd Hotel to be thronged with climbers, and good ones. Corporal Morris of the Valley team found out that this was in fact the case, so Lees spoke to the manager, Miss Tootwell, and asked whether Briggs had asked for Valley's help. Briggs had left for Snowdon with the six men he then had available, and, having realised that the RAF team was the width of Wales away, left it that Miss Tootwell would call on the climbers in the hotel and not telephone RAF Valley. Nevertheless, someone had indeed telephoned for the RAF.

Lees commented in the log that *Longlands* would not then have been suitable territory for the Valley team. Only he knew *Longlands*, and only one other member, Hancock, had climbed on Clogwyn D'ur Arddu before. All climbs there were in the higher grades and beyond the abilities of the ordinary mountaineer.

Mannings afterwards commented that this was a 'classic example of a call-out which could have been avoided', and he had discussed it at length with SATCO, 18 Group and the Llanberis police. He added that if the experienced advice of the NCO i/c (Lees) had been taken it would not have been necessary; however, Group, who ordered the call-out, had been informed of the situation. A large amount of energy, time and taxpayers' money had been wasted. Curry replied that 18 Group were now fully aware of the position and had made the appropriate promises. He concluded: 'This is how the British lost the American colonies. you cannot govern or understand things until you have been or are on the spot.'[7]

4 – The Fall of Jock Smith

The weather was beautiful, that Whit weekend of 1957 in North Wales. It was the sort of day when you could look forward to reaching the top and looking round, and feeling, almost literally, on top of the world: a blue sky, just feathers of white cloud. Perfect. You could forget the days and nights struggling against rain and wind and snow and ice.

The Aberdonian, Jock Smith, was not really a hillman but he had been attached to the Valley team as a driver. With his sunny nature, he was one of those who make the best of whatever situation they find themselves in. Therefore he did not restrict himself to driving, as he was quite entitled to do; he took part in all the team's activities and enjoyed them. Everybody liked Jock Smith.

In 1957 he was to be demobilised soon. Determined to take what new experience he could before the opportunity was lost, he asked Johnnie Lees, as they went out on the Whitsun exercise, if he could do some more rock-climbing. Lees readily agreed and arranged for him to go on Tryfan with an experienced member, Paddy Andrews. Paddy was reliable, the rocks would be dry and warm. Perfect. Enjoy yourself, Jock.

The rest of the team would have liked to do some real climbing, too, but, remembers John Foster, 'the sadist with the three stripes decreed we were to go flogging over the Carneddau in all that heat'.[10] Foster and his group were dropped at the head of Llyn Ogwen and made their way through the farmyard, following Afon Lloer up to Ffynnon Lloer, a small lake nestling in the cirque between Pen yr Ole Wen and Carnedd Dafydd. There was hardly a breath of wind and the heat was oppressive. They threw themselves down on the slabs by the outfall, resentful that they had been prevented from doing any real climbing in such perfect weather, and disinclined to do more than the minimum. They spent the afternoon there sunbathing, then started back down toward Llyn Ogwen, following the north bank to Ogwen Falls, where they knew they would find a tea stall just off the A5. They were at Mervyn's about to order their teas, when a nurse they knew from the C&A Hospital came running along the road, calling out to them that Jock Smith had been hurt. Paddy Andrews, she said breathlessly, had collected the stretcher from Idwal Cottage Youth Hostel and had gone back up with it.

Lees had sent out another party that day: Derek Walker[11] and Jock Grant. Unlike the Foster group, they were able to do some rock-climbing, and they too were on Tryfan. Walker was on Gashed Crag; the Andrews/Smith party were round the corner on North Buttress. Grant and Walker reached the top of Tryfan, revelling in the beautiful weather at a beautiful spot. Suddenly Walker cocked his head: What's that? Far away, down in the valley, was a familiar sound: the bell of the RAF Land Rover ambulance. They descended as fast as they could and reached Williams's farm, Gwern Gof Uchaf, where they found the team assembling. They learnt that it was one of their own number who had been hurt. It could only be Paddy Andrews or Jock Smith.

The Foster group, abandoning thoughts of Mervyn's tea, had taken off up the hill toward Tryfan, up past the Milestone Buttress, not caring now about the heat which had caused them to grumble so much before. Then up Heather Terrace and on reaching Nor' Nor' Gully they could see a stretcher with a casualty being lowered down the right wall. Smith's face, Foster could see, was ashen; blood was dripping from the stretcher.

Gradually the other parties were able to put together what had happened. Andrews had led the first few pitches on North Buttress, then asked Smith if he would like to lead through; easy ground could be seen about twenty feet above. Smith was keen to do this and he went on. After running out nearly all the rope on the easy ledges and short steps above, he called out to Andrews that he was belaying. It was not long after that Andrews heard the dreaded sound of falling rocks, then Smith screaming out to him. Andrews climbed quickly and found Smith lying with a shattered leg on a large area of ledges about forty or fifty feet up.

As far as he could tell, Walker and Grant, not far away, had not heard the sounds of the rock-fall. Fortunately, Dr John Clegg had. Dr Clegg, only recently back from the Kangchenjunga expedition, was also on North Buttress with another doctor, and was above them when he heard the rock-fall and the scream.

They went down quickly and took charge of the still-conscious Smith. Andrews ran down to the Youth Hostel for the mountain rescue equipment, including morphia. On the way down, he asked the people he met to go to North Buttress and help. At the Youth Hostel, Andrews telephoned RAF Valley and asked for assistance. A passer-by saw the base camp near to the road and told those there that there had been an accident to one of the team. Clegg took the morphia from Andrews and administered it to Smith, conscious and in severe pain. There were many civilian climbers about and the lowering of Smith down the rock face began. Then Foster and his party arrived. Some of the civilian rescuers were former members of the RAF Mountain Rescue Service, many of them former Valley men. One of them was John Brailsford, who had only recently been in the St Athan team, and had now been demobbed; he was later to become a well-known climber and mountain guide.

Smith was taken down to the RAF ambulance, brought from Valley by the standby driver Pete Crumpton; a helicopter had also come out from Valley, but there was much turbulence in the Nant Ffrancon and the pilot told Lees that Smith would have a less bumpy ride to the C&A in the ambulance. As the carrying party neared the ambulance at Gwern Gof Uchaf, they could see a car parked just in front of it, so close that the ambulance could not have moved. Foster shouted angrily:

"Who the hell's that car there?"

A police inspector was close by. "It's mine," he said. "I'll go ahead with my bell going."

"That's alright, then," replied Foster, reflecting that he had never been spoken to so humbly by a policeman, a senior one at that, before. There was much tension in the party, which the inspector clearly felt.

It was 7 pm when the ambulance left. Smith's leg was amputated on his arrival at the hospital. A very subdued team drove back to RAF Valley.

Next morning, Lees went to see the Station Commander and suggested that they should try to find out the cause of the accident. This was agreed and Lees and Andrews immediately went back out to Tryfan in a Land Rover with Flying Officer Seeley, the team's officer, and the Officer Commanding Flying Wing. Lees, Andrews and Seeley followed the route that the Andrews party had taken the previous day. About one hundred and fifty feet above the start they traversed onto the left-hand rib of North Buttress. Andrews then led onto the belay he had been occupying when Smith had fallen. Seeley, courageous in his first experience of rock-climbing, was then brought up and firmly belayed. Lees led through as Smith had done, reaching the lower end of the series of great ledges which run across the Buttress. He belayed twenty-four feet up and brought up the other two.

There the three men found a large block about 5′ × 3′ × 1′6″ which obviously had very recently fallen from above. It was embedded at its lower end on the edge of the ledge fifteen feet above Andrews's belay. Then they scrambled together a further twenty-five feet or so up the ledges to where the stricken Smith had been lying when Andrews reached him. About ten feet higher than this they could see a further huge block. This, sized about 4′6″ × 3′6″ × 3′6″, had fallen vertically down a fifteen-foot wall onto Smith, who, guessed Lees, had probably been lying there, merely dazed by rolling and bouncing down the ledges above. The underlying slab at that point had evidence in the form of cracks, in many places to a depth of over an inch, and much powdered rock and chips.

They went on about another forty feet, seeing on the way more unmistakable evidence: more powdered rock and large chips. This further point was clearly where the block they had just been looking at below had been perched until something had caused it to fall. Looking more closely, they could see a few scratches and it was obvious that something else had fallen from above. But what?

Fifteen feet above that, after some more scrambling, they could see another ledge. It seemed to the experienced eyes of Lees and Andrews that Smith had been lying or sitting on the rock when it tipped over the edge, taking him with it. Then it had struck the second block, and all three, Smith and the two blocks, had rolled and tumbled down, one of the blocks finally crushing Smith's leg. That was the theory they arrived at. Now it had to be confirmed.

Several days later, Lees went to see Smith in hospital. Smith said he had looked at the uppermost block, and had judged it to be sound. He then had looped a rope sling round it as a belay. That done, he had sat on it near the outer edge. It tipped forward and fell over the edge, taking him with it. The theory was confirmed.

Lees, in his final report, made some pertinent comments. Smith was a permanent staff driver and there had been no obligation on him to become a rock-climber. Nevertheless, he had been enthusiastic about learning and had progressed very well since joining the team. It is useful, continued Lees, to have a driver who climbs as well, so that base camp staff on exercise can both assist in emergencies and 'dash up the mountainsides to recall the team if required'.[12] For that reason all permanent staff were encouraged at least to have a first try at mountaineering; in fact, Smith who volunteered for this job had done so because he wished to do some climbing. Lees had previously taken Smith and instructed him, and had found him a sensible and apt pupil on rock. He was certainly adequate, believed Lees, to lead this section on the Buttress. Lees then turned to Andrews. He had been a member of the team for nineteen months. He was a capable instructor and was fully qualified to lead much harder climbs than the North Buttress. Its standard, continued Lees's report, is the easiest rock-climbing standard; anything easier is scrambling – that is, rather athletic walking and usually performed unroped. 'The team' concluded Lees, 'has lost an enthusiastic and popular man. We are all sorry that such a friend has had such bad luck and I am glad to see him recovering so well.' Seeley agreed, adding that with a more experienced man than Smith this might have been avoided. He had been impressed by Smith's keenness and his forthright attitude. Both the team and the RAF had lost a valuable member. 'We all wish well with him in the future.'

The Flying Wing Officer referred obliquely to what may have been critical earlier comments on Smith: 'I gather that SAC Smith was not the disinterested [sic] driver mentioned in previous entries.' Both he and the CO commented on the mental resilience of Smith, and on the philosophical way in which he had accepted his misfortune. He returned to Aberdeen, where he ran a petrol station for many years.

It was Lees's task now to restore the shattered morale of the team. This he started by taking them out onto the Milestone Buttress for a rock-climbing and abseiling exercise, with Seeley, a positive action which drew favourable comments from several officers on the station.

Only a month later, on July 6th 1957, the team had been on exercise on the Snowdon Horseshoe. They were just finishing the evening meal at 6.30 pm when someone arrived: the grocer from Bedgellert. The Llanberis police had tried the local telephones but were unable to get through. A rock climber, he said, had been injured on Clogwyn D'ur Arddu (Cloggy). Pushing down the remains of their mugs of tea, they piled into the Land Rovers and arrived with warm tyres at Llanberis before 7 pm. At Llanberis the station master had offered the use of the Snowdon Railway, and arranged for the last train to go back up to the nearest point to Cloggy, between Clogwyn and Halfway Stations. To the team on board, it seemed painfully slow, but they were told that it was in fact faster than the permitted speed. They were met by two Norwegian climbers who had been with the injured man, William Herbert, and told them that the leading man had fallen, and Herbert had received head injuries whilst trying to prevent his companion swinging around on a long belay. The two Norwegians, on their way to look at a neighbouring climb, had helped both men down to a grassy slope above Middle Rock, at which point Herbert had collapsed.

At what Lees, in the log, described as a 'fast trot – most impressive' the party left the train. Belays were set up and the stretcher lowered 150 feet, the last sixty down vertical rock. Then it was taken onto the train and down to Llanberis, where the ambulance was waiting. The whole operation had taken, from the time they abandoned their mugs of tea, three hours.

Also waiting at Llanberis Station was the current Inspector of Mountain Rescue, Sandy Gordon-Cumming. He was on one of his periodic inspections and had arrived an hour previously. Passing comment was made to Lees about the teams going soft these days and travelling to rescues by train.

5 – The Classified Canberra

The RAF St Athan Mountain Rescue Team convoy was finding its way in the

The St Athan team is inspected in 1965 by Air Chief Marshal Sir Charles Elworthy, Chief of the Air Staff. The team leader, standing next to the Air Chief Marshal, is Sgt Mick Fearn, who fell to his death when leading a pitch up New West on Pillar in the Lake District very soon after.
Photo: Peter McGowan

dawn half-light through the twisting mid-Wales roads, windscreen wipers working overtime, condensation constantly having to be cleared from the glass. They were heading for Bethesda, in Valley's patch. In the leading vehicle was Ian Martin. Ian Martin, an engine fitter, had been a member of the St Athan team in 1950, until he was posted abroad in 1951. After his spell abroad, the mountains called him again and on his return to the UK he managed to secure a posting to RAF Valley. Towards the latter part of 1957, Martin had been on one of Lees's team leader courses and was posted back to St Athan as team leader. Now here he was facing his first major operation. It was the early hours of December 10th when he took the telephone call which told him that a Canberra B2, WK129, which had been testing a new navigational device for the Ministry of Supply, had gone missing. Fighting the sleep in his eyes, he learnt that it had taken off from Pershore, crewed by Flight Lieutenants Bell and Shelley, and was believed to be in North Wales. Because of the secret nature of the flight and the bad weather, St Athan had been brought in as a second team to help Valley. Martin roused Flight Lieutenant Tony Newbould, the team's officer, and the team was got together. They arranged with Johnnie Lees at Valley to meet at Bethesda and the convoy was under way at dawn on the empty Welsh roads through foul weather.

Some hours later when they arrived at Bethesda they were surprised to find that Valley MRT was not there. Cursing, the wireless operator set up his aerial in

St Athan gave great help to the local communities during severe blizzards in the winter of 1981-82.

the appalling weather and was able to contact the Valley team. They had moved to Abergwyngregyn, between Bangor and Conwy at the northern foot of the Carneddau. The St Athan team drove the few miles there and found the base. By then, it was snowing hard. They could see the Valley group, Lees at its head, returning from its search. Lees told Newbould that the blizzard conditions made things impossible on the hill and he was sending his team back to the station.

Lees, as serious as ever, told Newbould and Martin that he had had time during all this activity to find accommodation for them and the team. This was at the Bangor University College farm at Aber. It was almost as an afterthought that he added, dead-pan, that it was in fact in the pig-sties. Fortunately, he assured them, they were new and unused.

The team was still unloading in the gathering dusk when a policeman arrived. Someone, he said, had seen 'something unusual' on Moel Wnion, a 1900-foot outlier of the Carneddau between Aber and Bethesda. Coming from such a source, this report could not be ignored. Newbould, Martin and the team made their way up to the cairn on the top of Moel Wnion, but saw nothing. On their

Unusually, the whole team received an AOC's Commendation. *Photo: Crown Copyright*

return to base camp the two St Athan men worked out with Flying Officer Anthony Seeley and Johnnie Lees a plan of action for the next day. They had very little information to go on, probably because of the nature of the Canberra's mission. All they had been told was that it had been on an exercise and was due to come into the coast at a low level from the sea. A weather forecast was obtained; things were likely to improve. They decided therefore that provided this improvement held and they had reasonable visibility, they would cover as much of 100-odd square miles of the Carneddau as they could, with air support. Some of the Valley team knew the area and its people well and two of them would be sent round in Land Rovers to find what eye-witnesses they could.

When the Valley men arrived the next morning, Newbould, Lees and Martin split them up into groups. They had some air support and started their ground sweep search. The priority was initially to cover as much ground as possible, so they decided against going above the cloud base – between 2,000 and 2,500 feet – at this stage. Up to that level they just managed to achieve their first objective as daylight faded and had been able to eliminate all but the highest ridges of the

Carneddau. All they had found was old wrecks, mostly from the Graham-Scudamore era thirteen years earlier. Gwen Moffat, Lees's wife, a writer and a mountaineer, had heard about the call-out on the radio. She bought a newspaper to get a better idea of the location, then set off. On the summit of Foel Fras she met the St Athan team with Tony Newbould.

Back at the search base that evening they were starting to think about the next day's plan of action but had depressingly little to go on. Then they heard a Land Rover pulling up; one of the Valley airmen was back from talking to the local people. Someone in the Conwy Valley had heard an aircraft very low overhead and from the description it seemed certain that it was much lower than the Canberra should have been. Then the witness had heard a surge of power as if it was trying to climb urgently, but it was going in the direction of the Carneddau. This story seemed to tie in with something a northward-scanning radar monitor had recorded, when an aircraft at about this time had gone south and out of its scan.

With the new information, the high Carneddau had to be the next search area. The leaders decided to concentrate on the eastern and southern faces. As they slept that evening, the Valley team in their beds and the St Athan men in their pigsties, about 120 miles away, the Harpur Hill MRT convoy was finding its way in the darkness through Congleton and Chester to the north coast of Wales and the Conwy Valley. They arrived at Aber in the small hours of the morning and with this reinforcement there were now about a hundred searchers. St Athan were to cover Pen yr Oleu Wen and Carnedd Dafydd, Valley the eastern approach to Carnedd Llewelyn from the Conwy Valley side and Harpur Hill the southern ridges from Tal-y-Braich. They had a common destination – the summit of Carnedd Llewelyn. After that they were to go north or north-west to Yr Elen, Foel Grach, Foel Fras, Drum Llwydmor and Drosgl, and then return either to Aber or Bethesda. It was a tremendous search area.

The promised improvement in the weather did not last for long. As the teams set out at 4 am, to catch the dawn's early light, a blizzard raged, reducing visibility to about ten yards and severely limiting the length of sweep passible. The portable radios – never particularly efficient – were, said Newbould, 'next to useless'.[13]

Newbould and Martin with the St Athan team reached the cairn on the top of Carnedd Llewelyn in a howling gale and blizzard, nine hours after the start, at 1 pm. The communications problems meant that none of the teams really knew how the others had got on. Heading straight into the hard-driven snow, the Newbould team pressed on toward Foel Grach. A few minutes later, there was a shout from one of the airmen. The two leaders went over to him. In his gloved palm was a shiny fragment of metal with a jagged newly-torn edge. Here at last, they believed, they had found some firm evidence. A local, controlled search was put under way, and across the ridge on an east-west line some more pieces were found.

The team then fanned out in both directions, excitement mounting. Then, at last, the point of impact was found. It was on the face of the cliff, about fifty feet down on the east side, at about 3,300 feet. As so often tragically happens in the mountains, just another few feet, a little more power, a little more speed, would have seen the aircraft safely away. Further down there were some larger fragments: engine blades. The main part of the airframe had carried on over the ridge and ended up on the western slope. The largest piece by far, and the furthest away, was the tailplane. The devastation was complete.

Sadly, the team turned back down the hill. At the mountain base, a radio call was made to Rescue Co-ordination Centre at 18 Group to call off the search. As they got together with the other teams, they learnt that Harpur Hill had found the wreckage first, but had been unable to get through on the walkie-talkies to tell the other teams.

St Athan and Harpur Hill started packing up their gear and putting it into the vehicles. Lees sent his first shift up to Carnedd Llewelyn to stand guard until what was left of the bodies and classified equipment could be removed and the site then left in the hands of the police. The St Athan convoy wound its way back through mid-Wales in the late afternoon, the team very tired. Two things – appalling weather and lack of precise information – had conspired to make this a more gruelling and slow search than many. The consolation, such as it was, was that whatever delays might have been avoided, nothing done by the teams could have prevented the deaths of the aircrew.

Again the possibility of disbanding St Athan (or, it was even suggested, the whole service) came up in 1958, only six years after the previous such speculation. Some rumours had been circulating, sparked off by ill-informed newspaper reports and a Parliamentary Question had been tabled. Alastair Hetherington, then editor of the Guardian, was a powerful ally. A passionate mountain lover, he wanted to put a leader in the paper, and telephoned Mike Holton, unaware that he was by then Private Secretary to the minister who would be answering the question the next day. Holton was embarrassed though he knew that the answer would be acceptable.

But the matter did not die there and rumbled on as such arguments are inclined to do in the House of Commons.

An MP called Awbery, on April 29th 1959, asked George Ward, the Secretary of State for Air:

> ... if he is aware of the work performed during the past ten years by the Mountain Rescue Service of the Royal Air Force, both for civilians and members of the Royal Air Force; if he is further aware that the need for such a service is increasing and not diminishing, and that the skill acquired by these men will be lost if the service is not continued; and if he will now reconsider his decision to reduce this service by 50 per cent.

George Ward, the Secretary of State, replied that no such decision had been made, and that the government were simply reviewing the number and location of the teams to see if as good a service could be provided more easily and economically.

> Mr Awbery: is the Minister aware that it has been reported that there are only six teams in the country? They have done excellent work but they are being reduced to three. Will the Right Hon. Gentleman take steps to see that the work that these people have been doing is continued and that the number of teams is not reduced as has been suggested?

That report, said Ward, was quite untrue. He added that in the nature of things some teams were very much busier than others and it was therefore natural to see whether the busy ones should be strengthened at the expense of the others.

Awbery then asked for, and got, confirmation that it was a voluntary service; after which Mr Watkins MP stood up to remind the Minister that the St Athan team had a very busy time rescuing even military personnel in the Brecon Beacons. Ward asked Watkins to write on that subject, as he did not know what the position was with the St Athan team.

Sandy Gordon-Cumming, the then Inspector of Mountain Rescue, wrote to the teams: 'I don't suppose most of you read Hansard – at least not regularly – so I enclose a copy of the replies to recent parliamentary questions on mountain rescue.' He commented in the margin of the Hansard extract: 'I see St Athan have friends at court.'

In June, Marshal of the Royal Air Force, Sir Dermot Boyle, had found it necessary to reassure teams in writing:

> My staff tell me that there is no question of dis-establishing or moving your mountain rescue team. They will therefore continue to carry out their important task which brings great credit and distinction to our service.

Gordon-Cumming had become Inspector of Mountain Rescue in 1955, having been a Secretary of the RAF Mountaineering Association, and it was through the ubiquitous RAFMA network that he had been picked out to replace David Dattner. Later he was to become Deputy Captain of the Queen's Flight. He retired in 1969, and started a second career in the civil service, ending as Counsellor of Aviation and Shipping in Washington.

6 – The Amphitheatre Buttress

It was the end of a weekend exercise, that Sunday evening, December 1st 1957, and Valley had just returned from the hill to the base camp. A good day's climbing in the icy cold, a good meal then it was back to the workshops and offices and hangars of RAF Valley in the morning. But a call came through: there had been a fall on the 300-foot cliff at Aber Falls.

The A55 then was a single-carriageway road: journeys took much longer than the equivalent journeys now and, from the detail given, time was clearly important. Lees asked the Controller at Pitreavie to arrange a police escort to speed their progress. A police car led the way, lights flashing, with Lees driving the Bedford QL close behind. Thanks to some earlier intervention by Sandy Gordon-Cumming, the governor on the engine had been removed, and Lees was: '...waving my hand out of the cab window like whipping a horse to get the Police car to go faster!!'[14]

The convoy reached Aber Falls in what was probably then record time, and the men jumped out and ran to see what was what. A student had been climbing the cliff, had fallen on the ice and, by the light of flares, could be seen lying injured, still roped to his companion, on a ledge about 100 feet up. Police and firemen had been unable to get to him and it was clear that a long lower from above would be necessary. The team went above him with ropes and used a good tree belay as an anchor.

One of the team members on this occasion, Corporal Technician S R G Bray, known as Vic (as in Vicar of Bray, an example of the RAF's quirky approach when selecting nicknames), was wearing nails, so Lees asked him – and he readily agreed – to take the main part. The noise of the falls was deafening, so as the tree was well back above easy-angled slabs Lees went down to just above the nearly-vertical part to relay messages to the lowerers. He found a tiny ledge there – 'about the size of small chair seat' – and stayed there just above the falls.

Bray was on three, tied-together 120-foot ropes – the longest then available – and Lees kept paying out Bray's taut rope through a karabiner and was just able to hear him. 360 feet of rope was more than adequate, but it carried the risk of knots snagging in cracks in the rock. Bray reached a point level with the injured man but about twelve feet to his right. He traversed to reach the ledge and eventually got the injured man clipped on. Then he had to pendulum back with him and Lees had to unclip himself from Bray's rope. Bray swung and descended and with the help of a rope dropped to him by some firemen, met the rest of the team below. They took the man off.

As they did so, the last of the flares finally faded and died. Up above, wondering if he had been forgotten, was the team NCO, Johnnie Lees, on a... 'big greasy crag in Vibrams, on a ledge I daren't leave in the dark!' To Lees's relief, one of the team remembered him and he was retrieved.

Bray was awarded the Bronze Medal of the Royal Humane Society.

Lees has always been the first to say that mountain rescue is, no matter how skilled or courageous the leading players, a team effort, or it is nothing. That episode and the next one, over the turn of the year, are prime examples of team work in action, and of experience leading to a swift improvement in equipment.

High up in Carnedd Llewelyn is Craig yr Ysfa which faces north-east, and is divided into three sections: South Crag, The Amphitheatre and North Crag. The Amphitheatre is a huge gully, on the left of which is the Amphitheatre Buttress (see map p.159). It was here that Colonel Gerry Finch, Major Hugh

Robertson, Lieutenant Roger Eagle, an army padre Fred Jenkins and Finch's two teenage sons were climbing on January 3rd 1958. The men were members of the Army Mountaineering Association, which had been created a year or two before, Finch and Robertson being founder-members. Until then, mountaineering clubs in the army had been corps-based, which meant that at any one time a large proportion of the membership was likely to be posted away. The creation of an association with a wider base was designed to overcome that problem.

Fred Jenkins and one of the Finch boys had just completed the climb when they became aware of a disturbance somewhere below them. Further down, Finch, still climbing with his other son, heard Eagle, in the last party, calling out. Robertson had been trying to lead an ice pitch when he came off. He fell onto a ledge, and Eagle, second on the rope, managed to keep him on the ledge, which was about 200 feet from the bottom. He shouted to Finch that Robertson seemed to have bad head injuries.

Finch reached Jenkins and asked him to explore down the nearby Pinnacle Wall to see if there was a way of getting the injured man up by that route. In the meantime, he went off down to Ogwen Cottage as fast as he could with his two sons to raise the alarm. People at Ogwen Cottage got a scratch team together but it looked as if it was going to be a difficult rescue, so a call was put in to RAF Valley. That was at 4.30 pm. It was then dark and there was concern about the two men, one badly injured on the ledge, and about the possibility of frost-bite and exposure.

Leaving his sons at the cottage, Finch went back up with the Ogwen Cottage group. They had no sooner reached the top of the crag when, to Finch's amazement, they were caught up by Lees and the Valley team at 7.20 pm, about three hours after the alarm was raised at Ogwen Cottage. They had taken the vehicles down the Conwy Valley, then onto the track past Llyn Eigiau, finally managing to get them over rough ground well up into Cwm Eigiau. Lees had guided his team in the dark up the mountain and over snow-covered rocks. This was something of a relief, since unlike the Ogwen Cottage group who had spent the day on the hill, the RAF men were fresh and in dry clothes.

Jenkins got a line down from the top and Lees took Paddy Andrews, Vic Bray and Gerry Finch 750 feet down to the ledge to join Robertson and Eagle. Below them was 200 vertical feet of rock, overhanging in places. This would be a difficult descent at the best of times, but here they had a delirious man. Now Lees had to decide on the best way to complete the operation. It was dark, and the Buttress was covered in ice. The only way, it appeared, was a final descent down the remaining very steep 200 feet, with a man who was concussed and thrashing about.

Until very recently, the teams had been equipped with standard 120-foot ropes. But only a month earlier, in December 1957, Lees had been to an annual Mountain Rescue conference at the Air Ministry in Whitehall. Several points

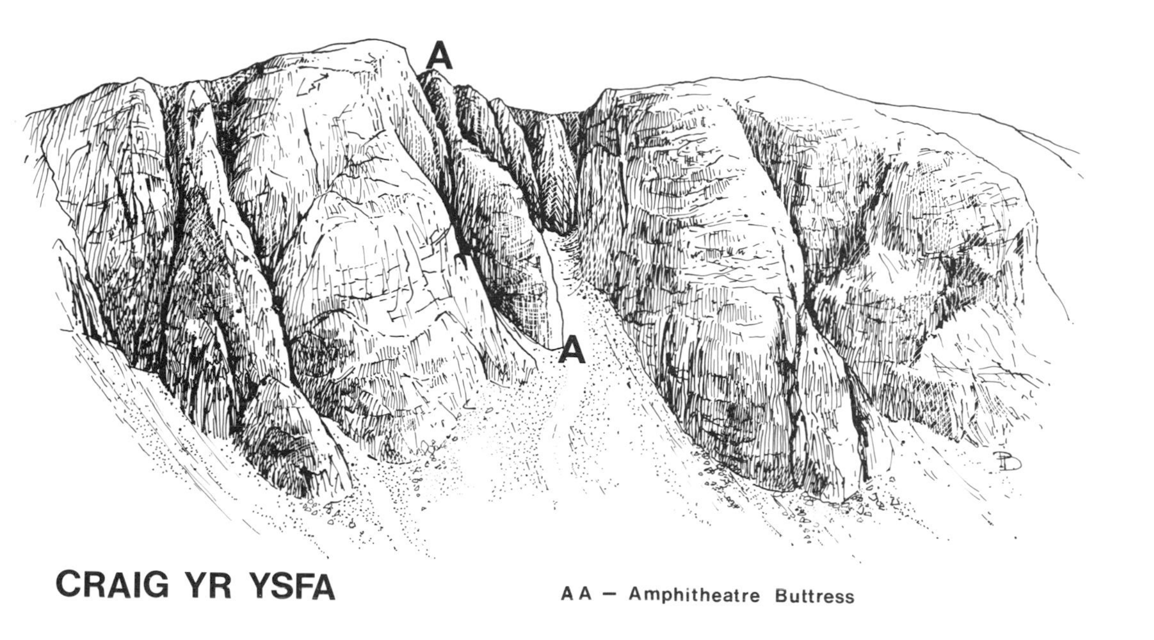

CRAIG YR YSFA

AA – Amphitheatre Buttress

Tragsitz: Descent of a cliff with an injured climber on the back of a rescuer. *Photo courtesy RAF Valley*

had been raised regarding equipment and almost at the end of the discussions, Lees had asked if 500-foot ropes could be provided 'to cater for exceptionally long stretcher or casualty lowers'. Sandy Gordon-Cumming, the Inspector of Mountain Rescue, agreed and undertook to investigate the supply.[15] The Aber Falls operation, less than two weeks after the conference, had emphasised the need. A drop of 200 feet would have entailed linking together two ropes, with, in those conditions, the risk that the knot would have jammed in a crack. Fortunately, Lees's far-sightedness was recognised and the 500-foot ropes had been supplied in time for the Amphitheatre Buttress call-out. But ropes are heavy and five hundred feet is a lot of rope. A plywood reel was devised which enabled a man to carry one of these ropes up on his back.

Eagle, by this time, had been on the ledge with the increasingly difficult Robertson for seven hours. He was beginning to suffer from the gathering cold and there was the danger of frost bite for both men. Lees decided that there was only one thing to do. He told the other men to lash Robertson to his back with a rope cradle. Then, with Robertson thrashing about and struggling to get free, he abseiled down, supported from above by a rope guided by his team-members. The combined weight on the rope was 28 stone.

Finally Lees reached the scree at the bottom, where by then team members were waiting with a stretcher. The physical strain of the descent compounded by Robertson's weight and his violent movements was enormous. Nevertheless, he still took more than his fair share of stretcher-carrying duties in taking Robertson to the ambulance where it had been parked in Cwm Eigiau. 'The RAF team' says Jenkins now[16], 'must have set up a record from one of the remotest spots in North Wales to the hospital.' Even so, it was 2.30 am by the time the ambulance reached hospital.

Robertson had a fractured skull and it was some time before he was up and about again. One of the first things he did was to visit Johnnie Lees and his team at RAF Valley to say 'Thank you'. He looked round the store and saw that they could do with more equipment. What, he asked Lees, do you most need here? After consideration, Lees plumped for a Tragsitz harness; a device designed for the task performed by the makeshift rope cradle on Lees's back which had brought Robertson down.

The Aber Falls and Amphitheatre Buttress incidents had brought home forcibly to Lees how much the teams needed something like a Tragsitz. A few weeks after these incidents he had been to see Wing Commander Cornish at RAF Valley, explained the need for the device and discussed how, given the right materials and some workshop assistance, he could probably design and produce one himself. Cornish agreed and wrote to the Air Ministry on his behalf. Before this had got very far, however, Robertson had made his grateful visit. He bought the harness the next time he was in Switzerland and had much trouble getting it through Customs.

The secretary of the RAF Mountaineering Association commented to Lees's boss in Whitehall:

There are three points that I should like to mention in connexion with the report [from the Army Mountaineering Association]. The main one is the outstanding performance of Flight Sergeant Lees which, in fact, is not dealt with very fully in the attached report. But I have it from eye witnesses as well as from Colonel Finch that Lees' presence and efforts shortened the time of rescue by several hours, which may well have made all the difference between life and death for the casualty.[17]

The Army Mountaineering Association had itself pointed out that: 'The fact that they had recently acquired two 500 ft. lengths of nylon rope was also of great assistance.'[17]

Then Mike Holton, instrumental after Beinn Eighe in bringing Lees into the service in the first place, took much pleasure in sending a telegram from the committee of RAFMA to Flight Sergeant Lees at RAF Valley:

PLEASE PASS AS PERSONAL FOR F/SGT J R LEES

CONGRATULATIONS ON THE RECOGNITION OF YOUR SERVICES TO MOUNTAIN RESCUE BY THE AWARD OF THE GEORGE MEDAL. FROM COMMITTEE AND MEMBERS OF THE ROYAL AIR FORCE MOUNTAINEERING ASSOCIATION.[18]

Three and a half years after this incident, late in 1961, Lees retired from the Royal Air force whilst leader of the Valley MRT. He had been instrumental, with a handful of others, in pulling the service round after a disastrous 1951, and in putting into place a systematic training programme which quickly became, and remains, admired throughout the mountain rescue world. He was awarded the BEM in the 1962 New Years Honours List.

He was the second of the giants of MR, after Graham. He remained, and remains, active on the hill, and now lives quietly at Bakewell.

7 – Aspain Point

A few miles to the north-east of Cadair Idris, on the other side of Dolgellau, is a range of hills, apparently gentle and rolling compared with those further north or even with Cadair Idris itself: the Arans.

Is there something ominous, the two Welsh teams wondered by the end of the weekend, about Whitsun? Jock Smith's disastrous fall on Tryfan only three years ago was still a sharp memory. Again, the Whitsun holiday in 1960 promised perfect climbing weather.

Compared to North Wales, there is not as much scope in South Wales – in the St Athan patch – for rock-climbing as there is in the north of the Principality. But the terrain provides several different sorts of challenge. Navigation standards have to be extremely high, as the area includes some of the trickiest high moorland and hill-climbing country outside Scotland. The Duke of Edinburgh's Award Scheme had used the area for many years, and had long asked the RAF St

Athan MRT to keep an eye on Boy Entrants from St Athan taking part in qualifying expeditions for the scheme's Gold Standard.

Machynlleth, in mid-Wales, was the site of the base camp that Whit weekend of 1960. It seemed at first that compasses would not be used; the only navigational skill on which the boys would be tested would be map reading. Not far away, though, to the south, a series of thunderstorms rumbled around the hilltops, returning time and again. This persisted through June 3rd and 4th. On the morning of the 5th it showed every sign of continuing fine for yet another day as a small group set out from Cwm Cywarch in the Arans to check a party of boys who were due to cross the southern col of Aran Fawddwy from the north and descend to Cywarch by the Drws Bach ridge. They turned off in the village of Dinas Mawddwy on a minor road leading up into Cwm Cywarch. Access to the Arans has always been a delicate matter and many walkers and climbers have brushed against local landowners in trying to reach Aran Fawddwy and Aran Benllyn. The jeep was carefully parked off-road at one of the agreed access points.

The four were Flying Officer F G Hodges, Flying Officer Michael Davies, SAC Michael Aspain and another airman. Geoff Hodges was the recently-established Officer i/c, having succeeded Tony Newbould the previous September; at the same time, Ian Martin had left to be replaced as team leader by Jack Hendren. Hodges had been climbing since a schoolboy, starting with, as he puts it, 'fumbling around the Berwyns'.[19] Their rendezvous was at the top of the ridge, where they watched the boy entrants start their descent. Glancing across to the south, though, they could see the persistent storm clouds. A small storm apparently detached itself from the main centre of disturbance and made its way with appalling speed towards the Arans. It is one of the hazards of a mountaineer's life to be caught in a storm and climbers are quite used to being soaked by rain and buffeted by wind. However, there was something about this storm that seemed ominous and Hodges decided that a speedy retreat was called for. They made their way as quickly as possible to the Drws Bach Ridge, which offered the fastest and safest descent to low ground.

The storm caught them up on the ridge. They were right on the apex when lightning struck and all four of the party fell. Hodges, dazed, looked around. Davies was just getting to his feet; the two airmen, who had been close together, were lying still. Hodges and Davies examined them. It was immediately clear that Aspain was dead, but the second airman was apparently just stunned. Davies immediately started artificial respiration on him and Hodges made a fast and dangerous descent of the nearest gully to get help. To his great relief, lower down he met Sergeant Hendren and more of the team who were on their way up. Jack Hendren and his group had had a job of their own and Hendren, the work completed, had decided to meet the Hodges party. The Hendren group carried on up the hill and Hodges went down to break the news to the officer in charge of

The memorial cairn at Aspain Point. *Photo: F G Hodges*

the Duke of Edinburgh's Scheme, Squadron Leader P M Dunstan. He alerted the other rescue services at Cywarch.

Within half an hour of the disaster, the storm had gone. A shaken St Athan team went up to the ridge later that evening to recover Aspain's body. The second airman made a full recovery.

Mike Aspain, whose Air Force trade was a miller, was 18 when he died. He had been a popular member and the team talked over with Hodges the possibility of leaving some sort of memorial. After these discussions, Hodges arranged with a mason in Tadcaster, Yorkshire, to make a memorial stone in Cornish granite, with a brass plate:

This Cairn was erected by Royal Air Force St Athan Mountain Rescue Team in memory of S.A.C. Michael ('Mike') Robert Aspain, who was killed by lightning near this spot on 5th June 1960 whilst serving with the team.

Hodges, by then Flight Lieutenant, took the stone to St Athan. Then he visited the summit of Pen y Fan in the Brecon Beacons and obtained a piece of old red sandstone to be built into the cairn. Pen y Fan was the highest point in St Athan's area and it seemed appropriate to include a piece of that in the memorial. The Stafford team joined in the exercise of hauling the 150-lb block of granite up to the Drws Bach. Fortunately, it had snowed the previous evening and they were able to put it onto a sledge for the long drag up from the Cwm Cywarch where they had set up their base camp. There were plenty of boulders at the site with which to build the cairn, but of course sand and cement had to be taken up as well. Hodges slogged up with the sandstone block on his back, rather, he feels, like Atlas holding up the heavens.

As the cairn took shape, an aluminium cassette containing the names of those who had taken part was cemented into the base and the Pen y Fan boulder was cemented into the southern face. The point chosen was not the exact spot where the disaster took place, but on the high point of the ridge, commanding views to Pen y Fan to the south and Snowdon to the north; the greater part of the length of Wales.

Some time later, a steel case was made in the RAF St Athan workshops for visitors' signatures, and placed in a niche in the cairn. The cairn now appears on the Ordnance Survey maps and teams find it a very welcome point of reference in bad weather, especially in the early hours of the morning during an exercise in torrential rain. Geoff Hodges comments:

Michael Aspain's generous and kind nature would have been pleased had he known that his memorial would be of help to other walkers on the hills. 'Still are they pleasant voices ... awake, for Death he taketh all away, but them he cannot take.'[20]

A letter arrived a couple of months later for Davies from Squadron Leader J R Sims, who was by then the Inspector of Mountain Rescue:

I have now seen the report on the accident suffered by the St Athan Mountain Rescue Team on Cadair Idris on the 5th June, 1960, and on the part you played.
I would like to thank you for your interest and help with the team, particularly on this occasion, and for your great presence of mind in applying artificial respiration resulting in the probable saving of a life. I was very heartened by your prompt and efficient behaviour under the most unpleasant circumstances and hope that you have no ill-effects.
Please give my regards also to Hodges for his energetic work and wish him good fortune in his next posting. I hope his shock is now completely cured.[21]

Very shortly after this, Hodges was posted away, but managed to get back to St Athan in September 1962. He still has a cherished possession: a prismatic compass, dated 1944, with the fixing screw which Aspain repaired for him.

8 – Boots Grooved Heel

Early in 1962 the Air Ministry put on an exhibition of Air Force activities, in which Mountain Rescue was featured. One of the government visitors was the Right Honourable Ernest Marples, then Minister of Transport. He was obviously genuinely interested in the display, and let it be known that he was an enthusiastic climber, and would like an opportunity to see one of the RAF teams in action. He was a member of the Climbers' Club and had recently spent some time with the Italian Alpini.

Very shortly after this he was in Hong Kong on government business, at the same time as Squadron Leader John Sims was there inspecting the RAF Kai Tak team, the leader of which was then Archie Hay. He and Sims met and as is

Boots Grooved Heel. *Photo: J R Lees*

Ernest Marples climbing with J Ellis Roberts

the way when a cabinet minister speaks, wheels were quickly put in motion and Sims invited the Minister to visit Valley.

By that time, the team leader at Valley was Flight Sergeant R A Bennett, generally known as 'Tony'. Bennett got in touch with John Ellis Roberts, a local civilian mountaineer who was in charge of the sub-unit equipment stored in the police station at Blaenau Ffestiniog. Apart from his work with the RAF, Roberts was custodian of the University College of North Wales's climbing hut in Cwm Orthin, just above Blaenau Ffestiniog, and is now Head Warden of the Snowdonia National Park. Bennett asked Roberts if the Valley team could have the use of the hut for the weekend of the 14th and 15th April and added that it had to be nice and clean, as it would be used by a VIP. He invited Roberts to join the team for the occasion, and John Sims also was to be there.

The ministerial car took Marples to Blaenau on the Saturday morning April 14th, where he transferred into one of the team's Land Rovers, which took him up the rough mountain track to the hut. The team was under canvas nearby. It was a beautiful day. Roberts was asked to lead Marples up some rock climbs on Craig y Wrysgan and Clogwyn yr Oen, with Sims and one of the Valley team members following on the same route with a camera. Then after lunch he was given a demonstration of stretcher-lowering and Tragsitz use down the full height of Clogwyn yr Oen (500 feet). When the 'casualties' reached the foot of the cliff, they were put into the ambulance and taken down the mountain track, brass bell ringing furiously, to Tanygrisiau, a village just outside Blaenau Ffestiniog. A field there was used for helicopter evacuation and on cue a 22

Squadron Whirlwind arrived, took the casualties off, did a couple of circuits and returned them to the team.

The Minister dined that evening in the Cwm Orthin hut on food prepared by the team, after which he was treated to a march past with one of those present playing the bagpipes, followed by a tour of the usual mountaineers' watering holes in Blaenau Ffestiniog. Marples stayed overnight in the hut and the Sunday, in contrast, started dull and damp – too rainy for serious climbing, remembers Roberts. Marples had promised his wife and his minders that he would not do any serious walking, but having escaped from London, he was going to seize every opportunity. He asked for a map, a compass and some directions, and was taken by Land Rover to the Stwlan Dam road. Then he strode off into the mist, quickly disappearing; visibility by then was about twenty yards.

When the Land Rover returned to Cwm Orthin, second thoughts caused the team to think along the lines of: If this Minister of the Crown goes missing, whose fault will it be? Quickly small parties were sent out from Marples's departure point in the hope that they would catch him up and keep him discreetly in sight. None of them found him. As the parties returned empty-handed during the afternoon, the weather was improving, but nevertheless the Minister was still missing. A vague unease soon turned to real concern. More parties were got together and were about to be despatched when Marples returned, striding back out of the mist. He had had a most enjoyable day. After leaving the Land Rover near the Stwlan Dam, he had gone over the Moelwyn, then down into Cwm Croesor and had found a farmhouse near to Croesor where he was served a cream tea. Refreshed, he had then climbed over Cnicht before returning to the Cwm Orthin hut.

Mountain rescuers are never slow in taking the opportunity, when it arises, to let someone with influence know when there is a genuine grievance. The service, since the very first days in 1943, had suffered from a lack of really good equipment. True, since Beinn Eighe in 1951 the clothing had been improved and army battledress was no longer considered adequate; and as a result of two major call-outs in Turkey by the Akrotiri team in 1959 and 1960 (Chapter VII), at least the high-altitude teams had crampons. Nevertheless, the service as a whole was for many years plagued by the notorious standard-issue boot, listed in armed forces fashion as Boots, Grooved Heel. Boots, Grooved Heel had been with the service almost from the start. Reputedly they had been designed for the Norwegian campaign (by the Germans, said some cynics). In 1951 it was said, in preparation for the first major conference:

Boots, ankle, grooved heel – These are quite good boots, but are issued with only hob nailing. Clinkers have been obtained, and put in by members of the team.
The best nailing is No. 6 Swiss tricounis round the welt and muggers in the sole with clinkers in the heel. The life of the boot is also longer with this type of a nailing than with clinkers in the sole.

Len Hammon in a Brays-Drew Tragsitz

Tony Bennet. *Photo: J Ellis Roberts*

It is a skilled cobbler's job to put in the nails satisfactorily and it is suggested that either the boots are issued suitably nailed, or that the O.C. of the Mountain Rescue team is permitted to have a contract with a local cobbler who is experienced in nailing climbing boots.[22]

The conference itself was not so sanguine as the person who drew up the agenda. The decision was:

The present nailing of these boots is not suitable. The Royal Marine Commandos may be able to offer assistance in this matter. A.D. Rescue to investigate.[23]

At the next conference it was announced that a different type of mountaineering boot was to be provided some time in the near future. Nevertheless, Boots, Grooved Heel were still listed the following year.[24] In 1955, Sergeant Bevis of Kinloss MRT was writing to the equipment officer at RAF Kinloss, with the Boots, Grooved Heel still proving unsatisfactory. The matter had been raised in the previous December's Mountain Rescue Conference, when it was said that some of the boots were to be improved; now there seemed to be some doubt about that, reported Bevis.[25] Hopes were raised again during the 1956 conference, when delegates were told that there had been trials, which 'had gone well', of new types of boot, and a bid would be made for one of the types tested.[26] A year later, one of the team officers told the conference that he had applied for the new Vibram-soled boots but had been issued with the old type.[27]

Eventually, though, the teams said a not-very-reluctant goodbye to Boots, Grooved Heel and welcomed Boots, MR. For about five years the subject went dormant, only to be stirred up again by, of all people, a cabinet minister. Sitting in the Cwm Orthin hut chatting to the team in the evening, Marples casually picked up one of the standard issue boots, and commented that, as a climbing boot, it was not very impressive. The team members quickly let him know that they shared his opinion. Marples undertook to use what influence he possessed. Within three weeks there had been a meeting between himself, Julian Amery (the Secretary of State for Air) and Squadron Leader John Sims. This was in Marples's house in Eaton Square, where he had invited them to tea in the large kitchen, surrounded by copper saucepans and photographs of his French vineyard. There was serious money here, felt Sims.

The three men agreed that the standard RAF mountaineering boots compared most unfavourably with several well-known continental designs and that this should be rectified. After being offered and accepting a lift back to the Whitehall office in the ministerial car AM 1 (an interesting experience in itself for a squadron leader), Sims reported:

It would take about a year to test fully a new (continental) type of climbing boot. If it proved possible for British Industry to copy this, a further delay would be involved before boots were obtainable in quantity. The Service is now short of Mountain Rescue Team Members, and one of the ways of encouraging volunteers is by the provision of better mountaineering equipment; irrespective of this it is Air Ministry policy to recommend the provision of the most appropriate equipment for specialised mountaineering tasks. I therefore favour the acceptance of a suitable proprietary design bought from continental sources such as the Art.304 made by 'La Dolomite' Montebelluna, Treviso, or the 'Summit' made by Munari. Such boots are available now, in sufficient quantity to re-equip Mountain Rescue Teams at wastage rates.[28]

The same minute concluded by asking the Assistant Private Secretary to obtain Amery's agreement. Sims was cautious, at this stage, about Marples's idea that he should approach one of the Italian manufacturers, well known to him, directly: 'I can see many complications if, by using Mr Marples good offices, we bypass the usual contractual procedures.' Julian Amery wrote to Ernest Marples on June 6th:

I thought you might like to know how we are getting on with the question of boots for the R.A.F Mountain Rescue Teams.

The total number we require is only about 250 pairs, with occasional follow-up orders. We have accordingly come to the conclusion that it would be cheaper and save time to buy a suitable proprietary design straight from continental sources rather than to develop a boot of our own. I gather we shall probably go for either the "Summit" made by Munari, or the Art.304 made by "La Dolomite" Montebelluna.

This is rather less ambitious than the plan we discussed together and we shall not, of course, get the publicity which might have followed from developing a special R.A.F. boot. But what the Mountain Rescue Team want is a good boot as soon as possible.

I am most grateful to you for drawing my attention to the deplorable boot we were using and for putting us on the right track for getting something better.[29]

Marples made a handwritten reply:

Dear Julian,
It has just struck me that you can get the best of both worlds, ie –
1. 'a good boot as soon as possible' (to use your words)
AND
2. the kudos of an R.A.F. designed boot.
Suppose you choose ART 304. I could then get Gianni Munari to make some minor modification to his standard boot eg alter the tongue to make it more waterproof. He could work something out. It wouldn't cost more and it could be called the RAF boot.
I know how his factory works and I am sure it could be done.
Anyway for what it is worth the idea is tendered free of charge!

Yours ever

Ernest.[30]

This was received with enthusiasm. Amery (in a letter drafted by Sims) replied:

I believe you have found the solution. If Munari can copy the Dolomite boot Art.304, with slightly stiffer sole, I have good hopes that not only will our Teams be better shod, but that our recruiting may be helped by some well placed publicity.[31]

Marples wrote to Munari on those lines on July 12th, noting to Amery: 'He will be meeting me at his factory on 4th August. I will report back to you after that date.'[32] Munari gave a pair of the boots to Marples to take back; he had to pay import duty, a bill which ended up on Sims's desk. Eventually several pairs were tried by the teams, but frustratingly no consensus could be reached within the service. The problem was shelved; Marples's efforts and influence had come to nothing.

But discontent continued; six years later, in the 1968 conference, John Hinde said that:

...although the service Mountain Rescue boot was a good hill-walking boot, its life with normal use in the Scottish teams was only six months or so, and it was common practice for the MRT members to spend quite large sums on buying their own mountaineering boots. Since no one type or make of boot suited each individual or team, he proposed a Boot Allowance of £10 per member on completion of each year's satisfactory service with a team.[33]

No particular comment is recorded, but the IMR was left to look into it. Next year, however, they were told that trials by the Scottish teams were taking place of 'Boots, Army, Ski, Marching'.[34] It is Sims's belief that, though the Marples episode seemed to end so unsatisfactorily, it did in fact start people thinking and pave the way for the eventual official approval of local purchase – much more satisfactory all round.

Even so, boot problems persisted. On the files only a few years after those conferences is a gently chiding letter from the then ILR (Inspector of Land

Rescue, the later title), Squadron Leader David Lofts. Approval had been received for, yet again, a new type of boot. Mention had been made of the fact that it would be repairable. Clearly a civil servant had caught on to this, and, conscious of the Treasury peering over his shoulder, had made a suggestion of which Lofts thought very little:

2. We are, however, at a loss to understand your reasoning that, because the new boot will be repairable, the initial purchase of the replacement items should be reduced by 50%. This repair facility cannot come into operation until boots – bought on the initial purchase – wear out and can only therefore affect the requirement for further purchases.
3. Your comments would be appreciated as it is possible to foresee a situation where a user would wear out the unrepairable Mk IV boot, only to find that no replacement was available due to this restricted purchase.[35]

Boots were not the only item of equipment to give problems. Sometimes it seemed that the Mountain Rescue Service was regarded as a dumping ground. But Gordon-Cumming, Sims's predecessor, knew how to obtain an unfavourable assessment from an acknowledged expert. A letter from his Whitehall office to Lees at RAF Valley was dated April 1957:

Dear Johnnie
Thank you for letting me have the broken ice-axe. You will see from my round robin that you were quite right.

That probably refers to the hated British Bulldog ice-axe, placed by experienced climbers in the same league as Boots, Grooved Heel. Then he continued.:

Disturbed, no doubt, by Sir Frank Tribe's revelations on stocks of A.T.S. underwear the Army have had a panic sale of all A.T.S. equipment including the small rucksack which we use. Consequently we have to find a replacement and I am being pressed to accept the large pack on standard R.A.F. webbing equipment. It seems obvious to me on first sight that it is useless because it has two narrow straps and, having no drawcord will let everything in it get wet. However, I must show willing and accordingly enclose one for you to test. Would you please let me have a report of your views, couched in suitably official language – say in a week or ten days – and let me have the rucksack back. You had better send it back dirty enough to suggest prolonged and enthusiastic trials.[36]

Following protocol, the report in the following month was in the team officer's name and addressed to the Under Secretary of State for Air. The writer had the honour to submit the report of the suitability of the pack as directed. Then it confirmed Gordon-Cumming's supposition that the contents get wet and added that smaller items could fall out and get lost. It was also confirmed that the straps were unsuitable. The concluding paragraph said: 'The test pack is to be returned separately.'[37]

Suitably grubby and scuffed, no doubt.

Peter McGowan in the 1960s. *McGowan coll.*

9 – A Good Rescue

Within the RAF teams, there gradually developed a tradition of joining in various mountaineering events, competitive or not. One of the keenest participants was John Hinde. Another was Peter McGowan. In November 1968 McGowan and Hinde had been the leaders of a north-south trek in Scotland, consisting of three from RAF Valley and three from RAF Kinloss. Then in May 1969 there had been the interesting relay traverse of the 'Roof of Wales'. Those concerned were the team members and the candidates on that year's Team Leaders' Training Course: Corporals Oldham, Gilligan, Hemmings, West and Foster. The walk was to take eight days and cover 456 miles. The relays consisted of two men at a time, and there was to be one relay walking throughout all twenty-four hours of each of the eight days. The event started at Newport and went by the Black Mountains, the Brecon Beacons, Black Mountain, Radnor Forest, Plynlimon, Cadair Idris, the Arans, the Berwyns, the Arenigs, the Rhinogs, the Moelwyns, Moel Hebog, Snowdon, Moel Siabod, the Glyders and the Carneddau. Thus it covered all the main mountain groups in Wales.

Not all were RAF events. In October 1971 there was the Karrimor Two-Day Mountain Marathon. In the 'Standard' entry list, for RAF Valley, were D Wood and P McGowan; but over in the 'Elite' list, along with such elite names as Jos Naylor, Chris Brasher and John Disley were, for Valley, Don Shanks and D Forster. Both classes had to cover 21 miles and 19½ miles respectively over two days. The event was based at Capel Curig but the route was not known to the competitors until they checked in and picked up their route sheets.

McGowan had joined the Mountain Rescue Service as a volunteer in the late fifties. He passed out as team leader in 1965 and his first team was Leeming. After two relatively quiet years he took over Valley in October 1968. That year, by Valley standards, had itself not been all that busy for some months. A boy had fallen on Snowdon in February, three walkers on three separate occasions had needed help in August; apart from that, nothing. Such a contrast to 1967 and, for that matter any other earlier year since 1951, the year of Black Easter.

Then came October, and it was almost as if accidents were waiting to happen, waiting for Sergeant Peter McGowan to arrive. On four different dates in October, three walkers went missing on Snowdon (all safe), a walker had a heart attack on Glyder Fach (dead), a walker fell on Snowdon (injured), and a light aircraft crashed on the Carneddau (pilot dead). Things quietened down in November but on two successive days in December, just after Christmas, there was a climbing accident on Cwm Glas Mawr (one injured) and on Snowdon a climber fell down a mine shaft (safe, but shocked). In January (1969), a girl fell on the Watkin Path on Snowdon; she was safe.

In February, the team had to search on one occasion for two soldiers on Foel Ganol, on another for an RAF Regiment airman on Cwm Eigiau and, between those two, deal with a climbing incident on Tryfan: the soldiers suffered from exposure but otherwise all were safe. The pace continued in March, firstly with two walkers in trouble on Pen yr Oleu Wan and then with a boy down another mine shaft, this on Pary's Mountain, Anglesey: again all were safe. A breathing space came in April, but in May four people were found suffering from exposure in Cwm Eigiau, and a walking incident happened on the Miner's Track. June saw a Gnat aircraft crash at Moelfre, just off the Betwys-y-Coed to Corwen road: the pilot was safe.

Then came July. On the 5th, a Saturday, McGowan, with others, was on a training walk of some twenty-five miles in the Rhinog Mountains, and had completed nineteen miles of it. Then in the late afternoon he picked up a radio call. A leading rock-climber, Malcolm Howells, had been trying to open a new route on Trwyn Y Gorlech on the northern coast of the Lleyn Peninsula. This was on a vertical cliff of about 800 feet, which fell sheer into the sea. A huge rock had fallen away from the cliff, and he with it. He had stopped about half-way down when he hit a narrow grassy ledge after plunging about eighty feet, and was badly injured. His companion had secured him to a rock on the ledge and climbed down to the foot of the cliff to get help.

A helicopter of 22 Squadron was called out, but on arriving at the spot found that it could not get close enough to winch Howells up. It was therefore sent to pick up McGowan, Corporal Robinson and Junior Technician Matheson from their position near Llanbedr, and firstly it took them to their base camp to get some equipment. By the time they reached the cliff it was 7.15 pm and time was pressing.

An S.55 Whirlwind drops off a patient at Gobowen, Oswestry, in 1959.
Photo: the late Mark Woodward, courtesy of H J Budgen

This cliff was new to McGowan. Using a 500-foot rope and karabiner brake, he abseiled 200 feet down where he found a small ledge and was joined there by Robinson and Matheson. Then they climbed down a further 200 feet to join the injured man and McGowan assessed the injuries as best he could. Howells was badly shocked but conscious. He had a fracture and a deep cut in his right leg – injuries which were beyond the first-aid capabilities of the Mountain Rescue men, but which obviously needed urgent attention. They had no-one else they could call on and darkness was approaching. With no-one at the top of the cliff, the use of a stretcher was ruled out. McGowan seriously considered bringing in the helicopter again (it remained on standby in a nearby field) but decided that the risk was still too high.

Lees's piggy-back rescue of Major Hugh Robertson on the Amphitheatre Buttress eleven years earlier had passed into Mountain Rescue legend and it must have gone through McGowan's mind when he was assessing the situation. The injured man, twelve stone, was strapped by Robinson and Matheson into the Tragsitz on McGowan's back and all then descended the remaining 400 feet to the base of the cliff. There were very few natural belay points on the way down and the ropes had to be anchored to pitons hammered into cracks in the rock.

Even at the foot of the cliff the ordeal was by no means over. It was now dark and there was a further 400 yards of a steep crag to be descended, followed by some 100 yards of steep scree. That part of the journey alone, from the foot of the cliff, took one and a half hours, and there was very little his two companions could do to assist McGowan. Finally, the casualty had to be carried a further mile along the beach in a stretcher and taken to hospital. The whole operation had taken seven hours and before it even started McGowan had covered nineteen miles on the training walk. Where does the additional energy come from for an effort like this? If it's serious enough, McGowan says now, 'A button gets pushed'. He remembers this as 'A good rescue'.

Clearly Malcolm Howells himself did not disagree with that.

Dear Pete

I feel I must write and thank you and your mates for the job you did in getting me to hospital after my accident in the 'Rivals' last Saturday. You probably don't realise how grateful I was to be brought down unless you have spent a few hours on a ledge sufficiently injured to be helpless. You may be interested to know I was stitched and plastered in Bangor and driven back to London on the Sunday after the rescue and then after several days' hopping around on crutches, examination in our local London hospital revealed that the wound was infected and the ankle injury wrongly diagnosed so I am now back in hospital with the prospect of a three week stay – a real drag.

He enclosed £5 for 'a night's drinking' and added:

Let me finish by saying that after ten years' experience climbing at all grades of difficulty I am still absolutely amazed at how you were able to carry me over those rocks at the bottom of the cliff. I could hardly believe it at the time and I can still hardly believe it now, all I can say is that if I see you involved in any rough stuff at any time I'll be on your side for safety reasons.[38]

Only two days later, on Monday July 7th, there was another incident, one that well illustrates how easy it is for British mountains to be underestimated. In the case of Snowdon, this risk is compounded by the existence of the railway which gives a deceptive air of suburban normality to the area.

Some are tempted to take the train to the summit, then walk down. That was exactly what two women, members of the Scottish national hockey team, set out to do on that Monday. One became stuck in a gully, and had to stay there overnight. John Roberts, accompanied by search dogs, reached her during the night and with food and clothing, but was unable to extricate her. McGowan and his team were called in at dawn to help with the evacuation.

10 – The Unexpected Burden

Tony Jones is a big rumbustious character with a voice to match which you can hear in the next Welsh valley but one. As Dr Anthony Jones, he is Warden of the University College of North Wales in Bangor, and is a marine geologist at the Marine Science Labs in Menai Bridge. Born in India, he spent his formative years in South Africa, then moved to North Wales. He had become interested in mountain rescue as a member of the Cape Town Section of the Mountaineering Club of South Africa. He joined the Ogwen Valley Mountain Rescue

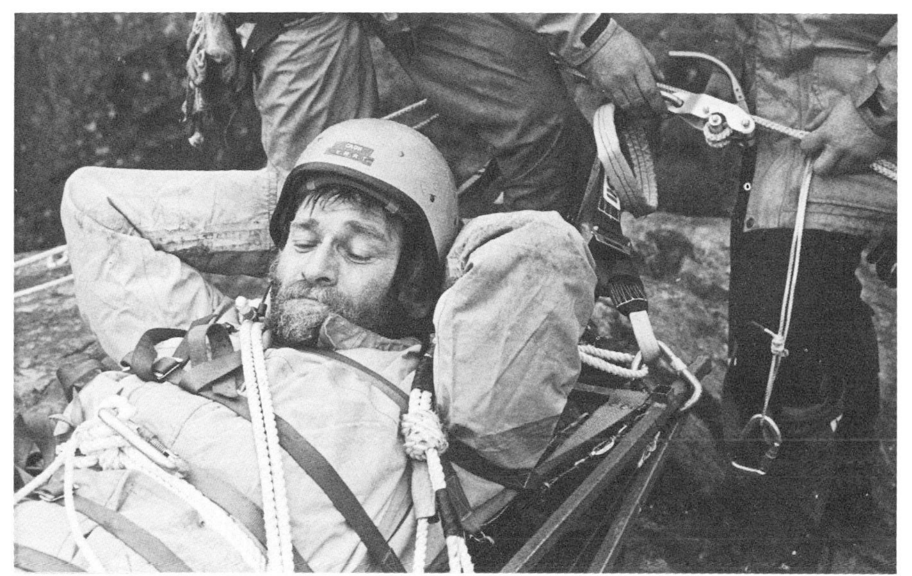

Tony Jones acting as 'victim' in stretcher-lowering practice. *Photo: Jones coll.*

Organisation (Oggy) in 1964 and became a team leader in 1967. It is largely to his credit that the Ogwen Valley team has its excellent reputation with the RAF teams. It is one of those civilian mountain rescue teams which often works hand-in-glove with the nearby RAF team, in this case Valley. Tony Jones himself says generously:

Anyone with a real interest in MR would, in those days, become involved with the RAF. Remember that there were far fewer civilian MRTs. The RAF had much to teach and still do. It was about 1964 that I first went out with the Saints[39]. One cannot work rescue in North Wales without a close contact with the RAF.[40]

One example of the close co-operation between civilian and service teams happened on February 7th 1970, a Saturday. On this exercise Sergeant Jack Baines was in charge of the Valley team and he had taken out a group on a weekend exercise based at Llanberis. For the exercise he followed a route which took his party south to Moel Elio, across to Foel Gron, Foel Goch and Moel Cynghorion, then on the western slopes of Snowdon to Clogwyn Du'r Arddu from where they reached the railway track. It was at this point, at about 2 pm, that they received a radio message from the base camp down near Llanberis: someone had been injured in Cwm Glas.

Cwm Glas Mawr (big green hollow) lies between the railway and the main Llanberis Pass road, and both for climbing purposes and scenically it is the best part of the north-east flank of Snowdon. It falls in one continuous magnificent drop from Garnedd Ugain to the road, a total of 2,900 feet. At its upper end is

Parsley-fern Gully, the 500 feet of which provides a good snow route in winter, but an unpleasant scramble in summer. From where Baines was standing with his party it could be reached from above, but the route was not easy for an inexperienced party in snow and ice conditions; and he thought it wiser to take them down the railway track and round by road to the foot of Cwm Glas. Having reached this point through wind, snow and hail, he learnt what had happened.

Martin Britnell and Gordon Robinson had been climbing *Parsley-fern Gully*. Britnell was leading through the cornice at the top when it collapsed and both climbers fell approximately 800 feet. Robinson had leg and head injuries, and Britnell a chest injury and lacerations to the face. However, Britnell had been able to get to a mountain hut to raise the alarm. An advance party of the Valley team with civilians – including Tony Jones – went to the scene of the accident.

A helicopter had been asked for because of the weather and the distances involved, but when it arrived the captain from 22 Squadron was unable to help because of the failing light and the foul weather. Apart from the snow and hail, it was gusting, estimated Chris Briggs, at up to 90 mph. The helicopter made eight attempts, but had to leave the rescue to the climbers.

The Jones party parked at the foot of the cwm at about 4 pm, and confidently expected to see the stretcher party descending very shortly. Jones and two others started off up the cwm, only to find the stretcher in the lower cwm and not up at the victim. Casualty bags and first-aid equipment had gone ahead of them, and they found a moderately easy route into the upper cwm. The helicopter was signalling to them, but the Jones group had no radio and could not understand the hand-signals the helicopter crew were making. It was 5.30 pm when this party reached the victim.

When the rescuers – led by Bill Jepson – had reached Robinson to their surprise they had found very close to him two snow-covered bodies. They were able to establish that they had fallen earlier in the day and their names were John and Patricia McCarten. No alarm had been raised for the McCartens, and it was not possible to say exactly where they had fallen from. Jones gave what first-aid he could to Robinson, who did not seem to be too seriously hurt. Neither Robinson nor Britnell had been aware of the bodies so close to where they were lying. The helicopter had stayed nearby, and at the team's request dropped two Neil Robertson stretchers to help the MRT take the injured man and the two bodies down to the road. The St Athan team had been contacted and by this time they also had arrived. Robinson, having been given a painkiller, was put onto one stretcher, and he started his journey down with the main RAF party and Chris Briggs. As the Robinson stretcher crew began the descent down the cwm, Jones turned to the two bodies. Looking at the man, he found no pulse and no breathing, but could not find much serious injury. Most of his torso was bare, and Jones suspected that exposure had caused his death. The young woman Patricia McCarten had severe skull and spinal injuries. Both seemed to be

Joe Wiggins climbing in Stob Coire nam Beith. Though at opposite ends of the country, the photograph indicates the conditions in which the McCartens met their death.

reasonably well-equipped though there was no sign of packs or ice-axes.

There were only six left to carry down the two bodies and McCarten's was heavy. Jones's knee was beginning to play up and he was not sorry to meet some more of the St Athan team lower down so that the stretcher burden could be shared. It was very dark by now and it was with relief that they finally saw flares which someone from lower down had sent up to light their way; in fact they were nearly hit by one. It was at about this point that Jones had what he described as a short but conclusive argument with a local press photographer who wanted to get a shot of a body on a stretcher. The whole incident had taken 9½ hours, from the call-out at 2 pm to the conclusion at 11.30 pm. However, by the end of the day, the Valley team had spent a total of 13½ hours on the hill.

John McCarten, aged 28, had been a scientist at the Atomic Energy Authority; his wife Patricia, 26, a school teacher. In Tony Jones's rescue diary is a letter from John McCarten senior, the father of the dead man, addressed to Dr Jones and the other members of the OVMRT:

> Words fail me, but I want especially to thank you for the firm stand you took at the inquest and for sympathy and understanding for the spirit of those who loved the mountain. In due course I will contact you again about support for your good work.

The coroner in question, with whom Jones had crossed swords before (and has since), had criticised people who climb on mountains and need to be rescued. Jones pointed out to him strongly that the McCartens were experienced climbers and that had positions been reversed they would have been among the rescuers.

Chris Briggs died at the age of 78 when this book was being written. His first mountain rescue work was during Black Easter in 1951 and, along with Hamish MacInnes and Johnnie Lees, he was one of the outstanding characters in mountain rescue in this country. A Yorkshireman, he went to North Wales when he was 34 and bought the Pen-y-Gwryd Hotei; not because he wanted to become a hotelier but because he was in love with Welsh mountains. It is a measure of the importance of the PYG Hotel to climbers that in 1993, when this book appears and RAF rescuers meet in Bangor to celebrate 50 years of RAF Mountain Rescue, the members of the 1953 Everest Expedition will already have gathered at the PYG to celebrate their 40 years; for it was from the PYG that they did much of their training.

11 – Four Boys Missing

The early 70s seemed to be a time for disturbing incidents involving children. In 1971 in the Cairngorms there was a disaster in which six schoolchildren died[41]. Then on February 20th 1972, fourteen young men and three teachers from Dulwich College were descending Snowdon alongside the railway. Underfoot was frozen snow; suddenly three of the youths slipped and went over the edge of Cwm Brwynog, known to experienced climbers as a hazardous spot. All three

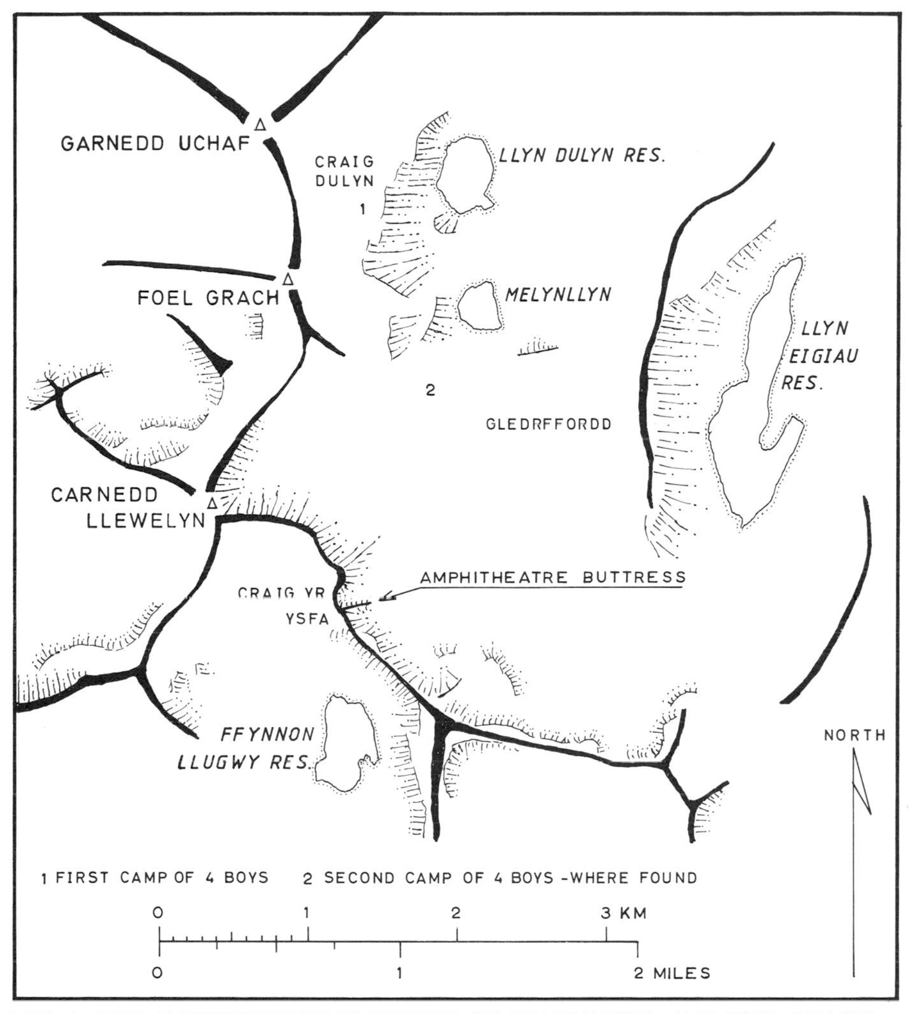

MAP 6 THE AMPHITHEATRE BUTTRESS OF CRAIG Y YSFA; AND FOEL GRACH

The Carneddau, long after the end of the war, continued to keep the North Wales team busy. In 1958, Johnnie Lees recovered a concussed and violent man from the ledge where he had fallen on the Amphitheatre Buttress (see p. 137). In 1973, four boys on a Duke of Edinburgh's Award walk missed their target of Foel Grach and spent two frightening nights in the cold and wet (see p. 160).

were killed and the Valley team was brought in to recover the bodies.

Those two incidents together focused public attention on mountaincraft, especially where young people were concerned. Only three days later, on February 23rd, the ILR, Squadron Leader David Lofts, went to a Thames TV studio to take part in a programme called Tea Break for a discussion on the subject with Ken Wilson, then editor of *Mountain*, and Peter Ledeboer of the Mountain Leadership Training Board.

Not that the problem was a new one. Thirteen years previously, in the days when Lees was the team leader, a school party from Welwyn Garden City had got into trouble on Fox's Path. Lees made some caustic comments in the log, and the officer i/c at the time, Flight Lieutenant J C Andrews, added:

> This matter of clueless school parties has been to the fore in a number of recent accidents. I wrote an article for the Times Educational Supplement or a similar publication. I would like it to be read by schoolmasters as it appears the majority of this class do not read books on mountaineering or articles on mountaineering safety which are published from time to time in journals. Well done Lees for that prompt action in that case.[42]

The excitement in the John Warren Comprehensive School at Hoddesdon in April 1973 was palpable. Graham Brown, Christopher Dell, Terrance Hankin and Stephen Attwood were working their way through the Duke of Edinburgh's Gold Award Scheme, and the next weekend – Easter – they were due to go to North Wales with the teacher Roger Baldwin. They were experienced for their age – about 16 – having already been on previous schemes and exercises, mostly in the Lake District; now they were off on a 50-mile qualifying walk. Arriving at the Hertfordshire Snowdonia Centre in Nant Gwynant, near Bedgellert, they settled themselves in and checked their equipment over: tent, whistles, torches, sleeping-bags, polythene bags, matches, stove, the first day's supply of food, emergency rations, warm clothing. Then the route: Capel Curig, Aber, Bethesda, Llanberis, Nantlle, Bedgellert. They were well prepared. Further food would be collected on the second day at Aber.

On a very cold and damp Good Friday, April 20th, they set off, aiming for their first checkpoint, the shelter on Foel Grach. They were crossing, though they could not know it, Graham's Graveyard. As night approached they found themselves getting colder and colder. Christopher seemed to be going into hypothermia, and, though only three-quarters of a mile short of the destination, they decided to stop, camp and eat. Although they did not reach the Friday checkpoint, nobody thought to tell the police until the Sunday.

Finding what seemed to be a reasonable spot they set up the tent and lit the stoves; the hot food – sausages, potatoes, peas – was welcome. Tired, cold, still frightened, but better for the meal, they climbed into their sleeping-bags. They cannot have been far from the spot where Ken Archer's Anson had crashed thirty years earlier and caused Graham to sit down and work out a systematic search

A search and recovery, 27th Sept 1967, involving Valley MRT, Ogwen Valley & C Flight of 22 Squadron. L to rt. John Calnan (team leader), John Dumbill, 'Buck' Buchanan, Ron James, Pat Donovan

In 1985 the Royal Air Force's Escaping Society awarded its trophy to the Mountain Rescue Service, in a small ceremony at RAF Valley. Front row, centre, Inspector of Land Rescue, Sqn Ldr Gordon Blackburn; second from right is War Off Ray Sefton. Back row, l to r, Flt Sgt Kas Taylor, Flt Sgt Pete Weatherill, Sgt Dick Allen, FO Mick Taylor, Flt Sgt Don Shanks, Sgt Trevor Loftus, Sgt Scoobie Patterson, Sgt Peter Kirkpatrick, Chief Tech Alister Haveron. *Photo: Crown Copyright*

and rescue plan, and where, a few months later, he and Scudamore found the teetotal crewman, wrapped in a parachute, fast asleep in another Anson's gun-turret.

In the morning, Christopher seemed still to be in hypothermia and the others thought he ought to rest; they stayed where they were, which were their instructions in case of any sort of trouble. By the end of the day, however, he seemd to have recovered. Sunday dawned and they moved on. Two other boys, Graham and Terrance, started to get intensely cold, and when the time came to pitch camp that evening – still about 500 yards short of their **first** checkpoint – they, in their turn, were too cold to help, though Christopher seemed to have recovered. By this time, the fact that they were missing had been reported.

Two blows added to their misery. The matches were damp; the stove could not be lit and they were able to eat only a little cold, uncomforting food. Then when they were turning in for the night, they found that the sleeping bags were also wet. They decided to sleep in the polythene bags, two boys to a bag (it would have been better, commented Tony Jones, had they slept two to a sleeping-bag, wet though they were).

Generally speaking, their morale remained fairly high, but they went into something of a downward spiral of increasing cold and depression on the third day. To keep their spirits going then, they sang hymns. Elsewhere, people who were very familiar with those hills had gathered, made plans and were already searching. Their transistor radio reassured the boys that a search was on for them, and from that point they became quite happy again.

The Ogwen Valley team on the Sunday had already picked up someone with a suspected broken leg and sent him off to hospital. No sooner had they finished this when, at 3.45 pm, they were told of the four boys and that nothing had been heard of them since they started out from Capel at 9 am on the Friday. An initial search by vehicle was immediately started. It was quite a fair evening, but with cloud on the hilltops. Tony Jones decided to call in RAF Valley and spent the night planning the parties, routes and climbs for the Monday.

Forty people from the Valley and Ogwen Valley teams started out at 7 am on Monday, walking the hills, but at 5 pm had found nothing. Parties coming off the hill reported foul conditions, with white-out on the tops, 'so party searches not all that effective.'[41] Two Ogwen Valley leaders, Ron James and Tony Jones, were joined by the Valley leader, Has Oldham, that evening to plan the next day's searching. When they had finished, a massive operation had been set up for the Tuesday.

The MRT of RAF Stafford, exercising in the Lake District, was called in and the search-and-rescue helicopters of 22 Squadron were on standby. Until that time the weather had been too bad to consider the use of a helicopter: one of the searchers had said that at one time it was a complete white-out – they were completely blinded by driven snow. With the three main teams and their helpers,

A base camp for a big joint call-out in North Wales

Past and present: Colin Pibworth retired from the Air Force to live in North Wales. Here he is with 'Heavy' Whalley when the latter was deputy team leader at Pib's old stamping ground, Valley.

450 were involved on the Tuesday morning. As well as the RAF teams from Valley and Stafford, and Ogwen Valley, there were civilian MRTs of Derby, Rhinog, Llanberis, Dyfed Powys Constabulary, Stockbridge; there was a contingent from the Search & Rescue Dog Association; there were parties from the London University Mountaineering Club; there were two groups of National Park Wardens, from Snowdonia and Merioneth; and there were other helpers too. The communications, crucial with so many different organisations involved, were under the charge of Dave Curtis, a civilian who often worked with RAF Valley.

A 22 Squadron Whirlwind took Tony Jones over Craig y Dulyn, just east of Foel Grach, when the weather started improving at 11 am, and they found an orange plastic bag which, they felt, had probably been in the boys' kit. Then, later, a boy could be seen moving below, without any kit. Joy very nearly turned to horror, for when the helicopter landed he started, in his weary, confused yet excited state, running straight towards the tail rotor. The navigator, Flight Lieutenant Stan Burt and Tony Jones together jumped out, grabbed the lad and began to calm him down. Then he was able to point up the hill towards their camp.

The helicopter moved up there and picked up the other three, but the pilot, Flight Lieutenant Gordon Mitchell, had to dump some fuel before he could collect Jones. By 11.40 am the four boys and the searchers had been dropped off at the Ogwen Valley premises. Cheerful and apparently fit again, the boys were plied with tea, soup and sandwiches, and questioned by reporters. At the time that Stan Burt and Tony Jones had picked them up, they had been down to their emergency rations of mint cake, chocolate and glucose tablets.

All search parties were called in, but it was 6.15 pm by the time some of the Ogwen Valley people were able to leave. Tony Jones was angry, as other rescue leaders had been angry in previous years. He was quoted as saying:

> The boys should never have been out in that weather. When they set out it was cold, wet and just horrible.
> I did not go out that day and the boys should never have set off, either. When you are only 15 and 16 you have not much in the way of reserves, either mentally or physically, if things go wrong.[44]

Still, as a mountain rescue operation it was a classic. The boys had shown a great deal of common sense – arguably more than the school authorities – and the many rescue teams involved had worked together very well. Finally, there had been some superb flying in dangerous conditions by Gordon Mitchell, Stan Burt and their winchman Master Aircrewman Stanley Ormeston.

12 – An Empty Lorry

In normal circumstances, a team gets called out. Just occasionally, it virtually has to call itself out.

The lorry had been standing empty by the Lower Cwm Bridge near Crickhowell on the edge of the Brecon Beacons, with the keys in the ignition. Nobody took much notice at first; then a report came in that a man was missing. Eventually the name was linked to the lorry. He had a history of disturbed behaviour: drug addiction, attempted suicide, psychiatric problems leading to detention, nine months in Colchester military remand centre. A Jehovah's Witness, he was said to be very 'troubled' in his faith. He was 22, married, with one child.

On April 19th 1977, the day after the lorry first appeared, the police undertook a sweep search of the immediate area, with the help of Longtown and Brecon Mountain Rescue Teams. News of this appeared in the press, and Flight Lieutenant C C Wyver, the officer i/c, telephoned the police to offer the help of the RAF St Athan team. There were no plans for any further searches, he was told.

Two days later, PC Clayton from Crickhowell police station telephoned at 2.15 pm to say that the team's help would be appreciated after all. He said that the intention was to do a sweep search of the area surrounding Lower Cwm, starting at 9 the next morning and involving other rescue services. Wyver agreed. A Tannoy call brought the team members into the section and they were briefed at 3 pm. They prepared the vehicles and equipment and stood down until 6.45 the next morning. An early breakfast at the airmen's mess at Llantwit Major, then they were on the road by 7.25 am, the radio vehicle going ahead with Wyver and the deputy team leader so that they could check the location of the search base with Crickhowell and radio the information back to the convoy. They arrived at the bridge just before 8 am, closely followed by the other vehicles.

Brian Davies of Longtown MRT was acting as controller on behalf of the police, but was much hampered by the lack of a communications centre. Wyver offered him the use of the St Athan radio van, and this was gratefully accepted. From then on the vehicle was manned by Wyver, Davies and his assistant. The civilian agencies found that this revolutionised their communications. Full contact could be kept with the various search parties throughout the operation, allowing full monitoring – a novelty for them. However, there was trouble in keeping in touch with Rescue Co-ordination Centre (RCC) at Plymouth, and this was by no means the first time. The choice of frequencies was limited and because of the technical vagaries of high frequency transmission, messages sometimes had to be relayed by way of Northern RCC in Pitreavie.

The usual sweep search pattern was adopted, with different teams allocated different areas. St Athan drew the area alongside the stream called Grwyne Fawr, and started at 9.50 am. This was an extremely difficult patch, with much undergrowth and afforestation, but they were finished by mid-afternoon. They moved on then to the southern part of Partrishaw Hill, which with its open high ground and lower enclosed slopes was much easier to work. Finishing here at 6.45 pm, they returned to the search base. No trace of the missing man had been found by anybody. There was a brief moment of excitement when a hypodermic syringe was found, but someone knowledgeable in these matters identified it as the type used to inoculate sheep.

A helicopter from 22 Squadron was, by chance, in the Brecon area at the time. Gallingly, however, the radio van could not contact either of the RCCs, and the helicopter could not be brought into the search. Wyver asked in his report if the radio equipment could be changed for a better model.

127 people had been involved in the fruitless search. The St Athan team now decided to return to station. Their original intention, if the search continued over an extended period, was to work from St Athan, and therefore no rations had been taken. They had been prepared to stay in the search area overnight, using Compo rations. But the late return meant that special arrangements had to be made for an evening meal, and at Wyver's request the police telephoned the Station Duty Officer.

The St Athan team had for a long time experienced problems with its motor fleet, especially the Bedford RL, then the RAF's standard 3-ton truck. On the run home that evening, the RL, which had been the subject of complaints in numerous reports over the previous months, could manage only 18 mph on one particular 1 in 26 incline about 3½ miles long, and this effort caused the exhaust pipe to glow red hot. Wyver yet again asked that the suitability of this model be looked at, as it had visited the MT section far too frequently. It was 9 pm before they got back to St Athan, to enjoy the food which the officers' mess cook, Corporal Thompson, had cheerfully prepared for them during several hours' extra work on this Saturday evening.

Had St Athan MRT not offered its services, they would never have been called upon. In contrast to the rapport built up between Valley and the civilian rescuers and police in North Wales over the previous 25 years, the convention in the south of the Principality seemed to be that the choice of mountain rescue team was left to the Committee of the South Wales Mountain Rescue Association. This had six co-ordinators who were all members of civilian teams and they tended to select the teams they knew, usually the one with which they were directly connected. One of the problems of this policy was that civilian teams had manning problems during working hours; not a problem shared by the RAF. Another was that, at that time at least, they were not as well-equipped as the RAF teams.

Flight Lieutenant Wyver made the point in his report that the Committee was depriving itself of much of the best expertise and equipment in the saving of human life. He suggested that the police forces in South Wales should be made aware of the services which could be offered by RAF St Athan's MRT. He and the team leader, Sergeant T A (Tom) Taylor, had already made first informal moves, but liaison was, he felt, needed at a higher level. For instance, he pointed out, the police had been under the impression that if they called on any RAF services, MRT or helicopter, they would have to be paid for; and they were surprised to learn that an RAF team could be on the road within 30 minutes of receiving a call.

Three years later the Civil Mountain Rescue Committee in its annual accident summary said:

> As always the RAF has given enormous help to injured mountaineers. The Service deserves the utmost gratitude both for the rescues it has performed over the years, the knowledge that is available to help when needed and for providing training in helicopter rescue for team members.[45]

But what of the poor disturbed and confused owner-driver of the abandoned lorry, who had taken up 1016 man-hours, excluding travelling time? He later turned up many miles away in England.

13 – Blizzard

Until a series of major public disasters at the end of the decade, the 80s were, on the whole, routine for the Welsh teams. Routine, but busy, probably busier than ever before. But the busyness was generally of the type concerned with cragfast climbers, ill-prepared walkers, would-be or actual suicides, lost young parties, missing children. Many were tragedies for the people most closely involved; but for the experienced mountain rescuer, these things, tragic though they are, are the stuff of everyday action, which do not stimulate more than a brief Report 'A', written, filed, forgotten. For the new young mountain rescuer they act as a maturing agent, helping to prepare him for the big one; until he goes out on his first real call-out, he has probably never seen a body. But then for some, nothing was quite sufficient preparation for what was to come in 1988 and 1989.

In the meantime, then, St Athan and Valley turned out to help where they could, very much now part of the local communities. In December 1981, St Athan had been below strength for some time, but had recently been successful in recruiting seven novices. Whilst they were welcome, it did mean that the experience level across the team had dropped considerably. The novices, however, were about to get their baptism of fire.

The winter of 1981/82 was a bad one and it hit South Wales in all its fury on December 13th. That weekend the Saints were returning from an exercise somewhere in mid-Wales, with the Team Leader, Sergeant Trevor Loftus, in charge. They had been driving through a blizzard and finally were stopped by blocked roads in Brecon. The police, overwhelmed by the conditions, spotted the convoy vehicles and asked for help in recovering motorists from buried cars. Loftus agreed, and nine such were recovered and taken to Brecon Police Station. But it did not end there. A pregnant woman was on her way to hospital, whether in the family car or an ambulance the records do not say. She, too, was collected and was taken to Brecon Hospital. One would think that if anything could get through deep snow, it would be a snow-plough. But no: the team picked up two snow-plough crews and brought them out. Lastly, an armed soldier was reported to be missing in a lorry in deep snow somewhere on the A4067 which runs north-south in the valley between the Brecon Beacons and the Black Mountain. He could not be found, but turned up in Trecastle, not very far away, the next morning. Why was he armed? What was the lorry carrying? Again, the records do not tell us.

Their tasks done, the team finally reached St Athan; three weeks passed. Then on January 8th, the South Wales Police asked them again for help in icy, blizzard conditions.

The only emergency services able to operate (a perfect example of 'Whensoever' in action), the team worked in three- and four-man crews from the Mountain Rescue Section and from police stations at Barry and Llantwit Major, handling no less than 102 incidents. Still working when the snow ceased and the temperature dropped considerably, they met drifts of up to 20 feet, and fog.

Over the next four days, the team took to hospital – Cardiff Royal Infirmary, Llandough Hospital, Sully Hospital, or the RAF's Princess Alexandra Hospital, Wroughton – five women whose pregnancies were near their time, ten people (with the help of 22 Squadron) who had suffered heart attacks, a renal patient for emergency dialysis and 27 other people who had suffered various injuries. Two were picked up who had taken accidental overdoses, and three attempted suicides. Four emergency drug deliveries were made, and food and milk were taken to old people and to babies. Co-operating with 22 Squadron, dialysis-machine technicians were taken to Pontypool, doctors to emergency cases and maintenance engineers to Aberthaw Power Station, the source of South Wales's electricity.

Ten dead were recovered from otherwise inaccessible houses; they searched for lost people in deep snow on the roads and recommended afterwards that 12-foot probes should be issued to all teams. The modern Bell stretcher, with which the teams were then equipped, needed snow runners fitted in the light of this experience.

During this arduous period, the MRT's fleet had been augmented by crash ambulances and Land Rovers from the MT pool, and a total of 2,563 miles had been driven. Then, on January 12th, conditions eased sufficiently for the Saints to be stood down, the last of the vehicles returning from Barry on the 13th. Gradually the civilian ambulance services resumed their normal work, but helped for a time by the army.

Tragic though it is for many, a period of intense activity like this is always a good morale-booster for an RAF team, the status of which is visibly raised both on station and in the community. Loftus was able to report that a number of new recruits had come forward as a result of the publicity, initially from the December operation but even more from the January one. This was helped by the corporate AOC-in-C's Commendation presented to the team during a ceremony in March. Similarly, the team's officer, Flight Lieutenant P S de-Camps, commented that whilst training had suffered, this was more than outweighed by the experience gained and the interest generated. His team was now up to its full quota – an enviable position to be in. This was particularly gratifying for him, since in the previous quarter's report he had had to admit concern over the manning levels and an unacceptable onus placed on experienced members.

Chapter 3 – Footnotes

[1] Letter to writer 17/1/92
[2] Conversation with writer 13/2/92
[3] Note to writer 24/1/92
[4] Ken McCoy to writer 23/1/92
[5] Report 28/9/55
[6] Letter to writer 5/2/92
[7] Valley MRT log
[8] Station Air Traffic Controller
[9] Station Standing Orders
[10] Letter to writer 15/1/92
[11] Letter to writer 5/2/92
[12] Valley log 3/6/57
[13] Letter to writer 24/4/92
[14] Letter to writer 20/1/93
[15] Conference minutes 5/12/57
[16] Letter to writer 5/5/92
[17] Quoted in a letter from Wing Commander C W Cornish, Air Ministry, to Group Captain J T Shaw, RAF Valley, 5/3/58
[18] Telegram RAFMA to Lees 30/4/58
[19] Letter to writer 29/5/92
[20] Description of the Aspain incident sent to the writer May 1992
[21] Letter Sims to Davies 8/8/60
[22] Appendix to agenda for 1951 conference
[23] Appendix to minutes of 1951 conference
[24] Air Ministry to Commands 13/3/53
[25] Sgt H A Bevis to Sqn Ldr H B Pashley 27/6/55
[26] Minutes of conference 6/12/56
[27] Minutes of conference 5/11/57
[28] Sqn Ldr J A Sims to APS to S of S 21/5/62
[29] Julian Amery to Ernest Marples 6/6/62
[30] Ernest Marples to Julian Amery 9/6/62
[31] Amery to Marples 3/7/62
[32] Marples to Amery 12/7/62
[33] Minutes of conference 26/2/68
[34] Minutes of conference 19/2/69
[35] Sqn Ldr D Lofts to S9e3(Air) 27/7/73
[36] Sqn Ldr A R Gordon-Cumming to Sergeant J R Lees April 1957
[37] Flying Officer C M Seeley to Under Secretary of State for Air 14/5/57
[38] Howells to McGowan 14/7/69
[39] The St Athan team
[40] Letter to writer 6/1/91
[41] Chapter IV Section 10
[42] Valley log 21/4/60
[43] Tony Jones's records
[44] Daily Express 25/4/73
[45] Quoted in quarterly report of ILR Squadron Leader G J. Blackburn, 7/8/80

The West Freugh MRT, returning from exercise in the Lake District in 1952, pauses for a brew-up on the Dumfries road. Flt Lt John Berkeley – later for many years a GP in Fort William – is second left, leaning against the Humber radio van, formerly ambulance. *Photo: David Horton*

West Freugh's Humber radio van in 1954. Readers of a nervous disposition are advised not to look too closely at the tread on the front tyres. The unsophisticated left-turning indicator can clearly be seen: a small steel semaphore arm operated by the driver who tugged on a piece of wire. For turning right, he used hand signals. *Photo: R Mackay, courtesy Keith Ford*

CHAPTER IV – ROOM AT THE TOP

Scotland: 1951-1992

There is always room at the top. Daniel Webster 1782-1852

1 – Kinloss and Dattner

Encouraged by the success of the Snowdonia course the previous October Air Ministry Rescue confirmed the second course for February 1952, based at the Rothiemurchus Hut near Aviemore. Owned by the 51st Highland Division, for 1s 6d (7½p) a head it provided good basic accommodation: bunks, cooking utensils, heat and light. Flight Lieutenant John Berkeley of West Freugh was to be the course leader, helped by Flight Lieutenant Mike Mason, then at Edzell, Mike Holton of the Air Ministry, and Sergeant Johnnie Lees from Valley. Spread over twelve days, the course was intended to cover 'general mountain craft'. In the event, the weather prevented any high-grade climbing, and such ice as was present was not suitable for instructional purposes.

However, the snow was deep and soft during the first week, making climbing very strenuous and a good test of stamina. Frequent snow storms provided opportunities for navigational training. A thaw came during the second week, removing the loose snow and leaving the hard snow underneath. From then on, harder snow-climbs could be tackled.

Two extra opportunities were provided by the course: to break in a new type of mountaineering boot and to test the recently-authorised nylon ropes (replacing hemp). The latter followed on a detailed report to Squadron Leader Sinclair – the Mountain Rescue supremo at the time – from Mike Holton as recently as October 1951. Joss Gosling was one of the trainees and his diary records:

Wed 20 February The whole team demonstrated snow and ice work and the use of stretchers to the Press on Castle Hill.
Thurs 21 February While the cloud level had been very low most days of the course on the Cairngorms, we watched the sunshine on the Monadhliath Mountains across the Spey Valley ever[y] day. Being our last full day, seven of us decided to follow one of the few tracks which lead in to the heart of the Monadhliath's with the Land Rover.
Our first attempt on a track just north of Loch Alvie proved unsuccessful due to a locked gate, so we pressed on to another track half a mile south of Kincraig and this time we managed to get two miles until a deep snow drift stopped us. We climbed out and walked to the summit of An Suidhe (1776ft) a really pleasant top with a magnificent view of the Cairngorms and Spey Valley spread out before us. After a short rest we returned to the Land Rover and adjourned to the "Pot Luck" at Aviemore for refreshments and returned to base.[1]

Kinloss was acting as the host to the course and by this stage Flight Lieutenant David Dattner, replacing Dawes, was the team officer.

David Dattner is a man who has aroused as much controversy as any. Originally an air gunner, then a wireless operator/air gunner, he graduated to be a senior signals instructor on the V Force. The controversy arose through his methods of training in first-aid for the Mountain Rescue Service, particularly at Kinloss. He had a number of team members at Kinloss who found it difficult to face death or trauma in crashed aircraft.

This is what concerned me, when they refused and were sick all over the place when you came to anything you really needed to rescue. I mean, if there was any blood they didn't want to know and if there was a dead person they certainly didn't want to know, and this as I said is why I started all this other business and very successfully I might say, because it made a lot of difference, *a lot of difference.*.[2]

There was an episode with a crashed aircraft containing thirteen bodies, when Dattner looked round, he says, and found he was alone on the hill. The whole team had left him and was down at the bottom again. He went to get them, literally kicking them back up the mountain, telling them that if they did not want to do this sort of thing they should just join a mountaineering club. He believes that his rough-and-ready technique seemed to work, and the young men then accepted the horror of the situation and got on with their work. However, he realised that there was a need for serious education. His radical form of training came in two phases. First of all he taught the team members how to use a hypodermic syringe for morphine. He had a supply of morphine but nobody would use it except himself. He explained in great detail when to use it and he made them plunge the needle into his legs.

Each kid had to do it ten times without anything to squeeze because I made sure they weren't going to kill me, so I took out the plunger.

The second phase was teaching them how to sew up a wound. Dattner would cut himself: then rather than using a surgeon's needle for the sewing process, he would use a hypodermic needle and thread nylon through the length of its cavity. Why? is a question that comes to mind. Assuming the sewing-up is a reasonable thing to do in the first place – which is, to say the least, open to argument, since there are other ways of closing a wound in an emergency – why use this strange method? Because, replies Dattner, if he had tried to use the 'fancy surgeon's way of doing it' it would have taken too long to teach them.

Infection, predictably, was a problem. Dattner admits he was always in trouble in this respect.

I was in hospital several times and the doctors criticised. I said "Look, I don't want any criticism; if you've got a better method, tell me".

He said, "No, we haven't got any better method".

I said, "Shut up then; you're paid to look after me if I'm hurt. I'll do my thing if you can't think of any better way of doing it. Don't interfere, just get me better each time I come in here."

Squadron Leader David Dattner briefing the Kinloss team, September 1951. He was later to be Inspector of Mountain Rescue. *Photo: Joss Gosling*

In spite of all the criticism his methods have engendered over the years, Dattner still claims now that they paid off and he is still glad he used them. They seemed to be as much concerned with getting the team members used to handling traumatised bodies, alive or dead, as with repairing them. He mentions a car crash that one of his convoys came across – four people with much blood spurting: he does not believe that the team members would have gone anywhere near those people without his training.

In April 1952, Kinloss MRT was involved in an episode where a woman survived but the men did not. Only two months after the course, the Kinloss team was back very close to the Rothiemurchus Hut. Not far from Aviemore is Glenmore Lodge, a training centre for mountaineers; and there has been close liaison between RAF Mountain Rescue and the Lodge's staff. David Stead, aged 20, from Leeds, and Margot Weaving, aged 21, from Chester, were climbing from here on a morning in April 1952 with an instructor, John Harvey, from Manchester, who was about 30. They were nearing the end of a week's course and were climbing in Coire an Lochain when all three fell about 500 or 600 feet, roped together.

Margot Weaving found herself lying in deep snow. Gradually she regained consciousness and tried to make sense of the situation. Not far away she could see Stead and Harvey, ominously still. Her own legs seemed to be strangely twisted; blood was coming from somewhere. She was there for many hours, unable to move, with nobody coming near, hungry and cold.

Harvey, Stead and Weaving were not missed until the course members met at the dinner table that night. At 7 pm, two search parties were organised at the Lodge from the forty people there. Fortunately it was known roughly where they would have been climbing. Meanwhile, in the gathering darkness, Weaving had remembered the advice she had been given at the beginning of the course: "If you get into any sort of difficulties at night, keep flashing your torch."

After what seemed an age, she became aware that people were approaching and called out to them. When the Glenmore Lodge parties reached her, they decided that it would be unsafe to try to take her down in the darkness, and made her as comfortable as they could for the time being. Harvey and Stead, they concluded, were beyond help. Then as the dawn light started streaking the sky, they put Weaving on their new Duff stretcher, and began to take her down, as well as the bodies of Harvey and Stead – a four-hour descent – and on the way were met by the RAF Kinloss team with David Dattner.

Dattner saw the two bodies covered with blankets. Then he had an angry conversation with someone from Glenmore Lodge:

"Who put the blankets over their heads?"

"I did."

"Were they dead when you did this?"

"Of course they were."

"How do you know they were dead?"

"You could tell."

"You bloody well can't tell! First of all, if somebody's frozen stiff it's like rigor mortis, and there's a way to determine this. Secondly, did you do any tests at all? Thirdly, what right have you got to suppose death when you're not competent to suppose death?"

He told the unfortunate person from Glenmore Lodge how to confirm death and not to take the obvious signs at their face value.

Dattner was right. Exhaustion-exposure – the combination of very cold conditions with extreme exhaustion – leads to the cooling of the inner parts of the body, the body core. That in turn leads to declines in the functions of the brain, heart, liver, lungs and muscles. Someone suffering from exhaustion-exposure can look, to the untutored eye, like someone who is dead. Many such people have been revived.

The armed forces do not easily take to people with ideas that are radically different from accepted practice, and the Royal Air Force is probably as conservative as the others in this respect. Nevertheless, Dattner was made Inspector of Mountain Rescue (IMR) in March 1954, succeeding Group Captain R E G Brittain, and moved from Kinloss to London. The first conference at which Squadron Leader Dattner presided was in April 1954. After being introduced by Squadron Leader Sinclair, the Chairman, he said that he wished all teams to understand the standard which he would expect. This he put under four headings: discipline; training; co-operation with non-service climbing bodies; the need to weed out climbers whose standards of knowledge and behaviour fell below those required in military Mountain Rescue Teams.

He remembers reporting on one team when he was in the IMR post, commenting that the Officer in charge was not doing his job properly. A group captain came back at him: "How dare you speak about one of my officers like this?"

The report on the file reveals that there was a lack of team spirit; the officer, though keen, was inexperienced; and although the standard of first-aid was high, that of navigation was low.

It is remarkable that Dattner's unusual training methods did not come to the attention of senior officers; or if they were known, that they were not stopped. It is even more surprising that a team officer with such controversial methods should have been selected to act as Inspector. Teams, team leaders, team officers, all talk amongst themselves. Surely these things were discussed? Clearly, therefore, the fact that under his guidance, Kinloss had improved out of all recognition had been seen and approved of in Whitehall despite those unusual methods.

But, it has to be acknowledged that for many people, David Dattner was a charismatic leader of men; some would go through fire and water for him. Some who served under him remember him with affection. Not all, though. One flight sergeant who was a flight engineer on Sunderlands at 57MU, Wig Bay, Harry Hawthorn, remembers Dattner visiting the team during his IMR period and demonstrating the Dattner methods of first-aid. Hawthorn told Dattner that he was putting himself at grave risk and was putting the team in an invidious position, declined to take any further part in the proceedings, and walked out.

In June 1955, after just over a year in the post, Dattner handed over the IMR mantle to Sandy Gordon-Cumming, who remembers Dattner's training techniques with something akin to horror.

David Dattner, who with dark film star looks can be seen in many newspaper cuttings of the time struggling through the Cairngorm snow followed by the Kinloss team, is at the time of writing in Israel running a children's home. After his retirement from the Air Force and before going to Israel, he was involved in helping deprived children, initially refugees from the Holocaust. He would take children from London to the Snowdon Ranger Youth Hostel to give them a breath of air for a few days. The hostel warden there was Joe Gianelli, who had been a climber in the '30s and '40s. (He was a close friend and climbing companion of Gordon Leigh, whom he met at RAF Llandwrog during the war.) Joe's little son Glyn enjoyed these visits and still remembers them well[3]: he in turn became an RAF rescuer in the '70s.

Life at Kinloss continued. The team had a lively turn-of-the-year – 1954-55.

A 5-day call-out on the "Ben" in the early 80s: two climbers. Kinloss attended.
Photo: Kinloss team member

On December 19th, a navy team left the top of Ben Nevis and aimed for the Carn Mor Dearg arête. Unfortunately, they were off-target and were descending a convex slope which proved to be fatally deceptive. The leader, Lieutenant Harding, suddenly became aware of Petty Officer Hunt glissading past, losing control and then his ice-axe, and sliding over the edge. Following him was Petty Officer Richardson, running and desperately trying to kick steps; Richardson, too, lost control and disappeared. After this came Midshipman Cass, Petty Officer Laws and Wren McWhirter. Of the original party of eleven, five had gone. The remaining six split up, three descending to the bodies of their companions, three to get help, which brought out the Kinloss team.

Then, on Boxing Day, an army officer went missing. He had left the head of Glen Nevis, heading north, and hoping to get to Spean Bridge. The search proved fruitless and was eventually abandoned. His body was found seven years later, well away from his stated route.

2 – Death on the Hill

Mountain rescuers – who must perforce become hardened to seeing death, often violent death – find it difficult to reconcile themselves to one of their own number going in this way. We have already seen how Mick Aspain met his death in Wales in 1960; but Aspain was not the first.

SAC Alan Grout was an engine fitter at RAF Kinloss. On August 19th 1956 the team was out on exercise in Ardgour, using for the first time the new long-wheelbase Land Rover ambulance. Grout had very little climbing experience and this was his first time with the MRT.[4] In the absence of Corporal Cathcart, who that day was off duty, one of the team members, Sergeant Smith, planned the exercises as he knew the area well. The team was divided into leaders and seconds. Grout was put with a more experienced man, Ward, who took him through belaying, calls, rope technique, and short pitches. Then he and Grout started up the North Face of Garbh Bheinn, graded as difficult but with many different routes.

Ward, misled by a cairn at the bottom of a face to the south of the main north face, started to climb. When he was about a hundred feet up he told Grout to follow him up. This Grout did, but traversed out to Ward's left instead of following the leader's route. When Ward could see what was happening, he told Grout to traverse back so that the rope would be above him and thus effective in holding a fall. However, Grout carried on up and reached a safe spot on a grassy slope.

If he had stayed there, all might have been well. Unfortunately, he tried to get just a little further up, to a ledge at the top of the climb; and this took him farther from the security of the rope. Then Ward saw him slip on the grass, slide helplessly down the slope on his belly, roll over onto his back, tumble up to his feet and finally pitch over the edge. Only the last fifteen to twenty feet was free fall, but with his rolling tumbling down the initial distance, his total fall was estimated by Ward to be between fifty and seventy feet.

Desperately Ward tried to take in the rope to reduce Grout's fall, and indeed he did manage to pull in a great deal. Not enough; Grout fell the length of the active rope, and then swung, a huge long pendulum, with sickening violence against the cliff face. Ward could see that Grout's head had struck and that he hung apparently lifeless on the still-swinging rope. When the shaken and silent team got him down, they could see that he had extensive injuries to his head and face, and guessed that he had been killed instantly.

About a year later, in August 1957, the team camped on the west shore of Loch Linnhe. Ralph Stephenson, who had not been in the RAF at the time of Grout's death, was in the team when a commemorative cairn was built.[5] They had with them all the necessary cement, sand, memorial stone, buckets and trowels, and the next day carried them up Coire an Uibhair. Looking up from the coire bottom, they found an ideal site east of the summit of Garbh Bheinn where Grout had been killed. This face, says Stephenson rightly, ...is impressive, rocky, seamed with gullies and with no evidence of man's intrusion.

The site, then, was ideal. Not so the weather. Preparation of the small site and laying of mortar began, but as soon as mortar was put down it was blown away by the wind. Eventually they gave up the unequal struggle, left the materials, and retreated back down the hill, chilled to the core, to be given rum at the base camp

Building the Alan Grout memorial after his death in 1956. *Photo: Kinloss MRT*

before returning to Kinloss.

A few days later, Stephenson with Paddy Hannon and Benny Paterson returned to the spot and found the stones and what was left of the cement. This had deteriorated somewhat, but they managed to grind the lumps down to some extent, and eventually it was usable.

The cairn stood about five feet high, with a polished stone plaque:

IN MEMORY OF
ALAN GROUT
KINLOSS MOUNTAIN RESCUE TEAM
DIED AUG 19 1956

That job done, they laid a wreath at the foot of the cairn, and took photographs which were sent to Grout's parents. Every August for many years afterwards, Alan Grout's parents sent a wreath which the team placed on the cairn.

On March 15th 1957, in the period between Grout's death and the erection of his cairn, the Mountain Rescue Team at RAF West Freugh had closed. One of its members was an airman called Ian Clough, already being noticed within the service as a climber, and he was transferred to Kinloss. Clough, from Baildon in Yorkshire, was one of those people, like Scottie Dwyer all those years before, whose whole world was climbing. He read about climbing, practised climbing and spent all his RAF pay on climbing equipment. His nickname was 'Dangle' from his habit of practising pegging and climbing with etriers and Prusik loops. He was famous for the assorted hardware he had hanging from his belt.

Clough was in a different class, and it soon became clear that he was raising the standard of the team's rock-climbing at Kinloss generally. His enthusiasm caused him to be late in returning to base camp on one exercise, delaying the team's drive back to Kinloss. He, and the man with him, Michael Bucke, were summarily drenched with water from the Nevis. The same enthusiasm caused him, with Hannon and John Alexander, to be nearly benighted at the infamous 'Mantrap' of the North-east Buttress on another occasion. Using combined tactics they managed to climb the pitch, and reached, well after midnight, the CIC Hut just below the North Face of Ben Nevis. Clough went to hospital the next day with frostbite.

Stephenson climbed with him one day in November 1957. They left Loch Duich at six in the morning, when it was still dark, to climb the first 2900 feet over steep boulder- and heather-strewn terrain. Then they traversed the Five Sisters and went over four other tops before dropping down to the Cluanie Inn. Stephenson is sure that Clough planned everything, including his RAF service, as an adjunct to his climbing ambitions.

In going out with Kinloss MRT, Clough was very much in his own territory. He recorded many first ascents in the area, including one with Terry Sullivan, which he named Kinloss Grooves in 1959.

Discussing the history of climbing in Glen Nevis, Kevin Howett says:

> After a lull through the 1950s when the only visitors were the RAF for training, Ian Clough and Terry Sullivan blitzed the main section of Polldubh in 1958/59. Their routes remain amongst the best here – Resurrection, Phantom Slab, Damnation, Flying Dutchman, and Kinloss Grooves.[6]

Another first ascent by Clough was *Point Five Gully* in early 1959. This was a controversial ascent because Clough and other members of the Kinloss team sieged the route with fixed ropes for five days.

Towards the end of the decade and the beginning of the next, Ian Clough was one of Britain's leading alpinists. In 1962 he achieved, with Chris Bonington, the first British ascent of the North Face of the Eiger. Immediately after that he abandoned plans to go to teacher training college and accepted an invitation from Derek Walker to go on an expedition. Walker, whom we first met in North Wales under the tutelage of Johnnie Lees, had left the Air Force in 1957. In 1962 he went to Patagonia for a second time, taking with him Ian Clough, Chris Bonington and Don Whillans. Walker and Clough climbed the north tower of Paine, Bonington and Whillans the central tower. Two years later, Clough was with Don Whillans again, this time on the Rock and Ice Expedition to Gauri Sanka, when they had to turn back just below the summit. Back in Patagonia in 1967, wintering over until 1968, Clough organised and led an expedition to the Fortress, Walker joining him there from Punta Arenas, where he was then headmaster of the British School.

Then came the assault on Annapurna in May 1970. Whillans and Dougal Haston had made the first ascent of the South Face. Clough was bringing down one of the last loads of the expedition on the very last day. Within a short distance of the base camp, and literally within minutes of the end of the expedition, an enormous serac fell on him.

Hamish MacInnes, who had shared rescue work with Clough in the region around Glen Coe, commented:

> It seems ironical, looking back on the way he was killed on the South Face of Annapurna a few years later, how chance and bad luck caught him unawares in the last few minutes of the expedition. He was probably the ideal team member in rescue work. He had a competence on the mountains both in winter and in summer which would be hard to equal. His mechanical knowledge regarding rescue work was first-class and his attitude to those who were unfortunate in coming to grief was sympathetic and considerate. His loss to our team is something none of us like to speak about for we all feel it personally.[7]

But let his old friend Derek Walker have the last word on Ian Clough:

> So that was the end of Ian Clough who was one of the most notable ex-members of RAF Mountain Rescue, superb climber and one of the least selfish people I'd ever met.[8]

A generation later, RAF Kinloss was home to yet another outstanding climber. Al McLeod joined the RAF Mountain Rescue Service in the winter of 1983/1984 and although this was his introduction to mountaineering, his talent quickly became obvious. By 1986 he was on his first Himalayan expedition, when he played a major part on the British ascent of the south-east ridge of Shivling. The following year he climbed the North Face of the Eiger, the first RAF mountain rescuer to achieve that. By 1988 he was recognised as one of the RAF's leading climbers, and that year he was on the British Services Everest Expedition, and reached within 1,000 feet of the summit, beaten back by weather and winds. Six years after he had taken up mountaineering, and aged only 28, he died, soloing the North Face of the Matterhorn.

3 – Hogmanay in Glen Doll

Those who are neither mountaineers nor rescuers can sometimes be heard saying that if someone gets themselves into trouble on a mountain, that is their problem, and public money should not be spent and others' lives put at risk to get them out of it. Hardly ever will you hear this complaint from those closely involved. In fact, express that opinion within earshot of a mountain rescuer – RAF or civilian – and you are likely to be told, in fairly pithy terms, that you are talking a lot of, well, nonsense. Some of the rescuers have turned the argument on its head: a popular car sticker reads: SUPPORT MOUNTAIN RESCUE – GET LOST!

Rescuers themselves are also mountaineers in the wider sense, and all are acutely conscious that even the best of them may need the help of a rescue team one day. It is a matter of pride at Kinloss that it once helped Chris Bonington out of trouble, albeit a rather young Chris Bonington, on the South Gully of Ben Nevis, in February 1955.

Then, the RAF teams are there anyway, and need to be kept in training. There is no better way of honing a team's skills in recovering aircrew than using them in recovering lost climbers. Apart from the team leader and a handful of other permanent staff, they are volunteers, and give up much of their personal time for training.

There is more validity to the other complaint that is heard. It is this.

From time to time a rescuer or a mountaineer will protest publicly at the foolishness of people who underestimate British mountains, and go up – to take a commonly-quoted example – in slacks, shirt and plimsolls. Certainly it is very easy to be deceived, especially in a tourist centre like Snowdonia or Fort William.

From the bar of the Royal Victoria Hotel in Llanberis, Snowdon can look deceptively benign on a summer's day. There are scores of people milling about. The mountain itself looks beautiful. And there is that quaint little railway which takes you to the top. Alongside the track is a path, the Llanberis Path. What could be easier than to walk up there to the café at the summit, have some lunch and return in the afternoon? Nothing, until the weather suddenly comes down. And those who are not familiar with mountains can have no conception of how quickly conditions can change, how lethal they can become and how dangerous that path can be.

Pilot Officer Jim Cockburn, the officer in charge of RAF Kinloss MRT in 1959, made some comment on this subject when Kinloss was given an award by the Aberdeen Press and Journal. After mentioning those with insufficient clothing, and often without map or compass, he added:

> They come to the top even when the cloud is down to 2000ft or so. I can only suppose that a watchful Providence is looking after them, or perhaps they follow the trail of sweets papers and orange peel left behind by those who have been up before them. Judging by last summer, cairns will soon become redundant.

He added that people sometimes wondered why the RAF teams assisted with civilian rescue operations. He pointed out that in the event of an aircraft crash the RAF would almost certainly need civilian assistance. It was, therefore, only fair that the RAF should help in civilian rescue when the occasion demanded it. He was speaking after a period of seven years when there had been more than forty deaths in Inverness-shire alone: " grim reminder" he said, "that Scottish mountains deserved respect, especially in winter."

The Press and Journal had presented to both Kinloss and Leuchars MRTs framed copies of a strikingly dramatic picture taken by Gordon Bisset, a staff photographer, the previous New Year, 1959. Both teams were descending Glen

Doll with the body of one of five lost walkers, all of whom died in atrocious weather. Bisset was justifiably proud of the picture and had been impressed with the devotion to their task of the two teams. At the ceremony with Cockburn were Flight Lieutenant Ian Hamilton and Flight Sergeant Bill Brankin of Leuchars, and Flight Sergeant Ian Martin of Kinloss.

The five lost men were all members of the Universal Hiking Club of Glasgow: Robert McFaul, Frank Daly, Henry Duffin, a man called Devlin, and 17-year-old James Boyle. Daly was 40, the others in their 30s, and they had decided that on New Year's Day, a Thursday, they would walk from Braemar Youth Hostel across Jock's Road, the twelve-mile mountain pass that links Braemar with Glen Doll, then down to Glen Clova where there is another youth hostel.

Heavy snow fell after they had left and eventually the fact that they were overdue was reported to the police. Parties of police, gamekeepers and others went out from Braemar and Glen Clova on the Sunday, three days after the beginning of the fateful walk. At the same time, the RAF was informed, and Leuchars was called out. On the first day of the search, young Boyle was found dead in a gully overlooking Glen Doll.

Relatives of the others met searchers as they returned from Jock's Road, only to be told that there was now no hope. For the time being, the police called off further searches:

There is absolutely no hope now.
As an exhaustive and careful search has been made of the whole area between Braemar and Glen Doll there is now no hope of finding the missing persons alive.
And as conditions are extremely difficult and dangerous the search has been abandoned and will be resumed as soon as conditions are suitable.
Search by unorganised bodies would be most dangerous and should not be attempted at the risk of further loss of life. Grateful acknowledgement is made to all who so willingly assisted in the search.[9]

The five men had dropped dead one by one. Instead of trying to find shelter together, they had just carried on until they had dropped from exhaustion and exposure, their bodies spread out over a stretch of miles.

It was not until the following spring that the last body was found, after the worst of the snow had melted. The Leuchars team found his body frozen into a waterfall, where it looked as if he had been hoping that there was a cave behind the fall in which he could shelter, but finally had been overcome by the cold.[10]

A further unpleasant touch to this whole episode, but one which carried the saving element of farce, occurred when a stringer for a popular newspaper got wind of the most recent macabre discovery, and went out to the site seeking 'news'. He lifted a corner of the blanket on the Thomas stretcher so that he could photograph the body. Now relations between the popular press and the RAF mountain rescue teams have frequently been uneasy. One team member saw him doing this, and warned him: "Look, mate, do that once more and you've got a problem."

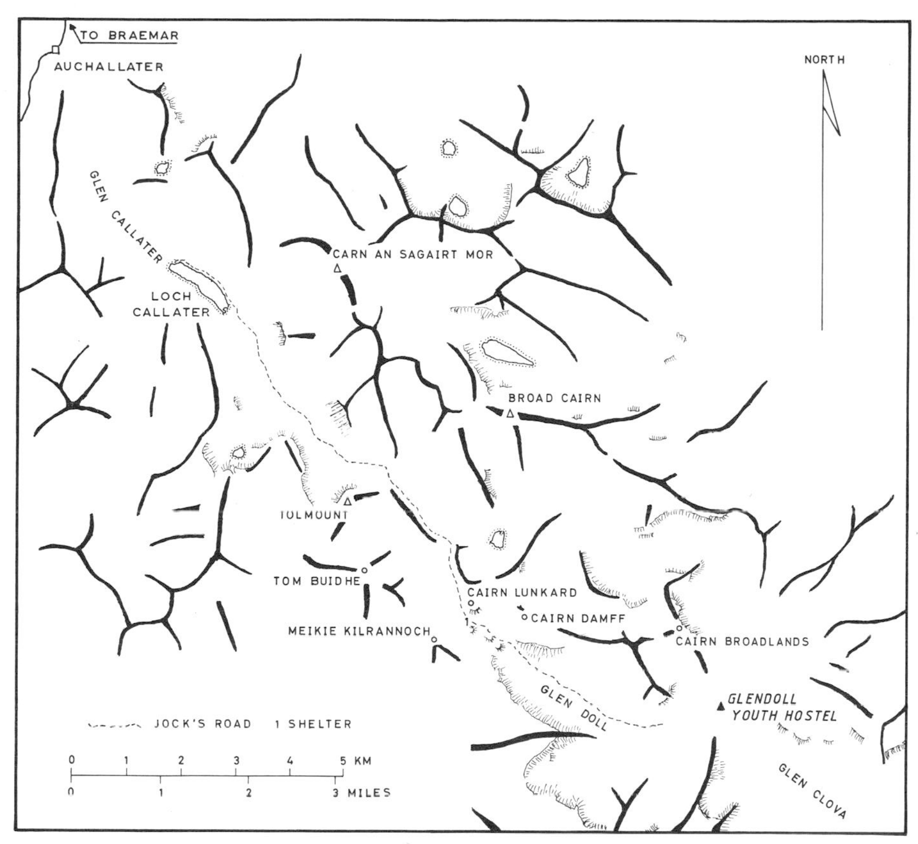

MAP 7 JOCK'S ROAD

The deaths of McFaul, Daly, Duffin, Devlin and Boyle over Hogmanay, 1959

Kinloss and Leuchars MRTs returning from Glen Doll, New Year 1959. *Photo: Gordon Bisset, Aberdeen Journals Ltd*

The journalist moved away. But soon afterwards he was seen trying again, and as forecast, he did have a problem. Several burly mountain rescuers moved to his side. One grabbed his (doubtless expensive) camera, and smashed it with an ice-axe. The journalist became very excited, and, in Sandy Gordon-Cumming's words, said that he was going to report them to everybody from Jesus Christ downwards. "Look," came the reply, "there's twenty-five of us here, all extremely accomplished liars. We all of us saw you trip over that rock and fall on your camera. Think about it, mate!"

However, it has to be recognised that the press have a legitimate job to do (even though it seems that sometimes they could do it more sensitively), and often the requirements of that job can conflict with what other people see as the proper thing to do.

By 1959, Sandy Gordon-Cumming had left the IMR's desk in Whitehall, and was back flying aeroplanes again – the Javelins of 29 Squadron from RAF Leuchars. For the first time, he joined a Mountain Rescue Team, and was the first ex-inspector to do so who had not been with one in the field before his Inspectorate posting. During Gordon-Cumming's time at Leuchars, a Javelin from the squadron he was commanding flew into the Moorfoot Mountains south of Edinburgh. The journey there included a spectacular, police-escorted, headlong dash down Princes Street. He went out with the party to locate the wreck, and when he finally reached it could see that, although the crew never knew what had happened, they and the aircraft were not as badly smashed up as might have been expected.

Before Gordon-Cumming had been up to the wreck and seen what sort of state it and the crew were in, again he had brushed up against a reporter, who said: "I want to come up there with you and take some pictures." Gordon-Cumming did not want published in the press pictures which forced the widows of his pilots to imagine what their husbands might look like. "Terribly sorry," he replied, "got secret equipment on board." He then explained, fingers crossed, that he would have to submit any pictures to the CO for vetting, and the journalist might end up facing a 'D' Notice. The journalist seemed to accept this and left.

Gordon-Cumming went to see the senior policeman on the site, and told him about the incident and that in his opinion the journalist or a colleague would be back in the morning, better briefed. "Aye, I've thought of that," said the policeman. "I've just declared the whole place a foot and mouth area."[10]

4 – Test Flight

Johnnie Squier, at supersonic speed in his prototype English Electric Lightning P1, knew something was badly wrong and did not hesitate. He pulled the blind, the canopy flew off, the seat fired and he found himself shot out into space

40,000 feet above the sea, turning over and over as he arced up, then dropped. He dropped like a stone through the danger area of oxygenless intense cold before the parachute opened automatically at about 10,000 feet with a whoosh and a crack of the cords. Then he was able, in relative peace, to look around as he swayed beneath the canopy towards the Irish Sea far below. He felt badly shaken from the firing of the ejector seat, and it had left his ears ringing intolerably. Still, he was alive. So far, so good, he thought wryly, with a mind to the uncomfortably cold sea in which he would splash down an unknown number of miles from the Galloway shore, with just an inflatable dinghy between himself and drowning or freezing. It was, after all, October.

At the age of 39, Squier was, after a career with the RAF, a test pilot for English Electric. His trade is populated by people who are natural optimists, and he reflected that, as he was on a test flight, his progress would have been carefully monitored and the Air-Sea Rescue people would have seen him coming down. Already the choppers and the launches would be starting on their way.

Hitting the sea, even though he was prepared for it, was an unpleasant shock; he seemed to keep going down, and about thirty feet under the surface he pulled the cord of his Mae West. Inflating on cue, it pulled him sharply back to the surface. Bobbing around in the waves, Squier then was encumbered by the parachute which had just saved his life, and he had to get rid of it. The next move was to find the dinghy pack and inflate that. That, too, worked, and with some difficulty he climbed aboard, then put the covers up, located the food and solar still for future reference, and waited to be picked up.

We first met John Hinde in 1947 when he tried and failed to join St Athan MRT, and then two years after that when he was in the Kinloss team. In the intervening years he had been out of Mountain Rescue, having postings as diverse as Southern Rhodesia, South Wales, Dyce. Then in 1957 he had gone to Leuchars.

On October 1st 1959, they were called out for Squier and the team left Leuchars at 1.50 pm. No-one knew precisely where to start looking, or even whether he had come down over land or water, but it was felt that the best starting point was somewhere in the Kirkcudbright Bay area. They found a farm on the peninsula south of Ross where they could camp. Whilst John Hinde and a couple of others walked across the peninsula and back (seeing the aurora borealis on the way), the team leader and Gordon-Cumming were trying to work out where Squier might come ashore. In the past there had been a shipping disaster in the area (to the Princess Victoria) and they found out where the bodies from that had drifted in. That gave them a good starting point.

Squier was not picked up as he had confidently expected. Darkness crept across the sky and he fixed the light to the top of the dinghy and settled back for the long night to pass, relieved that at least the weather was fair.

On October 2nd, the whole Leuchars team searched along the coastline and

In 1959 the test pilot Johnnie Squier had to eject from an early English Electric Lightning, no. XL628, over the Irish Sea at a high mach number; the fin collapsed after he brought the aircraft out of a roll. This was the first recorded ejection from a British aircraft flying faster than sound. This example, no. XL629, a contemporary of Squier's machine, first flew on the 29th September 1959, and was wihdrawn from use in January 1976. This photograph dates from 1966, and the aircraft is now the gate guardian at RAF Boscombe Down. *Photo: H J Budgen*

across the shore hills. After three and a half hours of very strenuous walking, Hinde received a message on the walkie-talkie recalling his party. Gordon-Cumming and the team leader had been told that the Lightning had been seen near Black Combe in Cumberland. The team packed up and made its way through Carlisle and then south through Penrith, west to Keswick, across the Whinlatter Pass, then south again along the coast to Ravenglass. Near Bootle it was accommodated at an army camp in relative comfort (by Mountain Rescue standards), using the gymnasium for sleeping, cooking and eating, with a bar, billiard tables and baths nearby.

But Squier was still in his dinghy. He had woken after a little sleep to find dawn on the way; he looked around him. There, on the horizon, was land. He started paddling. The current was against him and the land seemed to get no nearer. His persistent earache from the seat explosion and the resulting shock made matters worse. However, eventually he felt that he had turned the corner. Now the tide was in his favour; by the hour the land was getting nearer. Then, manifestly it was within reach. He summoned up more strength, and soon heard the blessed sound of the dinghy scraping over the beach and felt the solid land through the rubber floor. Tumbling out of the dinghy, he scrambled over rocks for about two hundred yards, with difficulty remaining on his feet in the breakers.

Eventually he made it to dry land and staggered up the wide beach after having been at sea for about thirty hours.

From the top of the beach he could see a village, and the first building he reached was a school. The amazed staff told this sunburnt, salt-caked, dishevelled, extremely tired man in a flying suit that he was at Garlieston, in Galloway. He was sat down and given much tea and sympathy; somebody made a telephone call.

Garlieston is just the other side of Wigtown Bay from Kirkcudbright, well within the Leuchars team's search area before it had been diverted by a false sighting to Black Combe. Leuchars MRT had been joined at Bootle by the teams from Leeming and Harpur Hill before the message came through about Squier's safe landing.

After a day's searching all were, in Sandy Gordon-Cumming's words, absolutely knackered, and it was too late to go back that night. They decided to find a pub and have a beer or two.[11] All three teams went out into the near-empty countryside, and eventually came across a very remote little pub which obviously never saw more than a handful of customers. Milling around outside, they finally pushed in through the door one of their number, a young airman from Lancashire. He went up to the empty bar. After an interval, an elderly lady – or, or quote Gordon-Cumming, an aged crone – came shuffling through from the back.

"Aye – what can I do for you?" she asked.

"Eighty pints please," said the Lancastrian in an accent you could cut with a knife.

The landlady looked pointedly over his shoulder to the otherwise empty room. "Pardon?" she asked.

The airman, as if talking to someone inattentive or deaf, turned his voice up a decibel or two.

"Eighty f...... pints!" he shouted; and the seventy-nine other men trooped in to reinforce his point.

Although they had been told of Squier's arrival ashore, next day the three teams stayed to look for wreckage of the Lightning. However, for the men the urgency had gone out of the operation, and they felt cheated by being diverted from a search area that their leaders had worked out for themselves and had proved to be correct.

A little desultory searching went on during the morning with the three teams, but the weather was very hot and dry and most of the day much time was spent in eating and sleeping. Something had to be done to pull the show together and the teams were given the task of searching Black Combe by various routes. Hinde led three team-mates, Alan O'Rourke, 'Sinbad' Roberts and Vic Salvadori, and the Hinde party was the first to the summit. The mountain gradually became crowded as the other teams arrived. Not only the other teams. Hinde noted:

Old dears materialised from somewhere, and asked a lot of questions. I don't blame them. They had to be shown how our T46s worked.[12]

After a spell on the summit, with a little searching but mostly spent admiring the views through the haze, they made a very fast descent. Hinde was carrying the T46, but had an additional handicap of which he was not aware until he reached the bottom of the hill. One of his team-mates, Malcolm Speed, had planted a rock in a pocket of his haversack.

That night, some of the team slept outside in the heat.

All very tired, the three teams returned to their stations the next day. Gordon-Cumming can remember falling asleep whilst driving the ambulance. Hinde was annoyed because he felt that nothing had been achieved and he had missed a climbing weekend. It had not been a happy call-out, on the whole. The only bright spot as far as some were concerned, had been when they had thrown Pete Davis, leader of one of the other teams, into a convenient static water-tank – a traditional punishment for some misdemeanours. Exactly what he was being punished for cannot now be remembered.

Squier had spent a night in hospital in Stranraer, awaiting specialists from London, and his wife and two daughters on their way from their home in Preston. He suffered nothing worse than shock and earache. For Squier, apart from the initial emergency, everything had gone right, every last piece of life-saving equipment had worked. It is not always so.

Just over a month later, on November 10th 1959, another aviator had to make use of the ultimate life-saver, and he too ejected. The pilot of a Royal Navy Scimitar from Lossiemouth, flying at 20,000 feet somewhere over the Cairngorms, found his aircraft had double hydraulic failure. He sent a message at 1.35 pm that he was baling out. Prestwick air traffic control was alerted, and in turn informed the RCC at Pitreavie. A helicopter left RAF Leuchars for a first search and went to Kingussie, to be joined by a Navy helicopter from Lossiemouth. Other aircraft involved included five Sea Hawks, a Shackleton and a Dragonfly. Before the day was out, every available aircraft from within the range of the search area had been put on notice to start searching the next day.

The Leuchars Team made its way to Blairgowrie and Pitlochry, and then alongside the railway, through Glen Garry and over the snow and ice of the Drumochter Pass. The road conditions were treacherous, and as if to emphasise the fact, there on its side on the Pass was a 3-tonner belonging to an SAS unit which was on detachment at Glenmore Lodge. Pressing on to Kingussie, the Leuchars men set up sleeping quarters in the drill hall, with a cooking tent in the entrance to the kirk.

The Air Ministry had appealed for information from the public. The pilot was believed to be using a yellow parachute, which would show up better against the snow-covered ground than the usual white. Darkness fell at 5 pm and the main search ceased. But then the Leuchars team received local reports of flares, lights and shouts not far away, and late that night, John Hinde with four of the team, a policeman and some gamekeepers, drove south through Newtonmore and then on a small side road to Cat Lodge. They combed a wood three times in the snow and darkness, from the road to the back of the River Spey. Nothing was found and Hinde concluded that what the witnesses had seen were searching aircraft, though where the 'shouts' had emanated from was anyone's guess.

Breakfast was early the next day, the 11th, a Wednesday. Leuchars was to join up with the Kinloss team and a party put together by the Navy from Lossiemouth. A civilian team from Arbroath was also due to join them as soon as it could make the journey, travelling overnight. Then Wing Commander Gordon-Cumming received a message that the pilot had been found at 4 am. He had landed safely west of Callander, many miles to the south and walked down.

Again, there was a feeling of anti-climax; tensions relaxed, nobody wanted to do much in particular, and the morning was spent passing time in local cafés. But the ejection seat had to be found. A new base camp was set up in the Pass of Leny, near Callander, John Hinde travelling down in the Navy bus. They found time on the way down to look at the burial place of the Clan MacNab on the island in the River Dochart near Killin. He was struck by ... A wild backcloth of sky and river and old trees and the pure white Ben Lawers in sunshine.[13]

A second search started that evening until dark on the western shore of Loch Lubnaig, but there was no sign of the seat there. After supper, Hinde and another team member, still frustrated after half a day in the bus, climbed Ben Ledi (2882′) in the moonlight and often waist-deep in snow.

The next morning, after a three-way football competition (Leuchars-Kinloss-Lossiemouth), the team returned to RAF Leuchars, leaving the Royal Navy to look for its aeroplane and ejection seat.

5 – Jean and Nigel

The van had been there since Sunday morning – parked by the side of Loch Morlich, in the shadow of Castle Hill and very near Glenmore Lodge. For all that day nobody took any notice. Many climbers brought their vehicles up to the Highlands, left them in a remote spot and went off into the hills. When it was still there on Monday, well, probably they had bivouacked; probably they were on holiday. But at home, those who loved the engaged couple Jean McBain and Nigel Milne were worried when they did not return home. Phone calls were made, initial enquiries undertaken. Where had Jean and Nigel planned to go? What were they driving?

Before long the van, covered in snow, was found, but with no sign of the two young people. Now people were really worried. The weather, for mid-April, was severe, with frequent snow and blizzards. A massive search was started from

Glenmore, but soon RAF Kinloss MRT was brought in, and then, by Tuesday evening, April 12th 1960, Leuchars. Spreading the net as wide as possible, they were to search the southern Cairngorms.

The Leuchars convoy set out to rendezvous with Kinloss, which was under "Admiral" Bob Sharp, on the Tuesday evening. Lieutenant Commander Robert Sharp RN was the only naval officer ever to command an RAF Mountain Rescue Team. A torpedo and anti-submarine warfare specialist, he was appointed to RAF Kinloss as the Maritime Liaison Officer, initially for a short period which was then extended, and in the event he stayed from June 1958 until July 1961. A keen climber, he had been a member of the RN & RM Mountaineering Club since 1947. On arriving at RAF Kinloss, he had been surprised and delighted to find that there was a Mountain Rescue Team there, and immediately volunteered and became a member of the team. A few months later, the Officer i/c was posted elsewhere, and Sharp was asked if he would take over. Mrs Sharp was heard to comment that whereas other naval officers brought back fish or birds from a weekend away, all he brought back was dirty clothes.

In the ambulance with John Hinde in the Leuchars convoy was the former IMR, Wing Commander Gordon-Cumming, now a member of the team; his replacement in the comfort of his Whitehall office was Flight Lieutenant John Sims, who had taken over the previous November after being in charge of RAF Valley MRT.

The team slept that night in a barn at Auchallater, then took a Land Rover past Braemar and up to Derry Lodge. Here they split up, the Hinde party following Glen Luibeg with the massive Beinn Macdui ahead of them. First they went to the top of Carn a' Mhaim (3329′), assaulted by weather which was deteriorating by the minute.

Struggling north along the ridge to the bealach, they were almost blown off on several occasions. Keeping in touch with the other parties every fifteen minutes by radio, Hinde and his two companions ('an Englishman, a Scotsman and a Welshman') went due north across the corrie of the Tailor's Burn, then up to the summit of Beinn Macdui (4296′). Hinde recorded:

> This summit is only 110′ lower than Ben Nevis and in conditions of today it was absolutely frightful. I would have turned [the] party back long before on a normal exercise, but we pushed it a bit for the search.
>
> Gale whipped spindrift horizontally across iron hard icy ground. Kicking steps up the last few hundred feet of corrie to summit we were actually blown up the slope.[14]

At this point another radio call was due, but conditions were so terrible that they ignored it; it was just too cold to put the aerial up. Instead they pressed on north-east from the summit and then down to Coire Etchachan.

This was turning out to be one of the worst call-outs in Hinde's considerable experience. Hard though it was, it also had its element of farce, which John Hinde could still see – or, at least, remember later in the warmth of RAF

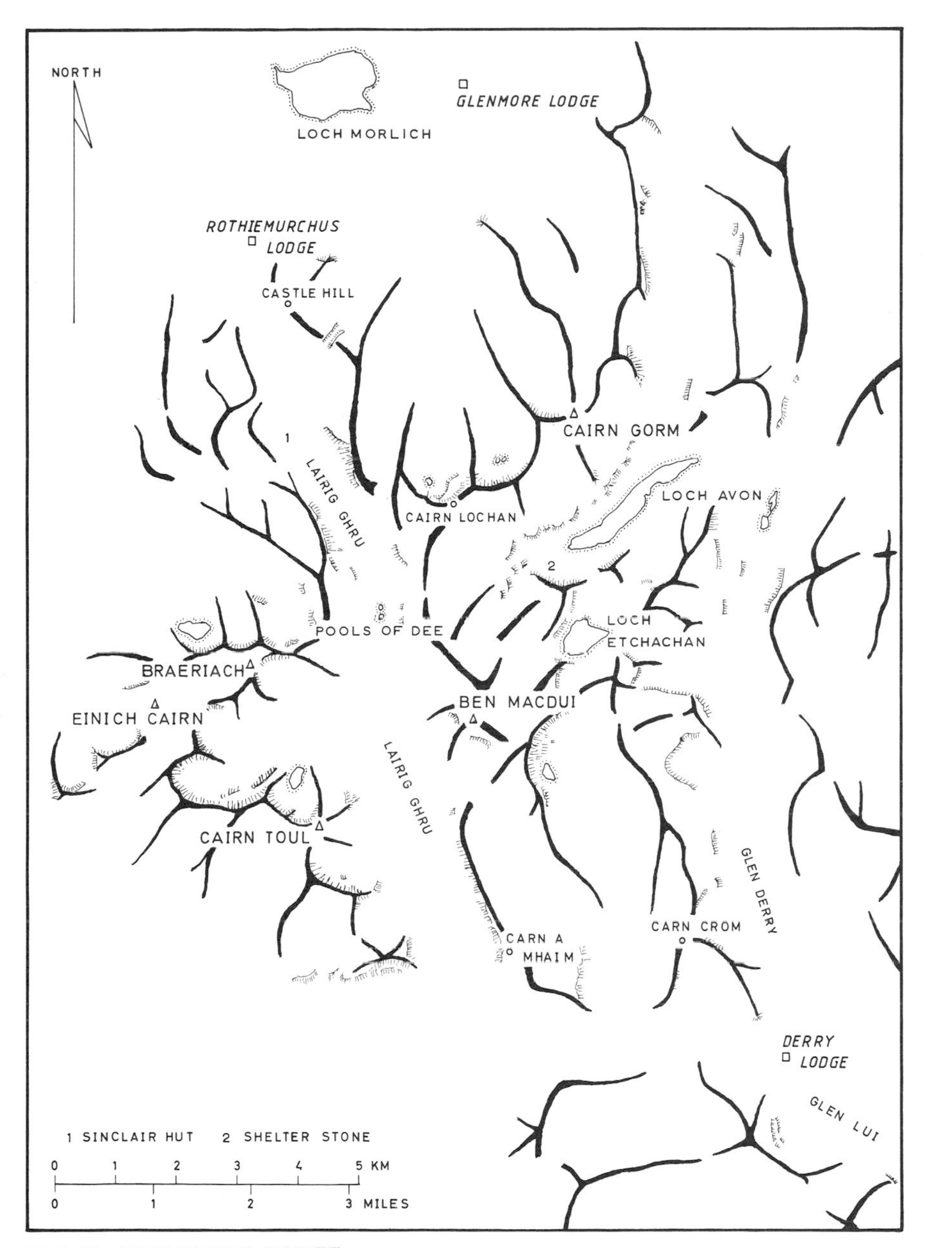

MAP 10 THE POOLS OF DEE

Where Neil Bailey died in 1981. This general area was also the scene of the Jean and Nigel search in 1960.

Leuchars – despite the immediate suffering. The Welshman he describes as a strong athletic youth, who was wearing track-suit bottoms and no overtrousers. With the hard-driven snow, the track-suit trousers were getting heavier and heavier, and the waist elastic was not really equal to the job. Taff was desperately hanging on, therefore, to the waistband of the trousers, more interested in that than in using a map and compass. Hinde therefore took the full strain of white-out navigation, and worried about Taff:

We carried only tiny rucksacks, which we called day-bags, containing a few bars of chocolate, a prismatic compass, binoculars and a Verey pistol: no bivvy bags, no spare clothing, no good waterproofs (just Ventile which was allegedly windproof – as it was then – clanking like suits of armour in the hard frost). Conditions were desperate; probably as hard as I had known up to then. I kept thinking, "If this guy hurts himself, or if he collapses with exhaustion, what do we do? Do we dash off and get help, or do we stay and die with him? If it is I who collapse, do I want them to stop for me? – Not likely."
I know that if we stop, even for a few minutes, we shall get so cold that we shall never move again. We are not even friends, just people thrown together because of volunteering for mountain rescue duties. In fact, I can't stand him. Why should we perish because of each other? There will be nothing we can do to help ourselves because we have no tent or sleeping bags.[15]

In Coire Etchachan they found the loch completely snowed over. They were due to return over the Derry Cairngorm ridge, but as Mick Fearn and his party were covering that, Hinde felt justified in going down to the mountain hut in Coire Etchachan, built about six years earlier. There they found three schoolboys who had wisely decided to stay there until the weather abated, and also Mick Fearn and his companions. There was little firewood and they found themselves getting colder and colder. The Hinde and Fearn parties therefore decided to return to Derry Lodge, a further five miles or so. Hinde's relief on getting himself and his party back to this safe spot was palpable. Back there on the Macdui Plateau, with difficult navigation and a weak party member, they had been many miles away from any help. Even if the radio had been fully effective, any help would have arrived too late.

The wireless that the teams carried then was their heaviest item of equipment. It weighed over twenty-eight pounds and was carried in two connecting sections, one on the back and one on the chest, with an aerial which was about twelve feet long. It was never very effective and on that day was just as useless as the heavy binoculars and Verey pistol. The same weight in survival gear might have been more useful.

On their way back to the lodge they had to run the gauntlet of three press photographers when crossing the bridge. Bill Brankin, Sandy Gordon-Cumming and Corporal Williams, the other party, had not yet returned. The Hinde and Fearn parties left the Land Rover for them and returned to Auchallater.

That night, Hinde drove the ambulance back over the Devil's Elbow to

Leuchars in fresh snow and total darkness, and learnt that because of the conditions the search was being called off. There had been many people out looking for Jean and Nigel over the two days. Part of the problem was that nobody really knew where to look. They had been staying at the old Glenmore Lodge and had been seen walking towards Bynack More. Nigel's body was found before very long, on wild moorland. The search was switched to that area, but still Jean could not be found.

Teams went out for weeks after; then even they stopped. Her brother, though, came to the area weekend after weekend and carried on looking. He never gave up. Finally, he found what was left of Jean, in the late spring, when the snow had nearly gone. She was a further five miles into wilder country, yet further away from people and houses.

Easter was close, and Leuchars could expect a busy time. But if they thought they might get some respite on the intervening day, they were mistaken. The day after they were withdrawn from the Jean and Nigel search, Thursday April 14th, an F100 of the US Air Force crashed near Dalmally. It was just a case of recovering the body of the pilot. Before the team reached Crianlarich, however, there was a message that the police had brought the body down. The convoy carried on to Glen Coe for exercises, setting up basc camp in Hamish MacInnes's barn. On the Saturday of the exercise, they helped to recover a fallen climber and took him to hospital in Fort William.

Then, on Easter Sunday, they woke to a morning of bright sunshine. Hinde, with two others, rounded off the Easter weekend by rescuing a cragfast sheep. When he reached the ledge, it was clear from the amount of droppings that it had been there for a long time. Having secured a rope they tied it round the sheep, pushed it off the ledge and lowered it down. Untying the rope, they watched the confused creature scamper off over the hill.

Two more sad notes from this year for Leuchars. The officer i/c in 1960 was a pilot from 43 Squadron, John Cleaver. The following year, he ejected – his second time – from a Hunter over Cyprus, and was killed. Hinde received the news in May 1961 when he was in Wales, and thought back to a day only seven months earlier when he had climbed with Cleaver and Flight Lieutenant John Robertson in the Cairngorms.

Then Mick Fearn, who had led one of the Jean and Nigel parties, became a team leader in 1962, his first team St Athan. Three years later, during the Whitsun weekend of 1965, he took St Athan on exercise in the Lake District. On the last day, Sergeant Fearn was leading a pitch up *New West* on Pillar (2,927 feet) in Ennerdale. The rock was damp and slippery, and he fell. The running belays between himself and his second failed to check his fall, and he was killed.

6 – Operation Boom-Boom

Within two months, the Kinloss team found itself involved in two major searches in the same area, in the Cuillin Mountains of Skye. In June 1960, John Oswin, Harold Middleditch and James Sampson were staying in Glenbrittle in the shadow of the Cuillins. On the Sunday, in perfect weather, they went by boat to Loch Scavaig intending to return over the Dubhs. Bad weather set in at 6 pm when they had reached Sgurr Dubh an Da Bheinn. However they continued toward Sgurr Thearlaich, which entailed steep rock-climbing in crossing the Thearlaich-Dubh gap. Here Oswin fell from the chimney on the north side of the gap and fractured his skull.

Sampson, a Canadian who had not long before been a flying officer in the Canadian Air Force, tried to climb out on the other side of the gap, but he also slipped and jarred his back. It was getting darker now, and was raining heavily. Sampson and Middleditch lay where they were, shouting from time to time through the dreadful storm. Nobody responded. Oswin, the most expert of the three, remained still, obviously unconscious and probably dead. The night seemed to be never-ending, but eventually they started to see the beginning of the dawn streaks in the eastern sky. They started shouting again through the persistent storm.

Mrs MacDonald, the Glenbrittle postmistress with whom they had been staying, had become alarmed the previous evening; she had expected the three men back for dinner by 8 pm. She waited and waited, then finally raised the alarm at midnight. The RAF Kinloss team – on the island for a two-week exercise – was combined with police and holiday climbers to form search parties.

In the early morning Sampson and Middleditch could see a party of climbers passing them. Desperately they shouted, and were heard. The party was not equipped for such a rescue, but passed the word on, and some considerable time later the RAF Kinloss team arrived. Led by Ian Martin and Bob Sharp, they helped the two survivors to safety, and then recovered Oswin's body from the gap, with some spectacular stretcher lowers.[16]

At the wheel of the Bedford whining its way through the darkness and up the steeply wooded slopes of Cluny Hill, Forres, was Corporal Ken Shaw, usually known, through the RAF's system of oblique puns, as Gubba (from G B, because of his surname). It was 10 pm, on October 18th 1960. Everybody concerned had been thoroughly briefed at 8 pm, in the Mountain Rescue Section, by Junior Technician D Ruddle, who had been put in charge of the operation. To assist him he had with him five other airmen. At the top of the hill they could just see, dimly outlined against the night sky, the Nelson Tower, built in 1806 to celebrate Nelson's victory at Trafalgar on October 21st of the previous year. Guarding the doorway of the tower were two old four-pounder cannon, which had (it was said) been used by one of Nelson's ships at the bombardment of Alexandria 150 years

Mountain Rescue Section,
Royal Air Force,
Kinloss

MRT/S.1/1/Air

OPERATION ORDER NO. 1/60

References: Map References: 45/012541; 45/013540

Time Zone used throughout this order: Zulu

Task Organisation: Detachment from M.R.T. (Jnr.Tech. D. Ruddle, R.A.F.)

1. SITUATION: A detachment of six airmen of the M.R.T. are to deploy to Cluny Hill and return to R.A.F. Kinloss.

2. MISSION: To remove one cannon from the castle, Cluny Hill (map. ref. above) to the Parade Square, R.A.F. Kinloss, (map ref. above).

3. EXECUTION:

a. The mission is to be carried out in five phases:

(1) Transport detachment to Cluny Hill.

(2) Remove cannon and load on to transport.

(3) Convey cannon to the Parade Square, R.A.F. Kinloss.

(4) Deposit cannon near Parade Square.

(5) Siting of cannon on Parade Square.

b. Transport will depart from Kinloss at 2130Z, 18th October, 1960.

c. Transport will return at 2230Z, 18th October, 1960.

d. Cannon will be sited by 0030Z, 19th October, 1960.

e. Detachment Commander is to brief all personnel proceeding at 2000Z, 18th October, 1960.

4. ADMINISTRATION AND LOGISTICS:

a. Transport to be provided by Cpl. G.B. Shaw.

b. Crow bars to be provided by Jnr. Tech. Ward.

c. Dress: optional.

d. Baggage allowance: clothes and additional 8 ozs.

e. Operational safety: responsibility of detachment commander, assisted by LAC. Serff.

f. Road Safety: responsibility of driver + shot-gun.

5. COMMAND & SIGNAL:

a. Code Name: The detachment will operate under the code name of "Operation Boom-Boom".

b. Callsigns: V/T Callsigns: ALPINE KILO ONE=TWO=THREE=FOUR=FIVE=SIX.

Acknowledgement Instructions: Nill

ago. Originally there had been six, but four larger cannon were taken away during World War II as scrap metal.

Shaw turned the lorry round, and backed it up as close as he could to the tower. Six men got out, the tailgate dropped quietly. As quickly as possible they lifted the nearer of the cannon on to the back of the Bedford. Four scrambled up after it to hold it steady, pulling the tailgate up after them. Shaw and another got back in the cab, and the lorry returned down the steep hill and back to RAF Kinloss two or three miles away. Swinging in through the gates only an hour after they had left, Shaw gave the guard-room his customary wave, then drove to the Mountain Rescue Section and parked the vehicle. There it was left, its cargo well out of sight. Nothing more happened until after midnight; then the six met up again to complete Operation Boom-Boom.

October 19th, 1960: early in the morning, and things were beginning to move at RAF Kinloss. One airman, up earlier than most, glanced casually across the empty Parade Square as he often did. The he took another look, for there, right in the middle of the wide expanse of tarmac, was what seemed to be an old cannon. Glancing round him first before stepping onto the sacred ground, he moved closer. It was indeed an old cannon.

Soon someone on Cluny Hill had noticed that a cannon was missing. It was not long before it was realised that Trafalgar Day was two days later. Working on this, they put two and two together and made five. Not far along the coast was a big naval establishment, Lossiemouth. No doubt – it was reasoned – a party of ratings or officer trainees, prematurely celebrating the Admiral's famous victory, were the guilty ones. The police were told and agreed. Angry telephone calls were made along sizzling lines to Lossiemouth. The officers at Lossiemouth, embarrassed, had to admit the logic of the argument, and apologised, promising to find out who was responsible and to return the cannon once it had been located.

In the meantime the Station Warrant Officer (SWO) at RAF Kinloss, not in the best of moods so early in the morning, was himself saddled with three problems: Who did it? Where did it come from? How do we get it back there?

Someone thought he recognised the cannon, and told the SWO. Reluctantly, he picked up the telephone and spoke to those in charge of the tower....

Despite his most diligent enquiries, he was unable to ascertain who was responsible. It seems strange that he did not immediately pin it onto Mountain Rescue with its reputation for outrageous behaviour. Nobody admitted to having heard, in the early hours of the morning, a three-ton Bedford being unloaded on the Parade Square; not a common occurrence. In the end, in the best tradition of the services, he called for volunteers, and detailed Flight Sergeant Raymond Bailes to take charge of the party which was to return the gun. Bailes and his seven volunteers manhandled the cannon, all seven hundredweight of it with its carriage, onto another Bedford, and returned it to where it had been undisturbed for many years. In the meantime, the SWO was still trying to find out who was responsible. He never did. The indistinct tyre marks found at the spot by the police were not enough to give them a real clue.

The smoothness of the whole operation must be a credit to Mountain Rescue training. A proper Operation Order was drawn up, with the duties of the key personnel properly defined. The motivating force behind Operation Boom-Boom was Corporal G B Shaw, who had an irrepressible and irreverent sense of humour and is remembered well throughout the service. Shaw later worked in the British Embassy in Saigon as a clerk, and, very sadly, was killed there when his Land Rover ran over a mine.

The team leader at this time was Ian Martin, whom we last saw on the Canberra search in 1957 when he was with RAF Valley. If asked, he will wisely, and possibly correctly, deny all prior knowledge of Operation Boom-Boom.

Ian Martin and Bob Sharp met again a couple of years before this book was written. Martin lives in New Zealand now, but when somebody in the service got wind of the fact that he was coming back to the UK on holiday, a reunion – known as the Sons of Ian Martin – was organised.

Finally, Bob Sharp makes one comment which is remarkable for a retired naval officer: "I can say that my time at Kinloss was the best time I have ever had during my service career."[17]

7 – Call-out in Glen Coe

Glen Coe strikes some as awesomely beautiful; others, perhaps influenced by the massacre of 1692, think of it as gloomy, a place to be hurried through, with Ballachulish and then Fort William, bright and bustling, offering a welcome at the far end. Going through the glen in that direction, you see the mass of Bidean nam Bian on the left, the highest in Argyll at 3,795 feet. Three great ridges, the Three Sisters, project towards the road: Beinn Fhada, Gearr Aonach and Aonach Dubh. It was on Aonach Dubh, the most westerly of the three, that four friends, Ronald Ralphs, a man called Davis, Michael Powell and Terence Brewer, were scrambling on Monday, September 19th 1960. Its most fearsome aspect is the north face, dominated by Ossian's Cave.

Ralphs hurt a foot on the way up and decided to return to Glencoe, helped by Davis; the other two continued and after completing their chosen route were descending the north face by way of a deep gully beside Ossian's Cave. Above this Powell fell at about 4 pm. Brewer heard him shout as he slipped over the edge of the gully. Shaken, he could just see him from above, moving but apparently badly hurt and unable to get up. They had not been roped and Brewer would not be able to recover Powell on his own. Shouting down that he would go and get help, he returned back down the mountain to Glencoe village and found Constable Sandy Whillans.

When the police had got together a few helpers, Brewer was so shattered by the experience and tired that he was unable to take the party to the point where the incident had happened, and unable to point out the gully in question. A major search was needed.

At RAF Leuchars, Hinde was in his caravan when the Tannoy cut through his slumber. Flight Sergeant Bill Brankin, then the team leader, asked Hinde to form an advance party with some of the best men and go straight to the police at Glen Coe. Then, if it seemed desirable, they were to go straight on to the hill.

At 2 am in Glen Coe, Hinde could see a light in Hamish MacInnes's cottage and guessed rightly that he was involved in the rescue. Hamish MacInnes is probably the most well-known figure in Scottish civilian mountain rescue. He came to mountain rescue in 1958 after a varied and colourful earlier career, much of it concerned with mountains. Mountain rescuers everywhere, and rescued climbers too, have reason to be thankful that MacInnes's fertile mind did not allow him to restrict himself to climbing and team organisation. Items of equipment bear his name – ice-axes, stretchers and others – and he was a founder of the Search and Rescue Dog Association (SARDA).

In Scotland, it is on the police teams that the first responsibility falls for recovery of civilian climbers, and they co-opt other civilian teams as necessary. But the civilian teams, other than the police, have problems with which the RAF teams are not afflicted. They have gone through periods of financial stringency; and most of their members have jobs to do, and cannot always get away.

Fortunately the RAF has managed to retain a policy of supporting the civilian teams where needed, often against Whitehall opposition. Chris Briggs in Wales and Hamish MacInnes in Scotland have been generous in acknowledging this help. MacInnes, in his book *Call-Out*, said:

> For many years the R.A.F. teams formed the backbone of mountain-rescue in Scotland and numerous climbers owe a debt of gratitude to them. Gradually, with the formation of civilian rescue teams in mountainous regions, the R.A.F. have modified their role and now provide support for local teams, particularly on protracted rescues and searches. Their usefulness is by no means diminished however, and it will be a sad day when the Ministry decides to disband them, for though their primary task is to locate crashed aircraft on the mountains, their secondary task – helping with mountain accidents and searches – is a very worthwhile one.[18]

In the same book, he paid tribute to John Hinde:

> John Hinde was then [1963] the Flight Sergeant in charge of the team. He had recently returned from an expedition in Alaska where he had his toes frost-bitten. Despite this handicap he was still getting about, though not back to his usual active self. John is a tall, quiet-spoken man and the fact that he is liked and respected by everyone in the rescue team is a high recommendation, for their assessment of fellow team members, and especially their team leader, is stringently critical.

The first helicopter rescue, 1960: Glencoe, Ossian's Cave.
Photo: Hamish MacInnes, Glencoe Productions

L to R: Dick Bywaters, John Hinde, Jack Baines, Grant Jarvis, 1961-62. *Photo: M Dixon*

Hinde went up to the MacInnes front door, and rang the bell. It was opened by MacInnes's wife, Dr Catherine MacInnes. She told Hinde that MacInnes, PC Sandy Whillans and two other climbers were still on the hill. There had been some more people who had taken the stretcher up, but they had returned. Hinde and his party went off to report to the police, and then returned to the foot of Aonach Dubh. As they did so, they met the rest of the team. By now it was 3 am.

They could see lights high up on the north face, probably, they thought, the MacInnes party, and Hinde took up a party of five. On the way they fired off several illuminating flares which provided them with a spectacular view of the north face but did not reveal anybody in the vicinity. They were getting nowhere, and decided to bivouac until daybreak, as Hinde wanted to search the foot of the north face, which would be too hazardous in the darkness. It was fortunate that it was a calm clear night; the star-studded sky was impressive.

The MacInnes party, including Constable Whillans, was doing exactly the same thing. They had spent a long time searching the face of Aonach Dubh until darkness forced them to stop. MacInnes can remember to this day that it was very cold and that they started again at first light.

Hinde woke with a start to see the beginning of daylight in the sky. He roused those who were still sleeping, and they forced their limbs into movement again. He split the party up into two, with Jack Baines, later to be a prominent team leader, leading one and himself the other. As the Hinde group got near to the top, one of the other group, Charlie Lyon, shouted: "Hamish is over there!"

They continued westwards, until they came to the great gully in the north face.

On the sloping shelf beyond Ossian's Cave they could see two searchers, but so far no-one seemed to have spotted anything. There was a bang from someone's Verey pistol, but the group could not see the flare. It was all getting very frustrating.

Carrying on up beside the gully, with the intention of traversing across the top of the north face and down the west face, they were not far from the top when one of the group, Mike Dixon, looked down. Was that something red down there? John Hinde looked intensely. His first reaction was that it was another rescuer. He stood up, cupping his hands round his mouth. "Are – you – OK?" he shouted. There was an answer of sorts from the red figure which sounded as if it could be "Yes!". They prepared to move on, but they were not sure. The figure in the gully had not shouted very loudly. In the absence of a clear positive message, they decided after all that they ought to go down and see what was what.

Climbing down into the gully, getting nearer, they heard the figure in red call again: "I've hurt my back!" They redoubled their efforts and had to abseil over some loose rocks. The slightest movement sent rocks tumbling down. As Hinde got closer to the injured man, he saw Hamish MacInnes also approaching, traversing down sloping grass and rock, and in fact MacInnes reached the man first.

It was now 9 am. They found a man with terrible head and face injuries, the most prominent being a very severe cut below the nose, as well as a back injury of unknown seriousness. At this point, MacInnes and Hinde were joined by the rest of the MacInnes party, including Catherine MacInnes, who dressed his wounds. The party had also managed to bring Brewer with them.

Hinde fired off a red Verey light to summon the stretcher. He and MacInnes then had to decide the best way to get the casualty and stretcher out of this rugged gully. Hinde and Dixon fixed belays and tied two 120-foot ropes together to reach the foot of a very steep and dangerous-looking pitch below the fallen man: there was an even steeper pitch below that. MacInnes and Hinde finally decided that whilst hauling the stretcher out of the gully would be extremely difficult, lowering it down would be impossible.

Waiting for the stretcher, Hinde and MacInnes filled the time by working out how Powell had fallen. His hat and coiled rope were on the top of a pinnacle and sixty feet below that was a clear imprint in the turf where he had first made impact. It seemed that after that he had pitched forward a further twenty feet on to broken rocks, where they found a large pool of blood. An anorak cord and further blood splashes showed where Powell had dragged himself for about twenty yards.

At 11.30 am, Bill Brankin and the rest of the team arrived with the stretcher. Powell was strapped on, and the very difficult evacuation begun, under MacInnes's direction. Firstly, they carried and hauled the stretcher up to the edge of the gully, using pegs as belays, with Hinde guiding the stretcher, and then down a very steep hillside. Four hours after Powell was strapped onto the stretcher, they reached the road. Hinde reflected wryly on how many willing volunteers they now had for the last half-mile.

At 3.45 pm, Powell was being put into the ambulance, which took him to hospital. There the medical staff confirmed severe head injuries, suspected spine injuries, condition 'satisfactory'. Powell's parents kept in touch with Hamish MacInnes for many years afterwards. Powell himself never fully recovered.

It was during the same year, on the very same face, though a little closer to Ossian's Cave, that a Whirlwind helicopter was used for the first time, again with Hamish MacInnes involved.

8 – Sputnik and Voodoo

In the spring of 1962 there was an event that, by its nature, has remained unknown, except to the privileged few, ever since, though at the time it created quite a stir in the service and involved a sweep search. A shepherd reported that he had come across what looked like a Sputnik high up on the moors in the Ardgay region. Sputniks, the early USSR spacecraft, were a subject of intense interest in the Western world at the time (this incident was before the Soviets publicised the sending up of the first dog). There was a good deal of scepticism about the shepherd's report – probably based on speculation about use of the local malt – and this was not diminished when Jack Baines and three others of the Kinloss team were discreetly brought into the section by telephone instead of Tannoy. When they looked at the wall-map, they saw that very close to the reported spot was an old wartime wreck; was this what the shepherd had found?

But no – at the reported spot was this strange object. It had obviously been there some time and important items seemed to have been removed. Buried nearby was a large number of bottles of colourless fluid – which might have been water – and such a heavy payload led one to wonder whether in fact there had been an animal aboard. To RAF eyes, the engineering seemed crude. There was what appeared to be a camera port with thick glass, and some sort of camera. No-one was told or was even allowed to speculate that the object was a spacecraft, but the brass recovery plate gave the game away. This was quartered by etched lines, with, in each numbered quarter, an explanatory picture:

1 Descent of Sputnik by parachute into open country.
2 A peasant – apparently Russian – riding a horse or camel finds the Sputnik.
3 The peasant goes to an Army officer in a town with onion domes and points out the direction of where the Sputnik can be found.
4 At an official ceremony the peasant is given a large bag of money or gold.

With the full team, a sweep search was made of the area. Some electronic bits and pieces were picked up and taken back to Kinloss.

What did we have here? The concensus was that it was a Soviet spacecraft of some sort. It was not spherical but box-shaped, however, contrary to popular mythology, not all Sputniks were spherical. What was the colourless fluid? Some thought water, suggesting that an animal or a person had been carried. Some thought distilled water, in which case it might have been used for a battery. Certainly the interior was large enough to have carried a man.

It did not seem to have crash-landed – it was in relatively good condition, suggesting a parachute. But then where were the parachute and the missing electronics? Had somebody from the intelligence services been up there and taken the interesting stuff, or had somebody walking over the moors just helped themselves to souvenirs?

When Kinloss's monthly report found its way to Squadron Leader John Sims in the Inspectorate Office, his curiosity was roused and he too asked questions. It was made fairly clear to him that information of this nature was on a 'need to know' basis, and that he did not need to know.

On March 3rd 1962 a skier called Billy Garden from Inverness went missing somewhere near the top of the Cairngorm chairlift, getting lost in thick mist. He was gone two days, having wandered south instead of north-west to safety, and descended down to Loch Avon. It appeared, from his story afterwards, that at least twice he got away from Loch Avon by way of either Coire Domain or Coire Raibert, then drifted down again through the other corrie, each time recognising in despair the sight of the loch in front of him.

In the depths of depression, he yet survived, two factors being what John Hinde describes as his 'great muckle coat' which went almost to his ankles, and the rings of ice round the tops of his boots which seemed to have prevented too much heat loss and therefore saved him from frostbite. After a couple of days he had been written off and the Kinloss team was looking for a body, when he appeared out of the mist into the arms of two instructors from Glenmore Lodge. They tied him in the middle of a rope between the two of them, and walked him out over the plateau and to the top of the ski-lift. John Hinde and at least one of his team members, Ian Sykes, can remember this strange party looming up out of the mist.

It occurred to someone in 1962 that since many of the crack army regiments had goats as mascots, why, then, should not an MRT have the same privilege? Permission was sought to have one officially on the strength, and the reply shows a nicely relaxed approach to an unusual request. Headed *Playing the Goat*, it says:

Permission is granted for the goat to be kept on the station but it must be emphasised that only the highest standard of hygiene and turnout will be accepted. The goat's quarters must be maintained in immaculate condition and the goat, its quarters and grazing area will be subject to the Station Commander's periodic inspection.

Regarding the goat's adoption as an official mascot, the goat's lineage and pedigree will

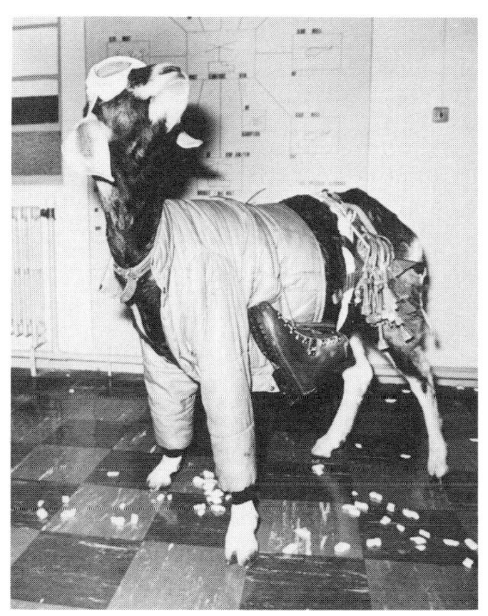

Hector, Leuchars team in 1982 carrying all the team leader's gear. Not the first goat in the service. *Photo: Leuchars team member*

The Glen Brittle Memorial Hut in the final stages of building, 1965. *Photo: John Foster*

first have to be obtained. It may also be necessary in due course to institute positive vetting procedure and in this respect past and present associates of the goat may render its adoption undesirable.[19]

Soon on the establishment, the goat lived at Kinloss for a few years, but gradually however became a source of irritation to the CO and his lady; he – the goat – ate everything in sight. Orders were given; threats were issued; promises were made; but still he continued to chomp his way through roses and spring leaves and just about everything else that was not ring-fenced.

Then in 1965 a totally unconnected event brought the running sore of the goat to a head. In Glen Brittle, just west of the Cuillin on Skye and the usual starting point for an ascent of Sgurr Alasdair, the British Mountaineering Council with the Association of Scottish Climbing Clubs had funded the Glen Brittle Hut as a memorial to mountaineers who had died in World War II. There was to be an official opening and Mike Holton was invited. By then he was a Principal in the Air Ministry, with the equivalent rank of group captain. Being encouraged, as part of his job, to go out and see the RAF in action, he did not find it difficult to arrange a visit to RAF Kinloss, giving him the opportunity of going to Glen Brittle with the team.

Arriving off the night train on June 1st, Holton was given the expected tour of RAF Kinloss. The Mountain Rescue Section was not on the programme, and he asked that it be added. In introducing Holton to those in the section, the conducting officer said that he did not know why the particular request had been made, but the team was able to tell him that Holton had been responsible for writing the first manual, AMP 299, thirteen years ago after Beinn Eighe. Later, Holton had drinks with the Station Commander who by this time had become aware of the MR connection. The Station Commander pulled him aside. "Look, Michael" he said quietly but with a touch of desperation in his voice, "if you've got any influence with these characters at all, please get them to do something about that bloody goat!"

The Glen Brittle ceremony was to take place on June 5th, on the same day that just a few miles away across the water on Iona a congregation of 700 was celebrating the completion of 25 years' work restoring the cathedral; and 600 miles south in the English Channel the Little Ships were celebrating the 25th anniversary of Dunkirk. A piece of land had been given by the owner of the nearby mountains, Dame Flora Macleod of Macleod; an appeal fund had been launched with Fred Pigott as the treasurer. The feu charter for the land reads:

> The feu duty shall be one shilling sterling per annum, to be paid at Whitsuntide, if asked for.[20]

Various people stayed at Glen Brittle – police, mountaineering clubs, RAF Kinloss MRT – on the night before the official opening. Few got to bed, and a crate of Talisker – the local malt – was consumed. In the early hours of the morning, through the Talisker haze, Holton spoke to John Hinde, asking him to keep the offending goat, metaphorically speaking, out of the CO's hair, but as so often with minor incidents like this, he never heard what the outcome was.

A great source of comfort to climbers in the glen, the hut is still there, its brass plaque unveiled by Dame Flora, then 87, reading:

GLEN BRITTLE MEMORIAL HUT
1939-1945
THIS HUT IS BUILT IN MEMORY OF
THOSE WHO FOUND STRENGTH IN
THE HILLS TO SUSTAIN THEM
EVEN UNTO DEATH
B.M.C. A.S.C.C.

Between the recruitment of the goat and the opening of the Glen Brittle Hut had occurred an incident that was to result in one of the biggest search-and-rescue operations.

Three Voodoos of the US Air Force went out together on a photographic reconnaissance on May 7th 1964, and on their return from Germany one was reported missing by the flight leader. Called out at 11.35 am, the Kinloss team was going initially to the Fort William area under Corporal Ray 'Sunshine' Sefton. Leuchars MRT was brought out at the same time under Peter Davis; the Voodoo was a very fast aircraft, and it was anticipated that a wide area would have

An RF101 Voodoo at RAF Bentwaters. *Photo: the late M Woodward, courtesy of H J Budgen*

to be covered in any sweep search. Kinloss had the help initially of 20 men from HMS Fulmar, Lossiemouth.

First instructions about the division of areas between the two teams had been vague, but this improved next day. They had to wait at Fort William for several hours until local information came in when a woman at Brae Roy Lodge said that she had heard an explosion at the end of a mountain road which comes off the road from Spean Bridge to Tulloch Station. Sefton sent a party off to check since it was not far from where they were based. It was not ideal searching weather, but all had experienced much worse. All the summits were visible at some stage or other through the intermittent hail and rolling mist, and there was a strong wind blowing. Before the Brae Roy Lodge party had returned, another and apparently more likely report had come in, and from several sources which gave it a misleading credibility. Some fishermen reported having seen a low-flying aircraft at Glenfinnan with wheels down. This seemed a likely prospect and an intense search was made of the area for two days. Only after the two days was the Rescue Co-ordination Centre able to establish that the aircraft had been a Scimitar on its way to Lossiemouth. Why it had dropped its wheels so far short of its destination was not recorded. On May 9th as the Glenfinnan search was called off, Hinde arrived to take over from Sefton.

By this time, the searchers were coping with heavy rain, and a cloud base down to 2,500 feet. Rain eased a little on the next day and the cloud base rose, but never enough to leave the higher summits clear. The HMS Fulmar party had to return to Lossiemouth, but the Leeming MRT was brought in, with eight men from HMS Condor, Arbroath. It was on this day, the 10th, that Lieutenant Browne of the USAF arrived. All the search leaders were brought together and Browne briefed them. His conclusions were that the most likely areas were along both shores of the great Loch Linnhe which runs from the sea opposite Mull, north-east to Fort William through the Corran Narrows. He based this on the debriefing from the pilot of the leading Voodoo, and managed to tie it in with various local reports of bangs and splashes in the loch. Searching of the new areas started and continued for the next five days with aerial support. Heavy rain resumed, with snow at times to add to the discomfort, and the cloud base dropped again. During this period, on May 12, two more RAF teams were imported: Valley and St Athan. Two civilian teams, Glencoe and Lochaber, had been helping during the 9th and 10th.

All mountain ridges and summits in area allocated searched whether or not in mist. Corries, glens and moors below cloud base scanned as far as possible with the aid of binoculars from neighbouring ridges.[21]

As the team had only three pairs of binoculars, Hinde put in a plea for an increase, suggesting double the number.

On the 14th, the weather suddenly improved and visibility with it. On May 15th an American C47 pilot saw the wreck, on the summit of a small hill, about a mile to the east of Creach Bheinn, seven miles east of Loch Linnhe. Infuriatingly, it had been struck off as searched some days earlier, and it can only be assumed that whoever made the report had searched the wrong mountain, perhaps Creach Bheinn. A party from Kinloss went there the next morning, but initially they could find nothing on the cloud-swathed mountain. Eventually they began discovering small pieces of aluminium alloy and then the remains of the pilot. On the north-east side of Creach Bheinn is a corrie, and the Voodoo had struck a steep loose cliff only about 30 feet from the lip, disturbing much rock, soil and vegetation. Hinde, in his report, concluded:

Recovery of all wreckage would be a hazardous and specialised task for trained Mountain Rescue personnel. There were some pieces of wreckage in the floor of the corrie, below the cliffs, about 800 feet lower than the point of impact, and tiny pieces were found two miles away.

Nevertheless, the RAF teams were told to leave evacuation of the dead pilot to the USAF, and they left at 4 pm to go back to their respective stations. Searching had taken nine days and had involved five RAF teams and two civilian ones, two parties of naval ratings and police from Fort William and Glencoe. American aircraft had flown 144 sorties, RAF Shackletons four, and British helicopters, RAF and naval, 71. It had been the biggest call-out ever and this must be a measure of the importance attached to whatever the Voodoo was bringing back from its reconnaissance flight.

Communications had always been a problem for rescuers in the mountains, right from the earliest days in 1943. High ground does strange things to the radio waves and to make the equipment more reliable in mountainous terrain it had been necessary to make it big and cumbersome – the last thing a climber wants. Frequently teams found it safer to rely on a coded system of flares. A new code was issued in December 1965 to convey the basic messages, by flares, light, sound or semaphore: 1 Help wanted here: 2 Message understood: 3 Position of base: 4 Recall to base.

Thunderflashes also could be used to attract attention. But still radio research continued. Kinloss MRT always maintained a close relationship with Glenmore Lodge, the mountain training centre. In June 1964, the month after the Voodoo search, a group of schoolgirls were on a course there, and Kinloss set up a control and aerial on the summit of Cairngorm, manned by an instructor. The girls went off into the hills and at pre-arranged intervals called in to control, noting their map reference and the strength of the signal as they did so. Replacement of radio equipment was discussed at the next Mountain Rescue Conference in May, 1965.

9 – High Mountains are a Feeling

> I live not in myself, but I become
> Portion of that around me; and to me
> High mountains are a feeling, but the hum
> Of human cities torture.[22]

Stand on the summit of a remote mountain and look around all 360 degrees of the compass and absorb the fact that there is absolutely no other sign of mankind right up to the remote horizon. Until you have done that, you can have little idea what motivates some people, from all walks of life, to go into the wild hills. Now, that mountain on which you are standing need not be in the Alps or the Himalaya; it can be here, in the United Kingdom. Until you have experienced that sense of scale in the Scottish Highlands, it is difficult to believe that the really wild places still exist in this country.

Airmen at all levels and from all trades and branches join Mountain Rescue for a variety of reasons: some because they want to rescue people, some because they can obtain cheap rock-climbing courtesty of the Royal Air Force. Some join just to do something they would not otherwise do and some because they want to experience the wild places. Many have a complex mixture of all these reasons, and some more. MR teams can have some experience of Byron's feeling of high mountains every week when they go on exercise (though few of them may be actively thinking of Byron when obeying the team leader's exhortations); but then the time is limited, the objective is precise and often there is little spare time to absorb that Byronic feeling. Perhaps it was for this reason that the custom developed in the '60s of going from side to side or from end to end of the Highlands.

An RAF MR team first traversed the Scottish Highlands in November 1962, on an east-to-west route (Glen Esk to Glenbrittle House) and included K D Shaw, R McKerron and A Ballantyne. Eleven Munros were, to use the jargon, 'bagged'. Munros are separate mountains in Scotland of over 3,000 feet whose separateness is decided by a height and distance criterion and are listed in 'Munro's Tables', compiled by Sir Hugh T Munro and published by the Scottish Mountaineering Club. Shaw was the first RAF man to climb all the Munros. Anyone who bags all 277 Munros is a Munro King, which today makes them sound like some sort of oversize fast food. Shaw and his companions took great loads of equipment with them in very bad weather, including tents, demonstrated later to be not really necessary.

Then in 1964 a well-known team leader, Geordie Armstrong, with D Golton and M J Raven, did the longer north-south route (Ben Hope to Ben Lomond), accumulating 37 Munros.

Two traverses were made in 1966, both starting in June, one north-south (A Ward, J Morrison, A W Bradshaw) and the other west-east (John Hinde, R S Shaw). The Hinde party slept under trees in good weather; otherwise in bothies varying in quality. They used derelict stalkers' houses, well-equipped mountaineering club huts, a youth hostel and a marble-quarry tea-break hut with permission from the night watchman to use the Calor gas stove. They found that a fire could be lit and wood was available in about a third of them, but they carried with them a Primus stove, which behaved perfectly. This party notched up 30 Munros, the north-south one 32.

In June of the following year, 1967, a party consisting of J M Gilligan, D Ward and S J Wagg reversed the long route and went south-north, collecting 26 Munros.

Pete McGowan (then team leader at Valley) with John Hinde of Kinloss led the 1968 north-south trek, each with two other airmen from his own MRT. By this time some informal rules had developed: no lifts could be accepted (except say, to a pub if the party then returned to the exact point of the lift); in very bad weather the route could be amended to avoid summits; but in that case others were to be included on good days. 300 miles, with a total climb of over 60,000 feet were estimated, and the expedition was expected to take 18 days, but 21 days were allowed in case of bad weather. 36 Munros were to be traversed. This was to be in November, the first time it had been attempted in winter, and new windproof and waterproof clothing, concentrated food and bivouac equipment were to be tested and some of the food dumped in advance in caches. McGowan needed only the ascent of Ben Lomond to put every Munro under his belt.

Highland landowners are rather sensitive about parties crossing their acres, and Hinde wrote to all on the route with a copy of the detailed plans, formally asking for permission. He added:

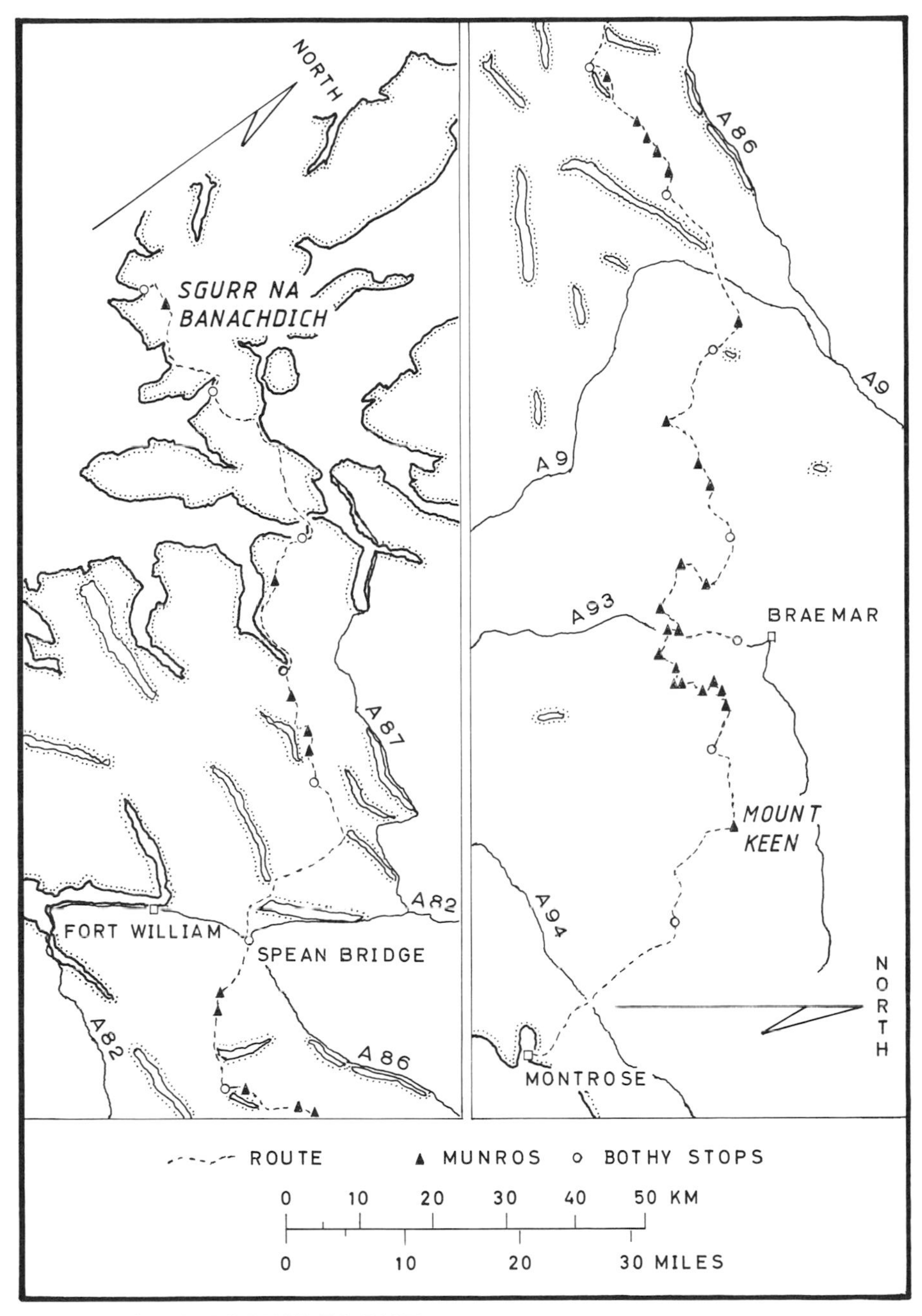

MAP 8 HIGHLANDS WEST-TO-EAST

John Hinde's route in 1966: 14 days' walking, 245 miles, 54,500 feet of climbing, 30 Munros

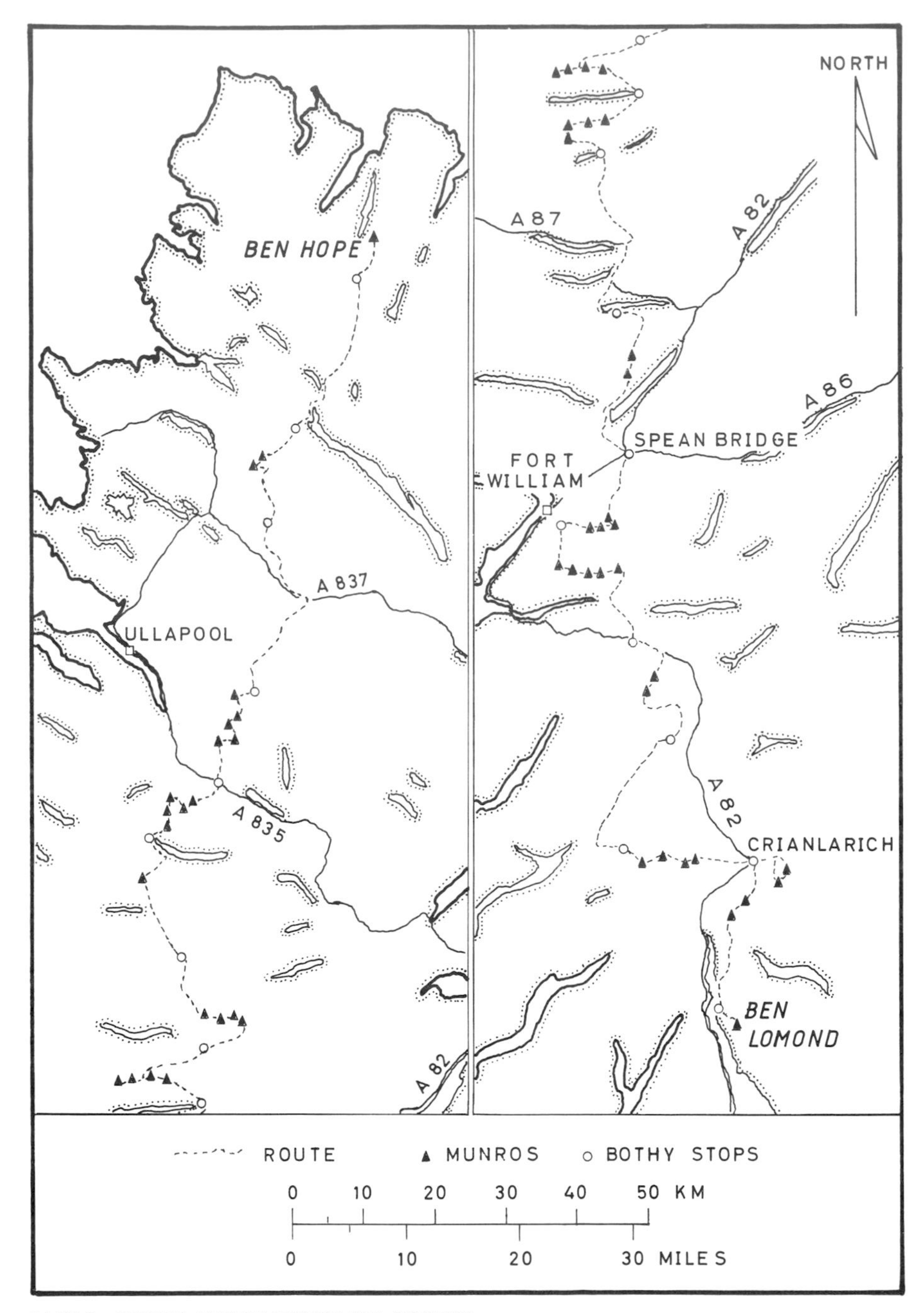

MAP 9 HIGHLANDS NORTH-TO-SOUTH

John Hinde's route in 1968: 19 days' walking, 328 miles, 90,750 feet of climbing, 48 Munros (though Peter McGowan attained 58 on the same walk).

I appreciate the trouble we might cause if hind stalking were in progress and we shall be only too pleased to amend our route if we are requested – either beforehand or in the event of being asked by a keeper or other person during the walk.[23]

Flight Lieutenant Dave Pierce, the Kinloss team officer, drove them to Ben Hope. They climbed it in moonlight, and near the summit were startled by a white snow hare breaking cover almost from beneath their feet. By day two, although the going had been good, the frozen ground beneath their feet had caused some footsoreness, and Corporal Blyth had a touch of frostbite. For the night of day five the bothy was a barn owned by a retired officer, Air Commodore Summerville, and by this time they had got over the fitness barrier and were well into their stride.

It is a measure of the remoteness of the northern areas of Scotland that it was the end of day six before the party reached a pub; this was the Achnasheen Hotel south of Fionn Bheinn. This point was a landmark in another sense: they had finished with the frozen peat of Sutherland, and were about to start on the east-west glen system that made their route so laborious. Blyth, the diarist, commented: Some of Scotland's most beautiful and hidden peaks are hidden in these glens. It was our intention to unveil all they contained.[24]

Next day, they came across a family of deer with a magnificent stag guarding his harem. At the summit, they could look back over six days' walking and see the snows of Ben Hope; the Black Cuillin of Skye to the west; and Ben Nevis, dwarfing everything else to the south.

Two days later, they had their first retirement, when Junior Technician Rabbits's ankle gave trouble and an evacuation by Kinloss MRT had to be arranged. Later they experienced the phenomenon of temperature inversion where low cloud settles in the glens leaving the high ground clear. The effect is ethereal and provides the conditions when Brocken Spectres can be seen – through the projection of a person's shadow, with a 'rainbow' halo, onto the cloud beneath.

Three quarters of the way through, McGowan had to sit an examination, and was collected and taken to RAF Kinloss. That night was the coldest yet, with their boots frozen as was the water in the dixies. One more day was planned before a two-day break, a day on which McGowan was returned to the route at the point where he had left it; he had some catching up to do.

After Ben Nevis, they met the Kinloss team out on exercise. The party as a whole had intended to complete five of the Mamores which lay between Glen Nevis and Kinlochleven, but McGowan had decided to cover ten, and persuaded one other, SAC 'Juff' Millgate, to join him. All of the others murmured appreciatively, says the end-of-trek report, and looked away when McGowan was seeking volunteers. They spent that night in the Scottish Mountaineering Club's hut at the head of Glen Coe having covered 19 miles and 8,000 feet, and were later joined by McGowan, who had covered his thirty miles and 12,000 feet.

1977: Peter McGowan retires from the RAF, handing over the Kinloss MRT to Flt Sgt Ray "Sunshine" Sefton. Sefton is in 1993 the longest-serving MR member, with Colin Pibworth the runner-up. Note MR badge on Sefton's sleeve.

Sq Ldr David Lofts, Inspector of Land Rescue, with a member of the team involved in the search for the children on Cairngorm, 1971.
Photo: David Lofts

One other forced retirement came before the end; four out of the six completed the route. Whilst the bulk of the party had walked 328 miles and climbed 90,750 feet, including 48 Munros, McGowan had covered 350 miles and 100,000 feet, including 58 Munros.

Again under McGowan's leadership, in 1976 came the first winter west-east traverse, part of that year's Team Leaders' Training Course. A further traverse that same year was east-west in May, which included SAC David 'Heavy' Whalley, later a noted team leader.

An April north-south journey came next year, again as part of the training course. It reunited McGowan and Hinde as instructors and included also Tom Taylor of St Athan, and Sergeant Don Aldridge of the US Air Force. It took place in winter conditions, more severe than those experienced in the November traverse of eight years earlier. Not only that, but the objective was to bag more Munros – 65 – than on any previous such expeditions. 350 miles of walking and 102,000 feet of ascent were involved.

The movement, started so modestly in 1962 by Shaw and his colleagues, continued, allowing others over the years to become, like Byron, a portion of that around them.

10 – Children on Cairngorm

Many of the service's rescues and recoveries are extremely difficult, either because of the terrain or the weather or both. But no matter how difficult they are, it is only when they involve a large number of people, or extend over many days, that the press become seriously interested. One such case was the Cairngorm search of November 1971; this was followed avidly containing as it did a dramatic mixture of distressed children, official error, extreme weather conditions and bravery. Fortunately a helicopter hired by a television news service was able to play a part in the recovery. When even experienced climbers and walkers can become snow-bound on the high ground, it seems remarkable that education authorities can send their charges up there in winter inadequately prepared and ill-equipped; but it has happened, and probably it will continue to happen. Of all incidents the MR service has experienced, it is probably those involving children that they find most harrowing.

On the weekend of November 21st-22nd 1971, the Kinloss team was on exercise in the Spey Valley near Newtonmore. Some of the troops did not like the look of the weather with its high winds and deep soft snow, and abandoned their planned walk around the hills surrounding Dalwhinnie.

Two trainee outdoor instructresses with six schoolchildren were not similarly deterred. They were on a two-day walking expedition over the Cairngorm Plateau. Before dark on the first day the weather came down, and with terrifying swiftness the group was in total white-out without shelter and had to bivouac in the open. It was not until the following day that a fellow instructor was able to report that they were overdue. A full-scale search and rescue operation was mounted, with nearby civilian mountain rescue teams and instructors from two mountain centres on the hill by 7 pm. In the high winds and driven snow, however, really effective night searching was not possible.

On that evening (Sunday), the Kinloss team had returned to RAF Kinloss after a rather frustrating weekend's exercise, when the team leader, Flight Sergeant George Bruce, took a telephone call between 9 and 10 pm, and before long the troops were again in the vehicles and on their way back to the Spey Valley. In the Joint Services Centre at Kingussie, they set up their base and Bruce was briefed by the Kingussie police.

He was told of the missing six children and two leaders, and that searchers from Glenmore Lodge were on the hill; he and his men would be needed at first light. At dawn he went to Glenmore Lodge for the search brief given by the Principal, Fred Harper. Kinloss was allocated a search area and Bruce agreed to set up a forward control radio link at Cairngorm carpark. An indication of the severity of the conditions is that Bruce was asked to provide four men to go to the help of one of the overnight search groups – all experienced people – which had a member suffering from hypothermia.

Kinloss established the radio link and Bruce sent his parties off. Spirits soared

A 22 Squadron Wessex puts a team down on the hill.

when the pilot of a Leuchars helicopter radioed back at 11 am that he had found one of the missing people, an instructress, trying to find her way to assistance. She was able to give some idea of where the children might be and the search areas were switched.

It seemed that the children were in open ground north of the Feithe Buide below the Curran Bothy. Bruce then had to call in his various search parties and redeploy them to this area. He radioed one of his groups which was on the plateau above the low cloud base, and gave them the new information, but other groups were not so conveniently placed.

A second RAF helicopter and a Royal Navy Sea King arrived. Bruce became aware of the naval aircraft as it flew very low over the road up the valley, keeping below the cloud base. It put down in the carpark and Bruce went over and spoke to the pilot, who agreed to take Bruce and try to collect the other groups and take them on to the plateau. The pilot tried several times, without success. Then another radio message came through: the Kinloss group already on the plateau had combined with a Glenmore Lodge group and found the missing children. The first impression was that they were all dead. Then another signal said that one child was still alive, though in a very bad condition. For the search parties to carry the survivors out would, therefore, not be fast enough; a helicopter evacuation was essential, even in these appalling conditions.

Bruce explained the situation to Lieutenant Hockey, the RN helicopter pilot. He agreed to do what he could, but he would need a guide who was very familiar with the terrain. Bruce said he would go himself and put one of his team in charge of the radio link. He positioned himself by Hockey's shoulder and guided him up Glen More and over the saddle north of Cairngorm and then up Strath Nethy into the Loch Avon basin so that he could keep below the cloud as long as possible. However, when they reached the head of the loch they had to cross the headwall and go up to cloud level. Bruce kept up a running commentary to the pilot, describing almost foot by foot the terrain in front of him, which he had walked so often with his team. Hockey, totally trusting a man he had never before met, was flying blind in the white-out conditions, and needed constant reassurance by Bruce that it was safe to ascend into the cloud. Then there was a slight break, and they could see a snow-field; here the pilot landed. Bruce checked his map; they were now very close to their target. Asking the pilot to stay there, he jumped down from the helicopter and moved forward to find the stretcher party, who should have been not far ahead. He pulled out his Verey pistol and fired flares over the ridge to attract the attention of the stretcher party. His silhouette broke the white-out for the pilot and Bruce could hear the engine note change, telling him that the chopper was moving forward in short hops.

Bruce, and the stretcher party, who had seen the flares, soon met. With the survivor safely aboard the helicopter, Bruce turned his attention to guiding the pilot out of the Loch Avon basin and down past Glenmore Lodge to the Spey Valley, picking up a doctor on the way. Then he followed the railway line which runs up the valley, and used that as a point of reference to guide the pilot to the hospital in Inverness, where both boy and instructress eventually made a reasonable recovery.

A long return down to the search HQ then had to be made by the foot searchers. There remained the problem of the five children and one instructress who had died and were still on the plateau. The searchers could not be expected to do any more that evening after a very arduous day and next morning the cloud base was again too low for helicopter work. A joint party of Kinloss troops and teachers from Edinburgh set out to recover the bodies and the evacuation began. Then the cloud lifted and an RAF helicopter could safely be taken up to complete the job, helped by a BBC helicopter which was there with a camera crew and reporter.

Bruce's memory of the incident is of a very harrowing call-out. He is proud of his team's performance and pays tribute to the work of the other searchers there.[25]

The Queen's Commendation for Bravery went to Bruce. The citation in the London Gazette said:

QUEEN'S COMMENDATION FOR BRAVE CONDUCT

X4136826 Acting Flight Sergeant Bruce G

For the part he played in the search for a group of young people missing in severe winter conditions in the Cairngorms. His control and co-ordination of the search and his courage, tenacity and skill in guiding a helicopter, in extremely difficult conditions, to pick up the boy survivor, played a vital part in the rescue.[26]

Four of his team, who had been in the party which found the children and dug them out, received commendations from the Air Officer Commander-in-Chief Strike Command: Corporal 'Bugsy' Rabbits, Corporal Mark Rowe, Junior Technician Ashby, and SAC Stewart McKenzie. The RAF helicopter pilot also received an award, but not, inexplicably, Lieutenant Hockey. (During the same year, Bruce took part in the Joint Services expedition to Elephant Island in Antarctica.)

11 – Jaguar in Glen Orchy

Glyn Gianelli, when we first met him, was a little boy living in the Snowdon Ranger Youth Hostel with his father Joe, and looking forward to the visits of David Dattner with the Jewish kids from the East End. As this is being written, he is on British Enterprise IV, somewhere in the North Sea. Between times, he has been in the RAF, a mountain rescuer at Kinloss and an air radar expert. Corporal Gianelli was with 202 Squadron, Sea Kings, at Lossiemouth in late 1979. From his father he had caught an enthusiasm for the mountains and was a member of the Kinloss Mountain Rescue Team not far away. It had been a quiet time for call-outs at Kinloss, but that was about to change for a couple of months.

It was Friday November 23rd; Gianelli was looking forward to the weekend exercise. In the middle of the afternoon, the helicopter on which he had been working was on a routine training flight, so there was not much for him to do. He was standing by the Operations desk when a call came in from RCC Pitreavie. Two Jaguars were out and the No. 2 sent in a Mayday: he had lost contact with his instructor in the No. 1 aircraft. They had been flying south-west down Glen Orchy intending to turn west at the main glen towards Oban on the coast. Suddenly the cloud had come down, and the leader told the No. 2 to abort and pull up: this he did. However, on pulling out of the top of the cloud, he could not see his leader and could make no radio contact.

Gianelli spoke to Pitreavie and on their instructions spoke to his Sea King on VHF, telling the crew to begin searching, starting down the A9 road and over Rannoch Moor to Tyndrum. Then he telephoned the Mountain Rescue Section at Kinloss and spoke to the deputy team leader, Terry Moore, to tip him off about a possible call-out. This came very quickly and Leuchars were instructed at the same time. Within the hour the Kinloss convoy had left.

They drove into Tyndrum in mid-evening under torrential rain. They had a friendly relationship with the Tyndrum Hotel and set up their base in a wooden hut behind the hotel, soon to be joined by the Leuchars troops. Flight Sergeant Jim Craig of Kinloss, with Flight Sergeant R G 'Spoons' Blyth of Leuchars, arranged parties of what Gianelli describes as 'the fittest Munro baggers'[27], to carry out a series of night searches round the Bridge of Orchy area. The rest of the two teams prepared gear for the next morning, but thankfully finished this task well ahead of closing time, and were able to receive progress reports in the comfort of the hotel bar.

In the early hours the overnight parties returned soaked through to the skin, and soon had hung up their wet gear from every hook and nail in the hotel's hut – a pattern that was to be repeated time and again over the next three days. After an early reveille and breakfast, the rest gathered at the search HQ some miles along the glen at Dalmally. Here they were organised into parties, with vehicles and designated areas. They had been joined by civilian searchers – Lomond MRT, Strathclyde and Central Police, Oban Coast Guards, Glencoe MRT. A helicopter search was carried out over the Ben Lui massif. Civilian teams were allocated to the southern side of the A85, concentrating on the Ben Lui massif, whilst the RAF teams were sent to the northern side of Glen Lochy.

Gianelli found himself in the Land Rover ambulance with two fellow-members, 'Cheeky' Sinclair and Nick Sharpe, sent via a very rough stalking track to search over a couple of small hills. At the end of the track a river had to be negotiated, which on the further side proved to be deeper than expected. Pulling its way up the bank on the far side, the Land Rover hesitated, then stuck, the exhaust gurgling like a motor-boat in the water. Clods of earth pulled out of the bank and pushed under the wheels were needed to give extra traction, and the Land Rover was able to pull itself up the bank. Several hours followed, searching round the neighbouring small hills, the intensity of the rain increasing, it seemed, all the time.

Finally the three men climbed into the ambulance and turned back for base, but found that the river, which had been difficult enough to cross on the way out, had virtually doubled in depth. Sitting in the Land Rover, the rain drumming on the roof, looking in despair at what seemed to be the Ganges in the monsoon season, Gianelli tried to raise the search HQ on the radio, as much for moral support as anything else, but was unable to get through. Finally, the three men took a deep breath, and decided that there was only one thing to do. With Gianelli driving and keeping the revs up, the vehicle dipped its nose into the water nearly up to the tops of the wings. At any second, they thought, the engine is going to cut out, but it kept going. They reached the far bank, released their breath and headed for base.

There, the news was that the Jaguar had been found by one of the civilian teams, just over the north-west ridge of Ben Lui. Impacting vertically, nose first, it had totally disintegrated, and there was no way at that stage of knowing whether the pilot had gone down with it or had ejected and was perhaps lying injured somewhere out on the hill. With no chance of any further searching that day, a massive sweep search would be needed starting early in the morning. The RAF Valley team was called in, and they flew that same night in a Hercules.

Sunday was another day of vile conditions. All MRTs went onto the hill and Leuchars tried to get the accident investigation people up to the wreck but with the lack of climbing experience on the specialists' part this failed, apart from the doctor and the photographer. One of the civilian teams, Lomond, found a flight document early in the afternoon.

Early on the Monday morning, the troops woke in the hotel's hut surrounded with the now-familiar drapery of drying climbing gear; but the weather had changed. The beginnings of the day's sunlight could be seen through the windows and the sky was clear. The search HQ were moved to Crianlarich. In the better conditions, the investigators reached the crash site. Airlifted in by a mixture of RAF and RN Sea Kings and army Wessexes, the MR men made a radial search of the area immediately around it, but no trace of the pilot could be found, so a series of sweep searches was arranged. The RAF teams started from the crash site and searched in an easterly direction, over the summit of Ben Lui and the surrounding slopes, but excluding the north face cliffs.

During this vast sweep-search operation, Gianelli was somewhere near the middle of the Kinloss line:

> Suddenly something caught my eye, just the merest glint amongst the stones, so I bent down and picked it up. It was just a small shard of perspex, no bigger than a matchbox, but obviously of recent origin. Any such leftovers from wartime wrecks would have shown some sign of ageing like discolouration from years of exposure to the mountain elements.[27]

He showed Terry Moore, in charge of that part of the line, and they very soon found more Perspex. It soon became clear this was the result of a canopy detonation. Moore radioed base and a few minutes later the Leuchars team, lower down, found the ejection seat. All these finds were between 1.30 and 2.30 pm.

They had the canopy and the seat: where was the pilot? Time was now of the essence. If he were still alive, he had been out on the hill for three nights in torrential rain, in November temperatures, probably in shock, possibly injured; his chances by now must be pretty slim. Calculations based on the wind direction and strength at the time of the Mayday led them to sweep south from Ben Lui onto the rough moorland expanses bound by a track which comes in from Loch Lomond side. After searching here all day, and ending up at the track, they had drawn a blank – it subsequently emerged that the wind information had been inaccurate. Land Rovers went out to pick them up and take them back to Tyndrum for a meal and sleep. A Sno-Cat had been brought in the previous day in hope that it could be used to take the crash investigators up to the site; that turned out not to be possible, but it was retained in case it might be needed to evacuate them.

Tuesday's weather was back to the previous foul mood. Small parties of experienced climbers were sent up to the steep ridges and cliffs of Ben Lui's northern and eastern aspects. Gianelli, with some others, went up there in a Navy Sea King, and climbed a ridge up the north face with Bill Batson, Sharpe and Sinclair. It was not pleasant climbing, mostly of scrambling standard interspersed by patches of snow. Weather and visibility were getting worse and as they reached

The Ben Lui Jaguar call-out, 1979. A casualty is brought in. *Photo: Paul Duckworth*

A Jaguar GR1A from RAF Lossiemouth, similar to that which crashed on Ben Lui in 1979, at RAF Valley. *Photo: H J Budgen*

the summit shoulder they could see only a few yards; the wind had increased, now accompanied by sleet. Underfoot the stones were covered in verglas, making it difficult to keep one's feet in the wind, even wearing crampons. Nothing of any interest had been found since Gianelli's piece of Perspex. Descent started down the north-eastern shoulder, when something started coming through on the radio. Gianelli recognised the voice through the static: it was Flight Seargeant Alister Haveron, team leader at Valley. The pilot's body had been found at the top of a gully just off the edge of the south-eastern shoulder. Kinloss tried to get in touch by radio, but something was blocking the transmission. Their operational channel seemed to have become obliterated by someone in permanent transmit, probably caused by a wet microphone. They wanted to reach the Valley troops to help them with the body down the steep slopes, but the treacherous terrain, the appalling conditions and the difficulty of communication made it hazardous even to reach them.

Batson decided that they should descend to below cloud level, and get a fix there. On their way down, they were picked up by a Sea King from RAF Lossiemouth. Gianelli remembers:

> ...The flying over the next hour must have been the most impressive that I have ever witnessed in the mountains; hovering for well over an hour within feet of the rock, just inside the cloud layer and buffeted by the lashing rain and wind.[27]

An RAF photographer was dropped and taken up the gully to photograph the grim scene, and then the body could be moved down by MRT men and put into the helicopter. Gianelli caught a glimpse of a black, cubic object falling and bouncing down the slopes a few hundred yards away. It was a Hasselblad body that the photographer had dropped when his camera case had burst open high up on the slope. It may still be there lying among the heather for any keen photographer who can face the climb. Nobody, in those conditions, felt like climbing down to collect even a Hasselblad.

What had happened to the pilot? Ejecting in those wild conditions, white-out and strong winds, made the chances of a safe landing virtually nil. He had died when he had landed backwards on a rocky surface, shattering his flying helmet. Two of the Leuchars team were assigned as wreck guards.

Within the month, on December 18th, they were out again, in extremely cold conditions, when an American F-11 crashed near Newton Stewart.

12 – The Third Man

In Aviemore Police Station the desk officer, on the first day of 1981, a Thursday, looked at the two young men who had come through the door. They seemed to be very tired and from their clothes were clearly climbers. "What can I do for you?" he asked.

They were English. They had left their car in the Cairngorm ski carpark, but on returning after a couple of days' climbing, they could not find it. It seemed to have been stolen; could the police help?

Yes, of course, the police would do what they could. But the man on the desk was worried about their appearance. He took them through into the office, sat them down in the warmth and rustled up cups of tea. Then, somewhat recovered, they were taken in a police car to the snow-covered carpark. After some poking around in snow-drifts the car was found, and when it was dug out the police helped the young men to start it. They had mentioned that they were now due to return to England, and the policemen wished them a safe journey. Just before they backed out, however, one of the men broke down and muttered something about a pal dying up there on the hill, and that they had been through a terrible ordeal.[28]

Once they were sure that they were not the victims of a practical joke in rather poor taste, the policemen made it clear that the matter could not be left there, and the climbers quickly returned to Aviemore Police Station under escort. Neil Bailey was the name of the Third Man (see map on p.191).

Flight Sergeant Ray Sefton, usually known as Sunshine, was leading the Kinloss team that day, nominally on exercise in the Fort William area. Possibly leading is not quite the right word on this occasion, for they had been celebrating Hogmanay in Fort William, and when the call came through at 8.15 pm from Aviemore, some of them were still celebrating. It was 9.35 pm before he was able to get the team and the vehicles together and point them towards Aviemore, which they reached just before midnight, settling themselves down in the bothy opposite the Red MacGregor.

They were up early the next morning, ready to go by 6.15 am, with the sore-head quotient unusually high, even for MR. Joining them at the Rothiemurchus Lodge were members of the civilian Cairngorm MRT, and also the less familiar CID officers and police photographer. It was not yet dawn when the party started along the forest paths, through the Chalamain Gap and up the Lairig Ghru in the teeth of a cold wind that blasted the last traces of alcoholic fog from the brain. By the time they passed the Sinclair Hut, they were in full daylight. Right at the top of the pass is a series of pools, the Pools of Dee, which indirectly help form the source of the River Dee. Here, when they reached it at 8.45 am, they found a bivouac bag and a partially covered tent. Digging around, the police were able to locate the body of Neil Bailey, dressed in an anorak and thin cord trousers, buried in a patch of snow by the edge of one of the pools. Bailey's body was then wrapped in the tent and strapped to the stretcher, and the return down the pass started at a brisk pace with frequent bearer changes. A Sea King had been called in and was waiting on a small flat area just above the Sinclair Hut to take the body to Glenmore Lodge.

What, then, had happened between the time the three friends started out from the Cairngorm Ski carpark and the time that two of the three called in at the Aviemore Police Station? The following reconstruction seems the most likely. It is based on the observations of Glyn Gianelli who was involved in the search,[29] on Sefton's official report and on his recollections.

Bailey and his two friends had come up from England, had parked the car and walked over Cairngorm from Coire Cas with the intention of spending the night under canvas. At Lochan Buidhe they tried to pitch tents, but were defeated by the weather. Giving up, they set out then for the Shelter Stone, but could not find it (it is just a cave under the largest boulder below Shelter Stone Crag) and spent an uncomfortable night in the open by Loch Avon.

The next morning was Wednesday, December 31st. Jean's Hut was the target now, but to reach that they had to breast Cairn Lochan where they met the full fury of a Cairngorm blizzard. In poor visibility and uncomfortably aware of the danger of the cliffs on Cairn Lochan, they went off course and ended up descending by the March Burn. Here, near exhaustion, Bailey slipped and fell into the burn. He was helped out but it soon became obvious, with his clothes wet through, that he was beginning to suffer from exposure. His companions helped him down to the Pools of Dee and here they tried to build a snow shelter. At this spot (it is not quite clear how) some equipment was lost; shortly after this, it became apparent that Bailey had died. Wrapped in a tent, the other two were fortunate to survive.

When they felt sure he was dead, Bailey's companions left him covered with the tent, and started out towards the Sinclair Hut, which they found quite full with sheltering climbers. Somehow, people made space for two more and there they rested overnight. Bailey's death was mentioned to no-one, either when they first arrived or in the morning. Before dawn they were up before anyone else and off down to the Cairngorm carpark in atrocious weather, and then on, when they could not find the car, to the police station.

Why had Bailey's friends behaved in this strange way? Why had they only as an afterthought mentioned to the police that they had left the dead Bailey up at the Pools? Gianelli comments:

> But, of course, the effects of shock on an individual are many and varied especially if one loses a friend in such sudden tragic circumstances. One can only surmise that nature's defence mechanisms can sometimes be a little too efficient in blocking out the harsh realities of occurrences such as these.[29]

Researchers have found that with minor variations the sequence of events in hypothermia is: abnormal behaviour, slowing, stumbling, weakness, repeated falling, collapse, stupor, unconsciousness, death. Research subjects who could be questioned afterwards reported apathy, sometimes preceded by a phase of anxiety. Sometimes there is a feeling of unreality and detachment, sometimes a feeling of drunkenness. Looked at from the outside, those suffering are judged by companions as showing irrational behaviour, irritability, aggressiveness, or unusual silence and apathy.[30] A much later research paper reported:

> Where the onset of hypothermia is slow, for example, in climbers and walkers, the first warning signs are changes in mood and impairment of motor function. The affected person becomes silent, withdrawn and unresponsive to conversation, walks more slowly and eventually stumbles and falls.[31]

We can see here what led to Bailey's death and the sequence of symptoms that preceded it. We can also see, perhaps, that a combination of their own hypothermia and shock at Bailey's death could well have led to the strange behaviour of his friends in the carpark. It was in these conditions that they decided, confusedly, to drive back down to Blackpool and break the sad news to Bailey's mother. Had it not been for the accident of the car being submerged in snow, this is what they would have done.

13 – Highland Wings

Over the last fifty years, the teams have grown accustomed to the idea that the chances of finding anybody alive in an aircraft wreck are not high, and are getting lower by the year as top speeds increase. The Ansons which George Graham and his enthusiastic but unskilled team pulled apart so that they could get to the injured crews were not exactly safe aircraft to crash in; but they had a top speed of less than 200 mph. Of a series of aircraft crashes in the Highlands in the 1980s, three will suffice to illustrate how contrasting the MRTs' work can be. As an exception to the general rule there were survivors, always a boost to MRT morale.

A curling championship was to take place in Aberdeen, and two aircraft were chartered to fly eleven Swiss curlers there from Gatwick, but an industrial dispute by air traffic controllers diverted the aircraft to Dundee. One of the aircraft landed safely at 8 pm, but the second, a twin-engined, six-seater Cessna 310, piloted by Stuart Palmer, disappeared from the radar a little later. It had hit the 1,000-foot Frankley Den Hill near Balbeggie, seven miles north-east of Perth, and burst into flames. Stuart Palmer managed to get out, as did four of his passengers, all badly injured, Horrified, they looked back at the blazing wreck which still contained two of their companions.

With all five in pain and shivering in the mist, it became obvious that nobody in the wide world outside immediately knew where they were; if they were to be found in time, the outside world had to be alerted. Palmer, despite a broken leg, managed to crawl in agony over 500 feet of rough ground until he reached a fence. He even managed to get over the fence; then he collapsed, and at that point he stayed throughout the very cold and damp night and into the next morning, a total of twelve hours.

Kinloss MRT were at Tyndrum for a weekend exercise, and RCC Pitreavie diverted them to Balbeggie to help in the search with civilian teams. Led by Corporal David 'Heavy' Whalley, they found Palmer who was able to say, "The others are up there. Oh my God, please tell my wife I'm all right."

One of the civilian searchers, Jim Fraser from Aberfeldy, found the rest of the passengers. All of those who got out of the blazing wreck survived.

One of the big aircraft incidents of the decade, however, (putting aside Lockerbie which was in a class of its own) was the Shackleton which crashed on South Harris on Monday April 30th 1990. In this case, location of the wreck was not the problem, but because of the way the wreckage and its contents had been scattered, and the way the casualties were embedded in the wreckage, it was a very distressing incident to work on.

Fortunately the previous year there had been a practice airlift of both Scottish teams to North Wales and this was of great benefit in getting the Kinloss team to South Harris. Whalley by that time was team leader with the rank of flight sergeant and with the team he secured the crash site. This was an RAF aircraft and the crew wore beacons, but a helicopter had to be used to locate them as some had become detached from the casualties. As this was done, the casualties were marked and the area mapped out.

A visit to the site by the Procurator Fiscal, with the police taking photographs and filming the casualties, was followed by one from Squadron Leader J Vinales, from Operations Wing, RAF Lossiemouth, acting as Incident Commander. Vinales commented afterwards to the OC RAF Kinloss on the great help given him by the team and the team leader: ...they were truly magnificent.[32]

It was some hours later before the Procurator Fiscal and RCC could give the all-clear to remove the bodies, two of which could be extracted from the wreck only with great difficulty; a distressing job. All were then put into body bags and put aside to be winched out by a Sea King of 202 Squadron. Then a night guard of six team members under Sergeant Patterson was put on, followed the next day by the accident investigation people, and in the evening the site was handed over to the crashguard from Lossiemouth. An airlift was provided for the lighter vehicles back to Kinloss, and the two Bedfords were driven back.

This was a sad call-out, however, all agencies worked well together and the Team carried out a difficult task with their usual professionalism.[33]

Not long after the Shackleton came the Canberra. This type had been in service with the Royal Air Force for a long time, and was by this time largely deployed on training duties. It could perhaps be regarded as the Anson of its time. This particular aircraft was seconded to RAF Kinloss from RAF Wyton, in Cambridgeshire. It was approaching Kinloss after a routine flight just before 7 pm one day in May 1990 in heavy rain and under low cloud. During the instrument approach, there seemed to be a surge of power in the engines, followed by an explosion. Although they were at a very low level, the crew of two ejected, landing about 200 yards away from the blazing wreckage. It had cut through overhead power lines, plunging much of the area into darkness.

Within minutes, the RAF Kinloss fire-fighting teams were there, soon supported by civilian fire brigades from Elgin and Forres. Where the crew members had landed the Mountain Rescue Team found the pilot dead and the navigator badly injured. A spinal splint, provided by the MRT, was put on by the Duty Medical Officer, and the casualty was evacuated to Raigmore Hospital.

Chapter 4 – Footnotes

[1] Gosling: climbing diary 20-21/2/52
[2] Dattner: in conversation with the writer 2/2/92
[3] Glyn Gianelli: letter to the writer
[4] Alan Coley in a letter to the writer, 14/5/92, and letter PO J A Coley to Squadron Leader A R Gordon-Cumming, 28/8/56
[5] Letter to writer 12/11/91
[6] Kevin Howett: Rock Climbing in Scotland (Constable 1990)
[7] Hamish MacInnes: Call-Out (Hodder & Stoughton 1973)
[8] Derek Walker: letter to writer 5/2/92
[9] Forfar police statement, reported in the Daily Express
[10] Sandy Gordon-Cumming: in conversation with the writer, 30/7/92
[11] Sandy Gordon-Cumming: in conversation with the writer, 30/7/92
[12] John Hinde: climbing diary 3/10/59
[13] John Hinde: climbing diary 11/11/59
[14] John Hinde: climbing diary 13/4/60
[15] Aberdeen Mountain Rescue Team 25-year Book 1992
[16] Martin to writer 21/1/92
[17] Bob Sharp: letter to writer 26/1/92
[18] Hamish MacInnes: Call-Out (Hodder & Stoughton 1973)
[19] Wg Cdr G McKenzie (OC Admin. Services, to Officer i/c Mountain Rescue, Kinloss, 19/7/62
[20] Feu = ground rent (Scottish law)
[21] Report immediately after the search by Chief Technician J Hinde, RAF Kinloss MRT
[22] Lord Byron: Childe Harold's Pilgrimage
[23] Letter Chief Technician J Hinde BEM RAF to landowners, 10/10/68
[24] Corporal Blyth
[25] Letter Bruce to writer received 21/11/92
[26] Report on Mountain Rescue Quarterly Returns, – 1 January – 31 March 1972. Squadron Leader D Lofts May 23 1972
[27] Letter to writer 29/5/92
[28] Letter WO R D Sefton to writer 26/11/92
[29] Glyn Gianelli to writer, 24/7/92
[30] L G C E Pugh: Accidental Hypothermia in Walkers, Climbers and Campers: Report to the Medical Commission on Accident Prevention (British Medical Journal 15/1/66)
[31] Investigation into the Nature of Exposure/Exhaustion – Progress Report No. 1 (Aberdeen university 1984)
[32] Letter Sqn Ldr Vinales to Group Captain R H Gould 3/5/90
[33] Flt Sgt D Whalley, Report A

A North American Harvard IV of the Fleet Air Arm crashed on Jacob's Ladder in 1952; Harpur Hill MRT attended. This is a still-existing example of the same mark. *Photo: H J Budgen*

F100 Super Sabre. Sabres kept Harpur Hill busy during the 50s. *Photo: H J Budgen*

CHAPTER V
BETWEEN BUXTON AND BAKEWELL

England 1951-92

> There was a rocky valley between Buxton and Bakewell,...divide as the vale of Tempe; you might have seen the gods there morning and evening, – Apollo and the sweet Muses of the Light...You enterprised a railroad,...you blasted its rocks away...and now, every fool in Buxton can be at Bakewell in half-an-hour, and every fool in Bakewell at Buxton.
>
> John Ruskin 1819-1900: Praeterita.

1 – Wings over the Peaks

Harpur Hill came in for a lot of criticism in 1947 after that disastrous exercise in South Wales (Chapter II). Much of it was unfounded, but in any case the team's performance during the '50s was enough to dispel any lingering taint on its reputation. Even whilst, many miles away, the Beinn Eighe searches were going on, Harpur Hill had been called out in April 1951 to a double Meteor crash on the Pennines in atrocious summer weather, and had shown up well.

Those with sufficiently long memories will remember the Harvard, the American trainer with the painfully piercing engine note. In January 1952 a Harvard, a navy plane, piloted by the 20-year-old Midshipman Brian Farley, was reported missing over Kinder Scout. It was five days before a group of walkers from Manchester, following the Pennine Way across Kinder Scout to Hayfield, spotted some wreckage near Jacob's Ladder. Closer, they could see that it was of a yellow aircraft, the wings ripped off, the nose buried in the ground, part-burned and, still in the pilot's seat, a human figure, the face hideously deformed by fire.

Glossop police were told and a small party of four police officers and two local people who knew the terrain well went to the spot. Harvard FT415 was found after a struggle through deep snow in the dark, at 8.20 pm. RAF Harpur Hill was told and the MRT was, by chance, not far away. The officer i/c, Flight Lieutenant Duthie, and two others were found and brought to the scene; the rest were sent for. Then followed the unpleasant task of removing the pilot's body and taking it down on a sledge stretcher.

On May 1st 1954, two de Havilland Vampires of 673 Squadron were going out on a camera gun exercise over the North Sea, but before it got that far one of them was struck by lightning in a cloud. Its pilot ejected, but his head was hit by the tailplane and his parachute did not open. His body was found, embedded in the ground, a few hundred yards from his still-smoking aircraft. Harpur Hill was called out. (One way or another, the Vampire was a particularly hazardous aircraft to be flying when trouble occurred, as the engine was behind the pilot, so a crash landing often resulted in the engine forcibly entering the pilot's compartment.)

The team's involvement with Sabres during the '50s both began and ended in a less than happy way. In December 1954, there was a call-out to recover the body of a Canadian pilot who had crashed in a Sabre near Holme Moss. On the way to the scene one of the MRT's vehicles collided with a plumber's van, wrecking the van and sending the plumber to Ashton General Hospital. After a delay the convoy carried on and then had a six-hour search before finding the pilot's body.

Then two RAF Sabres crashed on Kinder Moor in 1958. Some years later, the team, by then at RAF Stafford, went out on weekend exercise and sought, successfully, what was left of the wreckage, which was very widely spread, some near Edale, some near Glossop. A fuel tank was dug up from where it was half-buried on the Moor, but most of the wreckage, including the wheels, was more than a mile away. Again, the convoy met with an accident, this time on the way home.

Two Canadian Sabres were being delivered from Canada to Grostenquin in France, refuelling at Prestwick on June 26th 1959. They left Prestwick for RAF Wethersfield at just before midday, one arriving a little over an hour later. But where was the other? The last sighting had been ten minutes after take-off, when they broke formation at 5,000 feet before entering cloud, and there had been no radio contact.

At 2.05 pm two SA16s from the American 67th ARS at Prestwick, an Anson from RAF Silloth, a Valetta from RAF Kirkbride, and two Whirlwind helicopters from 22 Squadron at RAF Valley and 275 Squadron at RAF Leconfield were alerted. All the UK airfields were notified, as well as the French airfields at Marvelle and Grostenquin. An appeal went out over BBC radio and television; the coastal radio stations at North Foreland and Seaforth made special broadcasts to shipping. Very little response was received, and the most likely area appeared to be the Lake District if the aircraft had crashed.

As luck would have it, there was no team with this specific area. The MRT at RAF West Freugh, which had covered it, had been disbanded in March 1957. Normally Topcliffe would have been brought in, but was in the process of moving to RAF Leeming. Pitreavie therefore decided to bring in Harpur Hill and Leuchars MRTs.

At Harpur Hill the team leader was Sergeant Johnnie Steed (an alpinist who had started at Valley), who had qualified the previous year. Returning from the Summer Course in North Wales to find that the team had just left on exercise, he answered the phone at 4.30 pm to take the Pitreavie call. He then telephoned Glossop police, asking them to stop the convoy as they went through. There was nothing to be done then but wait for the call back from the team. This came at

5 pm; he told them to stand by and it was nearly two hours before Pitreavie telephoned again. Steed told the team to return to Harpur Hill to refuel and to pick up the officer (Flying Officer Rogers), himself and the rest of the team. By 9.30 pm they were all on their three-hour drive to Millbeck in the Lake District. Arriving there in the early hours, they were soon joined by the Leuchars team under Flight Sergeant Bill Brankin.

Searching in light rain the next day was unsuccessful. An aerial search was impossible with the cloud base of 2,500 feet, according to the Harpur Hill log, though records elsewhere show that at least one of the American SA16s and the Silloth Anson were up. On the 28th it was still raining and the cloud base was even lower at 1,500 feet. At 1.20 pm two airmen from Leuchars found the wreck with the dead pilot near the top of Iron Crag, south of Ennerdale Lake. One of them ran four miles to telephone RCC at Pitreavie, whilst the other stayed at the crash site and radioed the other parties.

It was a couple of hours before a 22 Squadron helicopter arrived from RAF Silloth to collect the personal effects of the pilot, and the team was then able to take the body to Whitehaven where it was handed over to the police. Part of the delay was because the Whitehaven coroner wanted the police to be present when bodies were removed. It was not until 9 pm that all parties finally returned to base, to stay overnight before returning to station. It had been a three-day operation.

One important point emerged from this call-out. Even where the MT drivers were not expected to go on the hill, they had to be used to sleeping out, sleeping rough, or sleeping under canvas, otherwise they could be more of a liability than an asset, and that is what proved to be the case here. A non-team driver was detailed by the MT section for this operation, and caused problems for Steed. This was obviously not for the first time, for a pained comment by Steed in the diary reads: 'It's happened again'.[1]

Bomber Command's mainstay heavy bomber for the second half of the war and the immediate post-war years was the Avro Lancaster, which had by the mid-50s been replaced in that role, but the design was so good and trusted that it was adapted for Coastal Command use, and called the Shackleton.

Shackleton No. WR 970, was on a test flight on December 7th 1956, piloted by Avro's test pilot Squadron Leader Jack Wales DFC, with a crew of three. Wales, who had won his DFC in Burma during the war and was Commanding Officer of 613 City of Manchester Auxiliary Squadron, had in the aircraft with him a flight engineer and two test observers, all civilians. People in the villages of Eyam and Foolow, near Buxton, saw Wales's Shackleton circling and getting lower. One of them was L du Garde Peach, the radio playwright, who commented to his housekeeper when he heard some strange changes in the engine note as if one of the four had cut out: "I think that chap's in trouble".

Losing one engine in a four-engine aircraft would not of itself be enough to cause a catastrophe, but the Shackleton was then seen and heard heading for the ground in a spin, engines at full blast. It then levelled off, and it looked as if it was going to get out of trouble. It just missed some houses, but the next thing was an enormous explosion and a plume of black smoke.

Harpur Hill set out under Flight Lieutenant Mitchell and Sergeant John Mooring, a medical branch NCO, to be met by a scene of almost total devastation, with fires breaking out whilst the team was trying to recover the bodies. For a long time they were unable to search the front part of the aircraft and it was five hours before the team could extract the last crewman from that portion of the fuselage, and two days before it could safely be said that the last limb from the last body had been found.

Nobody on the ground had been lost; the local people and the press were united in believing that Wales had struggled with the aircraft to get it away from the village. A V Roe & Co. Ltd asked the team to search a wide area in case any of the crew had been thrown clear, though there had been no reports of anybody leaving the aircraft. Afterwards Avro wrote to the Commanding Officer at RAF Harpur Hill:

> The party, under the command of Flight Lieutenant Mitchell, gave efficient and valuable service, particularly in the recovery of the bodies of the crew. This operation was carried out under extremely difficult conditions due to the state of the wreckage and the fact that outbreaks of fire were continually recurring.
>
> We would particularly mention Sergeant Mooring for his energy and initiative although we hasten to add that all members of the party behaved most excellently.[2]

So began a useful relationship between Harpur Hill MRT and Avro. Many of Avro's test flights took place over Harpur Hill's territory, with its hazardous terrain. Avro's liaison officer got in touch with Squadron Leader Griffiths at RAF Harpur Hill, and two years later, in November 1958, the team, under Steed, was invited to the Avro works at Woodford, Cheshire. Corporal Roche and ten airmen were shown round the Shackleton, Vulcan and the old and faithful Anson in detail, with special emphasis on break-in points. This became a regular occurrence, so that technical detail could be updated.

Only two days before the Shackleton crash – merely the biggest incident in a busy period – on December 5th 1956, an American military aircraft had crashed near Glossop. 18 Group telephoned Mooring to say that the team was to stand by; within half an hour this was cancelled. That evening they were on standby once more; again it was cancelled. Then three quarters of an hour later there were definite instructions to meet one or two USAF officers at Glossop Police Station the next morning.

After arriving on time and waiting in vain for the two officers, Mooring left a message that he was going on with the team to the crash site to recover the bodies. There the usual grim sight presented itself. One of the crew members

Sqdn Ldr Wales crashed during stalling tests of a Shackleton at Foolow, Derbyshire in 1956; Harpur Hill was called out. Ten years later, this Mark 3 Shackleton of 206 Squadron was photographed. It is fitted with the Autolycos exhaust trail detector for sniffing out submarines snorting on the surface – note the aerial on top of the fuselage. *Photo: the late M Woodward, courtesy of H J Budgen*

was still sitting in the burnt-out wreckage, the other spreadeagled face down beside it. Otherwise unrecognisable, the bodies were identified by an American dcntal officcr, Captain Scligman, who cvcntually showed up, and were taken by USAF ambulance to Glossop mortuary.

2 – Neil Moss

BUXTON read the destination blind on the bus as it left Leek at 11.30 am on January 17th 1952, a bleak day; but the crew and three passengers had no idea of just how bleak it was going to be for them. Before it reached the high spots of Brand Side and Axe Edge on the A53, it ran into a snowdrift near the village of Flash. There was no chance of getting it out, so the driver, Frank Moss, set off on foot towards Buxton, whilst the conductor, Jack Henning, stayed with it and the passengers. This was mid-afternoon, and people were getting hungry and cold. As dusk was falling, Moss was pleased to see a Land Rover approaching with Divisional Officer A J Reader of the local fire service at the wheel. One of his firemen lived at Flash and had been unable to get on shift, and Reader was going to pick him up. Reader collected Moss and two lorry drivers who were also snow-bound, and took them to Buxton. He had known the Harpur Hill MRT for some years and had helped to organise various joint exercises and call-outs, and from Buxton he telephoned the section.

Flight Lieutenant Fitton, the medical officer, Flight Lieutenant Duthie and Corporal Taff Austin, who had only that week been told about his BEM, met Moss and Police Sergeant Weaver, and managed to get within half a mile of the bus by 9 pm, then struggled the rest of the distance with blankets, food and hot drinks. With a sledge stretcher the passengers and Henning were taken to the MRT vehicle, each journey taking three quarters of an hour; and it was just before midnight, twelve hours after the bus had first left Leek, before the mission was completed.

Interspersed with the drama and the tragedies were times of high farce. For the short period of March 1955 to June 1956, Harry Appleby was the team leader, then to be posted to Nicosia. A physical-training instructor, parachute jumping instructor and remedial gymnast, he remembers Harpur Hill as a time bomb for two distinct reasons. Firstly, the station was a storage and issue unit for bombs, shells and small arms ammunition; and secondly, it was relatively quiet in Mountain Rescue terms, and one of his problems was to keep his permanent staff of six occupied and out of mischief. To this end, he rescheduled their programmes as soon as he took over. He admits now, however, that he did not take sufficient notice of the latent talents of his brilliant radio mechanic. Once having brought the equipment up to his own high standards, this genius became bored and found relief by serving his team leader with some unusual culinary creations when on the hill, such as corned beef and sheep dropping sandwiches. Appleby can taste the double-decker still.

He also had a talent for making the most of any dire situation he was in. Given fourteen days in the guardroom after an explosion in the Mountain Rescue Section, he occupied his time repairing the television sets of the families in the married quarters. This soon earned him the freedom of the guardroom, and before long, acting apparently on an impulse, he grabbed an RAF policeman's white belt and snow-drop cap from their hooks, and went out to man the barrier. Unfortunately, the first person to come along was the flight sergeant in charge of the guardroom.

Penistone police – a sub-unit of Harpur Hill – called in the team at 7 am on December 1st 1958 to look for three boys taking the Duke of Edinburgh's Award Test. They were navigating across the moor from Strines Inn to Salter's Brook Bridge, having started the previous day at midday. Strines Inn is on a little road which leaves the A57 Sheffield-Glossop road east of the Ladybower Reservoir, and the destination the boys were given took them a distance of about eight miles (as the crow flies) north-north-west across Howden Moors and Harden Moor, east of the Derwent Reservoir and the River Derwent, then dropping down sharply to the A628 Penistone-Hollingworth road at the Salter's Brook Bridge.

They were believed to be somewhere on Harden Moor.

Flight Lieutenant John Carter, officer i/c and medical officer, Flying Officer Hart and John Steed, team leader, took twenty-two of the team out, calling at Strines Inn on the way to make sure of the details of the story. They met six civilian volunteers and three policemen, one with a tracker dog, and split into eight parties with the civilians. Within half an hour the three boys were found, walking in from the moor to Salter's Brook Bridge – on course, if very late – and the other parties were recalled by radio and flares. One of the youths was affected by exposure and was taken to a pub where he was given tea.

To start at midday on a fairly long winter walk was an error of judgement for which Steed blamed the instructor; an error compounded by the boys apparently having lost faith in their one compass. Also they had no spare clothing or food, reinforcing a lesson which the service generally has always tried to broadcast over the years. No doubt it will continue to be ignored.

For high drama and public interest, however, nothing in the '50s matched the tragedy of Neil Moss. Never before had Harpur Hill, or any other team, been called upon to assist in a pot-holing incident. Rather casually, it was assumed that the pot-holing fraternity had an effective rescue network in place, just as mountaineers had. But this, apparently, was not the case.

In the Peak Cavern, Castleton, a young student called Neil Moss was trapped on Sunday afternoon, March 22nd 1959. Moss, an Oxford undergraduate, had descended into a recently-discovered extension with other members of the British Speleological Association. The party had two weeks previously found a shaft; and now it was to be explored, Moss volunteering to go down first. It was estimated to be 40 feet deep, but a 75-foot ladder was used in case the shaft proved to be longer. At 3.30 pm, Moss started on his way down, kicking the ladder before him. It started at a steep angle, but after about 12 to 18 feet it twisted then descended almost vertically to a blockage of boulders which might, it was thought, lead to another cavern. He reached the boulders, got off the ladder and shouted up that he was going to see if he could shift them.

He managed to a small extent, and in doing so jammed the ladder beneath him. Beginning to feel tired, Moss called out that he was coming back up to let someone else have a go. It was at this point that he himself became jammed: he could not raise either leg to get a foot onto the ladder. When he did not reappear, his companions dropped a rope. He tied it on, but when the others pulled it up, it broke several times. A fresh rope was sent for, and in the meantime, Moss, overcome by carbon dioxide, became unconscious (he had been using an acetylene lamp which increased the consumption of oxygen). At about this time, 6.45 pm, an official of the Derbyshire Cave Rescue Organisation appeared with two stronger ropes. The police were informed, but it was not until 10 pm that the call-out system of the DCRO was used. Moss was still unconscious and oxygen was called for; this arrived at 12.30 am. None of the DCRO members were on

the telephone and perhaps because the area was very foggy none of them had been contacted. The DCRO secretary, at 1.25 am, had to tell the police that more help would be needed. That was the situation when the RAF was called.

Buxton police telephoned Harpur Hill at 1.55 am. Having put his team on standby, Flight Lieutenant Carter obtained clearance from 18 Group to attend as the circumstances were unusual. Carter and Flying Officer Rogers, with ten team members, went over to Castleton, arriving at 2.55 am on the Monday. Led by experienced pot-holers to the cavern immediately above the trapped man, Carter called for oxygen, and then for two whole days the team, with pot-holers and others helping, struggled to get Moss free. A constant supply of oxygen equipment was maintained by the MRTs, and a telephone line was set up. Topcliffe was brought in from the Pennines to help, but all the efforts were in vain. As everybody worked in shifts to free Moss, they could see life slipping away from him. After two days, he died: lack of oxygen, carbon dioxide poisoning and exposure.

Then there was the problem of the body. Still it could not be reached, let alone freed, and the Home Secretary gave permission for it to stay, and it was sealed in, entombed in one of the caves which Moss had loved so much. It was March 26th before Harpur Hill returned to the station. 'Death by misadventure' was the verdict at the inquest, and the coroner went out of his way to congratulate the MRTs and other organisations, for their work.

Steed, the team leader, made the point in his report that the incident had attracted a great deal of publicity, and he felt it likely that they would be called in again. He recommended purchasing a small quantity of pot-holing equipment: helmets at fourteen shillings (70p) and carbide helmet lamps at 16 shillings (80p) each, and also suggested the use of RAF exposure suits as provided for aircrew in dinghy packs. Constructive though his suggestion was, the carbide lamps would not have been the best choice:

> The fouling of the air would also be increased by his own acetylene lamp going out adding the dissipating carbide fumes to an already bad atmosphere. There is no doubt that the acetylene lamp is a dangerous device in any kind of cramped space and I for one detest its use underground.[3]

Finally, having made some enquiries, Steed suggested the purchase of a guide book, 'Caves and Pot-holes of Britain'. As a direct result of that incident, Harpur Hill built up a small nucleus of members with caving skills.

Whilst it is beyond the terms of this book to analyse cave rescue methods, it is fair to mention that the Derbyshire Cave Rescue Organisation came in for considerable criticism after the incident, on the grounds that the rescue team was not called out soon enough, that some of the equipment such as ropes was defective and that its call-out procedure was inadequate. It is also fair to say that very soon afterwards the local clubs met and discussed the operation, and as a direct result the whole system was overhauled and has since been highly-respected.

Harpur Hill's successor, Stafford, no longer keeps cave rescue equipment, though it works quite frequently with the cave rescue organisations.

3 – The Stork Club

Two men had dinner one evening in the White Hart in Lincoln – a group captain and David Beardsall, the Quality Assurance Manager from GEC:

Nimrod, the Advanced Early Warning System, was about to be delivered to RAF Waddington. Chatting over coffee, Beardsall and the group captain realised that years before in the sixties, they had been stationed at RAF Leeming together. Leeming had been the home of No. 3 Flying Training School, and the group captain, then an acting pilot officer (APO), had been under flying training; Beardsall, then an air radar mechanic, had become a member of the mountain rescue team about three years after it had moved from RAF Topcliffe. There was good reason for the Waddington station commander to remember the time; with other APOs, he had been sent for a weekend with the MRT early in 1962. A night navigation exercise was arranged.

Beardsall, with his party of APOs, was dropped off early on the Friday evening at Dufton, just north of the exposed A66 which runs from Scotch Corner to Penrith, and which is so well known to drivers from the east and south of England heading for the Lake District and the Western Highlands. Using what is now the Pennine Way, they walked the 20-25 miles over Cross Fell to the village of Garrigill and thence to Alston.

It had been a hard winter, and they were coping with deep snow all the way. One of the APOs, fatigued and suffering from the cold, had to be helped before they reached Alston. Beardsall lent him much of his own clothing. Finally they reached Alston at 2 am, but there was a disappointment: in the field where they were expecting to camp there was no sign of the team. Obviously they could not stay in the open in those conditions, and reluctantly, they got the proprietor of an adjacent garage out of bed and told him of their dilemma. He opened up the garage and they slept in there as best they could, most of them making themselves comfortable on the back seats of various cars, wondering idly what the owners might have thought of the arrangement. Within the hour the rest of the team arrived, and told them that of the three roads into Alston, two were blocked by snow drifts, obliging them to make an enormous diversion across the Pennines and back again by way of Newcastle.

With the team complete, base camp was set up. Exercises were resumed and continued until an approach was made by a doctor from the local cottage hospital, telling the team leader, Sergeant George Bruce, that he had many patients in outlying farms, especially expectant mothers. He was worried because he could not reach them and felt that they would be safer in hospital. Could the team, he asked, bring some of them in? Few were on the telephone, so the doctor armed the team with letters of authority and off they went with the Thomas stretcher. Beardsall remembers now:

I think a few were rather surprised when they answered the door to a bunch of unwashed and unshaven scruffy-looking airmen, but they came with us and the exercise went without incident, although it was very tiring manhandling the stretcher over large drifts and deep ruts for many miles. On the second occasion we were met by reporters and photographers, who had come by train from Carlisle, as we entered Alston.[4]

The A66 (Scotch Corner – Penrith) has over the years been the scene of many call-outs for Topcliffe and Leeming. This is Leeming at work in 1990. *Photo: Paul Duckworth*

Brenda Raoul lived at High Ash Farm, and was expecting her first baby within a week or two. She was working in the house when she heard the knock on the door at noon. It had taken the team 1½ hours to reach her, and by 1 pm they were on their way. At 2.45 pm they had reached a spot about a mile from Alston where a snow-plough had cut a way through for the ambulance, and Mrs Raoul was put safely in it. Bruce, talking to a reporter at the time, said:

Everything went according to plan. We are hoping to be able to return to our headquarters at RAF Leeming, Yorkshire, tomorrow if the snow-plough clears the road.

The team was due to return to Leeming on the Sunday evening but was unable to leave the village because of snow-drifts. Standing on top of one of the drifts, Beardsall was surprised when he looked down to find that he was regarding the top of a telegraph pole with the wires disappearing under the snow.

Bruce, finding that the situation was no better the next day, telephoned RAF Leeming, and the station headquarters sent a telegram to the Post Office in Alston authorising travel warrants so that the bulk of the team could return by rail; the line to Newcastle had remained open. All except eight got away, but soon further snow blocked the line, and Alston was totally isolated. Making friends with the local publican, the group of eight, including Beardsall, were allowed to sleep on the pub floor – "the best bivouac we ever had" says Beardsall. Between games of darts, they continued to help the doctor and various people in the town. Messages kept coming from the Post Office to ring various numbers, reversing the charges – the callers newspaper and television reporters who had seen reports of the Stork Club – as it became known – and wanted a story. Some pressmen suggested that the team and the village might be running out of food, but in fact the team had ample Compo rations, and the villagers were used to being cut off and were prepared for it. Many of them invited the team into their homes for tea and meals.

When the railway line re-opened, Corporal Ray Tweddle went to Newcastle by train to be interviewed on television. Then, when they had been there a week, the rump of the team was able to leave; the snow-blowers had got through. Four vehicles left Alston squeezing between the cliffs of the packed snow piled high on either side, leaving behind a grateful Alston, and taking with them lasting memories of a village with tremendous community spirit.

Six years later, the men from Leeming were again able to help local people in an unusual way. It was early in 1968 and after the weekend exercise the convoy, Bedford 3-tonner in the lead, was returning to Leeming. In the back of the Bedford the troops were, for the most part, in the usual post-exercise semi-comatose state. However, Roger Quartermain saw something on the A66 which made him sit up and take action. About eight miles east of Brough, they met a private car going in the opposite direction which, when it had passed the convoy, skidded, rolled over twice and ended up in a hedge. Nobody had seen the incident except Quartermain and he had no means of communicating with the Bedford driver.

Behind the Bedford was the ambulance and Quartermain managed to convey to the ambulance driver that they should stop. That driver then signalled to the Bedford driver, the convoy stopped and, when Quartermain had quickly explained the situation, turned round and went back to the overturned car. Using the ambulance's searchlights, they found in the inverted car a very shaken family of two adults, two young children and two dogs. There were no serious physical injuries, but shock was clearly a hazard here. Extracting the children and their mother, the team put them into the ambulance in sleeping bags; initially the children were worried that it, too, was about to roll over, but they were reassured and before long the incident became an adventure for them.

Amazingly, when the team put the car back on its four wheels, there seemed to be no serious damage. With a short tow the engine started and when the interior had warmed up, the children were transferred there and the family was able to continue, about two hours after the accident. The mother's letter to Flight Lieutenant Bardern, the team officer, commented:

> To me, an ex-nurse, I marvel at the way my children's fears were allayed, the consideration and kindness shown to me, and the absolute calmness they showed. My two dogs were even given the same consideration!!! They turned a very frightening experience into a memory for the children when their prime adventure has turned out to be, "being rescued by the Mountain Rescue Team".[5]

4 – Working Together

Gradually over the years the incidence grew of multi-team search-and-rescue operations, and for certain types of incident the advantages of bringing in a second or even a third team became steadily clearer. But some incidents seemed to reveal a lack of awareness on the part of the rescue co-ordination people, of the MRT's capabilities and expertise.

RCC called out both Leeming and Stafford promptly when a Canberra crashed on Kinder Scout during the winter of 1963/64, and the two convoys reached search HQ at about the same time. This enabled the two teams to put maximum effort into the search without delay. But that same winter, two Rover Scouts went missing on Bleaklow, again in the Peak District. In that case initially there was no call-out and the team became aware of the incident only through BBC and press reports. The officer i/c took the initiative in telephoning RCC and eventually the team was deployed about 36 hours late.

Another Canberra had been reported missing on January 28th 1963 whilst on a low level flight. Leeming received a call from RCC, with no information as to the route, and was told that RCC would ring back. It did not and later in the day the team called RCC, to be told that the most likely crash area was either on a line east from the Isle of Man to the Lake District, or alternatively south from Penrith over the western Pennines. Corporal Ray Tweddle lived in Penrith and had often seen Canberras flying low over there: he suggested a first search in the Caldbeck Fells. With the weather bad and deteriorating, the team leader did not want to get snow-bound on the cross-Pennine journey, and asked RCC if he could move his team into the Lake District overnight, ready for the beginning of search at first light. RCC said No, stay where you are at RAF Leeming. It was not until 10.30 am that Leeming was finally sent into action, and by then only with difficulty could the Pennines be crossed to Caldbeck Fells, where the Canberra was soon found.

In a report some years later it was recommended that in such an incident, involving a large area, the future routine should be to alert the two nearest MRTs, and the officers or team leaders should decide whether one or both teams should actually go out. In the Caldbeck Fells case, went the argument, probably the best solution would have been to move Leeming to the west immediately and bring in Stafford or Leuchars as cover in the east.

All of the teams draw great benefit from climbing in each other's territory. Kinloss and Leuchars go to Snowdonia for a few days' training and experience the hazards of climbing on slate; Valley and St Athan go to the Cairngorms to experience on granite the heights and weather more extreme than those of their own patch. Probably, however, the teams which gain most from this tradition are the English ones. This is not to say that English mountains are hazard-free – far from it, as anyone who has become involved with the crumbling limestone of the

Peak District will testify – but in Mountain Rescue terms the areas have over the years tended to be much quieter than those on the other side of Hadrian's Wall or Offa's Dyke. Many a newly-qualified team leader has cut his teeth for a couple of years at Leeming or Stafford before moving to a more high-profile team.

For a week at the beginning of September, 1968, the Stafford team was based at Kinlochleven, Argyllshire, the objective being: ...to give the newer members experience in rock and hill-walking on the bigger hills of Scotland.[6]

Sergeant 'Teuch' Brewer was the team leader; he had obtained his team leader's qualification only that year, having joined Mountain Rescue as a volunteer in 1962. If the Stafford team thought that they were just in for a few days' improving exercise, they were mistaken. Arriving at Kinlochleven on Saturday August 30th, by 6.05 pm that same day they had been called out to a climbing accident in Glen Coe. On the Sunday they managed to get in a full day's serious walking, the only sign of anything untoward a terse comment in the log, in a different hand from Brewer's: ...2 fags and 3 matches to last all day – no matches were donated by Team Leader.

But after that there were several call-outs: one a night. After the third, on the night of September 3rd/4th, which took all night, the team rested whilst their gear dried out in the sun.

So it continued for the rest of the week, leading up to the Saturday, when, with the Kinloss team under John Hinde, they were due to cover the Ben Nevis Race. They arrived at Achintee early in the morning to be briefed on their positions for the race. Parties were stationed at key points on the mountain, each with a stretcher. At about 2,000 feet the cloud base was low, and soon after the 2 pm start the large number of runners started streaming through the mist past the waiting RAF people. Four runners were injured during the race and had to be stretchered off.

Chapter 5 – Footnotes

1 Harpur Hill diary 29/6/59
2 Quoted in the in-house history by David Lofts
3 James Lovelock: Life and Death Underground (G Bell & Sons Ltd, London, 1963)
4 Letter to writer 6/2/92
5 Quoted in 'Leeming Life' (RAF Leeming station magazine) March 1968
6 Stafford diary 1/9/68

CHAPTER VI – ASIAN DAWNS

Overseas 1954-76

It dawns in Asia, tombstones show
And Shropshire names are read;
And the Nile spills his overflow
Beside the Severn's dead.

A E Houseman 1859-1936: A Shropshire Lad

1 – The Secrets of Mount Suphan

Cyprus, in September 1954, saw the first overseas team, at RAF Nicosia. Later, Corporal Derek Bottomer was posted to RAF Akrotiri when the Cyprus troubles were at their height, and found that Eoka (the Greek-Cypriot nationalist organisation) had just destroyed in one its explosions the recently-built main hangar with five aircraft and all the services. He arrived to find a station bounded on one side by the Kyrenia Mountains and on the other by the Troodos Mountains, the main peak of which was Mount Olympus, 6,401 ft; a station where life was extremely frustrating, as security demanded that all personnel be confined to camp.

Not quite all. On frequent visits to RAF Nicosia, he noticed that every week, at midday on the Saturday, a convoy of vehicles marked MOUNTAIN RESCUE would leave, and would return a day or two later. Putting aside the small consideration that he was not, and had never been, any sort of walker or climber or mountaineer, he registered the fact that this could be the way to relieve the tedium caused by the security arrangements. 'I didn't think I'd fancy being behind barbed wire for 2½ years. So this was a way to get out.[1] He found the Mountain Rescue Section, and met Flight Sergeant Harry Appleby, the team leader, not long out from Harpur Hill. Appleby kitted Bottomer out straight away, and he went out with the team the following weekend. Uniquely, with the Nicosia team the wearing of RAF berets was obligatory, even on the most remote hills; unpopular, but better than the alternative, the possibility of being shot at as Eoka terrorists. Appleby remembers those times well:

There were very [few] occasions, indeed, when team members could go about their business without the encumbrance of a side-arm (pistol) or a Sten gun. For a short period of time non-NCO members were required to carry .303 Enfield rifles which proved an additional hazard when rock-climbing. Notwithstanding, I like the personal safety of being surrounded by team members that could discourage opposition with arms providing a healthy and rapid fire element.[2]

There had been a nervous incident in 1958 when the team was out in the

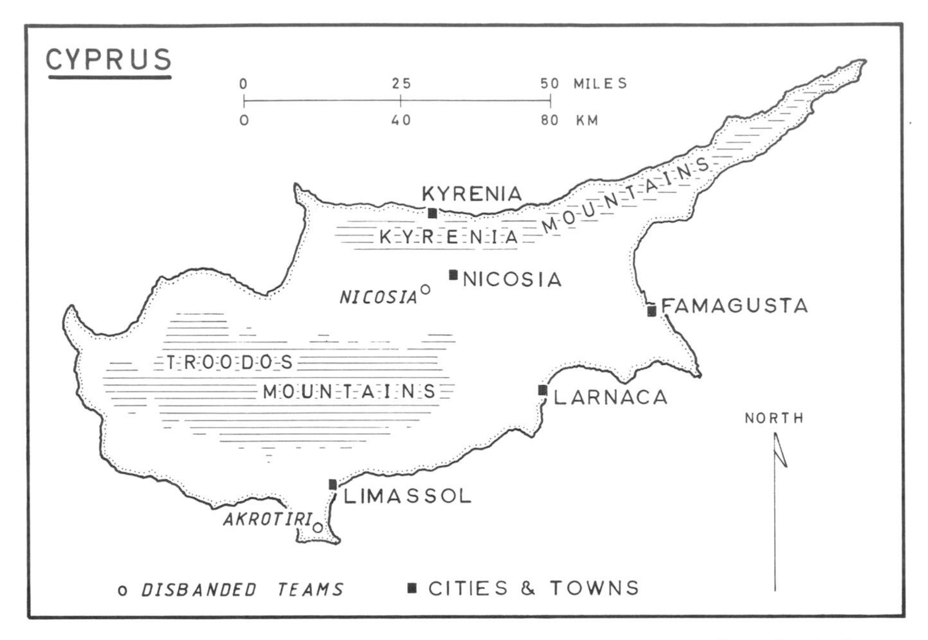

Troodos Mountains on a night exercise. After an unpleasant trek in the darkness avoiding thorn bushes and village goats, they suddenly became aware that in the darkness ahead of them were two shadowy figures with rifles to the shoulder, pointing straight at them. About to make a dash for cover, the three young men with Appleby were stopped when the flight sergeant hissed to them to keep still. "We're the Mountain Rescue!" called out Appleby. There was no response. "RAF!" he added after a few seconds. An English voice responded and positive identifications were made. Nobody had thought to tell Mountain Rescue that a contingent from a Guards regiment was out in that same segment of the mountains hoping to catch Colonel Grivas of Eoka. They were invited to join the two guardsmen in a small tent where they had been living for fourteen days on Compo rations, which Appleby's dog later refused to eat.[3]

Before long Bottomer was an enthusiastic member of the team. At Easter, 1959, he was one of a group which made a west-to-east trek across the 66-mile Kyrenia Mountains, taking thirty-two hours at an average height of 3,000 feet. This was the first time that this had been done, and was met with total incomprehension by the local rural population and the odd motorist, who assumed that the group was on some sort of punishment.

Although the higher Troodos Mountains were the usual training ground, it was not in Cyprus but in Turkey that the first major incident occurred. On April 25th, within three weeks of the Kyrenia trek, news was filtering through of a missing aircraft, an Avro Tudor freighter chartered from Air Charters Ltd of

Flt Sgt Harry Appleby (l) demonstrating the use of a snow shelter in the Troodos Mountains in 1959

London, on its way from London to Australia. Contact had been lost when it was on the Ankara/Bahrain leg, and it was estimated to be somewhere in the vicinity of the enormous Lake Van, surrounded by mountains of up to 13,500 feet. A highly-secret cargo bound for the Woomera Rocket Range was aboard and as the probable crash area was uncomfortably close to the USSR border, quick action was needed. Derek Bottomer recalls:

We were on exercise somewhere in Kyrenia Hills. I think this signal had come through that this aircraft was overdue, overflying Turkey ... going to Bahrain and South Australia, and we immediately went back to Nicosia. We were called back and put on standby. I know there was an air search going on, which went on for a long time, I think maybe a week.[1]

Two Hastings from 70 Squadron, RAF Nicosia, two Shackletons from RAF Akrotiri, and one each from Bahrain and Luqa, Malta were searching, with RAF Regiment men as observers. Maintenance parties for both types had to be flown in to keep the small fleet going. Within three days the search was intensified yet further. Crews were flying at 12,000 feet on oxygen and the searchers were getting little sleep. A Hastings of 70 Squadron, captained by Flying Officer

George Noble, spotted the Tudor on April 29th when the operation was on the verge of being called off and Noble's flight was to be the last. It was on Süphan Dağl (Mount Suphan), on the northern shore of Van Gölü (Lake Van), on the lip of a snow-capped plateau at about 13,000 feet, about two hundred feet short of the top. By this time the searching aeroplanes had logged up 50,000 square miles. Looking down at the stricken aircraft, the observers in Noble's Hastings were certain that nobody could have survived; nevertheless, survivors or not, it was important to get someone there very quickly.

Harry Appleby and his men were immediately sent into action. Another 70 Squadron Hastings was loaded with a Mountain Rescue Land Rover and two trailers, with the team's kit, and good-byes were said to families. It is not true, as at least one magazine article said soon afterwards, that Harry Appleby was told to stay in the section and that he disobeyed orders so as to be with the team. The team officer was Flight Lieutenant Richard ('Dickie') Robertson, and with them was the doctor, Flying Officer Ronald Ellis. Robertson was formerly a pilot with 208 Squadron and with 43 Squadron at Leuchars, flying Hunters in both cases; and at the latter a member of the aerobatics team. This was not his first connection with the rescue service: in Jordan, with 208 Squadron in 1958, he had organised the Desert Rescue Service.

They flew to Diyarbakir, where the Turkish Air Force provided a liaison officer, interpreter and three drivers with vehicles, and then made their way to the foot of Süphan Dağl and set up base camp as far forward as possible on April 30th. At the highest village, at about 9,000 feet, they were able to negotiate accommodation in the school house as a base camp. A small party was picked for its members' various specialities to make its way to the wreck: Sergeant Jack Emmerson was an engine fitter, but more importantly a Himalayan climber with altitude experience; Bottomer was an airframe fitter; Corporal Peter Whelan was an instrument technician; SAC Fred Costall was a radio man. Photographs had been taken by the Turkish Air Force showing that the aircraft was totally broken up.

Porterage was provided by the rest of the team of seventeen. In indifferent weather, it helped the Emmerson party to the high camp point, about 2,500 feet below the wreck, helped them pitch camp in the late afternoon and then returned down, leaving the Emmerson group there. After the Emmerson group had reached the wreck, the rest of the team was to join them later. It was expected that the final stage of the climb would be in cloud. Noble's Hastings shadowed the team, acting as a radio link between it and the RAF Rescue Co-ordination Centre at Nicosia. Bottomer continues:

> The next morning it was different – the weather was brighter and we carried on up the ridge and actually found ourselves separated from the main bulk of the mountain by almost a subsidiary peak. We found ourselves separated by a descent. The four of us descended down below the main base of Süphan Dağl. Other people had arrived, but they'd been airlifted so far. We saw them following our descent tracks...

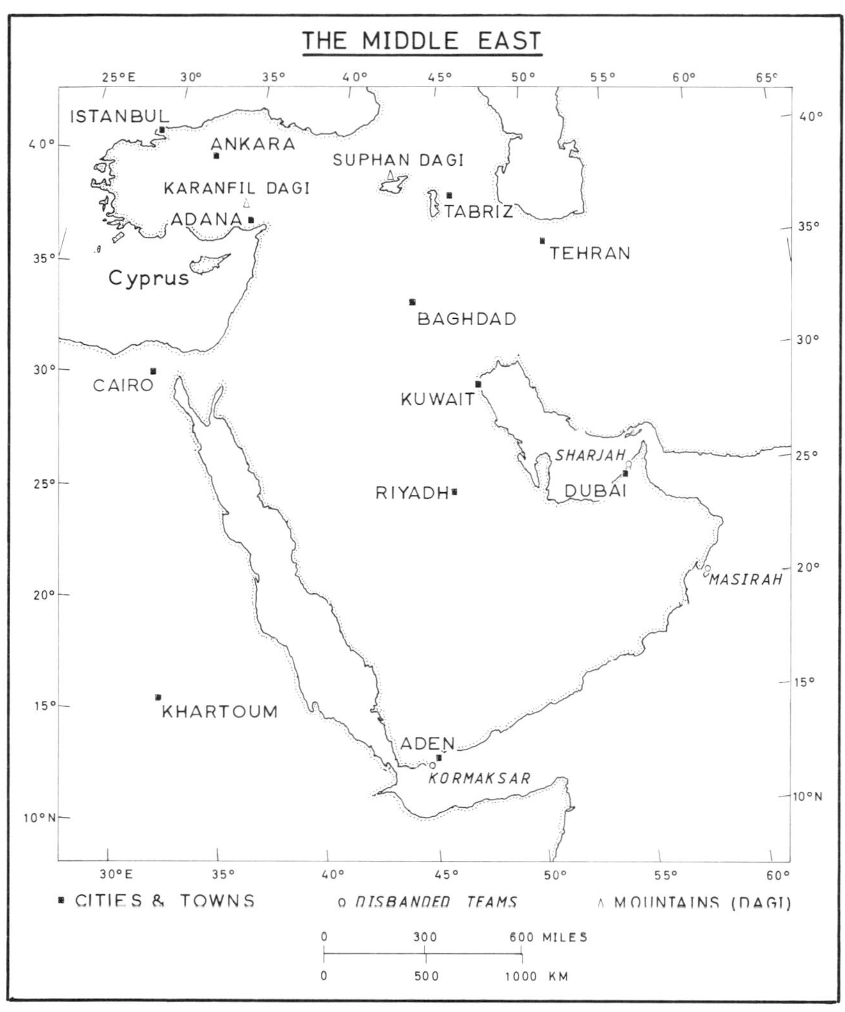

MAP 12 THE OVERSEAS TEAMS: 1960–76

For the team dates, see Appendices. This map also shows the locations of the two major Turkish operations which Nicosia MRT handled.

What they had seen in the distance were Robertson, Ellis and two of the team members, airlifted from the base camp by a Turkish Air Force helicopter, and the two parties linked up on the saddle between the two summits. Bottomer's narrative then continues:

...and I think at that time we decided that we didn't have enough tents to put everybody in... so Peter Whelan and I descended back down to a village. Jack Emmerson went down to our first night's camp and picked up one tent we'd left, and took it back up to the site where everybody was.

That rather understates it. Although Emmerson was by far the most experienced mountaineer, a founder member of RAFMA, with amongst other things a Royal Geographical Society survey of the Himalaya under his belt, he was totally exhausted when he arrived at the end of his double journey with the extra tent. Bottomer and Whelan, in the meantime, stayed at the base camp in the village.

Noble and his crew were due to return to Cyprus, and on May 1st another Hastings, piloted by Wing Commander Peter Parrott, the Officer i/c Flying at RAF Nicosia, was on its way to Diyarbakir with mail and emergency rations to be dropped, and with a relief crew to take over. A second Hastings which had tents, mail, cigarettes and rations was due to leave Cyprus later the same day. On this aircraft was what the press release described as 'certain equipment' provided by the Army. But the Parrott flight did not go according to plan. He took the aircraft over Suphan, but heavy static prevented any contact with the climbers. Visibility was very poor, and they were unable to drop supplies.

The first drop by Wing Commander Parrott at the base camp, recalls Appleby, was hectic.

Having some experience as a para instructor I knew the limitations etc required for the drop and located myself on a patch of flat ground near the village of Nurskincik – gave Wg Cdr Parrott the okay to drop only to be told that the drop was complete – using the Land Rover I was sitting in as a marker. I exited the Land Rover and discovered a C.L.E. (container) a 6′ × 1′ steel tube just ten feet away. I was just glad he was ex 604 Sqn![4]

The climbers, struggling through blizzard, lightning and freezing rain, had been unable to get any signals back to Rescue Co-ordination Centre since they started the last stage. That night they dug snow shelters in the side of the mountain, validating some training in the building and use of igloos they had gone through only a month earlier on Mount Olympus. Given the conditions, it is fortunate that Robertson had had the foresight to get crampons flown out to the team.

Crampons, up to that point, had never been issued, though many members who were also keen mountaineers used their own. Before the team left Nicosia, Dickie Robertson had sent a message to London asking for a supply of crampons to be flown out. At the time when this signal reached the UK, the IMR, Sandy Gordon-Cumming, was in a lecture on the Javelin hydraulic system at RAF Leeming. Hauled out of the lecture room to take a telephone message, he was told by the Air Ministry: "The Nicosia Mountain Rescue Team apparently need some things called – crampons. What do we do?" He thought quickly. Where could they be obtained urgently? What sizes would be needed? At that time in Seymour Street, near Marble Arch, was Robert Lawrie, a well-known supplier of

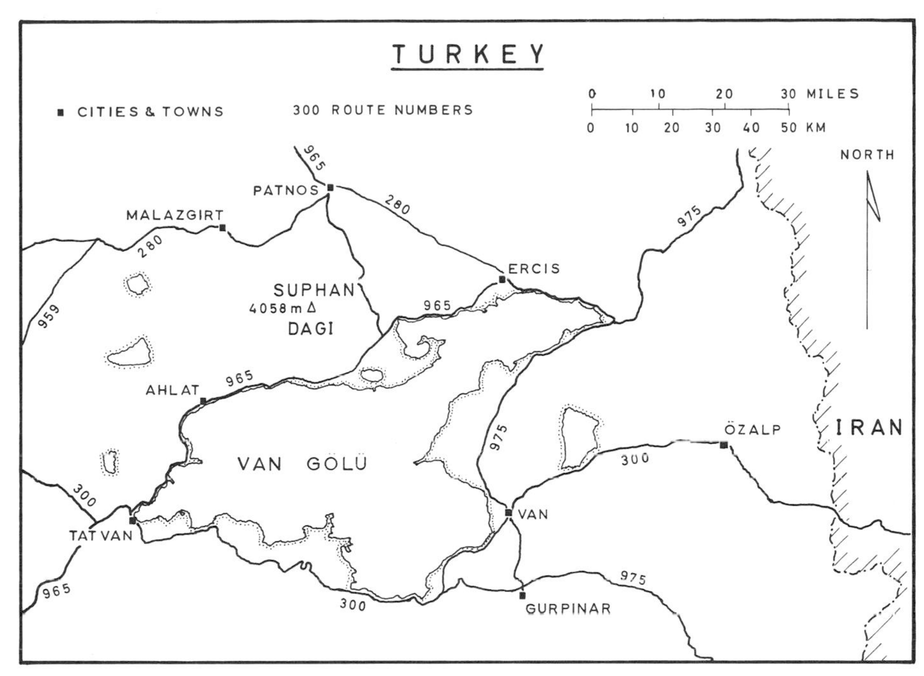

MAP 13 SUPHAN DAGI

Where the Avro Tudor crashed in 1959.

climbing equipment who had provided the equipment for the successful Mount Everest Expedition of 1953. Gordon-Cumming told his caller to send someone round there who should mention the Gordon-Cumming name and buy as many crampons as he reasonably could with a selection of sizes. Robert Lawrie came up with the goods, and the crampons were picked up by a despatch rider and flown out to Turkey by Canberra straight away.

Back at the base camp, Bottomer and his companions found that a demolition expert, Squadron Leader Ellery, had been flown in from the UK, his task being to blow up the wreck and its precious cargo. A message was received that there was an easier route on the far side of the mountain, and so Appleby, Bottomer and Whelan were airlifted with Ellery round to the point. They got above the snowline, but had not been climbing for long before it became obvious that Ellery was not used to being on the hill and was not going to make it. Appleby decided that the plan had to be abandoned otherwise Ellery would, says Appleby, have been the mountain's thirteenth victim. Now they found themselves on the wrong side of the mountain. It took them two days to get back; "No stroll," says Appleby:

Villagers and their livestock disappeared rapidly when we came into view – rustling of cattle being a major industry among the Kurds which is probably why our so-called

Turkish guides were well-armed. We did not know how well they liked Instant Nescafé until our abundant supply mysteriously disappeared. Turkish coffee was beyond their means and they drank tea with believe it or not, effervescent sugar cubes.
Last point – I think. The villagers were so poor that I did not see anyone with an overcoat – mostly just a jacket, open necked shirt, shoes, with in the main no socks.[4]

Another Hastings managed to find a gap in the weather on May 2nd, and the crew could see below tiny dots of people – some of the advance party – around the shattered aircraft, and this time was able to drop supplies. Further supplies were intended for the next day, including pistols and rifles as a protection against what the press release described as 'prowling bears and wolves, known to inhabit the upper slopes'. Appleby is sceptical:

Much play was made with bears and wolves – the bears were vegeterian and both kept below the snow line which was where their food lay not at 14,000 ft or thereabouts. The villagers had problems with the wolves and their livestock and kept dogs bred for the purpose of defending same.[4]

If the rifles were not intended for bears and wolves, then for what? Or rather, for whom, bearing in mind how close the wreck was to an important international border? Firearms were in fact never used in anger on this operation, whether against bears, wolves or the Red Army, but only during a shooting competition with the Turkish guides, employing the otherwise unusable remains of tins of food as targets, the Turks winning hands down.

A second party joined the first on the wreck on May 3rd, including the MO, Ellis, who confirmed that all on board were dead, and a simple burial service was held. Various documents were collected and handed over to the crew of a Turkish helicopter during a lull in the blizzard. Some equipment was salvaged, more destroyed with ice-axes, some mail and other personal items collected. Turkish mountaineering experts seemed to be surprised that the team had reached that far; until then, it had been believed that Süphan Dağl was climbable only in September.

Arms, ammunition and blankets were dropped during the morning of May 4th. Then on May 5th they were ready to start the demolition in earnest and plastic explosives were dropped that morning from a Hastings. But the explosives expert, Ellery, was no longer with them. Who was going to set the fuses?

Senior Aircraftman Gordon Hercod and SAC George Murphy went into the wreck, armed with the explosives, the fuses and some printed instructions given to them by Ellery, but with no specialised expertise. Setting the fuses as best they could from the unfamiliar instructions, they then left the wreck, retired to join the rest of the group, and waited and counted. For some time the teams had carried a camera with them to record evidence and such was the case here. All of the necessary pictures had been taken and were in the camera to be taken back to Nicosia for development, printing and technical scrutiny. As they were waiting for the explosion, however, someone spotted the official camera where it had been put down near to the wreck and then overlooked. It was too late to do anything about it and it went skywards in as spectacular a fashion as did the remains of the Avro Tudor.

After the explosions had finished, they were left with the uncomfortable knowledge that one charge had not gone off. They waited a long time but nothing further happened. The destruction was not complete, and Hercod, a wireless mechanic, went back into what was left of the wreck and reset the fuse. For this extraordinary act of coolness he received the Queen's Commendation for Bravery.

Murphy was one of the more experienced members of the team. He had in the past been at Topcliffe and had returned to Cyprus from an advanced mountain rescue course on Ben Nevis only three weeks before the Mount Suphan operation came up. It was Murphy who had adopted the Cyprus team's mascot, Sam, a pye-dog, somewhere in the Kyrenia Mountains. He and Hercod, good friends, later extended their connection into private life: they became brothers-in-law.

After the explosions, the ice-cap above them was believed to be unstable and likely to avalanche, and it became important to get away as soon as possible. At this stage the team had been six days and nights on the mountain in freezing temperatures and some were suffering from the altitude (oxygen was flown in, but more for the recovery specialists than for the team), some from the cold and some from sunburn. They made their way down to the base camp 4,500 feet below, where they rested, then by road to the airfield at Diyarbakir, to be flown back to Nicosia where there were some emotional greetings. A very happy magazine photograph of the time shows Harry Appleby being greeted by his wife Anne, herself a climber, and their Alsatian dog.

So ended the biggest operation, with the greatest risk to the largest number of people, in the most extreme conditions, at the highest altitude, that the service had ever experienced. It taught the whole service, not just Nicosia, a great deal, and shifted its direction yet further towards hard mountaineering. It had come very soon after Johnnie Lees's piggy-back rescue on the Amphitheatre Buttress in 1958, and the Jock's Road one-after-another disaster during the 1959 New Year. The '50s as a whole had been very active for the teams generally.

Süphan Dağl had its considerable effect, starting locally. Bottomer remembers:

> You see really, when we went to Süphan Dağl it was quite a – we were pretty green. I think there was only about one guy with us [Emmerson] who had any high altitude experience. And after that and the other Turkish air crash, the Nicosia team started to go back to Turkey on exercise and go to big mountain areas.... That was the start of it all. I think there was a sort of reallocation of areas of responsibility of teams which took in mountainous parts of Europe. I think this training has been stepped up and has got a lot

more professional. Year after year it's got more professional in outlook and equipment... I think that particular incident prompted a lot of new thinking so far as equipment was concerned – crampons and things like that...
Must have been a debriefing, some things which I don't know about and I think Dickie Robertson's gone to a Mountain Rescue meeting of committees and said look we must – should be equipping our teams better.[1]

During the Mountain Rescue Conference in London the following December, which Robertson and Appleby attended, two things emerged from the Süphan operation. Wing Commander C W Cornish said that:

...although he would not concede that a similar operation at high altitude was likely in the future, the M.E.A.F. report on the Mount Suphan incident showed clearly that oxygen would have been useful. He did not consider that expensive new equipment could be justified but would support proposals that equipment being developed for the Himalayan Expedition should be taken over by the R.A.F.[5]

These oxygen sets would serve three purposes:

portable medical equipment in the event of either crew or passengers of team members requiring oxygen for complaints such as pneumonia
to enable team members to operate more quickly and efficiently and to greater heights
to enable specialists (doctors, armaments experts, technicians) who may not be particularly fit to accompany the team to medium altitudes.

A footnote says that Ops. (Search and Rescue) agreed with the suggestion, had made a case and that financial approval was impending.

Flight Sergeant Lees, then the Team Leader at Valley, said that Mount Süphan demonstrated the need for a hard core of alpinists in the service, who could be collected and flown to the spot. Gordon-Cumming, the Chairman, agreed, and it was left to Cornish to look after the details.

There was one other outcome to Süphan Dağl – the largest number of awards for any one operation, up to that point and since. Hercod, as we have seen, received the Queen's Commendation for Bravery; Robertson was appointed MBE; BEMs went to Appleby, Emmerson and Murphy; the Commander-in-Chief's Commendation went to Whelan and Bottomer.

Nothing illustrates better than this episode the strange anomalies in the British award system. Nobody, reading the story of this call-out in detail, could argue that what Robertson achieved was superior to what Appleby, Emmerson and Murphy achieved; and to say that is not, by any means, to denigrate Robertson's performance. Now we see the British Empire Medal awarded to Appleby, Emmerson and Murphy, when clearly if they had held commissions, they would have been made Members of the British Empire at least.

Let Harry Appleby, writing many years after the incident, have the last word:

I count myself lucky in building a team which on the occasion went beyond my best expectations and, contrary to U.K. M.R.S. forecasts of the results, the boys did the Service and the R.A.F. proud.[4]

2 – Spy Plane

After the Mount Süphan incident the Nicosia team was given a week's special leave. Perversely – as it must have seemed to those who granted it – Bottomer and some others used it to go climbing in the Taurus Mountains of Turkey. Then in the first two weekends of 1960 advantage was taken of the first winter snows, and the Troodos Mountains of Cyprus were the venue for snow and ice climbs with some stretcher-lowering exercises. All were to prove useful very soon.

A Martin P4M Mercator of the US Navy's VQ1 Squadron based at Port Lyautey, Morocco, left Naples on January 19th with its crew of sixteen. Approaching the US base at Adana in southern Turkey it suddenly disappeared from the radar at 1.45 pm. Again, there was secret material involved; the Mercator, of which only 19 were ever built, was used by the USN for radar spying along hostile borders.

Provisionally it was arranged that a Hastings would leave Nicosia with the Mountain Rescue Team at 5 am next morning, but before long the Americans were asking that the search party leave immediately. Loading of the 70 Squadron Hastings started at 4.30 pm and a full Hasting-load of 18, with equipment and two Land Rovers, was got together from a total available of 26. Just as they were about to go, Jack Emmerson turned up, and because of his experience the recently-appointed officer i/c, Flying Officer K G Thomas, wanted to take him. Flight Lieutenant A Earle, the captain, agreed to stretch the passenger load to 19. An earlier Hastings, Playmate 41, with Wing Commander Parrott on board, had already arrived at Adana just after 7 pm that evening; the MRT aircraft, Playmate 42, touched down there at 9.40 pm. The following day was to be a heavy one with a dawn take-off immediately after the 4 am briefing by the USAF Search Controller, Major Jones; an early night was called for.

It had not been an easy flight for Earle, who had had to cope with an unserviceable tail wheel, making the aircraft very unstable when taxiing. Immediately on arriving, he and his navigator attended an aircrew briefing and arranged to attend the searchers' briefing early the next morning. Parrott signalled Nicosia to send out more of the team: another seven according to the main text of his report, another six according to Thomas's Appendix. Mysteriously, the list of MRT personnel involved, forming another Appendix, says that not six or seven but eight were sent out, not on the 20th but on the 18th; that was the day before the crash, which makes it yet more mysterious. There seems little doubt that the correct number was eight and the correct date was the 20th. Parrott's signal also asked for an RAF Regiment radio vehicle, as the MRT vehicle was away being modified, and it is likely that the discrepancy in numbers is due to counting one or two RAF Regiment radio operators as MRT personnel.

The new team leader, succeeding Appleby, was Peter Davis and with them was

Flying Officer Thomas (since Süphan there had been a complete change of management). However, Jack Emmerson remained a leading light in the team. Murphy was there too, as were Whelan and Bottomer. Davis, about to embark on his first operation with the Nicosia team, had qualified as a team leader in 1956, and before Nicosia had led Harpur Hill, Kinloss and Topcliffe. Thomas came to the operation with no prior climbing experience – always a trying situation for a new officer.

In the briefing, they learnt that Adana had received no flight plan, and that the first report of the Mercator received by the Adana tower had been at 1.30 pm, when it was approaching at 15,000 feet and starting let-down. Clearance was given, but very soon after that contact was lost. Radio communications in the area were notoriously unreliable and, with an 80-knot wind at 15,000 feet, there was a strong possibility of a navigational error, and the area of probability was quite large: a very mountainous countryside with peaks up to 12,000 feet and a general level of 7-8,000.

At 6 am the extra MRT members, the radio van and a second MRT Land Rover trailer with some equipment, as well as a servicing crew and spares for the Hastings, arrived. It was found that the RAF Regiment radio vehicle was equipped only for R/T (voice communication) and not for W/T (Morse). This could be a handicap, as when transmission conditions are poor (as they often are in the mountains) Morse will often cut through the static when the human voice will not. Hurriedly, a Morse key was borrowed from the Americans and, pooling their skills, the wireless operators from the MRT, RAF Regiment and 70 Squadron worked to adapt the equipment they had. It began to look, however, that they would not be able to establish ground-to-ground communication, and the USAF agreed to hold a listening watch.

Bottomer and other team members who had been on holiday in those mountains not long before formed part of the aerial search, and it was their Hastings, captained by Flight Lieutenant J L Martin, which spotted what seemed to be the wreck, at 11 am, on Karanfil Dağl (Mount Karanfil), 3059 metres, about 70 kilometres north-north-west of Adana. Including the two Hastings, four aircraft were on the search, and nine others from the USN, USAF and US Marines were still on their way when the sighting was made. First, what appeared to be footsteps in the snow were seen. Cloud was drifting over the scene, but the wreckage – if wreckage it was – was in a valley at about 8,500 feet on the north-west side of a 10,000-foot peak, only a small amount of debris showing above fresh snow. Quick sketches were made and an American aircraft diverted for a second opinion. Both aircraft were recalled to Adana and the crews interrogated, with the conclusion that, almost certainly, the missing aircraft had been found.

Thomas, Ellis, Davis and the lieutenant in charge of the American ground party had in the meantime been putting the convoy together, and the two Land Rovers with two 2½ ton trucks and an Air Police jeep were on their way by

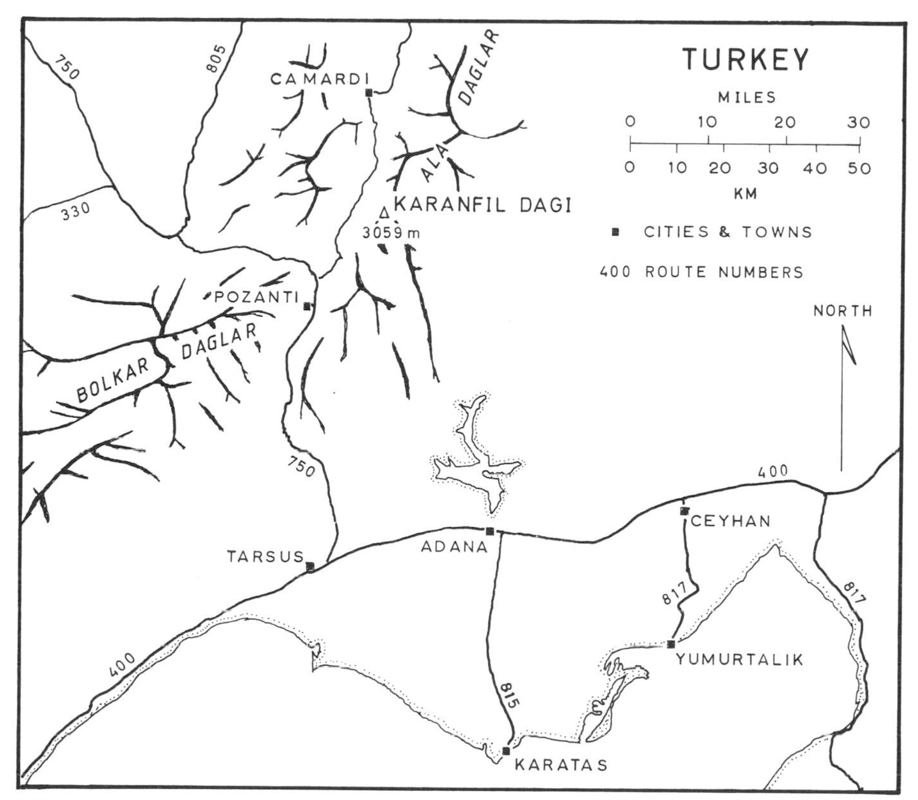

MAP 14 KARANFIL DAGI

Where the Martin Mercator crashed in 1960.

11 am, with an American who knew the district well in the leading Land Rover. Control of the search and rescue had been handed over to Thomas by the Air Police. 90 miles over good roads brought them to the village of Pozanti, where the road forks, the main road continuing to the left and a very minor one going off to the right. They took the right, which over the next 25 miles was a total contrast: little more than a mountain track, it took four hours with the vehicles getting bogged down and having to be pushed out several times. Seven miles south of the crash, late on January 20th, the American negotiated accommodation in a school with a village headman eager to help, and the weary team members were able to get some rest.

A team of fast climbers, led by Davis and Ellis, left at 3.30 am and drove to a point on a track closer to the crash site, near to a village called Kücükkaranfil Bagevleri, and started climbing at first light. A second party was formed with a

Turkish guide, who, the headman said, knew where the wreck was and could lead a party to it in three hours. Thomas thought this was an obvious exaggeration, but as he had plenty of men available he thought it was worth a try. He asked Jack Emmerson to lead a party of six. Apparently impressed by the headman's claims, the American Air Police agreed to let the headman take them on mules to the crash. The weather at this stage was good.

When the going got hard in deep snow the guide left the scene, having taken his party on a roundabout route and ending up close to the Davis route, where the two parties joined up. After a little further climbing they could see three corries, and they knew the wreck was in one of these. They split into three groups, one for each corrie. One party found the wreck at 10 am; there had been no survivors and initially they found only one body. They were unable to do much, as the Air Police, finding that the mules refused to go above the snowline, had returned to the schoolhouse. The Mercator had flown straight into a 60° rock wall, some of it remaining jammed into the mountain, but the main wreckage had fallen 200 feet down the cliff face burying itself in a small platform of deep snow. There was no difficulty in reaching the platform, but during the five hours from the base camp there had been trouble in negotiating the steep snow slopes. Following Mount Süphan, twelve pairs of crampons were held by the team. For those without, steps had to be cut.

Despite the lack of any recovery, Thomas regarded this first day, January 21st, as good with both the location of the wreck and the best route to it identified. But the extreme temperatures were proving a problem. Fortunately all of Davis's men were fit and no cases of frostbite occurred (except for one of the American naval officers), but all fluids – beer, Coca-Cola, intravenous fluid – froze up. Thomas recorded, as a matter of interest, what he wore at nights to give him enough warmth for adequate sleep: one Balaclava helmet, two pullovers, one shirt, one string vest, one pair of short underpants, two pairs of PT shorts, one track suit bottom, three pairs of socks. All this was inside two sleeping bags.

Conditions next day, the 22nd, were appalling. It took the team with one American enlisted man – "the only American to climb to the crash without the aid of a helicopter" commented Thomas sharply – five hours to reach the wreckage carring a Thomas stretcher, and there high up near the summit the temperature was −5° Fahrenheit (c. −15° Celsius). Cloud covered the mountain reducing visibility at times to a few yards and almost to a white-out, and an overnight fall of snow made the going very hard. Waist-deep snow had to be coped with, and though roped climbing was not necessary the steep snow slopes meant that ice-axes and crampons were needed. Not all succeeded in reaching the site. At the wreck short prayers were said. Only one of the bodies could be recovered by stretcher on this day and it was taken to a cave two miles from the base camp. Everyone was too exhausted to carry it the remaining two miles over rocky ground.

The crash point, from the base camp. *Photo: Crown Copyright*

The Mercator crash on Karanfil Dağı, January 1960

A fresh fall of snow that night obscured the day's tracks. Again cloud covered the mountain, stretching down almost to the base camp, and the wind was cold. Most of the team were feeling the effects of the first two days' exertions and only eight felt able to complete the climb on the 23rd, none of them American or Turk. American PVC body bags were taken instead of the stretcher to save weight. Another five hours' climb was called for in deep soft snow with poor visibility. Another body was extracted, but as a macabre result of the very low temperature it was frozen into a seated position, and, as it could not be fitted into the body bag, was replaced in the wreck. It was felt – wrongly – that this was probably the last time the team would visit the wreck, and the eight men gathered silently around. They reached base camp at dusk.

During the day two American naval officers had arrived to begin the investigation. They, and the enlisted men, were sleeping in the vehicles, and because they had brought no food were being fed by the RAF. Thomas told Lieutenant Commander Cartnell, the senior USN officer, that it was unlikely that any further bodies could be recovered until the spring. Cartnell accepted this judgement, but asked Thomas to keep the MRT at the site. Thomas promised to try to contact the Air Police, who had last been seen at the school house two days earlier, in which case Cartnell could stay with them and the MRT could return to Adana. Thomas and Cartnell therefore, on Sunday the 24th, went down to the school house, whilst a stretcher party went up to the cave to recover the body which had been stored there, a chore which the Air Police had agreed to undertake. Thomas and Cartnell reached the school house just as the Air Police were about to go, but their officer told them that several of his men were sick. Reluctantly, Cartnell agreed they would be little use to him. As the MRT's assistance remained necessary, Thomas and Cartnell drove up to Pozanti where a USAF radio truck had been positioned (the MRT's radio equipment had given trouble in the mountains right from the start). From the radio truck, Cartnell ordered further equipment. On the way back to the base camp, Thomas and Cartnell were intercepted by a Turkish Sikorsky helicopter. An American naval lieutenant aboard said that it was at their disposal until the end of the operation and at Cartnell's request Thomas agreed to keep the team there a little longer.

It was too late, by then, to do any further climbing that day, and the team, for the sake of international relations, held an Open Sports Day with the villagers who had gathered to see the helicopter. Events included tossing the tent-pole, throwing the rock, shooting and wrestling. Only the result of the last of these was recorded by Thomas in his report: ...the village wrestling champion easily defeated the MRT challenger.[6]

An ambulance brought beer and cigarettes; the general air of relaxation continued that evening when a party was held in one of the tents. By this time the Americans were supplying food, beer and cigarettes each day, the food in the form of 'C' rations which were generally felt to provide a much greater range than the British 'Compo' rations.

Early next morning, Monday the 25th, four members set off to the agreed helicopter dropping point, in perfect weather: no cloud, snow or wind. Nevertheless, when the machine dropped its first passengers at 9 am it was well below the site, but the party, unable to contact the helicopter, continued up to the crash. Then the helicopter took the team with the USN investigating officers to a point much closer to the wreck, only one and a half hours' climb away. Much work was achieved this Monday. Bodies and instruments were taken out of the wreck and taken down the mountain by the MRT and Turks, without the help of the helicopter. In view of this great progress, Thomas felt by the end of the day that his team had given all the help that the Americans could expect. For the first time several Americans had reached the crash, a well-worn track now reached the wreckage making it easy to find, and digging – the remaining job – could be done by hired villagers.[6]

Lieutenant Commander Garrison was taking over from Cartnell and both thanked the MRT.

Things changed yet again next morning, the 26th. As the vehicles were being loaded Thomas was approached by an obviously worried Garrison. He had had a sleepless night, and asked Thomas to keep the team there yet longer for several reasons: he considered it dangerous to continue the operation without experienced mountaineering advice; only a few Americans were fit to climb; in his opinion the villagers could not be trusted with bodies or equipment without supervision; he was not equipped to lead, organise or feed the new personnel arriving; and anyway with the RAF's help and the forecast good weather, the evacuation of bodies could soon be completed.[6] Thomas then was in some difficulty. He finally concluded that to turn down this request out of hand would have undone much of the goodwill built up in the past week, and he left Garrison six men including himself, Murphy and Whelan, sending the remaining 21 back to Adana with most of the equipment. Garrison, grateful, promised that the USAF would fly the six back to Nicosia when the whole thing was over. At the crash the remaining six with a few Americans and many villagers found several more bodies, the navigator's plotting chart, the secret material which had been carried and the black box.

They were disturbed in the night when twenty Turkish soldiers from a military mountaineering school arrived, led by their colonel. He had heard much of the RAF team and was delighted to have the opportunity to meet them and made an offer: he would like the team to go on a climbing expedition near his mountaineering school. There were now eighty people to continue the work – twenty Turkish soldiers, three Americans, six MRT members and over 50 villagers.

During the ensuing day, Wednesday January 27th, major excavations carried on but no more bodies were uncovered; they now had twelve of the sixteen. Later that day two more American officers arrived, both of whom lived in the Rocky Mountains and were experienced mountaineers. Despite Garrison's further pleas, Thomas felt that this altered the situation and decided finally that the MRT's contribution had to cease. He took the remaining party to Adana on the 28th, where they slept overnight, flying back to Nicosia the next morning, the whole operation having taken a week.

It had become obvious, both on this operation and Mount Süphan, that special conditions demanded special gear, but the equipment that Nicosia had used was the same as that issued to the UK teams, and Parrott recommended in his report that more crampons should be issued, one pair for each member. Icelandic special sleeping bags, special jackets, ski-goggles, three-man tents: all these were proposed. Most important of all was the matter of communications which also had been a problem at Mount Süphan. Radio contact had been haphazard throughout and a special issue of lightweight but robust walkie-talkies capable of a range of twenty miles was suggested.

> The M.R.T equipment used in this operation was barely adequate. In a rescue at higher altitude or where speed is necessary to save survivors, lack of better equipment might prove disastrous.[6]

Another problem at Mount Süphan had been sunburn due to ultra-violet radiation and Station Sick Quarters at RAF Nicosia had undertaken some research, coming up with an anti-sun cream which proved to be wholly successful at Karanfil.

Yet again the team had shown up well. Three in particular were named in Wing Commander Parrott's report: the team leader, Flight Sergeant P G Davis on his first Nicosia call-out; the officer i/c, Flight Lieutenant K G Thomas, who though of limited mountain experience had faced several difficult decisions and made them correctly; and SAC G Murphy. George Murphy, said Parrott:

> ...again showed his ability to improvise and to organise small parties of airmen to work in the most willing way. His good humour and strong personality at all times contributed to the morale of the team.[6]

Much goodwill had been built up with the Turkish forces, bringing a swift dividend. In April 1961, the team was already on its first high-altitude training expedition to Turkey, on Erciyes Dağı at 12,848 feet. Not able to make the summit because of deep snow, they nevertheless received good training, though without the benefit of the Turkish officer who was due to act as their guide. He turned up on the last day, his joining instructions having been delayed.

Only the next year there was another crash in Turkey, of a Fokker Friendship of Turkish Air Lines, on March 9th 1962. As well as the Nicosia MRT, the paramedics were taken in the search aircraft with the object of dropping if they could, to see quickly to any possible survivors. Flying over the wreck, they could see no sign of life, and in any case the Turkish government aborted the drop, so

Davis and the MRT went in to bring the bodies down. As with the Mercator crash, the MRT worked with the American and Turkish forces. Afterwards, the two NCOs concerned, Pete Davis of the MRT and Alf Card AFM of the paramedics got together and suggested that the two teams be combined. This did not quite happen, but it did result in some of the Cyprus and Sharjah men being parachute trained.

3 – Kai Tak

Although the Kai Tak team, in official terms, existed for a shorter time than any other since the war – 1961 to 1967 – there had been a team in place for some time before it was officially launched. To someone familiar with the Royal Air Force, that fact is not very surprising; like God, it moves in mysterious ways. What is remarkable is that the person who was largely responsible for getting the unofficial team rolling was an officer who, though he had never been a member of the Mountain Rescue Service, had already, on two previous occasions, encountered the Service in one way or another and had influenced its development from the outside. Tony Smyth was now a group captain and the commanding officer of RAF Kai Tak from 1955 to 1958. It will be recalled that in 1944 he had started the Aircrew Mountain Centre in Kashmir where staff included a doctor called Squadron Leader George Graham; then in 1951 he had been instrumental, when the MR Service reached a crisis, in drawing on the expertise of various people in the RAF Mountaineering Association. Now the long arm of coincidence, which has manifested itself at intervals throughout this Mountain Rescue story, was about to reach out again.

Originally, the task of mountain search and rescue in Hong Kong had been given to detachments of the RAF Regiment from Malaya. For a while the team seemed to run down but began to be revived in the mid-50s. On August 1st 1954, a Signals Centre had been established in Hong Kong. In addition to being the transmission and receiving rooms in the Station Headquarters, it also had two aerial 'farms' on land which has since been given over to housing estates. The Centre had a much larger number of airmen than other sections in RAF Kai Tak and therefore usually provided the bulk of those needed for various subsidiary activities. This was the case when in 1956 Smyth called for volunteers to join the Mountain Rescue Team which he wanted to get going with the help of Corporal R A L Christie – last time seen in Kinloss MRT during and after Beinn Eighe in 1951-52. Seven of the twelve volunteers came from the Signals Centre.[7]

Depending on the direction of the wind, it was necessary for aircraft to take off towards the mountains which were not very far away. An extension to the runway had been opened in 1951, but with the rapid development of aviation, it was obvious that if Kai Tak were to stay and be developed as an international airport (for the RAF was sharing a civilian airport) then much longer runways would be needed. Various other positions were considered for a new airport, but in 1954 the Legislative Council decided to develop Kai Tak by constructing a new runway which extended into Kowloon Bay. By the early '60s the airport was receiving Electras, Boeing 707s and Douglas DC8s. Clearly a demonstrable need for an MRT was growing.

Smyth also formed the Hong Kong Mountaineering Club in 1956, but the Mountain Rescue Team as much as the Club gained a name for rock-climbing. Their best effort was said to be *Sunset Crack* with *Cockscombe* on Suicide Wall, but they also visited Castle Peak, Ma On Shan, Monastery Slabs and other outcrops.[8] During this time Smyth and Christie, wearing Mountain Rescue hats, arranged a northern approach to Kinabalu (13,455 feet) in British North Borneo as a climbing enterprise. An ascent had never been made from that direction, the chief obstacles being jungle gorges and steep rock faces. As it happened, the progress proved so slow because of difficulties with local guides and with the non-existence of supposed trails, that the group of 20 was forced to withdraw from the North Ridge. Eventually Smyth fell ill with fever and they had to be satisfied with a dash to the top by the conventional southern route.

Although the team did not at this stage go onto the list of officially-recognised teams, some sort of half-way house was achieved. A station commander could form a land rescue team on his own authority but needed that of the Ministry of Defence before he could form a mountain rescue team.

> I am directed to [refer] to the above subject and to say that authority is given for the members of the Hong Kong Land Rescue Team to wear the Mountain Rescue Badge. This Badge is not yet available for issue, but delivery is expected in the U.K. during October.
> The scale of equipment for this team has not yet been completely approved, but in order to assist them with their immediate training difficulties three climbing ropes have been air-freighted to them. As soon as financial approval is given to the remainder of the scale you will be informed.[9]

Probably because of its in-between status, the Kai Tak team got no mention during the Mountain Rescue conferences in Whitehall over the next few years; nor were copy minutes sent to Hong Kong. Four years later an airman with mountaineering experience, Senior Technician Ron Peart from RAF Kinloss, volunteered to go to RAF Kai Tak in his trade. John Sims, the new IMR, knew of his expertise as a climber, and recommended that the proposal be accepted.[10]

Smyth stayed at RAF Kai Tak until June 1958, when he was posted to the Air Ministry in Whitehall as Deputy Director of Operational Requirements. During this long interim period, after the team had been re-formed by Smyth and Christie but before it was formally approved, it had no proper equipment except what could be begged, borrowed or stolen. Flight Lieutenant B J Lemon OBE was the officer i/c, a pilot with 28 (Army Co-operation) Squadron, then equipped with Venom Is. Lemon, in 1961, had a hair-raising experience with a Venom, when a cowling came off in flight and wrapped itself round the tailplane.

Struggling with the aircraft, he brought it back safely to Kai Tak, and for that received the Air Force Cross in the 1961 Birthday Honours List.

Training took place on the sports afternoon and also at weekends, much of it on the outlying islands and in the New Territories. Gerald White, one of the team members, recalls the location of sufficient beer for the exercise was the biggest problem, though if one knew the ropes it could usually be found by the Chinese villagers. Until Peart was sent out, there was, in 1956-57, only one UK rescue-trained man in the team and the team therefore developed as a land rescue team with a mountain rescue bias, rather than a mountain rescue team in the usual sense. 'I can recall that in the intense heat of the day 4 men could only carry a stretcher with [a] 10 stone patient for about 15 minutes, particularly over the rough Hong Kong terrain.'[11]

What finally persuaded the authorities that a Mountain Rescue Team was justified was a horrific USAF crash. This was in November 1960, when a C47 (Dakota) took off from Kai Tak. Air Traffic Control lost radio contact very shortly afterwards and the team was put on standby. A minute or two before midnight a monk walked into the police station at Wan Chai on Hong Kong Island, and said that at 6 pm the scrub at the top of Mount Parker had been burning and he could smell fuel. Tropical rain was teeming down on the Bedford as it turned out of RAF Kai Tak on the first stage – on its way to Jordan Road where a car ferry had been made available especially. Local radio had got hold of the news, and was broadcasting a non-stop account. This brought the local people out in great numbers, making their way to the site, and the police had to be brought in to keep the junctions open.

Fighting their way in the rain through the dense scrub, insect-ridden mud and: '...millions of mosquitos, most of which bit me...'[12] on Mount Parker (1,500 feet), the team members finally reached the smoking wreck. Amazingly, one person was still alive: Airman 1st Class Ricard Ferron, from Westbrook, Maine had survived because at the time of impact he had been standing by the open doorway of the C47. Given an injection, he was taken away on a stretcher for emergency treatment, suffering from internal bleeding and, of course having lain in the rain for several hours. A detachment from the Durham Light Infantry had been brought in to assist the RAF team and they took away the remains of the crew and passengers from the sad scene, with parts of the aircraft and suitcases and other belongings of the passengers spread over a wide area. A guard was put on for three days, .303 Lee Enfields being issued to the RAF. There were thousands of Chinese milling around, looking, thinks White, for souvenirs.

Some time after this incident, a formal request went from the office of the Far East Air Force Commander in Chief at RAF Changi in Singapore to the Air Ministry, requesting that:

...the name of the Rescue Team at Hong Kong be changed to the Royal Air Force Kai Tak Land-Mountain Rescue Team and the team be afforded official recognition under the terms of A.M.O. A.88/61.

It is considered that with the advent of increasing jet traffic through Hong Kong which is recognised as being one of the world's most dangerous terminal airports there is an increasing need for a streamlined highly efficient rescue team. The future re-equipment of No. 28 Squadron with newer and faster aircraft emphasises the urgency of this requirement.[13]

Squadron Leader Runchman made the point that the terrain in Hong Kong and the New Territories consisted of inaccessible mountain with extremely steep scrub and secondary jungle slopes with rocky outcrops, necessitating expert stretcher-handling and search and navigation techniques. He added that the aircraft approach to the runway lay between hills with a height of up to 3,500 feet. In some parts of the year meteorological conditions were unstable, sometimes causing the airport to be closed within minutes, the only diversion for fighter aircraft then being Sek Kong, which was almost certain to be closed at the same time. A slightly chilly response came three months later:

I am to say that although it is agreed that a requirement exists for a Mountain Rescue Team in Hong Kong, it is not considered necessary for the establishment to be as great as that of the United Kingdom teams. It is recommended that the full-time staff be restricted to the N.C.O. for the post of team leader and the remaining members be drawn from volunteers. On the M.T. side there is no objection to your proposal to establish one 3-ton truck for the use of the team.[14]

Still, the necessity had been acknowledged in principle. Squadron Leader Runchman was at the 1961 conference and by this time the team had a full-time leader, Sergeant Archie Hay.

From time to time we have recorded the death of a Mountain Rescue member when on MR duty, but never, until now, more than one at one time. But on September 1st 1962 Typhoon Wanda hit Hong Kong when some of the Mountain Rescue Team were then on Lan Tao Island, and they picked up the warning of the typhoon on the radio. They quickly struck camp and moved, for safety's sake, into an empty stone hut. Back at the MR section the operator lost radio contact. When it was possible other members went over to Lan Tao and found their five team-mates dead in the wreckage of the hut which had collapsed at the height of the typhoon. It was the first time that any RAF personnel had met their death by typhoon.

By 1963 Sergeant Jack Baines was the full-time team leader and was representing Kai Tak at the annual conference in the Air Ministry.

As part of the defence cuts of the time, it was decided to disband Kai Tak in January 1967. In anticipation of this, the team leader, then Sergeant D C Reeve (the author of *A Guide to Rock Climbing in Hong Kong*) was given the task of training ten officers of Hong Kong's Civil Aid Services. Mountain Rescue was not the only victim: 28 Squadron was also disbanded, as was the Marine Craft

WHAT DO YOU MEAN HE'S HAD A HARD DAY ON THE HILL?

The writer, the artist, the map artist and the publisher of this book are or were all mountain rescuers. This was sketched in the pub at the end of the day by Pat Donovan, the artist. The character on the left is alleged to be Jack Baines, now of The Ernest Press. *Drawing: Pat Donovan*

Unit which apart from its major anti-piracy and air-sea rescue duties, had also on many occasions taken the MRT to the islands for training.

Ironically, within a few months of disbandment the team's former members were back to work again. Hong Kong at that time was experiencing quite a lot of trouble with communist terrorists, and on August 28th 1967 Sergeant Workman of the Royal Army Ordnance Corps was defusing a bomb on Lion Rock when there was an explosion, Workman being terribly injured. Former MRT members including their medical officer, Flight Lieutenant L G Street, volunteered to bring him down, but an army doctor had already reached him to find that he had died.

However, gradually the Civil Aid Services (CAS) was taking over. This body had been formed in 1952, but had been content to leave mountain rescue to the RAF. The RAF team's disbandment coincided with a great increase in hill-trekking in the area, and only three of the RAF's 18 call-outs in the team's five and a half years had been aircraft crashes. The CAS had been created with the nucleus of the wartime Air Raid Precautions members, and at the time of the changes provided: a civil defence organisation in war-time; an emergency organisation during a period of economic unrest (not necessarily accompanied by civil disturbance) and a disaster organisation in peacetime. As years went by the importance of the civil defence element diminished, and in 1963 training for this stopped completely. With this changing pattern it was decided that the CAS should form a Mountain Rescue Team to replace the RAF one, and the RAF was asked if it would provide the training. Recruitment was from within the CAS and the criteria were high: very fit; capable of walking over hills in soaring summer temperatures; able to appreciate the art of survival during cold winter nights on open mountains; able to carry a heavy load; with a good knowledge of first-aid. Response was good, and training initially under Reeve and then under Chief Technician Baines followed by others, on detachment from the RAF, began.

Two teams were established, one on Hong Kong Island and the other in Kowloon. Each of the regional teams was divided into sections, geographically based, with eight members in each. Then in 1975 the two were combined. Easily recognised in their red shirts and helmets, they were well-equipped.

RAF help in the training of the CAS people continued for many years; for example, in 1976 a group went to the Outdoor Activities Centre at Grantown-on-Spey for a one-week course. After this, they reported to RAF Kinloss for a three-day course which took them to the Central Highlands, Loch Lomond, Loch Ness and Ben More. Yet more training followed, this time a rescue exercise in Torridon. Valley then was the host in Snowdonia, and BBC television, curious to know why all these Hong Kong Chinese were in North Wales, was also in action there. A 24-day Mountain Craft Course at Plas-y-Brenin National Mountaineering Centre closed the extensive programme.

4 – The Mystery of Wadi Mukeiras

On the Mukeiras Plateau very near the Yemen border, at the junction of Wadi am
Salul and Wadi Mukeiras, is a steep 3,000-foot rock face, consisting of alternately sound and unsound granite. 400 feet below the summit a gully starts and runs at an angle of 70° to 80° to Wadi Mukeiras about 2,600 feet below. Second Lieutenant Barclay of the 1st East Anglian Regiment Company, on Sunday April 12th 1964 was out with two fellow officers on a photographic expedition here which also involved some rock scrambling. He had told them that he had a 'little knowledge' of rock-climbing. At some point in the day, they reached the head of the gully.

"I'm going back to the summit," said one of them, "via an easy scramble."

"Let's go back the hard way," countered Barclay, and, deaf to his friends' appeals to his good sense, started immediately down the dried-up waterfall to a ledge 100 feet below, then contoured over and upwards towards the summit. They saw him fall, then slither and roll for about 300-400 feet over a near-

"This is what i call Mountaineering"

vertical pitch until he reached a ledge about eighteen inches wide which ran around that part of the cliff. There was a gap in the ledge and he fell through that, dropping a further four or five feet into what Sergeant George Paterson, the Khormaksar team leader, vividly described as: '...a natural box in the "Gods" of a theatre capable of seating four persons.'[15] About a third of his body was overhanging the precipice, approximately 450 feet from the top of this 3,000-foot cliff, and he was dead.

His companions raised the alarm and the Khormaksar team was alerted by RCC at 8.30 am the next day. Paterson was told that only a small aircraft could be used and, as a medical officer had to be included, he could not take more than nine including himself and his deputy SAC Bill 'Ginge' Tuke. He had to choose his men, therefore, with great care. They arrived at the scene at 12.30 pm on the 13th. Aerial reconnaissance by helicopter had earlier shown them exactly where the body lay.

Paterson decided that the only practicable route out was up the dried-up waterfall to the main face, and the only way to get there was 250 feet along a ledge which at times was no wider than eight inches, with a sheer drop of 2,400 feet below. That afternoon he asked the burly Tuke to go with him on this hazardous route to the body to assess the situation close at hand, and on the way they had to cross the heavily blood-stained strip which marked where Barclay had tumbled. Reaching the spot at 5 pm, they looked down at what had been a strong, athletic young man. If Barclay had still been alive when he reached that point, the slightest move could have sent him over the edge, and he would have landed far below on the bed of the wadi. So insecure was the body that they dragged it back from the edge, to await collection the next day. Working with a body in temperatures of 100°F was unpleasant in the extreme: Tuke, a brave and resourceful man, was violently sick after this operation.

Darkness setting in, no further action was possible and they had to get back whilst there was enough light. In the meantime, Paterson had noted that though Barclay's general clothing was sensible enough, given the climate, he was wearing Chukka boots – most unsuitable for the rock face in question. In Paterson's opinion at that stage, they may well have been the dominating factor in the fall (though he had cause to change his mind later). Barclay had no climbing equipment of any sort: no rope, no slings, nothing.

Next morning Paterson and Tuke led the rest of the team over the route they had rehearsed, taking 4½ hours in great heat to reach the body. With much difficulty, and with the work frequently broken by the necessity to use air fresheners, the body was got into the body bag. After a rest, they started to return along the 'eight-inch' ledge with their 11-stone burden. Paterson has much praise for Tuke. Although Tuke's experience with the team was limited, and he was considerably distressed at working with a body in that state and in those temperatures, he did not allow these factors to affect his cool-headed thinking, his nerve on narrow ledges at great heights, and his rope skills.

Balancing on the ledge the team took 3¾ hours on the first stage of the return, and a further 3 for the second stage to the top of the cliff. With the parts of rock formation unstable in the extreme, the team under Patterson's guidance often had to double- and sometimes treble-belay – hence the time taken on the rock-face – and the belays had to be tested at all stages; this was usually done by the heftiest man in the team, Tuke, who first had to be separately roped. Pitons were used, and in Paterson's opinion the recovery would have been impossible without them. 120-foot ropes were used and due to a lack of secure belays for about 200-300 feet of the route, there was virtually no rope protection; Paterson reported that 500-foot ropes would have much reduced the risk.[16]

To add a little more excitement, at one point below them there was a pool about 45 feet long infested with bilharzia. This invasive fluke, which leads to a most dangerous infestation in humans, having gained access to fresh water, enters the intermediate host, a freshwater snail. Large numbers in the secondary stage of development are liberated into the water and can then enter the human host by penetrating the skin or mucous membrane. This leads initially to rashes, fever, muscle aches, abdominal pain, headaches, coughs and sweating. The long-term effects are much more serious and can lead to renal failure, cancer of the bladder, and problems with the large bowel, liver and central nervous system.[17]

To get round the pool would have involved a long journey round the edge of the escarpment, so they rigged up a pulley system about ten feet above the surface of the pool, taking great care not to get a hand or foot or rope in contact with the water. Comments Paterson now:

> It was an incredible feat when you think of it, entirely a team effort, and not one of us could have claimed the patent, it just evolved.
> That is one part of the rescue which the authorities could not possibly have known about, because the pool was out of sight from all or any spectators, except from the air.[18]

Barclay's company had provided radio and motor transport, and the help of 14 officers and men. Evacuation was completed at 8 pm on the 14th, and the team returned to Khormaksar the next morning.

As Paterson's BEM citation indicates, the team was venturing into the unknown; at practically every stage, they had to improvise.

Throughout this rescue operation the team gave a most impressive performance; the task was frightening and unknown to them; their physical endurance throughout the 13 hours on the rock-face was in the highest traditions of the Royal Air Force and an example to all who watched. To Sergeant Paterson must go the highest praise for not only did he lead his team over this hazardous route but recovery would have been impossible without the personal reconnaissance he had made the previous afternoon. Only by his example; by his encouragement to the others and above all, by his courage and devotion to duty was this rescue made possible.[19]

Some time later, Air Vice-Marshal Johnnie Johnston, the AOC in Aden, called in on the Mountain Rescue Section to congratulate the team. Speaking quietly to Paterson, he said: "Did it ever occur to you that Lieutenant Barclay's death might not have been a climbing accident? What would you have thought if you'd known a bullet was found in the body?" During a long silence Paterson was remembering that the escarpment was close to the border. Eventually, "The Yemenis," he gasped. Johnston said nothing more and moved on, leaving Paterson to reflect uneasily that for two days they, too, had been as near to the border as had Barclay when he fell.

5 – Last Years Abroad

By 1971, the Near East Air Force (NEAF) team was based at RAF Akrotiri, Cyprus, and it seemed to have developed into a team which specialised in the unusual. In March, on exercise in Kenya, they had rescued the secretary of the Mountain Club of Kenya on Mount Kenya; he was suffering from pulmonary oedema. In July, one of their number, SAC McRae contracted cerebral oedema on the Alam Kuh Glacier in Iran. In August, they had given first-aid to an unconscious man after a swimming accident. Two of those three incidents had necessitated the use of oxygen, and the fact that they had oxygen was a direct result of the Mount Süphan and Mercator incidents of ten years earlier. Now, in December 1971 a most unusual call-out occurred, and again oxygen was called for. Flight Sergeant John Hinde, the team leader, was enjoying the usual cup of tea in the section at about 11 one morning when the telephone rang: "There's an aerial rigger, and he's stuck 260 feet up a 510-foot aerial tower."

There was an array of radio masts close to the station, at a place called Bitter Lake. This was a very swift call-out largely because the vehicles had just been washed and were standing outside. "We were actually in the vehicles heading for this tower within less than two minutes. And it was just one of those times when everything went absolutely perfectly," remembers Hinde with some pride. All the equipment they were likely to need was in the ambulance, right down to two 500-foot ropes. As they got within sight of the aerials, Hinde, with SAC David Oliver and SAC Ian Cunningham, the permanent staff driver, could see the unconscious man high up, with two of his colleagues by him – Corporal Sam Patterson and SAC Geoff Coleman. Wedged inside the framework of the aerial mast, semi-recumbent, the casualty had been tied to the mast and was being supported from beneath by Patterson whilst Coleman gave mouth-to-nose resuscitation.

Hinde, Cunningham and Oliver started making their way up the mast, Hinde and Oliver carrying 500-foot ropes. A race developed between Cunningham and Hinde as they started to put in running belays. Then they decided that running belays were not needed, and climbed straight up to the three men. Patterson and Coleman said that the man had stopped breathing several times, and it was clear that oxygen was needed: in fact, remembers Cunningham, "we thought he was a goner". Hinde shouted down to one of the team, Danny Daniel, at the foot of the mast: "Tie the oxygen bottles to the bottom of the ropes!"

When it arrived, oxygen was fed to the unconscious man for 15 minutes. He remained unconscious, though there seemed to be an improvement in his colour. Unconscious or not, Hinde decided, the man had to be got down. But how? For awkwardly wedged as he was inside the triangular framework of the mast, it would be impossible to get him into a stretcher, and the many guy lines would prevent a helicopter from getting close. There was nothing for it but to lower him somehow, and because of his condition, speed was essential; the chill factor caused by the biting cold wind at that height was doing him no good at all. He was secured into a climbing belt and chest harness. Then, still recumbent, he was lowered, lashed to Cunningham's chest, Cunningham guiding him down and trying, not always successfully, to protect him from collisions with the aerial.

News of the emergency had reached the Station Commander, Air Commodore John Stacey, who ordered a helicopter to stand off some way from the masts. Once down at ground level, the patient could be put into the waiting ambulance which was then driven clear of the aerial array to a point where the helicopter could pick him up and take him to the RAF hospital.

Within three months of this incident, John Hinde was on his way back to his beloved Kinloss and to his trade – engine fitter – prompting some comedian in the station magazine to offer him the gratuitous information: "No, John, they don't have propellers now!"

Hinde was replaced by Flight Sergeant Pete McGowan, who came to Akrotiri from a spell at Valley, where he had received his BEM; and by this time, 1972, he had been in the Mountain Rescue Service for eleven years. Like Hinde, he was an accomplished mountaineer in his own right, a member of RAFMA, and had been on several RAF expeditions. At this time the training programme was much curtailed because of severe defence economies. The team members, resourceful as ever, had kept themselves fit by walking and climbing in small groups around the island, and by playing football. Akrotiri MRT had in February sent ten people, five instructors and five pupils, to the Winter Course at Grantown-on-Spey. Then, with the team officer, Squadron Leader Mike Shannon, high-altitude winter training had taken place in Iran with mountain troops of the Imperial Iranian Army from the Shiraz Infantry Training Centre.

McGowan had not long been in place when, in the RAF Akrotiri station magazine, Flamingo, there appeared in the Mountain Rescue column:

> The team extends a welcome to our four new members, SAC Dave Wood 103 MU, SAC Ian McKinnon 27 Sqn, SAC Nolan Pol, and SAC John Corsie, ARSF. We all hope you will enjoy yourselves in MR and Cyprus.[20]

Three of these four were to go on the Mount Kenya expedition in March 1973, but on January 29th, at 7 pm, when several members of the team were relaxing in the section, a call came through bringing them to 'Immediate Readiness'. A chartered Ilyushin airliner, Egyptian-owned, had disappeared on its approach to Nicosia Airport.

As McGowan was in Scotland instructing on the course, the responsibility for the call-out fell upon the Deputy Team Leader, Corporal Neil 'Danny' Daniel, who had joined the service in 1962 at Leuchars, and that same year had also joined RAFMA. After spells in the MRTs of Khormaksar and Valley, he went back to Leuchars, then was posted to Cyprus and joined the NEAF team in 1970. A climber with much experience by this time (he had been on two expeditions, Mount Kenya and Alam Kuh, Iran, both in 1971, and on two major team exercises, Nejat VII and Nejat VIII, both in Iran, in 1971 and 1972 respectively) he was an Air Traffic Control specialist and was later commissioned in this branch.

He telephoned members at Akrotiri, Episkopi and Famagusta, and the sub-unit at RAF Troodos, then arranged for the convoy vehicles to be brought round to the section, checked the communications arrangements, made sure that radios with spare batteries were ready, and coped with updating calls from the controller.

1¼ hours after the first alert, the controller moved the team to RAF Nicosia, and they drove out of the gates of RAF Akrotiri at 8.15 pm. No sooner had they gone than Sergeant Bert Venman, of the medical team, arrived with a radio man, SAC Roger Rudling, and in Venman's new car they sped along the road to Nicosia to catch the convoy. Before Nicosia was reached a radio message told the team to go straight to the crash site, 2,500 feet up in the Kyrenia Range. An RAF Police Land Rover waited for them on the road to reinforce the message, and escorted the convoy at high speed through the city. On the roundabout near the airport a hitch-hiker was seen: fortunately he was recognised in time and one of the vehicles picked him up. It was SAC John Cuthbertson, who had learnt about the call-out when at home in Famagusta and he had dashed out hoping to catch the convoy. All the police checkpoints waved the vehicles through and, speeding on through a beautiful clear night sky, many members were getting their first sight of the Kyrenia Range.

After Kyrenia on the coast, they went on to Lapithos, then began climbing on forest roads and met a Land Rover from the British High Commission which led them to the site. The higher and the nearer they got, the more vehicles of all sorts hampered their journey – private cars, civilian ambulances, vehicles from United Nations units. People had gone out to help, but there was nothing they could do, and were descending now, going back home, visibly shocked by what they had just seen, succeeding only in obstructing those who could do something constructive. Pieces of misinformation were picked up by the men from Akrotiri as they crawled upwards through this melée: "There's nothing you can do." "It's a job that needs Commandos." "Seven helicopters couldn't help." They began to wonder what they were in for.

Daniel spoke to the senior policeman at the still-burning wreck, and it was agreed that two search parties, led by Daniel and Corporal Ron Cameron, would check the area round the site for any possible survivors. As expected, there were none: nothing, therefore, could be done until morning. A party of twelve from RAF Troodos led by Sergeant Ted Robinson arrived and with others prepared a camp site on the only flat ground – the road which was closed and guarded by the police. Tea was brewed, a radio call was put in to the controller and the opportunity taken to order extra equipment.

By 3 am, under the star-studded sky, the police were trying to doze in their Land Rover, and as many of the team as possible squeezed into the tent, the remainder sleeping where they could. 2½ hours later, they were on the move again.

For most of them, this was the first call-out of any sort, let alone one which exposed them to violent and hideous death; there had been 38 deaths. Their job now was to remove bodies from the wreck and it was a tribute to the Hinde and McGowan training that they did so efficiently and without question, even when McGowan was away. A pillar of strength in this was Sergeant Venman; never an outstanding hillman, nevertheless the burly Venman, it is Ted Robinson's belief, was provided by this incident with exactly the opportunity to respond magnificently and to give the team precisely the type of leadership that was required on the day.

By mid-afternoon, the job was done, the bodies were in vehicles to be taken down to Nicosia, photographed and, so far as possible, identified. One final brew of tea, then camp was struck and the convoy assembled. RAF Nicosia provided a meal on the way home and the main part of the team regained Akrotiri only 24 hours after the call-out. Some of the younger team members took several weeks

The Ilyushin crash of 1973: 38 dead, no survivors. *Photo: courtesy of Ian Cunningham*

to recover from the horrors of this episode.[21]

In 1975, with the reduction in RAF flying in Cyprus, the Akrotiri team was finally to be disbanded, and the '70s were to see first the contraction, then the removal of the Mountain Rescue Service from overseas stations.

There had been a team in the Arabian Peninsula since 1960, first at Khormaksar and then, after a short break in 1966, at Sharjah. In June 1971, the Mountain & Desert Rescue Team at RAF Sharjah was closed, as part of the withdrawal plan for the Persian Gulf. During the 4½ years that the team had existed, it had never been called to an aircraft incident, but had been kept on its toes with such activities as arranging desert survival courses for air-crew. In April 1970 Junior Technician Jones had assisted in the recovery of the body of a young Arab girl who had fallen down a well and been killed.

After a further short gap, a new 16-man team, under a delighted Sergeant Colin Pibworth who loved the Middle East, was opened at RAF Masirah on January 1st 1972. This provided SAR cover for the southern part of the air route from Akrotiri to Masirah. Early the following year, 'Pib's' BEM was announced. Pibworth is the first to admit that the teams in the Middle East were (through no fault of their own) never at the cutting edge of SAR work.[22] His service in the region – or anywhere at all – is probably longer than any other mountain rescuer's, but only two incidents stand out in his mind.

In 1943, a Bristol Blenheim of the South African Air Force operating out of Kutra Oasis had crashed, and the crew of six all died; they were buried on site. Twenty years later, on November 30th 1963, Operation Desert Blenheim was mounted under the team leader, Pibworth, with the officer i/c Flying Officer A F Jackson, when the Desert Rescue Team from El Adem disinterred the bodies of the crew, and took them back to Tobruk for burial in the big cemetery there.

Then in 1972, during his time at Masirah, he took the team out on an airborne search over '...my old stamping grounds of the Arab Emirates – looking for a commercial Caravelle that had wiped out its crew and passengers on the East Coast Mountains on a flight from Karachi to Dubai...'[22] Masirah, like Akrotiri, was to fall victim in late 1975 to the general contraction in the Air Force's overseas activities. For some time it had been operating on a part-time basis, but now the team which Pibworth had formed four years earlier was also disbanded. A short era had passed; there was now no Mountain Rescue presence outside the United Kingdom. But before that happened, there were at least three more major incidents involving Akrotiri.

6 – Mount Kenya

When the Akrotiri team returned from the Ilyushin crash, training restarted for the imminent Mount Kenya expedition, to be commanded by Flying Officer Brian Page, the Deputy team officer, and led by McGowan, with Daniel as the deputy.[23] On Saturday February 24th 1973, the expedition was flown to Nairobi in a 70 Squadron Hercules, the journey somewhat shorter than expected because the Egyptian government, grateful for the work done on the Ilyushin, now allowed the RAF aircraft to overfly Egyptian territory.[24] They were met by a sergeant from the Air Attaché's office and by Mr Minto Nuttall. Nuttall had previously been an RAF NCO and a member of Mountain Rescue, and now had his own business, Minto's Safaris, and had offered to look after the transport requirements. They were on the hill the next day.

By the Thursday, one party was on the Tyndall Glacier, but were uneasy about its condition, and decided to move off the glacier and do some rock-climbing instead on Point Pigott. Traversing over to the bottom of the climb, a steep wide gully, they started roping up. They had all just put their helmets on when a big stone-fall started from high up, tumbling down the gully for many seconds: everyone was hit before they could reach cover. Corsie took a blow on the helmet and was lying there dazed when Ian Cunningham dashed out in the thick of the fall and dragged him into cover. Corsie had bruised ribs and an injury to the left shoulder, and was helped back to base. Venman, in charge of the expedition's medical needs, was called up to give him treatment. His injuries proved not to be too severe, and he was able to continue.

Next day one party of four started their climb of a peak called after a Masai chief, Nelion (17,022 feet). On one rope were McGowan and Ian MacKinnon; on the second, John Cuthbertson and Don Shanks. Starting from a bothy called Top Hut, the vertical height of the route was 1,300 feet, but it was calculated that

L to rt. Unknown, Danny Daniels, Peter McGowan

about 2,000 feet would have to be climbed. From the 6.45 am start, they reached a spot called MacKinder's Gendarme at 9.30 am, by which time all were suffering from altitude and excessive load, and progress was desperately slow with many stops for breath. It was 3.35 pm before the last man reached the summit of Nelion, and all were truly exhausted, glad to bivouac in the warm and comfortable Lobonar Shelter on the summit.

Rising at 6.30 am, by 8 the four had started off on the traverse to a twin peak, Batian (the name of another Masai chief), reaching the summit by 10.15. They started the descent at 1 pm and had just completed the first abseil when McGowan saw that below him the rope had snagged on a rock. He told the other three to get well under the overhangs close by as it was obvious that as soon as he moved, the rock was going to fall. When they had moved, McGowan called: "OK – is all set?" and the reply came, "Yes!"

McGowan continues the story in his own words:

> They said Yes because the obvious thing was when you moved the rope the rock was going to fall directly down. It didn't do that. It fell, it ricocheted like a billiard ball and the rocks it kept hitting kept getting bigger and one kept straight in, hit him [MacKinnon] on the head and he fell....[25]

MacKinnon fell some 1,200 feet from the ledge where he was standing into an amphitheatre, down a couloir and then out onto the Krapf Glacier.

A radio call brought out team members from Top Hut, led by Phil Snyder (a local climber who had joined them) and Brian Page. Page met the three members of the summit party when they reached the bottom of the scree at 6.30 pm, and by this time confirmed to them that MacKinnon was dead. Other parties elsewhere in the Mount Kenya complex were gradually recalled. A large party left with two 500-foot ropes and a MacInnes stretcher, aiming for base camp, which some of them reached at 9.25 pm. A Park Warden, Bill Woodley, had received a radio message from Top Hut, and, flying over the accident site, had been able to direct the Top Hut party to the body.

On the following morning, Sunday March 4th, Page, McGowan, George Machar, Robinson, Shanks, Cameron, Corporal 'Sooty' Bullock, Corporal Bernie Cole, Cuthbertson, Cunningham and Snyder buried MacKinnon by the side of the glacier, the short, simple service conducted by Brian Page. Then everyone returned to base camp. At the expedition's request, The National Park wardens arranged for a small memorial to be set up; it is still there, checked at intervals by the wardens.

Understandably, the whole expedition was thoroughly demoralised that afternoon, and many wanted to call it a day and go back to Cyprus. Page and McGowan called them together in the evening and said that the team would stay on the mountain, and suggested a day of rest on the next day, the Monday. On that day Flying Officer Page had to go down to National Park HQ as the first stage of a journey to Nairobi for police investigations; he returned after two days and rejoined the expedition. It continued and finally finished as scheduled on Monday March 19th, returning in another 70 Squadron Hercules.

Nine months after it had welcomed MacKinnon, Flamingo carried this paragraph, with a black-framed photograph of a serious-looking, slim young man, with the beginnings of a widow's peak, and a moustache:

IN MEMORIUM

SAC IAN McKINNON

It is with deep regret and sorrow that we learned of the tragic death of SAC Ian McKinnon of 27 Squadron RAF Regiment on 3rd March 1973. Ian, a Scot from the island of Mull, was killed in a climbing accident whilst with the NEAF Mountain Rescue Team who were exercising on Mount Kenya. His death is a severe loss to the Squadron, the Mountain Rescue Team and to the Akrotiri Cross Country Club where he recently came second in the NEAF Individual Championship. All of us send our sincere condolences to his parents and friends at home.[26]

McGowan recalls MacKinnon well, the son of a Scottish judge:

He was a model airman. He was a big sports personality. He was the Squadron CO's driver. He was a member of the team. He was a pleasure to be with – a very mild nice guy – one of the people you'd least like to lose. That was a great shock.[27]

McGowan afterwards went to see the family, but they were still in such deep shock that they were unable to discuss anything connected with the accident. On the AOC-in-C's commendation for Pete McGowan in the following year, the citation reads:

By his outstanding qualities of leadership and organising ability he had brought the Team to a high level of proficiency. In a recent training expedition to Mount Kenya, during which a team member fell and was fatally injured, FS McGowan restored the morale of the Team by his personal example of self-discipline, courage and determination.

Venman, too, with his quiet efficient manner, had greatly helped in maintaining morale during a tragically marred expedition.[23]

It was proving to be a time of great change in the Akrotiri team, which had long found it difficult to attract sufficient recruits. In the month after MacKinnon's obituary appeared, Daniel was posted to St Athan and Cuthbertson and Dave Wood to Kinloss; Ron Cameron left the team; Cole replaced Daniel as DTL.

In the meantime, the mountains continued to extract their terrible price for man's impudence. Some of the MR Service – Chief Technician G Armstrong and Corporal I Jones of St Athan, SAC Tom Taylor of Leuchars, and McGowan – were included on an RAFMA Himalayan expedition, to the very difficult Dhaulagiri IV, in 1974. The advance party, Flight Lieutenant Addis, Jones, Taylor and McGowan, arrived in Kathmandu on February 11th, and the main party a month later. On March 13th they were all assembled at Pokhara, followed by a long trek to the climbing area. Then we come to McGowan's report for April 14th:

It was about 9 am when I reached the end of the moraine and I had only just set foot on the lower slopes of the couloir, when I heard a thundering explosion above me and looking up saw huge blocks of ice fall from the icefall on the left, down into the couloir. The column of eight men simultaneously made an immediate and quick movement to the right, seeking protection from the massive wave of ice and snow that now roared down the couloir towards them. Some made the protection of the rocks on the right-hand side of the couloir, whilst others stood no chance at all and were swept 2,000 ft down into the bottom of the snow basin. I moved quickly about ten yards to the right as the avalanche rushed past, then there was silence. After the cloud of powdered snow had settled, I was amazed to see the movement of four men high up in the couloir, for having witnessed such a destructive force sweeping down the mountain I could not visualise anyone escaping from its grasp.

Just above me in the avalanche debris I saw movement in the snow and rushing up, found two injured sherpas. Whilst the other climbers rendered first-aid treatment to them, I set off down the lower debris in search of the two missing sherpas. I found their twisted and broken bodies down near the bottom of the debris but there was little to be done for them, for they had been swept the whole way down the couloir and now lay in an area of complete disaster. Beside them in the devastation lay rucksacks, broken ice-axes, scattered personal equipment and even lengths of the fixed rope, that had been snapped by the force of the avalanche and carried down into the snow basin.

The two injured Sherpas were carried down to camp 1 on a makeshift ski-stretcher, but sadly, one died during the night and the other was evacuated on the morning of the 16th by rescue helicopter to Kathmandu.[28]

Dhaulagiri IV was abandoned from this point, but not solely because of the deaths of the Sherpas. Stringent defence cuts were in place at the time, and the RAF had withdrawn its airlift support, causing the expedition to spend a great deal of money air-freighting its equipment there, and they were very rapidly running out of cash.[29] All round, Dhaulagiri IV was a disaster.

Chapter 6 – Footnotes

1 Discussion with writer
2 Letter to writer 23/10/92
3 Letter to writer 31/10/92
4 Letter to writer 5/3/92
5 Minutes of Conference 3/12/59
6 Report dated 9/2/60
7 G L D Anderson: History of RAF Kai Tak
8 D C Reeve: A Guide to Rock-Climbing in Hong Kong
9 IMR, Squadron Leader A R Gordon-Cumming, to the Commander-in-Chief of the Far East Air Force at RAF Changi, August 1st 1956
10 Flight Lieutenant J R Sims to Records Office, Gloucester, 4/4/60
11 Gerald White: letter to writer received 23/1/92
12 White to writer 31/1/92
13 Squadron Leader F E Runchman to Under Secretary of State, 28/6/61
14 Squadron Leader A Lightowlers, for Deputy Director of Maritime Operations to Commander-in-Chief, FEAF, Changi, 27/9/61
15 Letter to writer 1/12/92
16 Report A, April 1964
17 Dr D Davidson
18 Letter to writer 1/12/92
19 BEM citation 21/4/65: 3142674 Corporal (Acting Sergeant Paid) George Henderson PATERSON. Royal Air Force KHORMAKSAR
20 Flamingo, July 1972
21 McGowan, in conversation with writer 28/2/92
22 Letter to writer 11/11/92
23 Mt. Kenya 1973 Report: FO B S Page, 18/7/73
24 Ted Robinson, in conversation with the writer, 6/12/92
25 McGowan, in conversation with the writer 28/2/92
26 Flamingo, April 1973
27 McGowan, in conversation with the writer 28/2/92
28 Flamingo, August 1974
29 Taylor, in telephone conversation with the writer, December 1992

CHAPTER VII – THE END OF THE PROLOGUE

Into the '90s

What's past is prologue.

William Shakespeare 1564-1616 (The Tempest)

1 – Anna Humphries

This book has had a geographical split from the point where the critical events of 1951 are described: the long, painful business of the Lancaster on Beinn Eighe and the contemporaneous brilliant performance of Valley MRT under Mike Mason supported by Colin Pibworth during Black Easter changed the outlook and direction of the service from that time on. However, towards the end of the '80s occurred three massive incidents which probably changed the direction of the service once more. For that reason, the geographical threads are now being gathered together to form, again, one central cord.

Auburn-haired Anna Humphries, in November 1988, was 15 years old. Her journey home to Hampton Wood near Ellesmere from Maelor High School in Penley was along a country lane which crossed the English-Welsh border between Shropshire and Clwyd. On Tuesday the 8th she left school as usual at 3.45 pm, and as usual was wearing her school clothes: V-neck jumper, white blouse, navy skirt, black ankle socks and black slip-on shoes; she was carrying her fawn shoulder bag with a brown strap. Normally she was met by her parents in their car, but on this terrible day they were held up in a traffic jam. It was for only five minutes, but it was enough. When they finally arrived and she was not at the usual spot, the alarm was raised. That evening, the police set up an incident-room caravan in the carpark of the Dymock Arms, Penley, but rapidly it became obvious that this was not big enough, and the operation was moved next morning to Penley Village Hall. Not only was it well-equipped inside, but an adjacent field provided a good helicopter landing site, there was good road access and there was ample parking space.

On the 9th the Valley team (under Flight Sergeant Peter Kirkpatrick and Corporal Andy Kelly) was called, then Stafford (under Sergeant Tony Emsley and Corporal G S Clethero) early in the morning of the 10th. One of Anna's shoes was found by the side of the busy A458, 30 miles away. By now, apart from the RAF, there were over 100 police from the North Wales and West Mercia forces (including dog handlers and underwater search team divers), coastguards, regular soldiers, Territorials and army cadets, civilian volunteers including the local hunt, SARDA, with 22 Squadron helicopters also involved. Other mountain rescuers in this non-mountain search were civilian ones from North Wales and the Pennines, including the Ogwen Valley team. Dr Tony

Jones, of the North Wales Mountain Rescue Association, was co-ordinating. Never, he reflected later, had he been on such a steep learning-curve.[1] Groups of people with very different skills – and some very willing helpers with no searching experience – had to be moulded into an effective force. To achieve this, the mountain rescue teams were broken up and their members used as party leaders.

At nightfall, all searchers returned to the village hall for the debriefing. The two RAF teams were accommodated at nearby RAF Shawbury, and after two days' painstaking, inch-by-inch but fruitless searching, Valley returned to station, leaving Stafford behind. They continued until Monday November 14th, when they were relieved by St Athan. Searching continued, still without success.

Anxiety and emotion were running high. A man who lived not far from Anna's home, a convicted rapist, had disappeared at about the same time as Anna, and his car was found abandoned. He had contacts in Dublin and it was strongly suspected that he could be there, as he had his passport with him, and a car similar to his had been seen near to the spot where the girl had last been seen. Five days after the first alarm, police were admitting that hopes of finding her alive were fading rapidly. Ports and airports around the country were being watched.

By this stage it was no longer a search-and-rescue operation; it was a criminal investigation for murder; the constraints had changed. Whilst the skills required for each have factors in common, they are not identical. Now the crucial element was not the preservation of life but the preservation of evidence: something which the RAF MRTs understood, fortunately, from their work with crashed aircraft. Now they were gathering evidence to help the police, not to find Anna; and not only did they have to garner every tiny shred of evidence – as they would when an aircraft crashed in the hills – but they also had to protect confidentiality for the sake of the integrity of the criminal trial to follow.

Searching was gradually stepped down. Then, suddenly, on November 18th, the eleventh day of the search, the atmosphere became electric. Some Mountain Rescue searchers found some items which had been in Anna's school bag – pencil case, text books and so on – at various locations. They reported to Search Control and almost immediately the resultant traffic on the radio network nearly overwhelmed the crew and the Communications Desk. The radio log had to be abandoned, and, comments Mick Randall:

> These events must have been the most intense in the history of mountain rescue comms. Unfortunately a voice channel recorder was not available to record it all for posterity.[2]

Intense activity continued until after dusk when the last person came in. Searching resumed the next day, Saturday the 19th, but then, on the Sunday, snow had fallen overnight; it would have been pointless to continue, and to do so would be to risk trampling unseen evidence underfoot.

> In the light of confidential information obtained in the course of their enquiries the Police

advised the Search Management Team to finally conclude their contribution to the Incident land and air search for Anna Humphries. However, the Incident would continue purely as a Police matter.[2]

Not in Dublin but in France, near Lyon, was the wanted man found. He was arrested and brought back to the UK. Three weeks after she went missing, Anna's body was found in the Severn at Bridgenorth, Shropshire. A man in custody was charged with her murder, tried in a Crown Court, found guilty and sent to prison.

Tragic as it was, this affair provided the teams with valuable experience in co-operating between themselves and, more importantly, with other agencies: police, civilian teams, the army, helicopters. It also provided a communications specialist who had considerable MR experience with an opportunity to examine the particular communications problems which an operation of this type raises. Mick Randall had retired from the Royal Air Force as Chief Technician in communications some four years earlier. In the '70s he had been McGowan's Deputy Team Leader at Akrotiri, where he stayed until the team was closed down as part of the defence economy measures. Then he went to Valley, where Jack Baines was in charge. His major incidents included the Jaguar search on Ben Lui in 1979, discussed in an earlier chapter.

During the search for Anna, Randall was assisting the Search & Rescue Dogs Association with its communications. Because of the problems with the equipment used at the time, the flat terrain and the extended search areas, high antenna masts were provided by the RAF and Ogwen Valley, and link stations set up. Ogwen Valley provided the civil SAR channel facility, and the RAF the military equivalent with the additional and valuable ability to work through RCC at Pitreavie, and with the 22 Squadron helicopters. Ground-to-air communications for the police air support and the transport pool came from the police. Back-up radio equipment, such as hillsets, were provided by the RAF and the Ogwen and Clwyd teams.

But there were shortcomings. The coastguards used Marine VHF Channel 0; some members of the public used Citizens' Band Channel 9; neither of these could communicate with the operational base. The police did not make available their 'On-scene Incident' Channel; a liaison officer had to forward messages to police officers. A VHF/UHF scanner receiver, believes Randall, would have been extremely useful to monitor events on various operational channels. A petrol electric generator would have provided back-up during mains failures (many – caused by overloading in the village hall), and the radio masts should have had hazard warning lights for flight safety. Finally, the necessity for link stations in turn necessitated much message relay traffic which took up valuable airtime and often prevented instant access for the search parties and operations staff with priority messages; Randall suggested that a dedicated admin channel would overcome that problem.[2]

The Penley search had been one of the most emotionally-charged that experienced rescuers, civilian and military, could remember. More were to follow in a short space of time; meantime, lessons had been learnt.

2 – The Maid of the Seas

Staff of the American diplomatic service were left in little doubt as to the unconfirmed but quite specific danger. A letter to all employees said that on December 5th, 1988 an unidentified person telephoned a US diplomatic facility in Europe with the warning that within the next two weeks there would be a bombing attempt against a Pan American aircraft flying from Frankfurt to the United States. Police and Pan Am had been informed; in the meantime, no assessment could be made of the reliability of the information. Embassy staff were left to decide what changes, if any, they would make to their personal travel plans, but they were not absolved from the obligation to use an American carrier.[3]

Those who did not work at a US embassy, or were not friends of those who worked there, were less fortunate. They were not given the opportunity of assessing the risk to themselves and families and considering a switch to another carrier.

Boeing 747-100 no. N-738PA, Maid of the Seas, had entered Pan Am's service straight off the Boeing assembly line near Seattle in February 1970. Since then she had been rebuilt in Pan Am's workshops with much new and lightweight material. On December 21st 1988 she flew into Heathrow from San Francisco, and there was then a six-hour turnround. She assumed the identity of Flight No. PA103, a flight which had started as a Boeing 727 out of Frankfurt, and left the stand at Heathrow for New York on time at 6 pm, carrying 243 passengers including three children and 16 crew. After take-off at 6.25 pm, she climbed steadily for half an hour and was in level cruising flight at about 31,000 feet for about seven minutes. At that point the crew were receiving Oceanic clearance from Shanwick Oceanic Control, but they did not acknowledge. At precisely that moment – just before 7.03 pm – the radar blip broke up showing multiple blips fanning out downwind for a considerable distance. 1.3 on the Richter earthquake scale was registered, and the seismological readings helped to predict the possible structural damage to houses and to locate the point of strike, and to determine whether the engines were working when they hit the ground.

Corporal Peter Higgins, Deputy Team Leader of Stafford MRT, was at home with his wife when the call came through, barely a month after Anna Humphries. He had been looking forward to the usual big Christmas exercise, this year in Scotland, in which all the MRTs were involved. St Athan MRT had already arrived at RAF Stafford on its way up, using Stafford as a staging post. Higgins had arranged their overnight accommodation and now he was at home for the evening. Tomorrow, the two convoys would start on their way to the Grampians. But then the phone rang. There had been a crash; a major crash. He made a disappointed face to his wife and she knew that the exercise was threatened. When she looked at him further, however, she saw firstly an expression of horror, then total disbelief. Higgins listened: a Boeing 747 had exploded at 30,000 feet over a town called Lockerbie, near the Scottish/English border, and had hit the ground in many pieces. All MRTs were to make their way there as soon as possible. That was the first he had heard of Pan Am Flight 103.

A jumbo jet, practically full, could mean about 400 people. Part of it had fallen on some houses; more deaths there, no doubt. He was not afraid of seeing death. He had seen it many times before and had assisted in extracting many bodies from many wrecks. But this, the sheer scale of it, was almost too huge to contemplate. Surely, surely, someone is having us on! He signalled to his wife and she quickly switched Ceefax on, punching in the code for the news headlines. There it was. An explosion in a 747 over Scotland. All must be dead. Could be a bomb. He made some essential phone calls, got into his climbing gear, had a cup of tea and was driven by his wife over to the Mountain Rescue premises on the station. One large convoy – Stafford and St Athan – was on its way within two hours.

RCC called out a 202 Squadron Sea King from RAF Boulmer, two 22 Squadron Wessexes from RAF Leuchars (one of which took a burns team from Edinburgh Royal Infirmary), three Royal Navy Sea Kings, a 33 Squadron Puma from RAF Odiham with a mobile air operations centre, four Wessexes from RAF Valley (one of which picked up a burns unit from Manchester), three Chinooks from 240 OCU and two from 7 Squadron. A Hercules from RAF Lyneham collected 25 firemen from Aberdeen along with two of their vehicles and survivor detection equipment. As well as Stafford and St Athan, the Mountain Rescue element was completed by Leuchars and Linton-on-Ouse, the latter now being the home of what had been the Leeming team.

At Lockerbie the initial picture was one of chaos – not surprising, said a senior officer from Pitreavie later – but the Leuchars team leader, Flight Sergeant David 'Heavy' Whalley, and a local police officer did a first 'recce' for survivors and those injured by fallen debris. Clearly little more could be done until daybreak and the MRT personnel were stood down, but for Squadron Leader Bill Gault and Sergeant Bill Batson, the Linton-on-Ouse team leader, staying on to work out a search plan overnight. (Gault, the then ILR, had by chance been driving through the area with his wife Roberta; he made arrangements for Roberta to continue on her way home, and joined his troops.)

Batson's clearest memory of the early hours, having arrived by a Sea King of 202 Squadron from Leconfield, is of frustration: frustration at the difficulty in finding any one person who knew what was happening; frustration at the endless round of meetings; frustration at not being able to give his waiting team the instructions they were waiting for.

With Flight Lieutenant Adrian Birkett, Sergeant Tony Emsley and Peter Higgins, Stafford MRT arrived at Lockerbie at 3 am and were told to report to Search Control at 6 am, as it was immediately obvious that little could be done in the hours of darkness. Accommodation was in a school gymnasium and most were able to get a little sleep whilst the civil authorities did what they could for people in the 40 stricken houses; no survivors had then been found.

Not until daylight did the full horror of the situation become manifest. Until that point the MR teams were working on the principle that there may have been some survivors – not from the aircraft, but perhaps from the houses. Cars had been engulfed in a fireball when the wings had hit the A74, which here forms the Lockerbie by-pass just to the west of the town, leaving a colossal crater of 140 × 40 feet, and had then scythed a huge gash through two rows of houses in the adjacent and parallel Sherwood Crescent. More of this debris reached the next road, the High Street, and beyond. Major parts of the fuselage fell near-vertically on the housing estate. All four engines fell on the town but caused little damage.

That was only the beginning, and awful as it was, it was not the most horrible – as the radar image had indicated, much lighter debris had been scattered by the wind over enormous tracts of the countryside, and in fact it was found eventually that some had reached as far as the east coast. For Stafford, St Athan, Linton-on Ouse and Leuchars, with civilian teams Tweed Valley, Moffat and Borders, that morning began with the grim task of searching for and recovering every piece of wreckage and human remains, large and small; a slow, painstaking, inch-by-inch search, with the help of the SARDA dogs.

Priorities had to be decided and the team leaders got together. Passengers were not the first priority – in Pete Higgins's words, "we couldn't do owt for them". As often happens, the MRTs were the first, uninstructed, to arrange a guard on the various parts of the wreck. Team members were allocated search areas and to Stafford fell the distinction of finding the Black Box half a mile to the east of Lockerbie. Close to the same spot were 65 bodies, the biggest concentration, and within the first hour nearly 100 had been found; further searching to the east of the town revealing baggage and parts of airframe. As darkness fell the Stafford team returned to station. On this first full day the MRTs generally had concentrated on the high ground; other agencies, such as police and army, on other areas.

After the demolished houses and the crater which replaced them the most abiding image of Lockerbie for most people is probably the sight of the cockpit and nose of the 747, half-buried in a field at Thundergarth Mains three miles from the town, the bodies of the crew still inside. Other images, rightly, did not get onto the front pages. Bodies – of adults, children and babies – were to be seen in fields, caught against fences like fish in a net, on rooftops, some still strapped in their seats. As well as all the passengers and crew, the disaster had killed eleven inhabitants of Lockerbie.

In the Black Box – actually bright orange – was a Digital Flight Data recorder (DFDR) with a duration of 25 hours and recording 20 parameters, and a Cockpit Voice Recorder (CVR) with a duration of 30 minutes. Data on the DFDR showed that the aircraft had been flying straight and level on the correct heading, and had just crossed the Scottish border when recording ceased abruptly. On the CVR were recorded the Oceanic clearances which were being passed at the time; this transmission was interrupted by a very brief noise (180 milliseconds), then all was silent. Amongst the wreckage recovered were passenger baggage and part of the framework of a baggage container which, when examined by Ministry of Defence scientists, showed evidence of the detonation of high-performance plastic explosive, which had been housed on the port side in the No. 1 Cargo/Baggage hold just forward of the wing.[4]

Relatively little credit in the media seemed to be given to the Mountain Rescue Teams involved, considering the MRS and the SAR squadrons, 22 and 202, were largely responsible for bringing order out of the initial chaos. Afterwards, however, Emsley was able to report, the day after his team had been stood down:

> This ... [is] the largest operation the MRTs have been involved with, the co-operation between teams, army Pol[ice] and SAR Helos[5] was excellent and will provide valuable experience for the future.[6]

Valuable though the experience was, it left, for some at least, a slightly dissatisfied feeling, a feeling that yet more could have been achieved. Bill Batson commented long afterwards:

> As for Lockerbie, well I'm still left with a feeling that we were pulled out too soon, and could have done useful work there, had we stayed.... This is not a dig at the RCC – I was just as keen to get home for Christmas as anyone else at the time, but on arriving back ... to free beer and normality, I had a very strong urge to turn the team around again and head back to Lockerbie.[7]

This is probably a common reaction with emergency agencies of any sort. Here they are, back in the comfort of their own home, or the Naafi, or the sergeants' mess, and what have they left behind? As they see it, an unfinished job and grieving relatives. Paradoxically, the teams that went straight on to Kegworth were probably more fortunate. But as ever in major incidents, there was a new lesson. Batson adds:

> Of course, everyone wanted to 'get it right' just like me, but as a result, there was a delay in any real action taking place. Certainly, a lesson I learned from Lockerbie was that it is not always possible to 'get it right' at the outset, and that it may be necessary to react on the information available at the time and modify the planning as more becomes available. Psychologically, even, this is a better solution, as the frustration [that word again!] of being in the centre of such a disaster and not actually doing anything is almost painful.

Corporal Duckworth, then DTL at St Athan, commented:

> All the troops worked extremely well. Not only together but with the other 3 MRTs and a high standard of morale was maintained in a very sensitive and difficult area of responsibility. This was the big incident we had always trained for and talked about. At the time it would have been nice to have had a PR officer on scene to represent the RAF SAR organisation. This would have taken the burden of press and TV from the shoulders of the search co-ordinators, giving them less things to think about.[8]

Pete Higgins's pithy comment to the present writer sums up the latter problem: 'We had to cope with many things at Lockerbie which were not very nice – including the press.'

Air Vice-Marshal D C G Brook, Air Officer Scotland and Northern Ireland, wrote from Pitreavie:

> Not surprisingly there was chaos at Lockerbie, but it was the training and organisation of the RAF MRTs which started to introduce some order there. For a start they arrived with full map coverage of the area, and within the first few hours FS Whalley, Leader of the Leuchars MRT and a local Police Officer had made an initial reconnaissance immediately outside the town of Lockerbie, including an initial search for any survivors or person injured by falling debris.
> It became clear that a comprehensive search would require careful planning, and that little could be achieved in darkness.

They had already been telexed the content of a letter from the Prime Minister, Margaret Thatcher:

> I WOULD LIKE TO THANK YOU, AND THROUGH YOU ALL YOUR MEN, FOR THE TRULY SUPERB JOB THEY ARE DOING IN THE AFTERMATH OF THE TERRIBLE CRASH AND PARTICULARLY IN ASSISTING WITH THE SEARCH AND RESCUE OPERATIONS. THE PROFESSIONALISM AND DEDICATION OF ALL THOSE IN THE AIR FORCE WHO I MET TODAY WAS IMMEDIATELY APPARENT, AND I AM MOST GRATEFUL FOR ALL THEIR EFFORTS.[9]

In the margin of the telex at Stafford was a note from the Station Commander to the team officer: 'I am sure the boys will also wish to see this one!'

Over the past 50 years the MRTs have handled many distressing situations. It is not easy for a young airman or airwoman who had probably not seen death in any form in their 18 years to cope with sudden, multiple death at its most violent and ghastly. Usually, the support of a strong but sympathetic NCO, aided by other, experienced team members, is enough to see the novice through. Lockerbie, however, was in a different league altogether; the sheer numbers of the dead involved made it so, and psychiatric help was offered and accepted (though at least one of the teams felt they had talked it through amongst themselves and had emerged with no lasting ill-effects, crediting what Batson calls the 'One Big Happy Family' principle).

A chilling flavour of the situation as it developed was given by the large-scale map used at the time to plot the debris and casualties as they were found: here, 'wreckage', 'two mail bags', 'panels/seats/clothing', 'wing spar', 'position of black box'; there, '4/5 bodies & cockpit', 'many casualties 65', '2 adults in seats + female casualty + 1 child', 'adult', 'adult, 'adult', 'child', '2 young children', 'one leg'.

Wing Commander Gordon Turnbull is the RAF's chief psychiatrist, based at the Princess Alexandra Hospital, RAF Wroughton. Turnbull in the '70s had been the team doctor with the Cyprus team, and was there when it was finally closed down in 1975. He has, therefore, a healthy respect for RAF mountain rescuers and their resilience. Wroughton's Psychiatric Centre had been taking an interest in what had become known as Post-Traumatic Stress Disorder since publication of a major paper in 1980, and Turnbull helped to develop PTSD techniques after the Hungerford Massacre. Royal Navy psychiatrists rapidly developed PTSD strategies during the Falklands War, as did the Army psychiatrists to cope with the stresses of conflict in Northern Ireland and the Falklands.

PTSD techniques were turned to by the RAF initially as a means of dealing with post-ejection phenomena and flying stresses; and then came Lockerbie. A team, skilled in debriefing techniques was set up, their techniques later honed by the Lockerbie experience so that the RAF was at the forefront during the events of 1991 – the release of prisoners of war after the Gulf War, and of the hostages Terry Waite, John McCarthy and Jackie Mann. All of these people were talked through their experiences in the special unit at RAF Lyneham.[10] Turnbull was assisted by his Senior Psychiatric Nursing Officer, Squadron Leader Bert Venman – the same Bert Venman who, nearly twenty years earlier, had been a member of the Akrotiri MRT at the time of the Ilyushin call-out.

Returning American POWs after the Gulf War spoke with envy of the RAF's reputation in these matters. One was reported as saying that as the plane door opened on his return to the USA, he was faced with a camera crew. Then after a military debriefing in Washington, he was simply put on a bus to his home in California. 'My life became absolute hell,' he recalls. "There was no privacy, and coping was a matter of trial and error."[11]

But although Turnbull's debriefing team was quickly set up after Lockerbie, before it could begin its work Kegworth happened, and for some the whole process had to be deferred. A conference had been set up at Pitreavie Castle to examine the facts of Lockerbie and to decide where improvements could be made. This was on January 20th 1989, but in the meantime an airliner had crashed at East Midlands Airport.

3 – Kegworth

Over the years the English teams have not been the most consistently active in emergencies, nor those with the most spectacular call-outs. That is no fault of

Leeming or Linton-on-Ouse or Stafford, but a reflection of the terrain they cover – the Peak and Lake Districts and the Yorkshire Moors – compared to the Western Highlands of Scotland or Snowdonia which Kinloss and Valley have to look after. But after Lockerbie they were not allowed to rest.

Seven days later, on December 31st, a farmer in the Lake District reported that a car had been parked on his land for a couple of days, and it was suspected that it belonged to a climber who had not returned. Stafford and Linton-on-Ouse were called out to search, but then were recalled by the police; it had been a false alarm.

On January 7th 1989, Stafford helped the Derbyshire Cave Rescue Organisation to extricate someone from Oxlow Cavern, who, without the proper tackle, had decided to 'have a look over the edge' of a precipice on the end of a sling, and was unable to get back.[12] He had fallen about thirty feet, landed on a pile of boulders, and escaped with nothing worse than cuts and bruises.

"Just turn round. I want to examine your shoulder blades," said the examining doctor.

"Why?"

"I want to see where your bloody wings are, that's why!"

On the same day, a crashed but empty car was found at Chapel-en-le-Frith and it was suspected that the driver had tried to make his way home over the moors in bad weather. As the search was being planned he was found safe and well. Incidents like these – relatively small in MR terms but desperately important to those involved and their relatives – are the everyday stuff of a team's life.

Still shell-shocked from the enormity of Lockerbie, and having only just returned from the Peak District and the two minor incidents, they learnt on January 8th that a Boeing 737-400 of British Midland Airways had crashed onto the M1 motorway just short of the East Midlands Airport runway. As well as Stafford, RCC Pitreavie called out the Linton-on-Ouse MRT, E Flight 22 Squadron, B and E Flights 202 Squadron, and SARDA. Flight No. BD092 had not long left Heathrow for Belfast when instruments indicated that one of the two engines was on fire. The passengers were told, at short notice, to prepare themselves for a crash landing.

This book is not the place in which to discuss the whys and wherefores of this crash, when the pilot very nearly made it to the runway at East Midlands Airport, Kegworth, between Nottingham and Leicester; nearly but not quite. It was tantalisingly in sight as the 737 hit the bank on the far side from the airport, skimmed across the motorway without hitting any cars, careered up the bank on the airport side, and came to rest, its back broken, against some trees.

Travelling up the M1 at the time was a minibus carrying members of an inshore lifeboat team, and they were some of the first on the scene. They organised a human chain with other arrivals and took out 18 survivors. Another very early arrival was SAC Matt Pickard, who was driving north along the motorway with friends when he saw the aeroplane bounce across the road in front of him. He tackled fires round the wreck, entered it, and rescued several people, and his actions earned him a Royal Humane Society Testimonial. Very soon afterwards the airport crash wagons arrived, immediately spraying foam on the still-burning engine. On their way were seven fire engines from Leicester, Loughborough and Coalville. As the scale of the disaster became evident, four more followed. Air Traffic Control had alerted the emergency services and four ambulances were on their way even before the 737 hit the ground. Quickly the motorway was closed off to all but emergency services and 30 more ambulances followed in 15 minutes. Others involved at an early stage were a unit of the Royal Signals, and an AA patrolman who just happened to be there.

RAF Stafford MRT under Sergeant Pete Winn arrived at 10.50 pm, about 1½ hours after the alert. There was still no central point of control and rescuers were going in and out of the fuselage with survivors and bodies, a fuselage precariously teetering on the edge of a slippery grass slope. One of their first actions, therefore, was to secure it with 250′ ropes to prevent the whole thing – wreckage, rescuers, casualties, bodies – slithering down. Other members joined the police and firemen in recovering people from inside, and formed a human chain to help with debris clearance. Aircraft fuel made the embankment extra slippery, providing a double hazard – further fire and an unstable working surface. A channel was therefore dug to aid drainage and steps cut in the grass slope.

There were at that stage conflicting reports as to the numbers of casualties. Linton-on-Ouse team arrived and made an extended search of the embankments. This was fruitless and work was again concentrated on the aircraft. One casualty in particular had severe spinal and pelvic injuries; he was stretchered down to the motorway for evacuation, and his extrication by both MRTs took seven hours, a very delicate operation.

Lack of a central control point obliged the two MRTs and the RAF helicopter crews to join together and act as a unit, and there was a feeling in the RAF that the civilian authorities, particularly the police, did not know what expertise the MRTs could offer. To be fair, it is hardly surprising that they were unaware of these things. In the Scottish Highlands and in North Wales the police had lived with RAF Mountain Rescue over many years; each respected the strengths and was aware of the weaknesses of the other. But there are not many mountains in the East Midlands, and until Anna Humphries and Lockerbie the emergencies wherein Mountain Rescue had been deployed in a non-mountain situation had been few.

Traffic was diverted off the busy M1 onto the A6, causing heavy jams which sometimes prevented emergency vehicles from getting to and away from the site; whenever necessary, the 22 and 202 Squadron Wessexes and the Navy's Sea Kings were used, but had trouble in putting down because of the high overhead motorway lighting. Casualties were taken to Derby Royal Infirmary and to hospitals in Nottingham and Leicester. Floodlights both on the crash itself and for search purposes on surrounding fields were provided by the RAF helicopters.

It was a very different scene from that of Lockerbie, and Winn commented that they had never handled anything on this scale before, and that it is quite rare to have had two major airline disasters in such a short space of time:

> We have learned a lot in terms of experience from them both. It has been a testing time for the lads. A lot of them had seen one or two bodies before but nothing on the scale of these disasters. It has made them mature very quickly.[13]

Terrible though it was, Kegworth had been therapeutic for some. Lockerbie had been dispiriting, demoralising; no survivors, and the dead had died horribly and in such numbers. At least at Kegworth lives had been saved. Thus ended a two-month period which must surely rank as the most demanding in the service's history, even including the war years when Ansons were dropping out of the sky or flying into peaks in Graham's Graveyard almost weekly.

4 – Changes

One of the RAF Llandwrog team from the 40s, Noel Bailey, has said:

> It may be difficult for anybody to imagine what it was like in 1941 when you look at a present day Mountain Rescue Team and its vast array of equipment. We had no helicopters, no fully equipped Land Rovers, no special clothing, no climbing boots, no walkie-talkie radio and worst of all *no* experience. What we did have, was our working battledress, rubber boots and RAF greatcoats. The Station Medical Officer, Flying Officer Graham, had his little black bag and a compass (Boy Scout type). Transport was borrowed from our M.T. Section.[14]

But some things do not change. As this book was being written in 1992, Junior Technician Alistair Brown of the propulsion bay at RAF Leuchars was rock-climbing with the Leuchars team in a quarry behind Stirling. A great flake of rock came away, and Brown with it, landing on a ledge. The rock landed on him, his leg was smashed, and he badly hurt the back of his head, necessitating major surgery. But like Jock Smith thirty-five years earlier who fell on Tryfan in an uncannily similar incident, Brown is a very resilient character of strong will. He is still in the Air Force and, some time after this incident, still getting used to his artificial leg, he was in the section prior to the annual formal inspection by a senior officer, accompanied by Squadron Leader Brian Canfer, the ILR. There was a call-out and Brown was able to do much of the preparatory work, making the turnout that much faster, and then escorted Air Vice-Marshal Blackley on a tour of inspection. Jock Smith and Alistair Brown would have recognised each other across the generations as kindred spirits.

Then there have been the changes in scale. True, the run-of-the-mill 'missing walker' searches are no better and no worse now compared to forty years ago; there are more of them. But the really big disasters – the Lockerbies, the Kegworths – are on a grander scale. The Lancaster on Beinn Eighe, the Aer Lingus Dakota on Snowdon, even Mount Süphan, were major events of their time, but tiny in comparison.

As experience has been accumulated over fifty years, the need for co-operation has been perceived. Until the early '50s, not only was there little or no working with civilian agencies – except on an ad hoc basis with the police – there was little co-operation between the RAF teams. The writer was the wireless operator with RAF Edzell MRT when the Beinn Eighe crash happened in 1951, but only learnt about it when researching this book; obviously nobody at Kinloss even considered the possibility of bringing in other teams.

From a scratch organization, created by enterprising medical officers to fulfil local wartime needs, using the people and the equipment which happened to be at hand, the MRS has grown into a professionally-trained, professionally-organised service which is the benchmark for mountain rescue across the world. In 1951, the views of RAFMA members and other experienced climbers, supported by influential outsiders such as Professor T Graham Brown, had at last been listened to in the Air Ministry.

Although nominally in charge, the officer i/c now (no longer necessarily a medical officer) really has the role of a facilitator, and the true centre of gravity moved long ago to the non-commissioned officer. This move accelerated from 1951, but unfortunately for a considerable time there was a red herring – a requirement that the team leader must be a Physical Training Instructor. A slightly dotty requirement when what is really needed is an NCO who is interested in and has expertise in the hills. Why assume that because a sergeant is superbly fit he will make a good team leader, when mountains bore him rigid and his real interests are football or marathons? Johnnie Lees comments:

> However it seemed silly to me, at the time, to change the Team Leader job from a Sgt (or F/S) of any trade to a branch of P.T.I. just to make it tidy. OK, I happened to be a P.T.I. but what was needed was a good mountaineer with some admin. experience – & it was often the case that P.T.I. recruits knew little about aircraft, whereas NCOs who'd worked on aircraft were much more suited to getting good relations with the working RAF to get key workers off for training – not a 'jolly', on 'sports afternoons' when flying hours & AOG were paramount – even if Command boxers or athletes could have time off! When an aircraft crashed and one needed to recognise bits and distinguish from existing wreckage! Trying to teach mountaineering to PTIs in 3 months was impossible though we did try v. hard.[15]

There was a time when it was thought naïvely that the emergent helicopters would take over the mountain rescue role, but realism prevailed: there are places a helicopter cannot get to, conditions in which it cannot be flown. Conversely, when it can be used, it can save hours in getting a climbing team to a casualty or a wreck, and then the casualty to the hospital. Both the present and the previous ILRs were formerly SAR helicopter aircrew members and the six teams and the two helicopter squadrons work very closely together.

Changes in the culture of the service have occurred over the years. Far more of the troops are climbers in their own right and the teams no longer work in watertight cells as they seemed to forty-odd years ago – now all of the troops are known to each other. (Incidentally, in 1951 they would not have been referred to as 'troops', that then being a noun left to the Army. Still less would one man have been described as a 'troop', which properly is a collective noun referring to a group of soldiers.)

Other cultural changes are on the way. There has been a tangible element of male chauvinism in the service, despite the fact that women's names show up in the rock-climbing guides as First Ascenders from the 1900s on, and that Scottie Dwyer (to name but one example) before, during and after World War II did some severe climbs with women. With the absorption of women into the mainstream RAF command structure and latterly the acceptance that they could have a role firstly as aircrew then as combat aircrew, also with the growing familiarity of seeing them as armed guards on the gate at RAF stations, it became ever more difficult to argue convincingly that they could not have a part to play in Mountain Rescue, especially as some of the most respected civilian teams have women members. Furthermore, demonstrably they were not, compared to men generally, lacking in stamina or physical courage. Squadron Leader Canfer readily accepted a change to the rules; and SAC Donna Flanagan at RAF Leeming was accepted as a novice in November 1992. Female trialists need to reach precisely the same standards in the trial period as their male colleagues. There has been some opposition to the innovation, as is often the case in close-knit male communities, but it is Canfer's belief that within two years all will be forgotten.

From time to time over the half-century of the service's existence, events have happened which have caused people to question either the need for its very existence or the way in which it operates. One such was the end of World War II in 1945, prompting the question: This service was formed to tackle the problems caused by wartime military flying; now that that will cease, do we still need the service? It continued almost by default. Although the number of flights dropped, there were still enough in mountainous areas to justify a rescue service; and gradually, largely unnoticed, the proportion of civilian climber search and rescue operations rose.

Secondly came the Lancaster crash on Beinn Eighe in 1951. The question was already being asked: Clearly the teams are not trained or equipped well enough to cope with major emergencies in terrain this rugged; should we train them up to that standard, or look for another solution? And the sub-text, largely unexpressed, was: Does this lot contain a bunch of mountain nuts who are merely looking for cheap climbing at His Majesty's expense? It was that subsidiary question that had prevented RAFMA's offers of help being accepted. But Beinn Eighe concentrated minds wonderfully.

In the Heath government of the '70s, the Chancellor of the Exchequer was Anthony Barber (described by at least one economist as the Demon Barber), who organised what became known as the 'Mini-boom' of 1971-73: extremely speculative and inflationary. Import figures shot up in relation to exports, Britain's competitiveness deteriorated, the spectacular profits were in financial services rather than manufacturing, a consumer credit explosion pushed prices up, up, up.... The stock market collapsed, fringe banks tottered, a truly enormous increase in the price of oil finally pushed the house of cards over.

It was in this highly charged atmosphere that there was a Defence Review to see how many millions could be saved here and there, and the Mountain Rescue network came under scrutiny in 1974. One of the proposals before the Air Force Board was to disband one of the UK teams. It was proposed by the Vice Chief of the Air Staff (VCAS) that the maximum acceptable 'Station to Incident Travelling Time' (SITT) was nine hours. SITT was defined as the time taken by an MRT to reach the top of any hill in the UK from its home station, based on these speeds:

35 mph by MT
2½ mph plus one hour for every 1,500 feet of ascent on foot
crossing time for ferries (extracted from the AA Members' handbook 1972/73: waiting times not relevant as the police would ensure that they awaited the arrival of the MRT)

Now the teams have AA routes and speeds on their personal computers.

An SITT of nine hours could be achieved if the high ground were divided into three areas:

Northern: north-west Scotland, Outer Hebrides, Skye (covered either by Kinloss or Lossiemouth, Kinloss being preferable)
Central: southern Scotland (south of Fort William/Aberdeen), Arran, Jura and Mull, and north of the line Barrow/Hull (could be covered only by Leuchars)
Southern: south of Barrow/Hull (coverable from St Athan, Stafford or Valley; little to choose between the three, Valley being preferable because of the helicopter unit there).

It was conceded that the service could not be justified on purely financial grounds (though the total cost was low – £90,000 a year – in relation to the cost of training a Phantom pilot – £400,000), but the VCAS believed that there was an important moral obligation to provide the means of rescuing aircrew from situations which might arise in the course of duty, as was met without question by the air/sea rescue facilities. An increase in the amount of low-level flying by fast jet aircraft over mountainous areas could only reinforce this obligation. Then there were additional tasks which Mountain Rescue accepted: coverage of Royal and VIP flights; crash investigation and recovery of bodies; assistance to service mountaineers; assistance at civil aircraft incidents.

Benefits included: assistance to the local community – including help to mountaineers and walkers; benefits to team members – such as opportunities to develop leadership, initiative, team spirit, physical endurance and a spirit of service and adventure; public relations and recruiting.

Neither the Army nor the Royal Navy had an alternative. True, the USAF had the 67th ARRS at RAF Woodbridge, part-trained by the RAF MRS, but it could not be an effective substitute. The VCAS suggested that the minimum requirement was the retention of Kinloss, Leuchars and Valley, but the additional retention of St Athan, Stafford and Leeming would result in SITTs well below the 9 hours maximum at relatively little extra cost, and would be welcomed by the civil authorities. Any decision should be postponed until after the Defence Review, which might result in deployment changes. That conclusion was a considerable improvement, from the MRS viewpoint, on his stance of a year earlier, when drafts of the paper suggested strongly that three teams should go and three remain. That had been a reaction to a proposal from the Economies Project Officer to disband the Leeming team and reallocate Leeming's SAR duties between the other five teams.

When the Board met, it agreed to postpone a decision, and Labour took power before the question was resolved. When the Defence Review redeployments were known in April 1975, none affected any of the MRS stations and the VCAS felt able to propose that the network should stay as it was. It seemed that the service could live, intact, to fight another day. But there was a sting in the tail of the Board's minute:

> Although the savings from their disbandment [St Athan, Stafford, Leeming] would not be great (£41,000 per annum) we may need to 'scrape the barrel', and as they are not operationally essential, I would suggest that it might be better to take yet another look at this in, say, 6 months' time.[16]

In the margin against this paragraph in the ILR's copy is scribbled in large capital letters with a black felt pen: 'BE READY!' Six months later the ILR, Squadron Leader Vernon, was indeed ready, picked up the challenge and tackled the problem from another angle. He queried the validity of the rather arbitrary 9 hours' SITT:

> This was calculated, with the present deployment of MRTs, on the worst possible case (the time for a man from Kinloss to reach the summit of Clisham on the Isle of Lewis – a journey involving 2 car ferries). This criteria produced an unbalanced picture of our requirement for the MRTs and lead to the conclusion that it would be possible to disband the Leeming, St Athan and Stafford MRTs without denigrating the military rescue service. The teams were granted temporary reprieve at that time because of their contribution to public safety in the mountains, and because the PR spin off for the RAF far outweighed the cost of the teams.[17]

He suggested that a more realistic yardstick would be the time taken to start search and rescue operations after the team members have been called from their normal place of work.

With present team deployments a search can be initiated in any hilly part of the mainland within 4 hours (in 90% of the areas within 3 hours). The withdrawal of any one of the MRTs (other than Stafford) would increase the surface SAR reaction time to the same area by 2 hours or more, a very significant reduction in capability. If the Stafford MRT were withdrawn there would be a localised slower reaction but overall times would still be within 3-4 hours.

He made two further points. Firstly:

The volunteer airman could carry out a normal day's work at his primary task, respond to a call-out, drive for up to 6 hours and then be expected to commence an arduous night rescue operation in hazardous weather conditions which preclude the use of helicopters. This I believe is asking too much. So long as our MRTs are composed of volunteers, with other primary tasks, we should keep travelling times to a minimum, in recognition of the fact that MR operations are arduous, normally prolonged, and often come at the end of a normal day's work.

Sccondly, aftcr pointing out thc pcrsonal timc dcvotcd to training for no financial reward and the 'initiative and adventure' benefits:

A further factor which must be considered is that the high standards of our MRTs are due in part to the long experience of many of the airmen, some have spent over 15 years on MRTs. Over the years the number of MRTs has diminished, Akrotiri and Masirah will soon be lost, and further reductions could make it increasingly difficult to maintain training standards.

He concluded:

Each team justifies its own existence in civilian rescues, RAF PR, and recruiting incentives. I wish to retain the UK MR service at its present size. Five teams are required to maintain the present military SAR cover and I believe that all 6 teams are necessary to maintain our present level of experience.

Vernon's new rationale and his arguments were accepted in their entirety. The UK network survived in full, though the overseas teams had soon gone.

Equipment and training constantly develop. Personal computers have been supplied to all teams since January 1992. One of the most difficult tasks can be handling questions from reporters when in the middle of a difficult operation. Now team officers, team leaders and deputies are all given media training. Medical training, too, is being extended, starting in 1993. Budgetary problems continue, but despite these a new signals wagon has been approved.

Similarly, structure and procedures have to change to suit changing circumstances. The ILR now has a 'No. 2', who acts as Chief Instructor, and the first, announced just as the final chapter is being written, is Warrant Officer

Alister Haveron. The creation of this new post at warrant officer level must help to open up a career path. Until now, entry into the permanent staff of the service has been something of a cul-de-sac.

Protective clothing now has to be worn at all aircraft crashes, and since October 1991 the service has been responsible for all military aircraft accidents – not just those in mountain areas – and for providing the initial crash guard. How long will it retain the name of *Mountain* Rescue Service? For the Anna Humphries search, Lockerbie and Kegworth, although not the first outside of the mountain areas, brought home to people that the MRS's work was not limited to *mountain* rescue.

5 – Wheresoever, Whomsoever, Whensoever

In 1953 a group of RAFMA members started to put together an expedition which was not merely the first with a high MRS content, but was also the first British Armed Forces assault on the Himalaya. This was the golden age of Himalayan climbing: during that year, Sir John Hunt led the first successful Everest expedition; one of his team was Wilfred Noyce, who had with George Graham been on Tony Smyth's staff at the Aircrew Mountain Centre in Kashmir.

RAFMA's president at that time was Air Chief Marshal Sir Ronald Ivelaw-Chapman, who had earlier been C-in-C of the Indian Air Force, and his influence there was invaluable. From RAF Lyneham, the UK contingent – Tony Smyth as leader, John Sims as deputy leader, Mike Holton as secretary, Donald Bennet, Johnnie Lees, Dan Stewart and Jack Emmerson, with Henry Jones as doctor and Lester Davies as transport officer – were to be joined in India by Nalni Jayal from the Indian Air Force. Originally the intention had been to explore the mountains around the Bara Shigri glacier on the Kulu-Spiti divide in the Pir Panjal range, but poor weather forced a change of plans, and they ended up exploring the Kulti Himal of Lahoul. Crossing the Rohthang Pass, one of the highest mountain passes in the world, they managed to climb eight peaks, seven of them virgin, between 18,000 and 21,000 feet. Their first climbs were Taragiri, Shikar Beh, Ashagiri, Sri Latta, Akela Lilla, Tila-Ka-Lahr and Tambu, and opened up the area to thorough knowledge. In the RAFMA magazine, Holton concludes: 'We left the day the monsoon arrived and 24 hours before the bridges gave way.'

This expedition in 1955 cost £1,300, including £3 for baksheesh. A budget of £8,760 was needed for another expedition to the same area 35 years later. Corporal Pete Higgins of St Athan MRT as the leader had SAC G S Clethero of Kinloss as his deputy, and the party was made up with four members of the Stafford team. They flew out of London to Delhi on September 25th 1990, but on arrival were advised by the British Consulate not to travel that night as student

The 1955 RAFMA Expedition: Back row l to rt Lester Davies, Donald Bennet, Jack Emmerson, Dan Stewart, Mike Holton, ———, Johnnie Lees; middle row Henry Jones left (with John Sims below), Tony Smyth centre in peaked cap

unrest was gripping the city. They finally escaped from the airport two days later. Because of the riots the Government bus was not running and they were obliged to hire a private one. Caught up in the riots on the outskirts of Delhi, they were stuck in the jam for nine hours. At long last, the driver forced his way across the central reservation and drove back to the airport. 'Morale was not high' says the report.[18]

All flights north were booked, so two taxis were hired. These reached the same point as the coach, with the same results. They joined a convoy of cars also going north led by a driver who claimed to know the routes, and met up with more riots from time to time, sometimes having to double back on their route to avoid trouble. A further unscheduled stop came when they met a mob burning an effigy of V P Singh, the Prime Minister, but they finally reached Manali at 6pm on the 29th. In 1955, the road had ended at Manali, and there the Smyth expedition had made its base camp. By 1990, the road had been extended to the pass, but the

Higgins expedition stayed in a hotel in Manali, then moved over two days up into the hills to Seri, and made base camp there.

Their main climb was to have been Deo Tibba (20,410 feet), to the south of the Smyth expedition area. In the event, they found Deo Tibba to be a peak too far, and settled for the appropriately-named Consolation Peak. 'This provided some excellent mixed climbing and ridge walking combined with steep precipitous drops into the Malana Nala and fantastic views of distant snow-clad peaks to the East.'[18]

One story will serve as an example of a team's involvement with the local community (there are many others). Sergeant Nick Sharpe took a phone call when he was in RAF Valley's MRT section with the duty crew, and found himself speaking to Christine Lewis. Her son James had had cancer diagnosed when he was very young in 1988. During his long period of unpleasant treatment, it emerged that what he wanted more than anything else was to 'climb a mountain', and Christine was organising a sponsored walk up Snowdon to raise money for a child cancer charity: would the MRT provide safety cover? Sharpe enlisted the help of his girlfriend, Liz Gough, and another team member, Rob Hannam. On a beautiful cloudless day they ascended Snowdon by the Miners' Track with James (now 5), and a small group of James's friends and family. Christine remembers that he said he felt he was in heaven; and one of the MRT members said to her: "He's too young to die with cancer. We'll take him back down to earth".

The idea developed, and in later years expeditions were made to Ben Nevis with the help of the Kinloss team. James had an operation in mid-1992 to remove a stomach tumour and in November his mother Christine was able to tell the writer that her son was in the clear. She added: "I would like to tell all who read your book that these people risk their own lives and the only way I can describe their 'true grit' is – There is no ending to anything but a memory of professional endurance dedication and love."[19]

Mrs Lewis could perhaps have added to that, the endurance, dedication and love of the wives of the members – something that has not been spelt out between these covers so far since we have concentrated on the teams themselves. As was acknowledged during the battle for the network's cohesion during the '70s, the volunteer members are expected to go on exercise two weekends out of three: this, year in, year out, is a severe strain on even the strongest marriage. Some marriages have buckled and broken under it. It is surely time that a public acknowledgement was made of the support which the womenfolk of the members give, support without which the service could not properly function. What form that acknowledgement should take is not for this book to say, but a start could be made by following the example of Leuchars MRT, which invites wives, fiancées, girlfriends of past and present members to the annual reunion.

At the summit; Rob Hannam on the left, Nick Sharpe with James in the centre.

The ranks of the Mountain Rescue Service were opened to women in 1993, as this book was being completed. This is the first Novice, SAC Donna Flanagan. *Photo: RAF Leeming MRT*

At least two major figures, one past (Peter McGowan) and one present ('Heavy' Whalley), have views on this. 'I cannot emphasise too strongly the importance of the wives' supporting and encouraging role to Team Leaders in carrying out what is and continues to be a very demanding and challenging role in guiding the RAF Mountain Rescue Service to the peaks of excellence.'[20]

Squadron Leader Canfer, the present ILR, recently adopted and distributed to the whole service an introductory set of notes which had been put together by Flight Sergeant Kirkpatrick for his own team. It is designed to give trialists an idea of what is in store should they be accepted and wish to continue. The last section is headed:

A WIFE'S COMMENTS ON THE MR SYSTEM – CATHY SCOTT[21]

Here I am being able to look at the MR system from the outside, having lost my husband and MR partner not to the love of the hills but to cancer.

I fondly remember meeting this triple relationship. The weekends alone, shopping alone, the rush on Friday nights, the mountaineering kit in the hall that was strewn across the living room the night before. You know it's the change of season, because the hill bag comes home to be turned out and sorted. Sunday night comes around; is it to be 7, 8, 9 or 10pm this time? "Hello dear, good weekend? Would you mind washing this kit, in case there's a call-out. Anything to eat. Come and talk to me in the bathroom." Well, I ask you, are you meant to put a feather duster somewhere appropriate at the same time?

So, the exciting kit. Open the poly bag, phew!! Oh God, what died in there? Oh, it's only a green sock soaking wet, inside out, screwed up and full of bracken, moss, dirt and stones. *Warning* beware the red socks – every new wife must face the dangers of a Pink Wash.

The chat is great, the sparkle in the eye, the mischief, the pride in achievement, the amusement in recalling someone's epic, the terminology, the new words all to be learnt. The harder the weekend the greater the need to wind down, hence the ritual Sunday night lovemaking and Thursday, because Friday they are away again. No need to put it into the diary, it's already booked.

Tell me how to beat this other 'woman' and hold on to her husband. My experience is to make friends, see no threat in her demanding and domineering manner; jealousy and resentment are two emotions better left alone, because of the damage they can cause to a relationship. I soon forgot any ill feelings when looking into my man's face as he described a climb, rescue or adventure. He was happy so I was too.

Trust is essential in this relationship. The partner must have a blind faith and trust to survive this MR temptress, and other offers of infidelity which can be available at some weekend bases. We tolerate such aspects only because of trust. Don't let us down, or yourself.

I admire the commitment of the RAF MRS and envy the desire to master the hills which radiates and oozes out of each and every one of you. May your years with the system be plentiful, but don't let it be totally consuming to the detriment of your relationship with the people who love you the most; your family.

I write for once as Cathy Scott not Scottie's wife.

The RAF Mountain Rescue Service is unique. It is unique in the mountain rescue context, for excellent as they are, the civilian teams consist of people who have jobs to go to and whose availability must in many cases be limited, no matter how extreme the emergency – whereas the RAF, if needs must, can arrange for all members to stay on a search and rescue until the job is done (though NCOs running workshops and offices have always grumbled, and will continue to grumble, at the unscheduled loss of staff). Then in the next context it is unique in the opportunity it gives for early responsibility, and especially for the fact that... 'the normal RAF rank structure is replaced by a meritocracy based solely on... proven ability within the MRS.'[21]

One would, perhaps, have to go back many years in the Air Force to get a situation remotely like that, when in Bomber Command a sergeant pilot was captain of the aircraft, no matter what the rank of his crew.

Also unique is the combination of skills possessed – mountaincraft, searching, paramedic, knowledge of airframes and engines, awareness of fuels and explosives, gathering and recording of evidence. The teams can boast total availability: anywhere, at any time, in any conditions.

Whensoever.

Chapter 7 – Footnotes

1 Dr A S G Jones, telephone conversation with the writer, 1/3/93
2 The Penley Incident: report by Mick Randall
3 Administrative Notice: *Threat to Civil Aviation*, December 13, 1988 signed by William C Kelly, Administrative Counselor, American Embassy, Moscow
4 Air Accidents Investigation Branch, Department of Transport
5 helicopters
6 Report 'A', RAF Stafford MRT, 24/12/88
7 Sgt Bill Batson, letter to writer 11/12/92
8 Report 'A', RAF St Athan MRT, 5/1/89
9 Telex HQ Strike Command to various units 18/1/89
10 Gordon Turnbull: Debriefing British POWs after the Gulf War and Released Hostages from Lebanon (WISMIC Newsletter, June 1992)
11 Reader's Digest, October 1992
12 Letter from Derbyshire Cave Rescue Organisation to Sgt P Winn, RAF Stafford MRT, 22/1/89
13 Sgt P Winn: Press interview
14 Letter to writer 3/10/92
15 Letter Johnnie Lees to writer 23/1/92
16 Air Member for Supply & Organisation to VCAS 1/5/75
17 ILR to Deputy Director Operations (RAF), 19/11/75
18 Report on Exercise Kulu Quest, January 1991
19 Letter Christine Lewis to writer received 5/11/92
20 Letter McGowan to writer 15/3/92
21 Royal Air Force Mountain Rescue Service (MRS) Volunteers (introductory handout to new trialists)

"Right! you don't smoke, don't drink, don't..."

APPENDIX 1 – BIBLIOGRAPHY

ALDERSON, G L D: History of Royal Air Force Kai Tak (Royal Air Force Kai Tak 1972)
ANDREWS, MICHAEL: The Birth of Europe (BBC Books 1991)
BIRKETT, BILL; CRAM, GEOFF; EILBECK, CHRIS; ROPER, IAN: Rock Climbing in the Lake District (Constable 1987)
BYRE, J & FRANKLAND, J: Race Against Time (Lyon Books 1988)
CAMPBELL, MALCOLM AND NEWTON, ANDY: Welsh Winter Climbs (Cicerone Press 1988)
CHURCHILL, WINSTON: The Second World War (Cassell 1948)
CRAM, GEOFF: see Birkett, Bill
DEIGHTON, LEN: Blitzkrieg (Cape 1979)
DOUGLAS AND CLYDESDALE, SQUADRON LEADER THE MARQUESS OF: see Fellowes, Air Commodore P F M; and McIntyre, Squadron Leader D F
DOYLERUSH, EDWARD: No Landing Place (Midland Counties Publications 1985)
DRASDO, HAROLD: Lliwedd (Climbers' Club 1971)
EILBECK, CHRIS: see Birkett, Bill
ETHERTON, COL. P T: see Fellowes, Air Commodore P F M
FELLOWES, AIR COMMODORE P F M; STEWART BLACKER, L V; ETHERTON, COL. P T; and DOUGLAS AND CLYDESDALE, SQUADRON LEADER THE MARQUESS OF: First over Everest (John Lane the Bodley Head 1933) (see also McIntyre, Squadron Leader D G)
FRANKLAND, J: see Byre, J
GRAHAM BROWN, T: Brenva (Dent 1944)
HIGHAM, CHARLES: Wallis (Pan)
HOWETT, KEVIN: Rock Climbing in Scotland (Constable 1990)
JONES, DR ANTHONY S G: Some Thoughts on the Organisation of Mountain Search and Rescue Operations (OVMRO 1973)
KAPADIA, HARISH: See Mehta, Soli
LAWRENCE, JOSEPH: The Observer's Book of Airplanes (Frederick Warne 1943)
LOVELOCK, JAMES: Life and Death Underground (Bell 1963)
MEHTA, SOLI and KAPADIA, HARISH: Exploring the Hidden Himalaya (Hodder & Stoughton)
MIDDLEBROOK, MARTIN: The Berlin Raids (Viking 1988)
MOFFAT, GWEN: Two-star Red (Hodder & Stoughton 1964)
MORIN, NEA: A Woman's Reach (Eyre & Spottiswoode 1968)
MOULAM, A J J: Carneddau (Climbers' Club 1966)
McLYNN, FRANK: Bonnie Prince Charlie (OUP 1991)
McINTYRE, SQUADRON LEADER D F, and DOUGLAS AND CLYDESDALE, SQUADRON LEADER THE MARQUESS OF: The Pilot's Book of Everest (William Hodge & Co Ltd 1936)
NEWTON, ANDY: See Campbell, Malcolm
NUNN, PAUL: Rock Climbing in the Peak District (Constable 1975)
O'BRIEN, TERENCE: The Moonlight War (Collins 1987)
REEVE, D C: A Guide to Rock-Climbing in Hong Kong (1968)
ROPER, IAN: see Birkett, Bill
SLOAN, ROY: Wings of War over Gwynedd (Gwas Carreg Gwalch 1991)

SMITH, DAVID J: High Ground Wrecks (Midland Counties Publications 1989)
STEWART, MAJOR OLIVER: The Royal Air Force in Pictures (Country Life 1941)
STEWART BLACKER, L V: see Fellowes, Air Commodore P F M
STYLES, SHOWELL: Snowdon Range (Gaston's Alpine Books 1973)
UNSWORTH, WALTER: Everest (Allen Lane 1991)
WILLIAMS, PAUL: Rock-Climbing in Snowdonia (Constable 1990)
WILSON, EUNICE: The Records of the Royal Air Force (Federation of Family History Societies 1991)

OTHER SOURCES

ANON.: Mountain Rescue (Royal Air Force Review January 1950)
ANON.: Tasks of the Civil Aid Services (Civil Aid Services Silver Jubilee 1977)
ANON.: The CAS Mountain Rescue Unit (Civil Aid Services Silver Jubilee 1977)
HOLTON, MIKE: In the Beginning (RAF Mountaineering Association journal 1988)
LEES, FLIGHT SERGEANT J R: How the RAF Mountain Rescue Service Began (Air Clues 1957)
LLOYD, FLIGHT LIEUTENANT J C: RAF Mountain Rescue Service (paper to the Alpine Club 6th February 1945)
LOFTS, SQUADRON LEADER DAVID: In-house history of RAF Mountain Rescue (1979)
LUK, C C: The CAS Mountaineers in the United Kingdom (Civil Aid Services Silver Jubilee 1977)
SMITH, DAVID J.: The Mountain Rescue Service (After the Battle)
SMYTH, GROUP CAPTAIN A J M, OBE DFC: The Expedition of the Royal Air Force Mountaineering Association to Lahoul, June 1955 (Himalayan Journal 1956)
WHITE, FLIGHT SERGEANT T E: Mission to Burma (RAF Upper Heyford station magazine December 1947)

"Straight up, i've seen them drinking in the N.A.A.F.I."

APPENDIX 2 – RAF MOUNTAIN RESCUE TEAMS 1941–1993

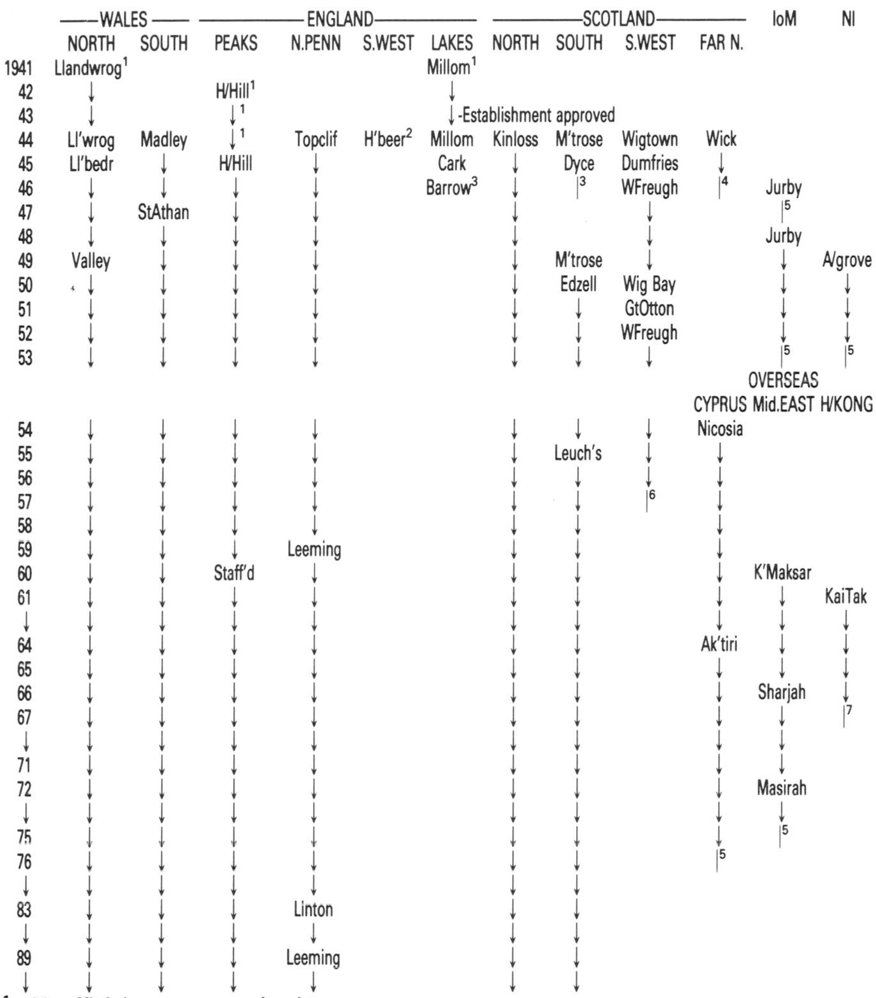

	WALES		ENGLAND				SCOTLAND				IoM	NI
	NORTH	SOUTH	PEAKS	N.PENN	S.WEST	LAKES	NORTH	SOUTH	S.WEST	FAR N.		
1941	Llandwrog[1]					Millom[1]						
42	↓		H/Hill[1]			↓						
43	↓		↓[1]			↓ -Establishment approved						
44	Ll'wrog	Madley	↓[1]	Topclif	H'beer[2]	Millom	Kinloss	M'trose	Wigtown	Wick		
45	Ll'bedr	↓	H/Hill	↓		Cark	↓	Dyce	Dumfries	↓		
46	↓	↓	↓	↓		Barrow[3]	↓	[3]	WFreugh	[4]	Jurby	
47	↓	StAthan	↓	↓			↓		↓		[5]	
48	↓	↓	↓	↓			↓		↓		Jurby	
49	Valley	↓	↓	↓			↓	M'trose	↓		↓	A/grove
50	↓	↓	↓	↓			↓	Edzell	Wig Bay		↓	↓
51	↓	↓	↓	↓			↓	↓	GtOtton		↓	↓
52	↓	↓	↓	↓			↓	↓	WFreugh		↓	↓
53	↓	↓	↓	↓			↓	↓	↓		[5]	[5]
										OVERSEAS		
										CYPRUS	Mid.EAST	H/KONG
54	↓	↓	↓	↓			↓	↓	↓	Nicosia		
55	↓	↓	↓	↓			↓	Leuch's	↓	↓		
56	↓	↓	↓	↓			↓	↓	↓	↓		
57	↓	↓	↓	↓			↓	↓	[6]	↓		
58	↓	↓	↓	↓			↓	↓		↓		
59	↓	↓	↓	Leeming			↓	↓		↓		
60	↓	↓	Staff'd	↓			↓	↓		↓	K'Maksar	
61	↓	↓	↓	↓			↓	↓		↓	↓	KaiTak
↓	↓	↓	↓	↓			↓	↓		↓	↓	↓
64	↓	↓	↓	↓			↓	↓		Ak'tiri	↓	↓
65	↓	↓	↓	↓			↓	↓		↓	↓	↓
66	↓	↓	↓	↓			↓	↓		↓	Sharjah	↓
67	↓	↓	↓	↓			↓	↓		↓	↓	[7]
↓	↓	↓	↓	↓			↓	↓		↓	↓	
71	↓	↓	↓	↓			↓	↓		↓	↓	
72	↓	↓	↓	↓			↓	↓		↓	Masirah	
↓	↓	↓	↓	↓			↓	↓		↓	↓	
75	↓	↓	↓	↓			↓	↓		↓	[5]	
76	↓	↓	↓	↓			↓	↓		[5]		
↓	↓	↓	↓	↓			↓	↓				
83	↓	↓	↓	Linton			↓	↓				
↓	↓	↓	↓	↓			↓	↓				
89	↓	↓	↓	Leeming			↓	↓				
↓	↓	↓	↓	↓			↓	↓				

[1] Unofficial or unrecognised team
[2] Disbanded – area taken over by Madley
[3] Disbanded – area taken over by W. Freugh
[4] Disbanded – area taken over by Kinloss
[5] Disbanded
[6] Disbanded – area taken over by Leuchars and Leeming
[7] Disbanded – RAF continued to assist Hong Kong CAS with training

MOUNTAIN RESCUE AREAS

The present (1993) main operational and training areas for each team are:
KINLOSS Grampian and Highland
LEUCHARS Tayside, Fife, Strathclyde, Central Lothian, Dumfries and Galloway

LEEMING	Northumberland, Durham, Cumbria, North and West Yorkshire
STAFFORD	Lancashire, Greater Manchester, South Yorkshire, Derbyshire, Cheshire, Stafford, Salop, Hereford and Worcester
VALLEY	Gwynedd and Clwyd
ST ATHAN	Powys, Dyfed, Gwent, Glamorgan, Devon and Cornwall

APPENDIX 3 – RECRUITMENT, SELECTION AND TRAINING THEN AND NOW

1943 After his review of methods (Ch. I Sect. 3), Graham reduced the call-up time by dividing the team into two groups, the advance search party and the carrying party. The advance group included three with some mountaineering or hill-walking experience, the Medical Officer, three nursing orderlies, a driver and a wireless operator. The carrying party were untrained personnel who were detailed to be on standby. Nursing orderlies were trained in mountain skills, and training of anyone who showed some aptitude took place 'whenever their normal duties permit': a rather grudging attitude to vital training quite common at the time. These days, anybody who is a member of a Mountain Rescue Team must be made available for MRT training as well as for call-outs.

Graham's training programme looks rather low-key compared with now. Usually it consisted of sending an inexperienced man out with an experienced one, though occasionally a larger exercise took place. Finally, Graham looked at search techniques. He made the point that, whilst searching is not difficult when the weather is good and clear, by definition one is most often searching when the weather is misty or rainy. As with many other team tasks, the ideal number for a search party is about twelve, and that was the number he suggested for the advance party. Every alternate member carried a portable radio, a prismatic compass and a map. The MO marked out the search area on the map and remained in charge from the ambulance. The team was spaced out at fifty-yard intervals on a line to one side of the area, and those with the compasses were given the bearing which would take them to the other side. It was important that the men with compasses should keep to the bearing, and that the other members kept in touch with whistles – a procedure which would seem very risky today.

1944 In March 1944 a Directorate of MR was formed in Air Ministry, under Flight Lieutenant Gill (whose responsibilities included Air Sea Rescue) and the teams were visited by Major Roxburgh, who had been appointed to supervise. Flying Officer T O Scudamore of Llandwrog said the visit was: '...encouraging and promising. The Air Ministry directorate provides a body to whom we can now turn for guidance and help, in the knowledge that sympathetic consideration, at the very least, will be available.'

Within the month, the teams were being visited by Sergeant Hans Pick. Sergeant Pick was an Austrian, a former police officer from Vienna, then in the 52nd Mountain Division, and he instructed the teams on map-reading, compass use, and rock-climbing. Pick made some very positive recommendations regarding equipment, mountain navigation training and movement in mountainous country, included in an undated report (apparently in November 1944) by Squadron Leader O H Warwick to the Director of Medical Services Overseas. Warwick had visited MRTs at Montrose, Llandwrog, Cark and Topcliffe, and one of his conclusions, with which few mountain rescuers would today agree in full, was that physical fitness was most important, but true rock-climbing ability was seldom necessary.

"Who got up last night?...and forgot to close the flap!"

Sergeant Gordon Leigh, a wireless operator/mechanic, joined the Llandwrog team as a volunteer climber in mid-January, 1944. Graham had left for his new posting on the Friday; Leigh arrived on the Monday and always regretted that he did not have the chance to meet Graham. Even in those busy times – aerial activity was beginning to build up to a climax – the team trained regularly, including those weeks when there had been a call-out. Leigh, like many others, got to know about this new service from two sources: official memos within Flying Training Command and by word of mouth around Ogwen in North Wales where he did much of his personal climbing. He was interested and not just because he loved the mountains:

I had two aims in joining the Mountain Rescue, First of all to make my knowledge of North Wales and my activities as a climber and mountaineer available for this what I considered important work, and secondly my cousin was killed while training as an air gunner in 1942. He was killed in a mountain crash in Eastern Scotland and although he died in the crash I understand that two of his colleagues died from exposure in this particular crash because it wasn't located for quite a long time. That was my aim in volunteering for Mountain Rescue and I think you'll find that most other volunteer members that joined had some sort of axe to grind in that direction as well.

1945 John Lloyd mentioned, in his talk to the Alpine Club in February 1945, that since the system had been put into operation in July 1943, it had saved twenty-six lives.

Two small movements towards the modern MRT style happened in March and May. Pick visited Montrose early in 1945 for training. He was at Llandwrog again in March, this time to train a support party of volunteers in navigation skills. Under Scudamore's and Pick's guidance, Llandwrog was moving away from Graham's concept of a very small skilled core with the support of an unskilled carrying party, and towards the modern pattern where all members, permanent staff and volunteers alike, are highly-trained.

1946 Gradually the training, like other aspects of mountain rescue, was put on a properly-recognised footing. Air Ministry Orders for September 1946 read in part:

Mountain rescue units are based at certain RAF stations.... The personnel of these units, drawn from station resources, are specially trained and equipped to locate and rescue distressed aircrews within a radius of up to 80 miles of their stations. The general and training policy for these units is laid down by the Deputy Directorate of Rescue. Implementation of this policy is the responsibility of the command concerned, which is also responsible for the local organisation of the units. Close liaison with the civil police and other local authorities is to be maintained to ensure efficient local co-ordination of search and rescue operations.

Kinloss had pointed out in September 1946 that, although flying activity was much diminished, many team members were being demobilised and their replacements, though keen, were inexperienced. The suggestion was made (adopted several years later) that members should be screened from posting for a certain period to enable teams to build up a nucleus of experienced members. Within two months, 18 Group Headquarters was calling for mountain rescue volunteers from various stations, those accepted to be posted to Kinloss.

1947 The first major exercise that can be traced was in South Wales, near Llandovery, on May 31st 1947 (Ch. II Sect. 2), organised by Warrant Officer Pitcairn, the Air Ministry instructor.

1948 Perhaps acting on the lessons from the 1947 exercise, the Air Ministry on January 12th 1948 wrote to all Groups and all Commands, but more particularly to the teams then extant – St Athan, Harpur Hull, Topcliffe, Wigtown, Kinloss – recommending at least one day exercise per week, one combined day and night exercise per month and various methods of search to be practised as frequently as possible. The purpose and duties of the service were spelt out. The full operational strength was to be 30 men, including: Officer i/c, preferably a medical officer; senior NCO i/c, preferably sergeant; two nursing orderlies; two drivers; one MT fitter; two wireless operators; one wireless operator mechanic; one ACH/GD (aircraft hand and general duties), to look after the equipment.

The officer commanding at Kinloss responded. He started off blandly enough on the training subject, setting out what was being done. Then, rolling up his sleeves, he commented rather sharply that it was not understood how airmen of the various trades could be mustered as suggested, since it was essentially a volunteer force. Warming to his subject, he said that the most essential trade had been left out – fitter armourer, preferably of senior NCO rank. This man should declare whether explosives are present and if so make them safe or otherwise dispose of them. One can see the logic of this, but so far as can be ascertained, it has never been RAF policy to ensure that each team had an armourer; though, in the nature of things, it is quite probable that many of the teams had one, just by chance.

The CO at Kinloss then put forward an argument that has been used many times: that certain trades could never be released from their normal duties for exercises: nursing orderlies, drivers and MT fitters. One can imagine what the officer i/c the Kinloss MRT thought of that. It is not an argument that would last five minutes today. Kinloss's CO continued:

A comprehensive syllabus of training and lecture programmes on the following subjects have been drawn up, lectures being held in off-duty hours: maps and map-reading; type 38 walkie-talkie and Lloyd 10″ searchlight; elementary first-aid; armament and handling of dangerous components;

elementary meteorology. Regular exercises are held as under and several of the MRS members of this station also take part in organised cross-country runs whenever possible. (a) One day exercise per week: (b) One weekend exercise per month in which a combined day and night exercise is held.

In August that year, Pitcairn was succeeded in his peripatetic inspection and training role by Flight Sergeant John Archibald, an energetic Scot. He had been brought up in Perthshire, and knew and loved the mountains. His leave was often spent on walking tours and on one of them he covered nearly 200 miles in the Highlands, sleeping in the open in the winter. In 1949 he was one of 22 servicemen selected for an evasion exercise which had been named by some comic 'Cornplaster'. The task was to walk from Bagshot, Surrey to Chivenor, Devon, a distance of some 180 miles, testing escape kit. 12 of the 22, including Archibald, finished the route.

1949 During Archibald's time a Scottish conference was called, oddly without Archibald being there; this was on October 3rd 1949 at RAF Pitreavie, which houses the Rescue Co-ordination Centre. As well as RAF search and rescue officers and representatives from the three Scottish MRTs, there were delegates from the army, Royal Navy, Ministry of Civil Aviation, the Scottish Home Department and the Inspector of constabulary for Scotland. Montrose, the newest MRT, was represented by Flight Lieutenant R A Dent, Flight Lieutenant A A Garson and Flight Sergeant W H MacDonald, West Freugh by Flight Lieutenant E W H Nourish, Kinloss by Flight Lieutenant D F Shepherd. On the subject of training it was agreed that exercises were necessary and that these should employ not only simulated casualties, but also an aircraft fuselage. It was suggested that sites of previous crashes could be used.

The army people, Lieutenant Colonel J L Maxwell from Lowland District and Major D Geddes from Highland District were there because the army was going to set up its own mountain rescue teams. RAF MRTs were to be used for training the new army teams and the army would be provided with the RAF's training syllabus. Both army officers were invited to arrange tours to and demonstrations at the various RAF stations to stimulate interest but army teams were not to be included in the proposed exercises until their training was further advanced. This scheme seems to have sunk without trace.

All teams, by now, had got regular training programmes well-established. Station Standing Orders at RAF Valley in 1949 included, on the subject of exercises: (a) These will be carried out regularly to give personnel practice in map reading, operation of walkie-talkies, and other rescue techniques. (b) There will normally be one week-end and three one-day exercises per month, the latter on Wednesdays. Combined night and day exercises will commence on Tuesday nights. (c) The officer i/c Mountain Rescue is to ensure that the strength of any one section is not unduly depleted.

1950 Archibald visited RAF Montrose MRT and by way of an exercise sent some search parties onto the hill. The present writer, who was then a wireless operator and probably looking forward to a quiet day in the base camp roaming the airwaves and making tea, has a vivid memory of Archibald issuing the friendly invitation: 'Right, laddie, let's go for a wee walk'.

It was a walk all right, but wee it was not.

He left his training and inspection post in September 1950 to take a commission. He was commissioned in January 1951, but sadly was killed in a private air crash in the June.

1951 Other NCOs were interviewed for the job, but in the event he was not replaced. If he had been, it seems doubtful that his successor, however dynamic, would have been able to avert the disaster of Beinn Eighe which took place only six months after Archibald's departure.

The service had been groping, painfully slowly, towards a comprehensive training programme. Several times the RAF Mountaineering Association had looked with some alarm at the well-meaning but haphazard arrangements which had prevailed, with occasional changes and improvements, since the end of the war. Part of the problem had been that the authorities had expected that military flying activity would drastically reduce after the end of the war, and that there would be fewer demands on the MRTs' services. The first part of the equation fell into place; the second did not. This was because of the growth in climbing and walking activity which began slowly in 1945 but before very long became something of an explosion.

The helpful overtures, therefore, of RAFMA, made by the Vice Chairman Wing Commander Beauman were rebuffed on several occasions. After all, had not experts in the past expressed the opinion that for mountain rescue of aircrew what was needed was not mountaineering or rock-climbing ability but simple physical fitness?

1952 onwards For the effect of the Beinn Eighe disaster on training policy, see Ch. II, Sects. 7 and 8.

1993 Teams are organised on a volunteer basis and the members, except those on the permanent staff, undertake such duties in addition to their normal station tasks. Units are on call at all times and members must be prepared to devote a considerable part of their spare time to training with the team in order to attain the high standard of fitness and proficiency necessary for work under the most arduous and exacting conditions. In view of the great amount of off-duty time, especially at weekends, spent on MR training, they are exempt from all station duties.

Teams are trained and equipped to search for, rescue and where necessary administer Immediate and Emergency Care (IEC) to crews and passengers of aircraft that have crashed or made forced landing in mountainous or otherwise inaccessible country and to service personnel needing assistance whilst engaged on official training in mountainous areas. In the event of a military aircraft accident anywhere in the UK, teams provide crash guards for the first 36 hours, if the location is over 5 miles distant from an RAF station. Where calls are made on the MRS to provide assistance in other incidents, help is given as an act of grace, subject to Service requirements. Operations are controlled by a Rescue Co-ordination Centre (RCC), which will normally alert and instruct a team to attend an incident. RCCs are at RAF Pitreavie near Edinburgh and Mount Wise near Plymouth.

The Kinloss, Leuchars and Valley teams have up to 36 members; those at St Athan, Leeming and Stafford have up to 25.

Weekly lectures and briefings are held reflecting the training syllabus. Routine training exercises are undertaken in all weathers, day and night, in all parts of the team's area. Members are expected to attend two thirds of the team's exercises and lectures.

TRIALS (Courtesy Flight Sergeant P Kirkpatrick)

The purpose of the MR trial is to assess the individual's personal and physical qualities so

that within 6 months of joining an individual will have fully integrated within the team, be fully fit and have attained a basic level of ability in many aspects of rescue and mountaineering. They should also display a sufficient degree of commitment, determination and maturity to endure physically and emotionally stressful situations.

Most trialists struggle physically with the mountain activities. However, a high level of fitness is not essential – pure effort and determination are equally respected – but a high degree of stamina and fitness must be attained eventually. A fit MRS member should be capable of carrying out an 8-hour mountain day, resting and eating for an hour, then undertaking a further 8-hour mountain night activity; and within that period go very quickly for an hour. They must be able to carry and lift considerable mountain loads on occasions.

The MRS may appear to be very unmilitary, but beneath its apparent casual attitude lies a code of conduct refined over the last 50 years. MR rank and status replace the normal RAF rank structure. Respect is gained through actions, not words. Junior members are expected to work hard. All members are expected to work as a unit, mix and contribute towards team spirit.

All MR personnel enjoy the mountains, but ability and enthusiasm for them are not always the central feature; willingness and selflessness in other matters is also required. Those who cannot integrate easily, whilst retaining an almost constant sense of humour, will not stay long in RAF mountain rescue.

On the trial the most common activity will be mountain walking, with a mixture of climbing and ridge walking. An assessment of the trialist's confidence in steep places will be made. Non-mountain activities include cooking and various menial tasks, which all help in assessing common sense and flexibility. Adequate training and supervision are given to ensure safety. The trial normally takes place over 3 weekend exercises.

Mountain Rescue Service Training Courses (*Courtesy of Flight Sergeant P. Kirkpatrick*) In addition to the normal cycle of training involving weekly exercises and lectures, the MRS runs dedicated residential courses in mountaineering, rescue and leadership. These are staffed by senior members of the system, with additional instruction given by external lectures as required. The courses objectives are: to produce climbers who can reach anywhere, at anytime and complete a rescue operation – and rescuers who can administer, plan, lead and participate in all facets of the MRS administrative and operational responsibilities.

The Summer Course The two-week Summer Course is held annually in Wales and designed to produce rock-climbing leaders capable of safely leading Very Difficult climbs in mountaineering boots. The students selected are usually junior members of the MRS who display the commitment, enthusiasm and potential to develop into rock-climbing instructors within their own teams. Incorporated in the training are elements of single man crag rescue work.

The Winter Course The two-week Winter Course is held annually in Scotland and is designed to produce winter mountaineers who can ascend Grade II routes and have developed a deeper understanding of winter navigation, hazards and survival techniques.

The Advanced Course The seven-day Advanced Course is held annually in North Wales and is directed at selected senior members of the MRS who display leadership potential. The course content involves a wide range of administrative, media, technical and operational instruction – which if absorbed would allow a graduate to control and lead a MRT in operational incidents. The course is a highly desirable stepping stone in an individual's development to the position of Deputy Team Leader.

The above courses reproduce many of the elements contained in any normal mountain training centre course, but additionally seek to present a higher degree of physical and mental challenges to the students. These 'extra elements' assist in the production of highly motivated mountain rescue personnel.

Team Leader Course This is not simply a course, but a complex training programme which will eventually produce a mountain rescue team leader. Initially any applicant for training must progress through a selection procedure which requires the candidate to demonstrate a wide range of mountaineering, rescue and administrative skills. Successful candidates will then be directed to improve on their weak areas, and also to attend individual training courses on media, communications and medical care before attending a two-week training and assessment course held bi-annually in North Wales. The process will take 1 year to complete and only produces approximately 6 team leaders each cycle.

The role of a RAF mountain rescue leader can be compared to that of a 'Player-Manager' of a fourth division football club. Many civilian MRTs have a network of officers with various responsibilities. However the RAF MRT have team leaders who largely act as a combined chairman, secretary, treasurer, trainer, controller and rescue leader – all aspects of the job which make it one of the most challenging and rewarding positions in the RAF.

An MOD perspective of the MRS (A message given to all new volunteers).

The primary task of the RAF SAR assets is to locate and rescue military and civil aircrews who have crashed or abandoned their aircraft. Despite considerable advances in technology and equipment the only guaranteed way to ensure all-weather overland rescue is the use of properly trained and equipped MRTs. Therefore the service which you have shown an interest in has an important operational role and should not be considered as a club or sports team.

The commitment and dedication required is considerable but it is more than matched by the advantages of belonging to a highly motivated, well trained and equipped professional organisation. There are considerable opportunities for early responsibility and the normal RAF rank structure is replaced by a meritocracy based solely on your proven ability within the MRS. There are numerous residential courses and whilst you will receive encouragement you will be able to develop at your own pace within the strict commitment required. Whether you are one of the first female trialists or simply continuing in the 50 years of male volunteers I wish you well. If you do fit in you have many enjoyable years ahead of you in the MRS.

APPENDIX 4

The Air Ministry Promulgation announcing the formation of the service after Flight Lieutenant Graham had been running the Llandwrog MRT successfully with Air Ministry blessing for six months:

AMO A67/1944 – FORMATION OF MOUNTAIN RESCUE SERVICE

1. A Mountain Rescue Service has been formed in order to facilitate the search for, and rescue of, aircrews who have crashed, or are believed to have crashed, in mountainous districts within a radius of 40 miles of RAF Stations Llandwrog, Millom and Wigtown.
2. This Service has been formed at the Stations mentioned in para 1 above; the crews are drawn from station resources and are specially trained in mountain rescue duties. These stations are provided with an ambulance, ancillary transport and WT and RT equipment.
3. Units responsible for taking action in respect of aircraft which are overdue, or which receive information of aircraft believed to have crashed in the districts referred to in para 1 above (in addition to taking any action outlined in para 6 of AMO A648/43, as amended by A68/44), are to telephone the appropriate Fighter Group Flying Control Liaison Officer giving the following information:

   Rank, name and unit of officer passing the information
   Source of information
   Map reference or pinpoint
   Date time of crash (if known)
   Number and type of aircraft
   Details of aircrew including parent unit

4. Mountain Rescue Searches are under the direction of the O i/c Mountain Rescue Service at the RAF Stations mentioned in para 1 above, who will be guided by information passed by the Fighter Group FCLO. The Duty Flying Control Officer at the airfield at which the MRS is based will be responsible for receiving and transmitting any information relating to the search.

27 January 1944

APPENDIX 5 – EARLY EQUIPMENT

1943 At this distance of time, one is surprised at the lack of radio communications during the Foel Grach call-out – the one which inspired Graham to put forward his formal proposals. Portable wireless was available and had been used by the army for some time. It was, however, heavy and cumbersome, and often unreliable especially in mountainous areas. Graham suggested that the ambulance should be fitted with radio enabling the leader to contact both the RAF station and the climbers with their portable sets. This was accepted. Long-range radio connected the ambulance headquarters with RAF Llandwrog. Short-range radio connected the HQ with the various search parties and with any searching aircraft, and the search parties with the searching aircraft directly.

Graham's new search parties, each consisting of two men of whom at least one was to be experienced enough to navigate across the mountains and give a grid reference, were equipped with the portable radio, a Verey pistol and cartridges, a compass, a one-inch map, a whistle and an electric head lamp. The Verey pistol was to be used when the wreck was found.

Then Doc Graham looked at the vehicles. The ambulance was the standard RAF Albion ambulance, too large to negotiate the mountain tracks. It was replaced by a four-wheel-drive Humber ambulance (which within a few years was converted into a wireless van). The only other vehicle at that stage was a jeep. The new ambulance carried enough equipment to carry out minor surgical operations, a Thomas splint and an oxygen cylinder, and food sufficient to keep the advance party going for twenty-four hours.

Someone who succeeded Doc Graham and admired him, Flight Lieutenant John Lloyd, said, talking to the Alpine Club in 1945:

> On November 20th [1944] the Unit received the news that an aircraft had crashed near Trawsfynydd [near Ffestiniog]. The ambulance reached the scene of the crash in an hour and forty minutes. Two of the crew were alive though seriously injured and one had a fractured spine. First-aid was given and the Humber started towards the nearest hospital about twenty-five miles away. On the way the patient's condition began to give rise to anxiety. Oxygen was administered and with its aid he arrived at the hospital in sufficiently good condition to undergo immediate surgical treatment.

To those who have never had occasion to carry someone on a stretcher down a mountainside, one stretcher seems much like another. But the general service stretcher is heavy and in other ways is quite unsuitable for mountain work. John Lloyd again:

> I have a horrid memory of being one of eight carrying two heavily laden General Service stretchers from the top of Aran Fewddwy to the farm at Eagair Gawr a distance of three miles involving a descent of 2400 feet. There was one man to each corner of the stretcher and nobody to relieve us when we were tired. The evacuation of those casualties took seventeen hours.

Seventeen hours to descend 2400 ft and travel three miles; seventeen hours with nobody to take over and provide a break; and for the casualties, seventeen hours over rough ground, carried by exhausted men.

Mountain rescue stretchers have changed over the years, and in fact many mountain rescue team members, both RAF and civilian, believe that what is suitable for the Welsh mountains is not ideal for the Western Highlands of Scotland. The first move towards a specialised stretcher came under Doc Graham who introduced the sledge stretcher. This was described at the time as being the best for mountains where the general pattern is a gentle slope for several miles. Lloyd described how, with a sledge stretcher, his team

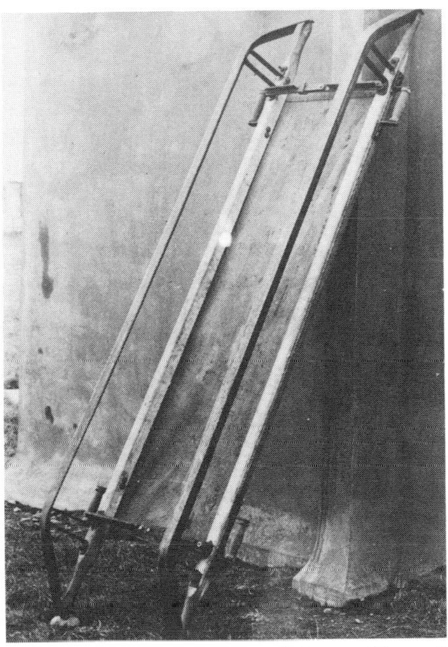

A sledge stretcher improvised from a General Service stretcher with old bed-irons bolted to it: Llandwrog, Dec 1944.

'Dinger' Bell, Kinloss MRT, about to hold a 'falling leader' (1 cwt). Little Tryfan, 1963.

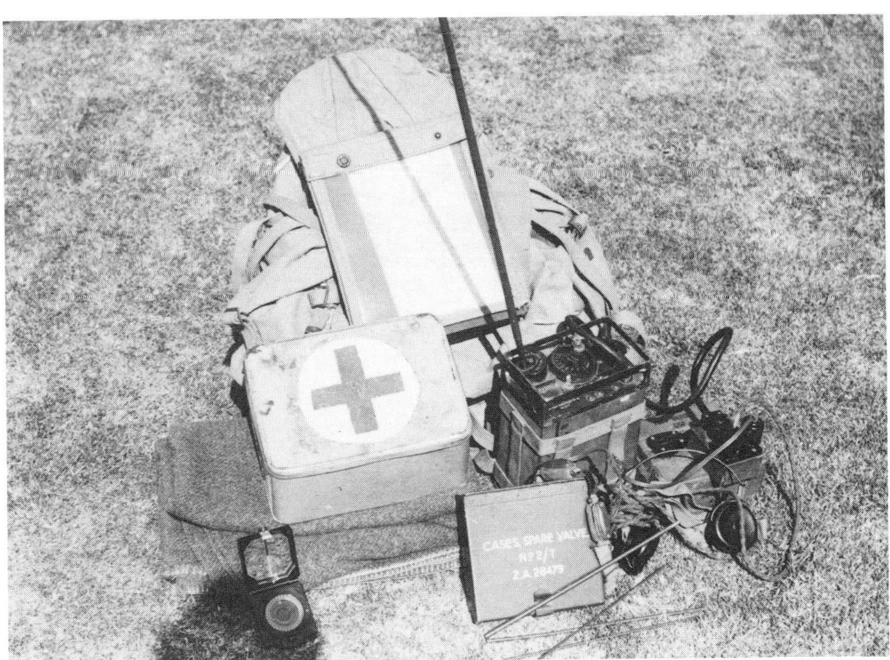

Some of the kit carried by two people in the West Freugh MRT, 1946 *Photo: K S Ford*

completed another evacuation from the top of Aran Fewddwy, not in seventeen hours but in little over four.

During the late '40s there were developed several types of sledge stretcher. The one used at Llandwrog was as simple as possible, the runners made of right-angled iron, taken as often as not from old bed frames, welded on to the whole length of a general service stretcher. Quite independently, Crichton's team at Harpur Hill had arrived at the same answer to the problem. Improvement though this was, within a few years it was recognised that a general service stretcher, however modified, was really not adequate, and two replacements, the Thomas and the Duff stretchers, were being considered.

The teams' equipment had by the end of 1943 been standardised: boots, ankle, grooved heel (nail with hobs) or boots, heavy greased; socks, wool blue/grey; frocks, white; smock/trousers, windproof; battledress, serge; coats, duffle white; helmets, balaclava; mittens, long wool; stockings, seaboot; rucksack, Bergen; carriers, Everest Mk III.

Thus appeared, for the first time, the infamous 'Boots, grooved heel' which were to plague the Mountain Rescue Service for quite a few years yet. They had, apparently, been designed for the Norwegian campaign; probably, said an old MR hand, by the Germans.

1944 In February, Dr D G Duff demonstrated his stretcher to the Llandwrog team. It was made of tubular steel with a canvas bed, and had a canvas belt to secure the patient. There was a footrest to support the patient when the stretcher was vertical. The whole structure was telescopic, and a single bicycle wheel could be attached.

A few months later, the new officer with Mountain Rescue responsibility, recommended the use of the Swiss army stretcher – the Koller. This was turned down, with no explanation, by Air Ministry. Later in 1944, probably frustrated by this, Pick made some modifications to the GS stretcher.

The Air Ministry promulgation of January 27th 1944 had mentioned the teams' vehicles and equipment. There is a brief record in Llandwrog's log in November 1944 of a Mountain Rescue conference held in the Air Ministry, at which medical equipment was discussed. No minutes or other record can be found of this, the first formal conference of many.

Success brings its own penalties; with growth, came the beginnings of bureaucracy: quarterly returns were also started in 1944.

The first list of standard vehicles is modest indeed. There was to be the Humber ambulance (4×4) mentioned above, and a 'car passenger Ford utility type 30hp V8', as well as a box trailer to be towed by the Ford. The Air Ministry does not seem to have made it clear how the teams were supposed to take an effectively-sized search party to the search area in a convoy consisting of one ambulance and one jeep. The present writer became very familiar with the Humber when it was later converted to act as a radio van, and at the most it would carry seven passengers, and six of those would have been in the back in semi-darkness, since the side windows were very small. It may well be, of course, that a 3-tonner or something similar was requisitioned from the MT people on an ad hoc basis, but the unreliability of this sort of arrangement is obvious, and indeed was pointed out to Group Headquarters by Kinloss in 1946.

Detailed instructions were issued for minor alterations to the Humber to equip it for its ambulance role in the hills, including such matters as an additional stretcher bracket and storage for Verey pistol and Aldis lamp. The most major work was to be the installation of wireless equipment on a table, which itself had to be specially built in. It was a few years before the impracticality of expecting a vehicle to double as ambulance and communications van was conceded. It carried an oxygen cylinder, enough surgical equipment to enable a minor operation to be carried out, a Thomas splint and a sledge stretcher. A tent was made up of old drogue material which fixed on to the rear of the ambulance, increasing the space available for treatment.

The members of the advance party carried a small first-aid kit which included two tubonic ampoules of morphia of ¼ grain, shell dressings, first field dressings and a tube of gentian violet jelly.

Its double role apart, opinions on the sutiability of the Humber seem to have differed. Flight Lieutenant Lloyd said in February 1945:

> There are two vehicles at present used in Mountain Rescue Work. The ambulance ... is a powerful four-wheel-drive Humber. The other is a Jeep. These two can negotiate tracks in North Wales which go right up into the Cwms. For instance they can easily be driven as far as the gate overlooking the two lakes in Cwm Silyn and at the other end of the range they can reach the derelict building close to Melynllyn under Foel Grach.

On the other hand, Flight Lieutenant Crichton said a year later:

> The Humber ambulance appears to be of dubious value for rough work because of trouble with back axles, apparently a not uncommon type of trouble with this four-wheeled vehicle.

1945 Technical development continued when pressure of work allowed. In March, the Llandwrog team tried out some new casualty bags, during an inspection visit by Flight Lieutenant Gill. These had an electrical filament.

Tom Scudamore chose for this exercise the area around the two Llynau Cwm Silyn, in the hills between Beddgelert and Penygroes. Firstly, the team climbed Craig Cwm Silyn by the easy western route, finding the bags easy to carry on an Everest carrier, or even, at a pinch, on a Bergen rucksack with a walkie-talkie radio. At the summit, Gill was put into one of the bags and carried some of the way towards the base camp. That was not so easy: six men were needed. The task was made a little easier by putting wooden poles through the handles, and converting the bag into a sort of stretcher, but it was not comfortable for the patient; the head had no support.

It was the heating system, however, which caused the real problems. The filament needed a 12-volt or 24-volt accumulater, and to say the least it was difficult to carry these. Scudamore, in his report, said that hot-water bottles and Everhot bags inside the casualty bags would do the job just as well, and in any case the power was needed for the radios in the Humber and the Aldis lamps at night. Despite these reservations, he concluded that the bags were most useful, and he was recommending them for adoption.

1946 In the meantime, the controversy over the Humber continued. The Officer Commanding RAF Kinloss seemed to be supporting Lloyd in September 1946: '...It will be appreciated that the Humber is an ideal vehicle for use in mountainous country when used as an ambulance only.'

For what it is worth, the writer cannot recall, through the mists of time, any continuing trouble with the vehicle (in its solo guise as a radio van) during 1950-51, and it was certainly taken into some pretty rugged parts of the Scottish Highlands; it went practically everywhere that the jeep did.

By September 30th 1946, RAF Kinloss felt able to say to Group Headquarters (following a visit of the Inspector General) that the then establishment of two jeeps and one Humber ambulance was proving to be inadequate. Kinloss proposed instead: jeep; Humber ambulance; 3-ton tender; wireless tender (4×4).

The main point made by Kinloss was that the Humber, when used for W/T as well as for ambulance purposes, could only accommodate two casualties, and when a heavy aircraft such as a Lancaster had crashed, several journeys had to be made between crash site and hospital.

Oddly, though, a further memo from Kinloss only just over a month later was complaining about an establishment of two jeeps, one Humber ambulance, one Commer W/T tender and one Bedford 3-tonner, and was proposing instead: Humber ambulance; Humber W/T tender and personnel carrier 4×4; three Humber heavy utility passenger cars 4×4.

This argument was to rumble on for some time between Kinloss MRT, Command, Group and the Air Ministry. In August 1947 the Ministry said that:

The 3-tonner held by Kinloss was established at Kinloss's specific request, although the department concerned did not consider it a suitable vehicle.
Whilst the signals tender [presumably the Commer] was not ideal and that a four-wheel drive would be better, nevertheless there should seldom be a need to drive the signals van across country, since the signals van would normally be set up on, or adjacent to, the main road.
The 4×4 passenger utility car was in very short supply.
The jeep, whilst open to the weather and with limited capacity, nevertheless is indispensable in negotiating country impassable to other vehicles, and the jeep must therefore stay on the strength.

The comment regarding the W/T tender seems to indicate a writer with little knowledge of mountains generally or of the Scottish Highlands particularly; or, for that matter, the modus operandi of the teams.

In passing on these Ministry opinions to 18 Group, Coastal Command added that the number of 'established' vehicles was to be kept to a minimum, and should additional vehicles be required for an extended search, they were to be requisitioned from the pool of normal station transport. Finally, throwing the dog a bone, the Ministry agreed that the 3-tonner should be replaced with a 4×4 passenger utility. However, it had earlier made clear that even if this change to establishment were to be agreed, this particular vehicle type was so rare that Kinloss's chance of actually getting one was rather remote.

Bruised, Kinloss accepted and withdrew to lick its wounds. However the Kinloss MRT officer was not one to let go. Having, despite the odds suggested by the Ministry's earlier comments, acquired a 4×4 Humber passenger utility to replace the Bedford, Flight Lieutenant Willits in a memo to his CO on July 28th 1948 was asking that the Humber passenger car should be replaced by a Thorneycroft 3-tonner. Advantages of the Thorneycroft over the Humber were said to include the greater carrying capacity, its ability to provide sleeping accommodation and to extract itself under its own power when apparently bogged down. Disadvantages conceded were a speed limit of 20 mph and the fact that its weight and size rendered some tracks and bridges impassable to it. This may at first glance seem perverse, especially as elsewhere in the records it emerges that the Thorneycroft did not perform as well as its Bedford equivalent.

By January 1948 transport consisted of the 4×4 ambulance, jeep, radio van and jeep trailer. Modifications were permissible to allow for local conditions, and extra vehicles

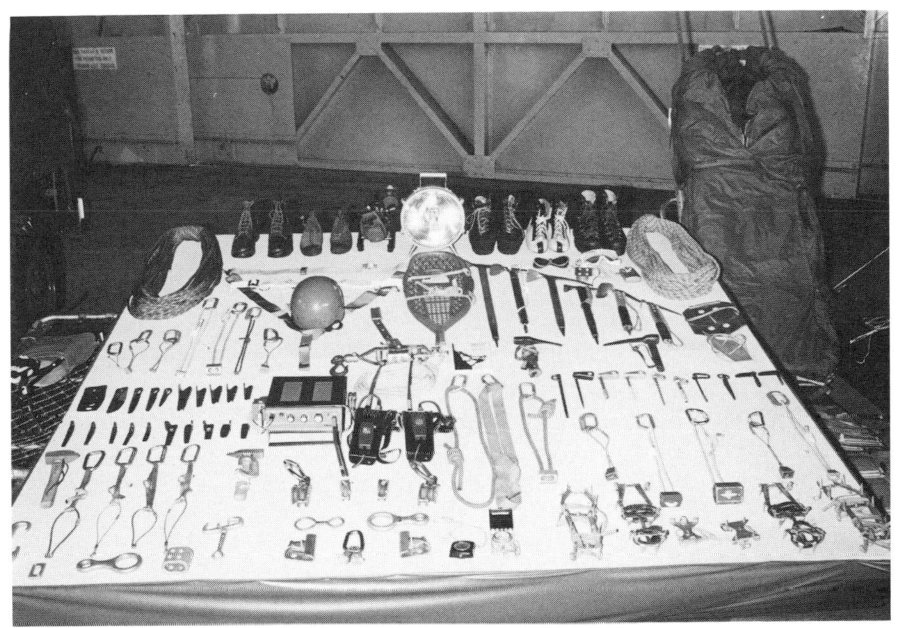

An RAF mountain rescuer's kit in the 70s. *Photo: Peter McGowan*

could be called for if a rescue operation proved to be unduly prolonged. On September 2nd 1948, the establishment was changed so that a Humber signals van 4×4 should replace the Humber 4×2: ie, four-wheel-drive to replace two-wheel-drive. this was the first appearance of the modified ambulance.

From the 1950s the transport gradually became based on variations of the Land Rover, plus two 4-ton personnel carriers. In 1979, for instance, a minor change was proposed by Flight Sergeant Sefton, bringing the scale to:

2 Bedford RLs containing: (a) full range of special rescue equipment, aircraft crash equipment, base camp kitchen equipment, rations, tentage, first-aid gear and searchlights. (b) 200 cu ft baggage, base snow shoes, 40 avalanche probes, 2 sheets PSP, rigid tow bar, 10 personnel, 1 mountain stretcher. Land Rover LWB Stretcher carrier/ambulance; Land Rover LWB FFR – radio equipment and pyrotechnics; Land Rover SWB – personnel and day bags; Cargo trailer – bulk fuel and oil.

APPENDIX 6 – TEAM LEADERS

TEAM	*LEADERS*		*QUALIFIED*
RAF AKROTIRI	1964	G Bruce	1962
	1966	D Betteridge	1955
	1969	J Hinde	1961
	1973	P McGowan	1965
	1975	E Henry	1971
RAF ALDERGROVE	1949	Knowles	–
RAF EDZELL	1953	Nelson	–
	1954	J McKinley	1953
		J Bulmer	1954
RAF HARPUR HILL	1942-46	D Crichton[1]	–
	1952	Jones	–
	1954	N Didsbury	1954
	1955	H Appleby	1955
	1956	P Davis	1956
	1957	J Steed	1957
RAF KAI TAK	1961	R Peart	–
	1962	A Hay	1954
	1963	J Baines	1963
	1966	D Reeve	1964
RAF KHORMAKSAR	1960	D Dewar	1957
	1961	C Pibworth	1961
	1963	G Paterson	1963
	1965	C Pibworth	1961
RAF KINLOSS	1946	C Gilbert	–
	1948	D Siddons	–
	1952	F Ward	–
	1953	J Lees	–
	1954	H Bevis	1953
	1955	A Hay	1954
	1956	D Cooke	–
	1958	P Davis	1956
		I Martin	1957
	1961	J Hinde	1961
	1968	G Bruce	1962
	1970	H Oldham	1969
	1971	G Bruce	1962
	1973	D Reeve	1964
	1975	P McGowan	1965
	1977	R Sefton	1967
	1979	J Craig	1976
	1980	R Sefton	1967
	1981	K Taylor	1975
	1986	T Taylor	1976
	1989	D Whalley	1986
	1992	J Smith	1986
RAF LEEMING	1959	N Collighan	1958
	1961	T Wilkinson	1960
	1962	G Bruce	1962
	1963	T Wilkinson	1960
	1965	J Tunnah	1963
	1966	P McGowan	1965
	1968	R Stevenson	1968

Trial of the Ellis stretcher by Stafford MRT, 21st July 1973. Cpl John Banks, deputy team leader, standing. *Photo: Crown Copyright*

Bell stretcher on a 'Pulley Tyrolean', early 1970s.

TEAM	*LEADERS*		*QUALIFIED*
	1970	J West	1969
	1973	E Henry	1971
	1975	A Haveron	1975
	1977	P Weatherill	1977
	1980	R Allen	1979
to RAF LINTON ON OUSE	1983		
	1984	P Kirkpatrick	1983
	1987	W Batson	1986
to RAF LEEMING	1989		
	1990	B Webster	1989
	1992	P Duckworth	1989
RAF LEUCHARS	1956	D Wilson	1954
		W Brankin	1955
	1963	P Davis	1956
	1965	J Hendren	1958
	1967	R Sefton	1967
	1970	J Tunnah	1963
	1973	R Sefton	1967
	1977	R Blyth	1967
	1981	M Taylor	1975
	1984	D Shanks	1977
	1987	D Whalley	1986
	1989	P Kirkpatrick	1983
	1992	W Batson	1986
RAF LINTON-ON-OUSE: see under RAF LEEMING			
RAF LLANBEDR	1945-46	T Scudamore[1]	–
	1949	C Staff	–
RAF LLANDWROG	1941	G Graham[1]	–
	1944-45	T Scudamore[1]	–
RAF MASIRAH	1972	I Jones	1972
RAF MILLOM	1945-	J Lloyd[1]	–
RAF MONTROSE	1944	B Harley[1]	–
	1945	S Duff[1]	–
	1949	Nelson	–
		W McDonald	–
RAF NICOSIA	1954	J McKinley	1953
	1956	H Appleby	1955
	1960	P Davis	1956
	1963	G Bruce	1962
RAF SHARJAH	1966	C Pibworth	1961
	1967	S Wagg	1966
	1968	R Shaw	1966
	1969	C Pibworth	1961
RAF STAFFORD	1961	T Wilkinson	1960
		I Burnett	1961
	1963	A Hay	1954
	1965	J Tunnah	1963
	1966	J Baines	1963
	1967	R Shaw	1966
	1968	J Brewer	1968
	1972	J Morrison	1971
	1974	R MacGowan	1972
	1975	M Taylor	1975
	1976	J Craig	1976
	1980	M Taylor	1975

TEAM	*LEADERS*		*QUALIFIED*
	1981	J Morning	1981
	1982	D Shanks	1977
	1984	J Green	1983
		J Patterson	1983
	1987	A Emsley	1986
	1989	P Winn	1986
	1991	J Smith	1986
	1992	J Chapman	1992
RAF ST ATHAN	1953	D Cooke	–
	1955	W Brankin	1955
	1957	I Martin	1957
	1958	J Hendren	1958
	1962	G Barry	1961
	1963	M Fearn	1962
	1965	L McNab	1964
	1967	C Pibworth	1961
	1969	J Tunnah	1963
		G Armstrong	1966
	1972	R Blyth	1967
	1975	C Pibworth	1961
	1976	E Henry	1971
		T Taylor	1976
	1979	T Heaton	1979
	1981	T Loftus	1981
	1986	R Foreman	1986
		M Troy	1983
	1989	P Kay	1988
	1992	D Carroll	1992
RAF TOPCLIFFE	1952	Aitchison	–
	1954	G Avenall	1952
		J Lees	–
	1955	D Betteridge	1955
	1958	P Davis	1956
RAF VALLEY	1952	J Lees	–
	1953	F Ward	–
	1955	J Lees	–
	1961	A Bennett	1961
	1967	J Calnan	1966
	1968	P McGowan	1965
	1972	H Oldham	1969
	1975	J Baines	1963
	1978	A Haveron	1975
	1982	P Weatherill	1977
	1987	P Kirkpatrick	1983
	1990	A Emsley	1986
	1992	P Kirkpatrick	1983
RAF WEST FREUGH	1945-47	W Pitcairn[1]	–
	1952	R Anderson	–
	1954	D Wilson	1954
	1956	J Caulfield	–

[1] In early years the team was often led by an officer rather than an NCO, though he was not necessarily known as 'Team Leader'.

"He's convinced that he had two Mars Bars"

APPENDIX 7 – SENIOR MOUNTAIN RESCUE PERSONNEL

AIR MINISTRY INSTRUCTORS		
Sergeant H Pick	Air Ministry	1944-1947
Warrant Officer Pitcairn	Air Ministry	1947-1948
Flight Sergeant J D Archibald	Air Ministry	1948-1950
INSPECTORS OF MOUNTAIN RESCUE		
Group Captain R E G Brittain	Air Ministry	1952-1954
Squadron Leader D Dattner	HQ Coastal Command	1954-1955
Sqn Ldr A R Gordon-Cumming	(a) Air Ministry	1955-1958
	(b) RAF Staff College	1958
	(c) RAF Leeming	1959
Squadron Leader J R Sims	Air Ministry	1959-1967
Squadron Leader J D Cooke	Ministry of Defence	1967-1970
Squadron Leader D Lofts	Ministry of Defence	1970-
INSPECTORS OF LAND RESCUE		
Squadron Leader D Lofts	Ministry of Defence	-1974
Squadron Leader J Vernon	Ministry of Defence	1975-1979
Squadron Leader G J Blackburn	Ministry of Defence	1979-1985
Squadron Leader R Foster	Ministry of Defence	1985-1988
Squadron Leader W Gault	Ministry of Defence	1988-1991
Squadron Leader B J Canfer	Ministry of Defence	1991-
CHIEF INSTRUCTOR		
Warrant Officer A Haveron	RAF Kinloss	1992-

APPENDIX 8 – AWARDS

Award	Name	Year / Reason
George Medal	Flt Sgt J R Lees	1958 Amphitheatre Buttress
Member of the British Empire	Flt Lt G Graham	1943 Services to MR
	Flt Lt R Robertson	1959 Mt Süphan
	Sqn Ldr J Sims	1967 Services to MR
	Flt Lt D Crichton	1946 Services to MR
	Sqn Ldr G Blackburn	1984 Services to MR
	Sqn Ldr W Gault	1989 Lockerbie
British Empire Medal	Cpl G McTigue	1945 Services to MR
	SAC M Brown	1952 Beinn Eighe
	Sgt J Mooring	1958 Services to MR
	Flt Sgt H Appleby	1959 Mt Süphan
	Sgt J Emmerson	1959 Mt Süphan
	SAC G Murphy	1959 Mt Süphan
	Sgt J Steed	1960 Services to MR
	Flt Sgt J R Lees	1962 Services to MR
	Flt Sgt W Brankin	1963 Services to MR
	Sgt G Paterson	1964 Wadi Mukeiras
	Ch Tech J Hinde	1964 Services to MR
	Sgt P McGowan	1971 Services to MR
	Cpl C Pibworth	1972 Services to MR & Desert Rescue
	Flt Sgt J Tunnah	1972 Services to MR
	Flt Sgt G Bruce	1973 Services to MR & Elephant Island Expedition
	Flt Sgt H Oldham	1976 Services to MR
	Flt Sgt R Sefton	1977 Services to MR
	Flt Sgt J Baines	1979 Services to MR
	Ch Tech J Craig	1979 Services to MR
	Flt Sgt A Haveron	1984 Services to MR
	Flt Sgt D Shanks	1986 Services to MR
	Flt Sgt K Taylor	1987 Services to MR
	Flt Sgt P Weatherill	1987 Services to MR
	Flt Sgt D Whalley	1992 Services to MR
	Flt Sgt P Kirkpatrick	1993 Services to MR
Queen's Comm. for Bravery	SAC G Hercod	1959 Mt Süphan
	Flt Sgt G Bruce	1971 Children on Cairngorms
	Sgt W Batson	1989 Lockerbie
	Sgt P Winn	1989 Lockerbie
	Flt Sgt D Whalley	1989 Lockerbie

AOC-in-C's Commendation

There have been many awards under this heading – too numerous to mention – but among the most interesting were two for Mount Süphan in 1959 (Bottomer and Whelan), one to the St Athan MRT as a team in 1982 for help to the local community in the blizzards, and three for Lockerbie in 1989 (Batson, Winn and Whalley).

APPENDIX 9 – AIRCRAFT

(Acknowledgements to Hugh Budgen for the information)

Below are details of the crashes and rescue described in the book. The left-hand column identifies the chapter and section; eg, I,1 refers the reader to Chapter I, Section 1. Brief technical information is included on the older or more obscure aircraft.

Avro ANSON 1939

Known affectionately as "Faithful Annie", this was a sturdy machine used for many training purposes. It served throughout the war in several marks, and on at least one occasion was, almost unbelievably, able to claim the destruction of a Messerschmidt Me 109, the Liftwaffe's main fighter.

MARK I:

ORIGIN – UK; PURPOSE – training and reconnaissance; CREW – 6; MAXIMUM SPEED – 188 mph at 7000 ft; CEILING – 19000 ft; RANGE – 790m; ARMS – 2 machine guns, 360 lb of bombs.

REF	DATE	IDENT	STATION	UNIT	WHERE CRASHED	DEAD	MRT
I,1	9/1/39	L9153	Prestwick	12ERFTS	Rhinns of Kells	All	–
I,3	20/11/42	N4981	Penrhos	9(0)AFU	Moel Eilio	All	Llandwrog
I,3	14/1/43	EG110	Llandwrog	9(0)AFU	Foel Grach	2	Llandwrog
I,5	30/11/43	EF909	Jurby	5AOS	Foel Grach	none	Llandwrog
I,7	20/2/44	LT433	Cark	SPTU	Lyncowlyd	1	Llandwrog
I,7	23/4/44	AX583	Millom	2(0)AFU	Drum Mt	All	Llandwrog
I,9	12/7/44	MG804	Mona	8(0)AFU	Foel Fras	1	Llandwrog
I,9	17/11/44	MG464	Jurby	5(0)AS	Grisdale Pike	1	Millom
I,10	2/1/45	LT471	Barrow	10 AGS	Black Combe	All	Millom
II,1	23/11/45	NL185	Halton	BmrCmdHQ	Edale	1	Harpur Hill
III,2	11/8/52	VM407	A'grove	23MU	Snowdon	All	Valley

Grumman AVENGER 1942

Often misidentified as the Martlet from the same stable – which is exactly what the Millom team did – but a bigger aircraft with a different purpose.

ORIGIN – USA; PURPOSE – torpedo bomber; CREW – 3; MAXIMUM SPEED – 271 mph at 12000 ft; CEILING – 23000 ft; RANGE – 1020m; ARMS – 5 machine guns, up to 2000 lb of bombs, 1 torpedo or 8 rockets.

REF	DATE	IDENT	STATION	UNIT	WHERE CRASHED	DEAD	MRT
I.10	16/1/45	JZ390	Inskip	763Sqn RN	Wastwater	All	Cark

Douglas BOSTON 1940s

ORIGIN – USA; PURPOSE – bomber; CREW – 3; MAXIMUM SPEED – 320 mph; RANGE – 1200m; ARMS – 7 guns, 2000 lb bombs.

REF	DATE	IDENT	STATION	UNIT	WHERE CRASHED	DEAD	MRT
I,3	17/10/42	Z2186	Bradwell Bay	419Sqn RCAF	Carnedd Dafydd	1	Llandwrog

Blackburn BOTHA 1939

Probably took the wooden spoon for lack of success, and was swiftly transferred to training duties from its original roles; also used as a target tug. It was grossly underpowered.

ORIGIN – UK; PURPOSE – Reconnaissance and torpedo-bomber; latterly training; MAXIMUM SPEED – 249 mph at 5500 ft.

REF	DATE	IDENT	STATION	UNIT	WHERE CRASHED	DEAD	MRT
I,4	28/8/43	L6202	HootonPk	11 RS	Llwydmor	All	Llandwrog

It was a de Havilland Dominie air ambulance like this which crashed killing crew and patient in the Lake District in 1946; West Freugh MRT attended. This particular example is seen here at Duxford. The Dominie was an adaptation of the pre-war airliner Dragon Rapide. *Photo: H J Budgen*

CANBERRA

REF	DATE	IDENT	STATION	UNIT	WHERE CRASHED	DEAD	MRT
III,5	10/12/57	WK129	Pershore	RRE	CarneddLlewelyn	2	Valley, St Athan, Harpur Hill

Douglas DAKOTA 1941

'Dakota' was the RAF name, which eventually gained general currency round the world, along with the original American designation DC-3; in different guises, it was also known in the American services as the C 47 Skytrain and C 53 Skytrooper, depending on how used and modified (there were many other versions). It was probably the most ubiquitous and long-lived of all the wartime aircraft, and examples are still in use by local airlines in various countries.

C-47:

ORIGIN – USA; PURPOSE – trooper or heavy freighter; CREW – 4; MAXIMUM SPEED – 230 mph at 8800 ft; CEILING – 24100 ft; RANGE – 1350m; ARMS – nil

REF	DATE	IDENT	STATION	UNIT	WHERE CRASHED	DEAD	MRT
I,8	8/8/44	C-47	?(US)	?	Portpatrick	?	W.Freugh
I,9	23/11/44	43-48473 C-47	US	27ATG	Dulyn	All	Llandwrog
III,1	10/1/52	EI-AFL	Dublin	Aer Lingus	Bwlch y Rhediad	23	Valley

de Havilland DOMINIE 1939

A twin-engined biplane, developed from the pre-war feeder airliner the Dragon Rapide.

ORIGIN – UK; PURPOSE – trainer, communications, ambulance; MAXIMUM SPEED – 157 mph at 1000 ft.

REF	DATE	IDENT	STATION	UNIT	WHERE CRASHED	DEAD	MRT
II,1	30/8/46	X7394	Abbotsinch	782SqnRN	Scafell	All	W.Freugh

Fairey FIREFLY 1943

ORIGIN – UK; PURPOSE – carrier-borne fighter and reconnaissance; CREW – 2; MAXIMUM SPEED – 316 mph at 14000 ft; CEILING – 28000 ft; RANGE – 1070m; ARMS – 4 cannon; 2 × 1,000 lb bombs or 8 rockets.

REF	DATE	IDENT	STATION	UNIT	WHERE CRASHED	DEAD	MRT
II,4	16/5/49	Z2108	Lossiemouth	766SqnRN	Lochnagar	All	Kinloss

Boeing B-17 FLYING FORTRESS 1941

The most well-known of the American heavy bombers, extensively used in the daylight raids on Germany.

B-17G:

ORIGIN – USA; PURPOSE – bomber; CREW – 10; MAXIMUM SPEED – 300 mph at 30000 ft; CEILING – 35000 ft; RANGE – 1850m; ARMS – 13 machine guns, 17600 lb of bombs.

REF	DATE	IDENT	STATION	UNIT	WHERE CRASHED	DEAD	MRT
I,11	8/6/45	44-6005	Valley	US311BSqn	Cadair Idris	All	Llanbedr

Handley Page HALIFAX 1940

One of the RAF's three main heavy bombers, it was not in the same league as the Lancaster in this function. However, it ran to many marks, and proved to be very adaptable, used later for paratrooping, glider towing and agent dropping.

MARK III:

ORIGIN – UK; PURPOSE – heavy bomber; CREW – 7; MAXIMUM SPEED – 282 mph at 13500 ft; CEILING – 24000 ft; RANGE – 1030m; ARMS – 9 machine guns, 13000 lb of bombs.

REF	DATE	IDENT	STATION	UNIT	WHERE CRASHED	DEAD	MRT
I,9	31/8/44	LL283	Dishforth	1664HUC	Portmadoc	1	Llandwrog
I,9	3/9/44	JD417	Lindholme	1656HCU	The Rivals	6	Llandwrog
I,9	22/10/44	LL505	Topcliffe	1659HCU	Great Carrs	8	Millom

North American HARVARD 1941

ORIGIN – USA; PURPOSE – trainer; CREW – 2; MAXIMUM SPEED – 208 mph at 5000 ft; CEILING – 21500 ft; RANGE – 750m; ARMS – 3 machine guns

REF	DATE	IDENT	STATION	UNIT	WHERE CRASHED	DEAD	MRT
V,1	14/1/52	FT415	Syreston	22FTS RN	Jacob's Ladder	1	Harpur Hill

Lockheed HUDSON 1940s

ORIGIN – USA; PURPOSE – Reconnaissance and bomber, trainer; CREW – 5; MAXIMUM SPEED – 284 mph; RANGE – 2000m; ARMS – 6 guns, 5000 lb bombs.

REF	DATE	IDENT	STATION	UNIT	WHERE CRASHED	DEAD	MRT
I,6	14/3/44	AM949	Dum Dum	357Sqn	Burma	5	–

JAGUAR

REF	DATE	IDENT	STATION	UNIT	WHERE CRASHED	DEAD	MRT
IV,11	23/11/79	XX762	Lossiemouth	2260CU	Beinn a'Chleibh	1	Kinloss, Leuchars, Valley

Avro LANCASTER 1942

This was the RAF's main heavy bomber of the war, and was used in many other roles and ran to many marks. The Beinn Eighe aircraft was a late version, the GR3.

MARK I:

ORIGIN – UK; PURPOSE – heavy bomber; CREW – 6-8; MAXIMUM SPEED – 300 mph; ARMS – 10 machine guns, 18000 lb of bombs.

REF	DATE	IDENT	STATION	UNIT	WHERE CRASHED	DEAD	MRT
II,6	13/3/51	TX264	Kinloss	120Sqn	Beinn Eighe	All	Kinloss

Consolidated B-24 LIBERATOR 1941

This must have been the most adaptable of all the American wartime aircraft, and was built in far greater numbers than any other type, even the B-17 Flying Fortress. Much used by the RAF.

B-24J

ORIGIN – USA; PURPOSE – long range bomber, transport, reconnaissance; CREW – 12; MAXIMUM SPEED – 300 mph at 30000 ft; CEILING – 35000 ft; RANGE – 2100m; ARMS – 10 machine guns, up to 12800 lb of bombs.

English Electric LIGHTNING

REF	DATE	IDENT	STATION	UNIT	WHERE CRASHED	DEAD	MRT
IV,4	3/10/59	XL628	Warton	E.E.	Irish Sea	–	Leuchars, Leeming, Harpur Hill

Martin B-26 MARAUDER 1942

Known by the American aircrews in its early days as "Widow Maker", which speaks volumes for its reputation.

ORIGIN – USE; PURPOSE – medium bomber; CREW – 7; MAXIMUM SPEED – 283 mph at 5000 ft; CEILING – 19800 ft; RANGE – 1100m; ARMS – 11 machine guns, 4000 lb of bombs.

REF	DATE	IDENT	STATION	UNIT	WHERE CRASHED	DEAD	MRT
I,10	1/2/45	44-68072	Ferry flight	USA-Burtonwood	Y Garn	5	Llandwrog

Martin MERCATOR 1950

The Mercator P4M-IQ was designed originally as a long-range patrol bomber, but was found to be very suitable for highly-secret electronic spy flights. Only 19 ever built. Unusual for several reasons, not least for the fact that it had two jet and two propeller engines, the small jet engines intended to boost the speed temporarily to get the plane out of trouble.

ORIGIN – USA; PURPOSE – originally bomber, then secret reconnaissance; CREW – 16; MAXIMUM SPEED – 280 mph normally, 420 mph boosted; ARMS – two machine guns.

REF	DATE	IDENT	STATION	UNIT	WHERE CRASHED	DEAD	MRT
VI,2	19/1/60	?	PtLyautey	VQ2 USN	Mt Karanfil Turkey	16	Nicosia

de Havilland MOSQUITO 1941

Famous for its moulded plywood construction, it was very successful in many roles not dreamed of when it was designed; one of the war's outstanding aeroplanes.

MARK XVI (others differed considerably);

ORIGIN – UK; PURPOSE – bomber, fighter, ground attack, reconnaissance; CREW – 2; MAXIMUM SPEED – 408 mph at 26000 ft; CEILING – 37000 ft; RANGE – 1370m; ARMS – 4000 lb of bombs.

REF	DATE	IDENT	STATION	UNIT	WHERE CRASHED	DEAD	MRT
I,9	25/9/44	HX862	HighErcall	60 OTU	Föel Fras	2	Llandwrog
I,9	1/11/44	W4088	Cranfield	51 OTU	Mynydd Mawr	2	Llandwrog

North American P-51 MUSTANG 1942

P-51O;

ORIGIN – USA; PURPOSE – Long range escort fighter and ground attack; CREW – 1; MAXIMUM SPEED – 437 mph at 25000 ft; CEILING – 41900 ft; RANGE – 2080m; ARMS – 4/6 machine guns, 2000 lb of bombs or 10 rockets.

REF	DATE	IDENT	STATION	UNIT	WHERE CRASHED	DEAD	MRT
I,11	17/5/45	44-726844	Debden	333FS (US)	Arran Fawddwy	1	Llandwrog

Airspeed OXFORD 1939

ORIGIN – UK; PURPOSE – advanced trainer and ambulance; CREW – 3; MAXIMUM SPEED – 182 mph at 8300 ft; CEILING – 19200 ft; RANGE – 550 m.

REF	DATE	IDENT	STATION	UNIT	WHERE CRASHED	DEAD	MRT
II,1	28/12/45	HN594	Seighford	21PAFU	Brown Knoll	none	Harpur Hill

SABRE

REF	DATE	IDENT	STATION	UNIT	WHERE CRASHED	DEAD	MRT
V,1	14/12/54	19234	Ringway	137(T)Flt RCAF	Holme Moss	1	Harpur Hill
V,1	26/6/59	23380	Prestwick	421Sqn RCAF	Iron Crag	1	Harpur Hill, Leuchars

SCIMITAR

REF	DATE	IDENT	STATION	UNIT	WHERE CRASHED	DEAD	MRT
IV,4	10/11/59	XD281	Lossiemouth	807SqnRN	Aberfoyle	–	Leuchars, Kinloss

Avro SHACKLETON

REF	DATE	IDENT	STATION	UNIT	WHERE CRASHED	DEAD	MRT
V,1	7/12/56	WR970	Woodford	AV Roe (test flight)	Foolow, Derbys	4	Harpur Hill

Boeing SUPERFORTRESS 1943

The largest bomber of the war, and the first to be pressurised, it was the Superfortress which was chosen for the Hiroshima and Nagasaki atomic raids.

ORIGIN – USA; PURPOSE – long range heavy bomber; CREW – 10-14; MAXIMUM SPEED – 357 mph at 30000 ft; CEILING – 33600 ft; RANGE – 3259m; ARMS– 12 machine guns, 12000 lb of bombs.

REF	DATE	IDENT	STATION	UNIT	WHERE CRASHED	DEAD	MRT
II,2	7/1/49	44-62276	Scampton	301BG US	Strachur	21	Kinloss

Republic P-47 THUNDERBOLT 1943

American fighter also used by the RAF.

ORIGIN – USA; PURPOSE – fighter, fighter-bomber; CREW – 1; MAXIMUM SPEED – 429 mph at 30000 ft; CEILING – 42000 ft; RANGE – 590 m; ARMS – 6 or 8 machine guns, 2500 lb of bombs.

REF	DATE	IDENT	STATION	UNIT	WHERE CRASHED	DEAD	MRT
I,8	6/9/44	41, 6246	Atcham	496 FTG US	Arran Fawddwy	1	Llandwrog

Avro TUDOR SUPERTRADER

REF	DATE	IDENTITY	WHERE CRASHED	DEAD	MRT
VI,1	23/5/59	G-AGRH Air Charters Ltd	Mt Süphan Turkey	12	Nicosia

VOODOO

REF	DATE	IDENT	STATION	UNIT	WHERE CRASHED	DEAD	MRT
IV,8	7/5/64	56-0013	Valley	7FTS US	Mynydd Mawr	All	Kinloss, Leuchars, Leeming Valley, St Athan

The last Wellington built (11,461 total). *Photo: Mark Woodward courtesy H J Budgen*

Vickers Armstrong WELLINGTON 1939

The Wellington's unique geodetic construction enabled it to take a great deal of punishment. In use throughout the war, it ran to many marks.

MARK X:

ORIGIN – UK; PURPOSE – medium bomber and reconnaissance; CREW – 6; MAXIMUM SPEED – 255 mph at 14500 ft; CEILING – 24000 ft; RANGE – 1325m; ARMS – 6 machine guns, 6000 lb of bombs.

REF	DATE	IDENT	STATION	UNIT	WHERE CRASHED	DEAD	MRT
I,7	16/5/44	HF519	Wrexham	26 OTU	Llanwrst	All	Llandwrog
I,8	16/6/44	HZ715	Wellsboro Mountford	22 OTU	Red Pike	All	Millom

Boeing 737

REF	DATE	IDENTITY	WHERE CRASHED	DEAD	MRT
VII,3	8/1/89	Brit. Mid. Airways	Kegworth	32	Stafford, Linton on Ouse

Boeing 747

REF	DATE	IDENTITY	WHERE CRASHED	DEAD	MRT
VII,2	5/12/88	N738-PA Pan Am	Lockerbie	259	Stafford, St Athan, Leuchars, Linton on Ouse

"You said that the next pitch was easy"

INDEX

''Jack roll us a fag''

''Dont worry its downhill all the way''

"I thought he had kicked that habit!"

''Mountain Giants, Demons, Trolls---you and your daft stories''

Valley, Stafford, St Athan and Linton on Ouse on joint ex

The 40th Anniversary reunion, ten years before this book was published. In the bac